THE GAME OF LOVE IN GEORGI...

CW00765602

EMOTIONS IN HISTORY
General Editors
UTE FREVERT   THOMAS DIXON

Interest in the historical dimensions of emotional life has grown rapidly. Focusing on the period 1500–2000, the *Emotions in History* series reaches across regional and national boundaries, bringing together studies from all parts of the world. The series recognizes the multifaceted nature of emotions, exploring them through the histories of science, medicine, and psychology, as well as literature, art, religion, politics, and economics.

Courtship in Georgian England was a decisive moment in the life cycle, imagined as a tactical game, an invigorating sport, and a perilous journey across a turbulent sea. This volume brings to life the emotional experience of courtship using the words and objects selected by men and women to navigate this potentially fraught process. It provides new insights into the making and breaking of relationships, beginning with the formation of courtships using the language of love, the development of intimacy through the exchange of love letters, and sensory engagement with love tokens such as flowers, portrait miniatures, and locks of hair. It also charts the increasing modernization of romantic customs over the Georgian era—most notably with the arrival of the printed valentine card—revealing how love developed into a commercial industry. The book concludes with the rituals of disintegration when engagements went awry, and pursuit of damages for breach of promise in the civil courts.

The Game of Love in Georgian England brings together love letters, diaries, valentines, and proposals of marriage from sixty courtships alongside an extensive range of sources including ballads, conduct literature, court cases, material objects, newspaper reports, novels, periodicals, philosophical discourses, plays, poems, and prints, to create a vivid social and cultural history of romantic emotions. The book demonstrates the importance of courtship to studies of marriage, relationships, and emotions in history, and how we write histories of emotions using objects. Love emerges as something that we do in practice, enacted by couples through particular socially and historically determined rituals.

Sally Holloway is a Vice Chancellor's Research Fellow in History and History of Art at Oxford Brookes University. She is a historian of gender, emotions, and visual and material culture in Britain over the long eighteenth and nineteenth centuries. After completing her AHRC-funded PhD at Royal Holloway, she worked on the Georgians season at Historic Royal Palaces, and taught at Queen Mary University of London, Oxford Brookes University, and Richmond, The American International University in London. She is co-editor of the volume *Feeling Things: Objects and Emotions through History* (OUP, 2018).

Praise for *The Game of Love in Georgian England*

'Holloway excels at showing the relationship between culture and practice, providing detailed and precise evidence for the replication of cultural "scripts" in individual relationships...a fascinating addition to the histories of marriage and courtship, and a significant work within a growing scholarship on emotions and material culture.'

Kate Gibson, *History*

'Eighteenth-century emotions have never been so keenly felt as in Sally Holloway's engaging and wide-ranging study *The Game of Love in Georgian England*. Holloway provides a thoroughly researched and lively account of the rituals, material culture and lexicon of love and courtship...The study is underpinned by an impressive range of contemporary source material, extending well beyond life-writings to include novels, plays and poetry, ballads and prints, medical treatises, newspaper reports and court cases, paintings, philosophical discourses, periodicals and conduct literature.'

Helen Metcalfe, *Journal for Eighteenth-Century Studies*

'As well as a vivid account of eighteenth-century courtship, Holloway offers much food for thought regarding the impact of social conventions and consumer culture on emotional experience and its expression. The language of romantic love was remarkably consistent across social classes in the eighteenth century while at the same time flexible in response to changing ideas and fashions. As she points out in her conclusion, it continues to evolve.'

Marilyn L. Morris, *Eighteenth-Century Studies*

'this is an impressive book which offers new insights into how Georgian men and women negotiated the processes of courtship, and provides an exemplar of how to "do" emotions history with objects.'

Elizabeth Spencer, *Women's History Review*

The Game of Love in Georgian England

*Courtship, Emotions, and
Material Culture*

SALLY HOLLOWAY

OXFORD
UNIVERSITY PRESS

Great Clarendon Street, Oxford, OX2 6DP,
United Kingdom

Oxford University Press is a department of the University of Oxford.
It furthers the University's objective of excellence in research, scholarship,
and education by publishing worldwide. Oxford is a registered trade mark of
Oxford University Press in the UK and in certain other countries

© Sally Holloway 2019

The moral rights of the author have been asserted

First published 2019
First published in paperback 2022

All rights reserved. No part of this publication may be reproduced, stored in
a retrieval system, or transmitted, in any form or by any means, without the
prior permission in writing of Oxford University Press, or as expressly permitted
by law, by licence or under terms agreed with the appropriate reprographics
rights organization. Enquiries concerning reproduction outside the scope of the
above should be sent to the Rights Department, Oxford University Press, at the
address above

You must not circulate this work in any other form
and you must impose this same condition on any acquirer

Published in the United States of America by Oxford University Press
198 Madison Avenue, New York, NY 10016, United States of America

British Library Cataloguing in Publication Data
Data available

Library of Congress Cataloging in Publication Data
Data available

ISBN 978–0–19–882307–0 (Hbk.)
ISBN 978–0–19–287099–5 (Pbk.)

Links to third party websites are provided by Oxford in good faith and
for information only. Oxford disclaims any responsibility for the materials
contained in any third party website referenced in this work.

For my parents
Lesley and Peter Holloway
with love

Acknowledgements

This book began ten years ago while I was studying for an MA at King's College London, and discovered an enticing cache of love letters written in code in the Bedfordshire Archives. The project has since taken me through a PhD, and research and teaching posts at several institutions. I am grateful to Amanda Vickery for supervising my doctoral research at Royal Holloway, University of London between 2009 and 2013, for shaping my methods of research and writing, and for determining how I 'do' history to this day. My advisor Jane Hamlett has also been unfailingly generous in her support of my research and career, providing incisive feedback, guidance, and reassurance when I have most needed it.

I gratefully acknowledge the Arts and Humanities Research Council for funding my doctoral research, and The Friendly Hand Charitable Trust for funding additional research trips. For their invaluable intellectual and emotional support, sharing of references, and reading of works in progress, thanks to Katie Barclay, Antonia Brodie, Polly Bull, Joelle Del Rose, Catherine Dille, Alice Dolan, Markman Ellis, Freya Gowrley, Hannah Greig, Leonie Hannan, Judith Hawley, Tim Hitchcock, Hi'ilei Hobart, Jane Mackelworth, India Mandelkern, Sally Osborn, Sarah Ann Robin, Beth Robinson, Clara Tuite, Susan Whyman, Ya-Lei Yen, and especially Tul Israngura Na Ayudhya.

My PhD examiners Thomas Dixon and Helen Berry both shaped how the thesis would look as a book by providing constructive critiques and suggesting new avenues to pursue, and writing a continual stream of references for which I am most grateful. My sincere thanks to Thomas for encouraging me to submit the book to this series, and for reading interminable drafts as I did so. A Visiting Research Fellowship at Chawton House Library gave me much needed time to think as I drafted my book proposal, while an Early Career International Visiting Research Fellowship at the Australian Research Council's Centre of Excellence for the History of Emotions was formative in writing the introduction surrounded by a stimulating and collegial group of historians of emotions.

My fellow convenors and attendees of the British History in the Long Eighteenth Century seminar at the Institute of Historical Research in London have been a continual source of encouragement and inspiration. Since I joined Richmond, The American International University in London in 2014, Michèle Cohen has been a much-valued mentor and friend, helping to sharpen both my language and arguments, encouraging me to own my voice as a writer, and translating declarations of love in French ad infinitum.

Most recently, this project has taken me to Oxford Brookes University, where I am thankful to be surrounded by a group of inspiring and supportive colleagues. I am particularly indebted to Joanne Begiato for sharing her extensive knowledge of eighteenth-century marriage and family life, championing my work, and providing judicious and measured feedback on my writing in many different forms.

Thanks to Fiona Mann for helping to prepare the final manuscript for publication, and to Sally Osborn for compiling the index. Adrian Seville generously showed me his outstanding collection of historic board games, one of which provides the cover for this book. The publication of images was made possible by a grant from the Scouloudi Foundation in association with the Institute of Historical Research. Cathryn Steele at Oxford University Press has ably shepherded the book from the initial proposal through the review process to publication, while the anonymous reviewers each provided important insights that helped to clarify and refine my key arguments.

Last but not least, my husband Dexter Bonner was always emphatic that a doctorate was not a pipe dream, but one I could and should pursue, and he ended up paying for it in more ways than one. I will never be able to repay fully the lifetime of encouragement, love, and support that I have received from my parents Lesley and Peter Holloway—a childhood spent in and out of National Trust houses is evidently apt training for the budding historian. This book is for them, with all my love.

Oxford
May 2018

Contents

List of Figures and Table

FIGURES

TABLE

List of Abbreviations

BAS	Bedfordshire Archives Service, Bedford
BCH	Black Country History
BI	Borthwick Institute, York
BIWLD	British and Irish Women's Letters and Diaries
BL	British Library, London
BLO	Bodleian Library, Oxford
BM	British Museum, London
CRO	Cumbria Record Office, Carlisle
DRO	Derbyshire Record Office, Matlock
EBBA	English Broadside Ballad Archive
ER	*English Reports*
ERO	Essex Record Office, Chelmsford
ESRO	East Sussex Record Office, Brighton
HM	Horsham Museum, West Sussex
HRO	Hampshire Record Office, Winchester
JJC	John Johnson Collection, Oxford
JRL	John Rylands Library, Manchester
KHLC	Kent History and Library Centre, Maidstone
KJV	The Bible, Authorized King James Version
LIRO	Liverpool Record Office, Liverpool
LMA	London Metropolitan Archives, London
LOB	Library of Birmingham
LSF	Library of the Society of Friends, London
LUL	Liverpool University Library, Liverpool
LWL	Lewis Walpole Library, Farmington, CT
MET	Metropolitan Museum of Art, New York
MOL	Museum of London
NRO	Norfolk Record Office, Norwich
NYRO	North Yorkshire Record Office, Northallerton
OBO	Old Bailey Online
OEDO	*Oxford English Dictionary* (online)
SHC	Surrey History Centre, Woking
TPM	The Postal Museum, London
V&A	Victoria & Albert Museum, London
WSA	Wiltshire and Swindon Archives, Chippenham
YCM	York Castle Museum

I had been trick'd once by *that Cheat call'd Love*, but the Game was over, I was resolv'd now to be married or nothing, and to be well married or not at all.

Daniel Defoe, *The Fortunes and Misfortunes of the Famous Moll Flanders* (London, 1722)

O, you novice at Cupid's chess-board! do not you see the next move? Check with your new knight, and the game is your own.

Maria Edgeworth, *Belinda* (London, 1801)

Introduction

But sure my Charming Conquerest cannot Be soe cruel were she but Sencible
what and unusuall Disorder she had occasioned; sure she wou'l[d] have some
tender Thoughts to allay itt; i languist by and Intollarable yet pleasing wound;
and can you blame me, if I ask the reason why my charmer may not Consent
to perfect my bliss.

William Martin to Hannah Smith, 1714

On 15 February 1714, the impassioned suitor William Martin of Cannon Street
in London wrote an ardent love letter to Mrs Hannah Smith, drawing liberally
upon the language of heroic love.[1] The fair maiden Hannah was his 'Charming
Conquerest' and the 'deare disturber of my Repose'. In presenting himself as a
chivalric suffering lover, he emphasized the disorder that she had occasioned.
He hoped that Hannah's 'Ravishing looks' did not conceal an 'Obdurate heart', as
her love 'wou'd crown my joy to all Eternaty'. The letter concluded with a flourish,
as his signature was underlined by ten ornamental swirls. William asked Hannah
to send a reply to the packer Mr Watts' on Bush Lane. Unfortunately it seems his
suit was unsuccessful, as a second suitor named William Denyer from Racton
in West Sussex mounted a new romantic campaign two years later. By this time,
Hannah was lodging with a carpenter near Guildford in Surrey. Her new paramour
harnessed Aesop's fables to describe how forgetting Hannah would 'be as vain as to
wash a black moore white'. He too contrasted the raptures and miseries of love;
Hannah was 'yᵉ subject of my meditation Day & night, and could I imagin 'twere
my fate to be forever excluded yoʳ favour in yᵉ cass I should Esteem my self of all
Men most miserable'.[2] Little evidence has survived about the lives of Hannah and
her admirers beyond these letters. Yet the precious status of love letters as treasured
possessions has ensured that they provide a lasting record of the emotional lives of
these ordinary men and women at the beginning of the eighteenth century.

As this book will reveal, the languages and customs of romantic love were
completely transformed as the century progressed. The epoch witnessed the uneven
growth of literacy, the professionalization of the Post Office, and the rise of the world

---

[1] 'Mrs' is an abbreviation of the term 'Mistress', and connotes social rather than marital status. See
Amy Erickson, 'Mistresses and Marriage: or, a Short History of the Mrs', *History Workshop Journal*
78.1 (2014): 39–57.

[2] W[illia]m Martin and William Denyer to Mrs Hannah Smith, 15 February 1714 and 22 January
1716 (new style), 3M51/684–5, Hampshire Record Office, Winchester (subsequently HRO).

of letters. The heroic love espoused by Hannah Smith's suitors was superseded by new cultures of sensibility and romanticism. The century was punctuated by the publication of amatory works such as Eliza Haywood's *Love in Excess* (1719–20), Samuel Richardson's *Pamela* (1740), Jean-Jacques Rousseau's *Julie, ou la nouvelle Héloïse* (1761), Johann Wolfgang von Goethe's *The Sorrows of Young Werther* (1774), and Jane Austen's *Pride and Prejudice* (1813). The rise of the luxury trade also transformed the material culture of love, producing a dizzying array of new romantic souvenirs such as *bonbonnières*, perfume bottles, and patch boxes. The emergence of shopping as a leisure activity saw the flourishing of stationers' shops producing elaborate cards, precipitating the evolution of Valentine's Day as a commercial celebration.

This book recreates the emotional experiences of courtship—the fêted 'game of love'—using the words and objects chosen by courting men and women to navigate their relationships. The period from *c.*1714 to 1830 saw a momentous increase in the volume of love letters written and exchanged by couples. While surviving sources such as the letters to Hannah Smith are comparatively scarce as the century opens, they grow in number with each decade. Maintaining a romantic correspondence rapidly became an important step towards securing an official engagement. The most numerous correspondences run to several hundred letters, which were carefully preserved and stored in bundles tied with ribbons or string. This book unearths these treasured missives in archives across England to rediscover the joy and heartache of courtship in the words of lovers themselves.

By focusing closely on experiences of courtship, the book offers fresh insights into this emotionally charged period in the life cycle. Couples saw themselves as navigating 'little Barks upon a troubled Ocean', struggling against tempests in order to reach 'the desir'd Harbour' of matrimony. Individuals hoped that by placing 'Love and Hope at the Helms', they could sail toward marriage 'with Safety'.[3] While the majority of studies have approached courtship as part of wider analyses of marriage and the life cycle, this book focuses wholly on how couples navigated their vulnerable 'little Barks' through this decisive time.[4] By concluding with the breakdown of relationships, the book disrupts the traditional or anticipated narrative of a linear trajectory progressing from courtship to marriage.

---

[3] A bark (from the French *barque*) is a small ship. John Lovell to Sarah Harvey, undated (*c.*1757), 161/102/2, Wiltshire and Swindon Archives, Chippenham (subsequently WSA). This formulation of courtship as a 'Tempest Tost Sea' leading to a 'Harbour of Rest' was also used by suitors in Philadelphia. See Nicole Eustace, ' "The cornerstone of a copious work": Love and Power in Eighteenth-Century Courtship', *Journal of Social History* 34.3 (2001): 517–46, at 522.

[4] Notable studies include Judith Schneid Lewis, *In the Family Way: Childbearing in the British Aristocracy, 1760–1860* (New Brunswick, NJ, 1986); Anthony Fletcher, *Gender, Sex and Subordination in England 1500–1800* (New Haven, CT and London, 1995); David Cressy, *Birth, Marriage and Death: Ritual, Religion, and the Life-Cycle in Tudor and Stuart England* (Oxford, 1997); Amanda Vickery, *The Gentleman's Daughter: Women's Lives in Georgian England* (New Haven, CT and London, 1998); Joanne Bailey [Begiato], *Unquiet Lives: Marriage and Marriage Breakdown in England, 1660–1800* (Cambridge, 2003); and Katie Barclay, *Love, Intimacy and Power: Marriage and Patriarchy in Scotland 1650–1850* (Manchester, 2011). The few exclusive studies of courtship include John Gillis, *For Better, For Worse: British Marriages, 1600 to the Present* (Oxford, 1985) and Diana O'Hara, *Courtship and Constraint: Rethinking the Making of Marriage in Tudor England* (Manchester, 2000).

In doing so, it recasts the story of courtship in a new mould, to recognize the very real fears of individuals that their relationships might stall before reaching the altar.

The sixty couples whose words populate the pages of this book represent a broad variety of social and occupational groups, enabling us to trace continuities and changes in romantic rituals across class divides. Studies of marriage commonly focus on couples of a given status, whether paupers, the provincial gentry, or the aristocracy.[5] The highest-ranking lovers in this book are noblemen such as John Kerr, Earl of Ancram (1794–1841), and Lady Diana West (1731–66), youngest daughter of Lord De La Warr. Genteel correspondents include the gentleman Samuel Whitbread II (1764–1815) and gentlewoman Mary Martin (*c.*1751–1804), plus politicians, soldiers, clergymen, and well-to-do businessmen such as the cotton-trader Joseph Strutt (1765–1844). Although the key requirements for gentility were 'land, lordship and local acknowledgement', genteel status was often claimed in their absence, primarily by 'the professionals, crown servants and lawyers, doctors, teachers and academics' and 'the married clergy'.[6] The book also features published novelists, poets, and philosophers such as Judith Cowper (1702–81), William Godwin (1756–1836), Mary Hays (1759–1843), John Keats (1795–1821), Eleanor Anne Porden (1795–1825), and Mary Wollstonecraft (1759–97), whose letters were preserved in greater numbers due to their fame and literary skill.

The majority of lovers studied in this book are lesser known men and women, whose courtships are brought to light from the 'dust' of the archives.[7] Writers of the middling sort include the tailor's daughter Sarah Hurst (1736–1808), flour merchant Thomas Kirton (1709–57), and ironmonger's daughter Olive Lloyd (1707–75). While defining the 'middling sort' can be problematic, the term is used here to refer to people 'beneath the gentry but above the level of the labouring classes; most of them worked for a living, although a growing number lived wholly or partially on rental income and other investments'.[8] Jonathan Barry argues that individuals who worked were rarely employed by others, but traded 'the products of their hands' (such as yeomen, husbandmen farmers, and artisans) or their 'skills in business or the professions' (including merchants, attorneys, and apothecaries).[9] As revealed in Chapter 6 of this book, the majority of breach of promise suits were fought between plaintiffs and defendants of the middling sort. At the lowest social level are the labouring classes, whom 'fortune' had 'not plac'd...among the number

---

[5] On marriages of the poor in England, see Steve Hindle, 'The Problem of Pauper Marriage in Seventeenth-Century England', *Transactions of the Royal Historical Society* 8 (1998): 71–89 and R. A. Houston, *Bride Ales and Penny Weddings: Recreations, Reciprocity, and Regions in Britain from the Sixteenth to the Nineteenth Centuries* (Oxford, 2014). On the gentry, see Vickery, *The Gentleman's Daughter*, Ch. 2. On social elites, see Schneid Lewis, *In the Family Way*, Ch. 1, and Kate Gibson, 'Marriage Choice and Kinship among the English Catholic Elite, 1680–1730', *Journal of Family History* 41.2 (2016): 144–64.

[6] Felicity Heal and Clive Holmes, *The Gentry in England and Wales, 1500–1700* (London, 1994), 7.

[7] See Carolyn Steedman, *Dust: The Archive and Cultural History* (Manchester, 2001).

[8] Margaret Hunt, *The Middling Sort: Commerce, Gender, and the Family in England, 1680–1780* (London, 1996), 15.

[9] Jonathan Barry, 'Introduction', in *The Middling Sort of People: Culture, Society and Politics in England, 1550–1800*, ed. Jonathan Barry and Christopher Brooks (London, 1994), 2.

of the rich and great'.[10] These include the coachman John Everard (b. *c.*1695), domestic servant Elizabeth Woollat (1729–74), and her upwardly mobile suitor Jedediah Strutt (1726–97), who later went into partnership with the industrialist Richard Arkwright. While working as a journeyman wheelwright in 1751, Jedediah asked his future wife, 'I am a servant and perhaps wou'd turn master, of what or who? or wherein shou'd I be better'd?'[11]

Evidence of these relationships has been preserved in thirty archives and museum collections. The sources traverse a broad geographical distance, situated in twenty-four counties across England from Cornwall to Northumberland, Gloucestershire to Norfolk.[12] Appendix 1 charts the occupation or social rank of each individual, their religious persuasion, dates and location of courtship, and the repositories where manuscripts can be located. Of these collections, only five sets of love letters have previously been published.[13] All quotations are taken from original manuscripts where possible.[14] These letters are interpreted in light of a diverse range of other primary sources, in order to construct a rich social and cultural history of romantic emotions. Sources include ballads, conduct literature, court cases, diaries, dictionaries, ephemera, medical treatises, memoirs, newspaper reports, novels, paintings, periodicals, philosophical discourses, plays, poems, and prints.

The material culture of love provides a further important resource, including love letters as physical objects, but also extending to garters, gloves, hair, miniatures, rings, signets, snuffboxes, and valentine cards. These items have been sourced from twenty-three antiques dealers, auction houses, archives, libraries, museums, and private collections. The selection of objects is partly directed by the survival of particular goods, which may be more durable (like rings) or have been preserved

---

[10] Jedediah Strutt to Elizabeth Woollat, 3 February 1755, D5303/4/1, Derbyshire Record Office, Matlock (subsequently DRO).

[11] Ibid., Leicester, 25 February 1751, D5303/1/3, DRO.

[12] In full, these are: Bedfordshire, Berkshire, Cambridgeshire, Cornwall, Cumbria, Derbyshire, Devon, East Riding, East Sussex, Essex, Gloucestershire, Hampshire, Kent, Lancashire, London, Norfolk, Northumberland, North Yorkshire, Somerset, Surrey, the West Midlands, West Sussex, Warwickshire, and Wiltshire.

[13] Published letters exist for the courtships of Mary Hays and John Eccles, Mary Berry and Charles O'Hara, Mary Wollstonecraft and Gilbert Imlay, Mary Wollstonecraft and William Godwin, and John Keats and Fanny Brawne. Unfortunately the letters of Imlay and Brawne have not survived. See A. F. Wedd, ed., *The Love-Letters of Mary Hays* (London, 1925); Lewis Melville, ed., *The Berry Papers; Being the Correspondence hitherto Unpublished of Mary and Agnes Berry (1763–1852)* (London, 1914); Roger Ingpen, ed., *The Love Letters of Mary Wollstonecraft to Gilbert Imlay* (London, 1908); Ralph M. Wardle, ed., *Godwin & Mary: Letters of William Godwin and Mary Wollstonecraft* (London, 1967); Harry Buxton Forman, ed., *Letters of John Keats to Fanny Brawne* (London, 1878). The first volume of Hays' correspondence with Eccles can be found in the Carl H. Pforzheimer Collection of Shelley and His Circle at the New York Public Library, while the largest proportion of Keats' letters to Brawne are in the Harvard Keats Collection. Many of these have been digitized at http://nrs.harvard.edu/urn-3:FHCL.Hough:hou00062, while others have been lost, and are only available in Forman's text.

[14] Quotations from the letters of Mary Wollstonecraft and William Godwin are taken from MS Abinger c40, Bodleian Library, Oxford (subsequently BLO), and of Mary Berry and Charles O'Hara from Add MS 37727, British Library, London (subsequently BL). The diary of Sarah Hurst has been published in Susan C. Djabri, ed., *The Diaries of Sarah Hurst 1759–1762* (Stroud, 2009). All quotations are taken from MS 3542–5, Horsham Museum, West Sussex (subsequently HM).

with particular care (like valentines). The objects available are also determined by the acquisitions policies of museums and private collectors, predicated on an object's age, authenticity, craftsmanship, material, value (whether aesthetic, intellectual, or rarity), and historical association.[15] Certain objects such as eye miniatures crying tears of diamonds (Figure 3.3) are shown here for their outstanding craftsmanship. Others such as a valentine created as part of a lottery (Figure 4.5) were chosen for their rarity, or as the first of their kind (Figure 4.6). All form part of the wider material milieu in which courting couples forged their relationships.

As will become clear in this introduction, the methodology of this book is fundamentally interdisciplinary, drawing upon anthropology, art history, literary theory, philosophy, and psychology to discover the cultural codes of love. The overarching approach is one of 'thick description', whereby individual relationships are situated among contemporary taxonomies and ideas about love in textual, visual, and material culture. Clifford Geertz argued that 'man is an animal suspended in webs of significance he himself has spun.' This book unpicks these 'webs of significance' in eighteenth-century culture to consider how the symbols, rituals, and meanings of romantic love were created and contested by individuals. In doing so, it endeavours to 'bring us into touch with the lives of strangers', and flesh out the hopes and fears of ordinary courting couples as they navigated the often fraught path to matrimony.[16]

STUDYING LOVE

Many historians have proclaimed an 'emotional turn' or 'affective turn' in recent historical scholarship, which has revealed the centrality of emotions to human experience, and their significance in driving social, cultural, and political change.[17] In endeavouring to define what emotions are, historians have engaged with research in a diverse range of fields, including anthropology, psychology, and neuroscience.[18] The field has provided a rich new interdisciplinary space to work out the interplay between culture on the one hand and biology on the other. Historians of emotions are thus uniquely situated to bridge the opposing 'universalist' approaches, that stress the universal nature of emotions as timeless neuropsychological processes,

---

[15] Susan M. Pearce, *On Collecting: An Investigation into Collecting in the European Tradition* (London and New York, 1995), Fig. 20.2, at 356.

[16] Clifford Geertz, 'Thick Description: Toward an Interpretive Theory of Culture', in *The Interpretation of Cultures* (New York, 1973), 310–23. In his definition of culture, Geertz notes, 'Though ideational, it does not exist in someone's head; though unphysical, it is not an occult entity', 314.

[17] See, for example, Rob Boddice, 'The Affective Turn: Historicizing the Emotions', in *Psychology and History: Interdisciplinary Explorations*, ed. Cristian Tileagă and Jovan Byford (Cambridge, 2014), 147–65, and Nicole Eustace, Eugenia Lean, Julie Livingston, Jan Plamper, William Reddy, and Barbara Rosenwein, 'AHR Conversation: The Historical Study of Emotions', *American Historical Review* 117.5 (2012): 1487–531, at 1487.

[18] For a useful overview of both historic and modern attempts to define emotion, see Jan Plamper, *The History of Emotions: An Introduction*, trans. Keith Tribe (Oxford, 2015), 9–25.

and 'constructionist' approaches, which argue that emotions are social ideas or judgements that can only be found in language.[19]

For biological anthropologists such as Helen Fisher, romantic love is a 'universal human experience' that is 'woven firmly into the fabric of the human brain'.[20] Fisher used brain scans of individuals who had recently fallen in love—as they gazed at a photograph of their beloved—to isolate its defining characteristics. She found that love is characterized by several distinct traits, including mood swings, emotional dependence on a person, sexual possessiveness, and obsessive thoughts. These create elevated activity of dopamine in the brain, similar to the feeling generated by a rush of cocaine. Such research suggests that love is not an emotion, but a basic human *drive* (such as hunger or thirst) located in the craving part of the mind.[21] There are obvious issues for historians here in fixing basic features of love that are unchanging for all people, in all cultures and time periods. Can a medieval troubadour really experience love in precisely the same way as an eighteenth-century man of feeling, or a millennial today? Surely not. New research in the history of emotions has worked to bridge this gap between the 'internal' neurochemical experience of emotions and their 'external' expression. As Monique Scheer has persuasively argued, 'emotional arousals that seem to be purely physical are actually deeply socialized', as socially and historically situated actions of a 'knowing' or 'mindful' body.[22]

Love is generally absent from lists of the pan-cultural 'basic' emotions created as a result of evolution: principally anger, disgust, fear, happiness, sadness, and surprise.[23] Psychologists such as Paul Ekman again argue that love is not an emotion at all, since it does not involve a unique facial expression, and is more long-lasting, potentially enduring a lifetime rather than seconds or minutes. Rather, love is an 'emotion complex' or 'emotion plot'.[24] Psychologists scrutinizing the semantics of love have likewise presented it as part of a 'constellation of feelings experienced in

---

[19] See John Deigh, 'Concepts of Emotions in Modern Philosophy and Psychology', in *The Oxford Handbook of Philosophy of Emotion*, ed. Peter Goldie (Oxford, 2010), 17–40, and Thomas Dixon, 'Why I am Angry: The Return to Ancient Links between Reason and Emotion', *Times Literary Supplement*, 1 October 2004.

[20] Helen Fisher, *Why We Love: The Nature and Chemistry of Romantic Love* (New York, 2004), 3. Cf. William R. Jankowiak and Edward F. Fischer, 'A Cross-Cultural Perspective on Romantic Love', *Ethnology* 31.2 (1992): 149–55.

[21] Helen Fisher, *Anatomy of Love: A Natural History of Mating, Marriage, and Why We Stray* (New York and London, [1992] 2016), 37–41; Fisher, *Why We Love*, 3–25.

[22] Monique Scheer, 'Are Emotions a Kind of Practice (And is That What Makes Them Have a History)? A Bourdieuian Approach to Understanding Emotion', *History and Theory* 51.2 (2012): 193–220, at 201 and 220.

[23] On love and 'basic' emotions, see Andrew Ortony and Terence J. Turner, 'What's Basic about Basic Emotions?' *Psychological Review* 97 (1990): 315–31; Paul Ekman, 'Are There Basic Emotions?' *Psychological Review* 99 (1992): 550–3, 'An Argument for Basic Emotions', *Cognition and Emotion* 6 (1992): 169–200, 'Basic Emotions', in *The Handbook of Cognition and Emotion*, ed. Tim Dalgleish and Nick Power (New York, 1999), 45–60; Jesse Prinz, 'Which Emotions are Basic?' in *Emotion, Evolution, and Rationality*, ed. Dylan Evans and Pierre Cruse (Oxford, 2004), 69–88; John Sabini and Maury Silver, 'Ekman's Basic Emotions: Why not Love and Jealousy?' *Cognition and Emotion* 19 (2005): 693–712; Ruth Leys, 'The Turn to Affect: A Critique', *Critical Enquiry* 37 (2011): 437–43.

[24] Charles Darwin, *Expression of the Emotions in Man and Animals*, ed. Paul Ekman, third edition (New York, [1872] 1998), 83.

romantic and conjugal relationships', which either derive from happiness or constitute a separate category comprised of affection, lust, and longing.[25] Couples in Georgian England described such a 'constellation' of emotions, from 'piercing thorns' of pain to the 'bright state of excitement' anticipating marriage.[26] The philosopher Paul Griffiths has distinguished between the more primitive 'basic' emotions (such as anger) and 'higher cognitive emotions' (such as love) that are more culturally differentiated. The experience of love is understood to be a relatively long-term process, which involves using 'traditional beliefs' in a society to recognize 'traditional desires' and guide an individual's actions.[27]

The language chosen by individuals to verbalize their love was beyond a simple *expression* of emotion. The anthropologist James M. Wilce has described a 'hot-as-molten-metal mental fusion' between language and emotion, arguing that forms of emotional expression 'help constitute social understandings and apparently internal processes'.[28] Thus while Jack Goody maintains that troubadours left 'no evidence of new feelings in general, unless we mean by that new forms of expressing those feelings', these new forms of expression would themselves have shaped the feelings of their users.[29] William Reddy has termed such emotion claims 'emotives' as they 'inevitably alter' the feelings they describe, 'sometimes very significantly'. The most pertinent examples for us here are 'I love you' or 'I am in love with you'.[30] The vocabulary used by lovers not only conveyed their love for another, but confirmed and intensified the experience of love itself. As Chapter 1 reveals, romantic lexicon provided an overarching framework within which couples could navigate their courtships through shared knowledge of the idioms of love, which changed in tandem with wider shifts to conceive of the 'chemistry' and 'electricity' of attraction.

Whose conception of love are we discussing here? Simone de Beauvoir famously argued that 'men and women understand love quite differently. That is why they do not understand one another.'[31] Katie Barclay describes love within marriage in eighteenth-century Scotland as 'signified by gender-specific loving behaviour that reinforced the social hierarchy between husband and wife', strengthening the patriarchal system 'with every act of love'.[32] As the influence of heroic love waned in the

[25] P. Johnson-Laird and K. Oatley, 'The Language of Emotions: An Analysis of a Semantic Field', *Cognition and Emotion* 3 (1989): 81–123; P. Shaver, J. Schwartz, D. Kirson, and C. O'Connor, 'Emotion Knowledge: Further Exploration of a Prototype Approach', *Journal of Personality and Social Psychology* 52 (1987): 1061–86; Christine Storm and Tom Storm, 'The English Lexicon of Interpersonal Affect: Love, etc.', *Cognition and Emotion* 19 (2005): 333–56, at 355.

[26] Hays to Eccles, 10 September 1779, Letter XL, in Wedd, ed., *Love-Letters of Mary Hays*, 79; Anthony Hamond to Mary Ann Musters, undated (*c.*1828), HMN 5/95/2, Norfolk Record Office, Norwich (subsequently NRO).

[27] Paul Griffiths, *What Emotions Really Are: The Problem of Psychological Categories* (Chicago, IL and London, 1997), 92, 241–5.

[28] James M. Wilce, *Language and Emotion* (Cambridge, 2009), 2, 8, 12.

[29] Jack Goody, *The Theft of History* (Cambridge, 2006), 268.

[30] William Reddy, *The Navigation of Feeling: A Framework for the History of Emotions* (Cambridge, 2001), 99–105.

[31] Simone de Beauvoir, *The Second Sex* (1949), cited in 'Introduction' to *The Philosophy of (Erotic) Love*, ed. Robert C. Solomon and Kathleen M. Higgins (Lawrence, KS, 1991), 1–12, at 3.

[32] Barclay, *Love, Intimacy and Power*, 109–10.

second quarter of the eighteenth century, the men studied in this book avoided styling themselves as a valiant 'ancient Hero', in order to express the 'undissembled Sentiments' of their hearts.[33] It remained far more rare for women to dissect their 'undissembled' love in courtship letters. After all, love was 'inseparable from assertions of status; love and power were intimately connected'.[34] Whilst women discussed love amongst one another, and in their diaries, they largely refrained from doing so with suitors. As Chapter 2 shows, appropriate feminine self-presentation in courtship letters underscored a woman's modesty and virtue. Suitors repeatedly reminded their sweethearts that while men 'may be pleased for the moment with a forward woman', they 'would not like to see it in a wife'.[35]

Love was understood as a long-lasting and intangible passion, and celebrated as an almost spiritual experience that went beyond words. In 1723, the poet Judith Cowper described her love for Captain Martin Madan in an unsent letter as 'so strong, so soft a Passion, mixt wth so much of an awfull regard'.[36] A woman's love was necessarily soft and delicate: she 'could not relish the coursest [*sic*] Food of Love, unless it had been season'd with that obliging Softness, and anxious Regard, in which the Delicacy of the Passion consists'.[37] In the second half of the century, the cult of sensibility encouraged men to examine the many different facets of their love, in order to emphasize their emotional tenderness, and delicacy of feeling. In 1779, John Eccles wrote to the novelist Mary Hays asking, 'But what is love, and how is it produced?' He concluded, ''Tis a passion that raises in the breast sensations most refined; a complacency replete with delight.' With love increasingly presented as a tender and refined sensation, the philosopher Mary Wollstonecraft wrote in 1796 that love was 'an affair of sentiment, arising from the same delicacy of perception' that enabled people to appreciate 'the beauties of nature, poetry, &c.' Such feelings were 'impalpable—they must be felt, they cannot be described'.[38] The term 'emotions' was only rarely invoked by writers to describe a very general inclination or perception, such as 'emotions of approbation' toward a suitor, or 'a mixed emotion' at continuing a relationship in the face of parental opposition.[39]

The eighteenth and nineteenth centuries saw a new celebration of romantic love in literature, philosophy, and art. The discourses underpinning romantic language are outlined in Chapter 1 of this book. In literature, notions of an ideal married

---

[33] George Gibbs to Ann Vicary, 22 June 1745, MS/11021/1/14, London Metropolitan Archives (subsequently LMA).

[34] Eustace ' "The cornerstone of a copious work" ', 518–19. In an extended version of this article, Eustace describes how expressions of love 'served to veil exertions of power...Like clouds that gauze without wholly covering': *Passion is the Gale: Emotion, Power, and the Coming of the American Revolution* (Chapel Hill, NC, 2010), Ch. 3, 110.

[35] Note by John Dewey, undated, 32M77/F/C31, HRO.

[36] Judith Cowper to Martin Madan (unsent), 1723, MS Eng. Lett. c. 284, f. 2, BLO.

[37] Bernard Mandeville, *The Virgin Unmask'd: Or, Female Dialogues Betwixt an Elderly Maiden Lady, and Her Niece, On Several Diverting Discourses of the Times* (London, 1709), 203.

[38] Wollstonecraft to Imlay, Sweden, 3 July 1796, Letter LV, in Ingpen, ed., *Love Letters of Mary Wollstonecraft*, 127.

[39] Hays to Eccles in Wedd, ed., *Love-Letters of Mary Hays*, 31 September 1779 and 27 October 1779, 109 and 149. On the changing languages of 'emotions', see Thomas Dixon, ' "Emotion": The History of a Keyword in Crisis', *Emotion Review* 4 (2012): 338–44.

love as the reward for virtue were popularized in epistolary novels such as Samuel Richardson's best-selling *Pamela* (1740). In philosophical treatises such as Rousseau's *Emile, or On Education* (1762), love *before* marriage was upheld as 'the law of nature'. The 'principle duty' of couples such as Emile and Sophie was 'to love each other'.[40] Loving marriages were taken as key markers of progress, in order to distinguish Enlightened Europeans from their 'savage' counterparts.[41] Sentimental artworks by Henry Singleton, Francis Wheatley, and others created idealized scenes of rural courtship, while conversation pieces by artists such as Thomas Gainsborough and Johan Zoffany monumentalized the affection and intimacy between married couples.[42] As Ruth Bloch argues in her study of eighteenth-century America, sex in the context of courtship and marriage 'had come to be seen as a conduit to a higher morality beyond the physical and profane', as romantic love was transformed into a 'civilizing and stabilizing' force.[43] A companionate marriage became 'essential to ye most lasting, most perfect happiness', with individuals engaging in courtship hoping to 'meet with proper Returns of affection from the person I love'.[44] In her study of parenting in Georgian England, Joanne Begiato has argued that children were 'imagined as the culmination of married love', an idea that garnered 'considerable emotional power' in an age of sensibility.[45] Yet as we shall see, the new ideal did not mean that decisions to marry were made on the basis of love alone.

COURTSHIP AND MATRIMONY

Following decades of fierce debate, historians have long agreed that marriage was neither entirely cold nor universally romantic.[46] There was no clear-cut distinction

---

[40] Jean-Jacques Rousseau, *Emilius; or, A Treatise of Education* (Edinburgh, 1768), Vol. III of III, Book V, 87.

[41] 'A savage is seldom or never determined to marry from the particular inclinations of sex...He discovers no preference of any particular woman, but leaves it to his parents, or other relations.' The whole marriage is completed 'with the most perfect indifference': John Millar, *The Origin of the Distinction of Ranks; or, An Inquiry into the Circumstances which Give Rise to Influence and Authority in the Different Members of Society*, third edition (London, 1781), 26–7.

[42] See Kate Retford, *The Art of Domestic Life: Family Portraiture in Eighteenth-Century England* (New Haven, CT and London, 2006).

[43] Ruth H. Bloch, 'Changing Conceptions of Sexuality and Romance in Eighteenth-Century America', *The William and Mary Quarterly* 60 (2003): 13–42, at 40.

[44] Elizabeth Woollat to Jedediah Strutt, February 1755, D5303/4/2, DRO.

[45] Joanne Bailey [Begiato], *Parenting in England 1760–1830: Emotion, Identity, and Generation* (Oxford, 2012), 22–3.

[46] For an overview of changing responses to Lawrence Stone's landmark work *The Family, Sex and Marriage in England, 1500–1800* (London, 1977), see Helen Berry and Elizabeth Foyster, eds., *The Family in Early Modern England* (Cambridge, 2007), esp. 'Introduction', 1–17. The authors conclude that Stone was 'emphatically wrong...to suggest that the history of the family was one of progression, in which the eighteenth century marked the arrival of a more civilised, loving and recognisably "modern" family', 16. In the same volume, Joanne Bailey divides responses to Stone into 'revisionist' (1970s–1980s) and 'post-revisionist' (1990s–2000s) phases, 'Reassessing Parenting in Eighteenth-Century England', 209–32, at 209–10. For post-revisionist scholarship, see David Lemmings, 'Marriage and the Law in the Eighteenth Century: Hardwicke's Marriage Act of 1753', *The Historical Journal*

between strategic unions on the one hand and marriages for love on the other, but a 'broad grey area in which both sentiment and prudence interplayed'.[47] Despite the new romantic ideals outlined so far, it is clear that love was one of a number of concerns compelling individuals to marry: marriage promised companionship, but also financial security, social advancement, and the continuation of a family line. Importantly, it was a key marker of adulthood, signalling the creation of a new household and economic unit. After seven years pursuing unsuccessful courtships, the Hampshire surgeon John Dewey finally found a wife aged twenty-nine after moving to America. He reported back to his first love Charlotte Lambourne of Winchester in 1817:

> I am at last without courtship married I know so little of my wife that I cannot give you any account of her I believe she loves me much I am afraid two well [sic] for her own happiness If I did not like her before marriage, I love her now quite as much as I wish, and intend making a good partner, indeed I think her very fortunate.

John's new wife was much younger than him, and he expected would be 'young enough twenty years hence to have a family'. While the presence of love evidently shaped how John perceived his fledgling union, he had grown to love his wife 'quite as much as I wish'. John's pragmatic decision to take a young wife he knew little of was motivated by his advancing age, previous romantic disappointments, and desire for children.[48]

The eighteenth century has also been presented as a pivotal moment in the history of sexuality, which witnessed a revolution in both sexual attitudes and sexual behaviour.[49] Tim Hitchcock and Henry Abelove have argued that sexual behaviour became increasingly phallocentric, moving away from fondling and 'long hours spent in mutual touching' during courtship, and towards full penetrative procreative sex. While first-hand records of changes in sexual activity are predictably scarce, this transformation is suggested by demographic shifts: the population mushroomed, illegitimate births grew exponentially, and a higher proportion of the population got married, with a third of brides already pregnant on their wedding day.[50] As one heavily pregnant young bride reassures her

---

39.2 (1996): 339–60; Vickery, *The Gentleman's Daughter*, esp. Ch. 2; Ingrid Tague, 'Love, Honour and Obedience: Fashionable Women and the Discourse of Marriage in the Early Eighteenth Century', *Journal of British Studies* 40.1 (2001): 76–106; Helen Berry, *Gender, Society and Print Culture in Late Stuart England* (Aldershot, 2003); Catherine Frances, 'Making Marriages in Early Modern England: Rethinking the Role of Family and Friends', in *The Marital Economy in Scandinavia and Britain 1400–1900*, ed. Maria Ågren and Amy Louise Erickson (Aldershot, 2005), 39–55.

[47] Naomi Tadmor, *Family and Friends in Eighteenth-Century England: Household, Kinship, and Patronage* (Cambridge, 2004), 193.

[48] Letter book of John Dewey, undated (*c.* September 1817), 32M77/F/C30, f. 14, HRO. For further evidence of motivations for matrimony in men's own words, see written proposals of marriage, including the proposal from Philip Yorke to Lady Jemima Campbell in 1740, L30/9/113, and from Jason Humberstone to Mrs Jane Parker in 1819, Z742/36, Bedfordshire Archives Service, Bedford (subsequently BAS).

[49] See, for example, Faramerz Dabhoiwala, *The Origins of Sex: A History of the First Sexual Revolution* (London, 2012).

[50] Henry Abelove, 'Some Speculations on the History of Sexual Intercourse during the Long Eighteenth Century in England', *Genders* 6 (1989): 125–30; Tim Hitchcock, 'Redefining Sex in Eighteenth-Century England', *History Workshop Journal* 41 (1996): 72–90.

husband-to-be in Richard Newton's print *Matrimonial Speculation* (1792), 'Never mind John, it may be all for the best', to which he replies 'If it does, I'll be D—d.'[51] In a patriarchal society, sexual intercourse with the 'opposite' sex was an important signifier of masculinity, and increasingly became required of men 'in order to demonstrate their "normality" '.[52] While historians such as Randolph Trumbach have argued that the century erected new boundaries between the 'normal' heterosexual majority and a transgressive homosexual minority, others have since cautioned against anachronistically searching for the origins of a modern 'gay' identity during this period.[53] The cultural obsession with heteronormative sex was bound up with a 'crisis of effeminacy' in the mid-eighteenth century, manifested by growing social anxiety about and hostility towards effeminate men, who were categorized alongside anarchists, papists, and foreigners as social deviants.[54]

The castrato was one such effeminate man, unable to father children, and consequently viewed as an exotic creature—a fascinating *thing*—neither entirely male nor female.[55] Helen Berry has brought to life the highly unusual marriage of the celebrated castrato Giusto Ferdinando Tenducci (*c.*1735–90) and his young pupil Dorothea Maunsell (*c.*1750–1814) in 1766, which was accepted by many of their contemporaries even though Tenducci was physically unable to consummate the union. The marriage was a companionate one, with Tenducci affectionately calling his wife 'Doro', and claiming paternity after she gave birth to a child in *c.*1769.

---

[51] Richard Newton, *Matrimonial Speculation*, published by William Holland, hand-coloured etching, London, 1792, 1948,0214.385, British Museum, London (subsequently BM). A similarly reluctant groom is shown being forced up the aisle towards his pregnant bride in *The Unwilling Bridegroom, or Forc'd Meat Will Never Digest*, hand-coloured mezzotint, London, 1778, 1877,1013.878, BM.

[52] Hitchcock, 'Redefining Sex', 84. In his revolutionary work in the history of sexuality, Thomas Laqueur argued that 'sex as we know it was invented' during the eighteenth century, with the creation of a new model of 'two new distinct and opposite sexes'. See *Making Sex: The Body and Gender from the Greeks to Freud* (Cambridge, MA, 1990), 148–9. Karen Harvey has problematized Laqueur's linear narrative of change, using published erotica to emphasize the continuing diversity of understandings of sexual difference in eighteenth-century England: *Reading Sex in the Eighteenth Century: Bodies and Gender in English Erotic Culture* (Cambridge, 2004).

[53] On the emergence of a singular and recognizably modern gay subculture, see Rictor Norton, *Mother Clap's Molly House: The Gay Subculture in England 1700–1830* (London, 1992); Randolph Trumbach, *Sex and the Gender Revolution*, Vol. I, *Heterosexuality and the Third Gender in Enlightenment London* (Chicago, IL and London, 1998); Randolph Trumbach, 'Modern Sodomy: The Origins of Homosexuality, 1700–1800', in Matt Cook, with H. G. Cocks, Robert Mills, and Randolph Trumbach, eds., *A Gay History of Britain: Love and Sex Between Men Since the Middle Ages* (Oxford, 2007), 77–106. For critiques of this approach, see Cameron McFarlane, *The Sodomite in Fiction & Satire 1660–1750* (New York, 1997), 5–19; Tanya Cassidy, 'People, Place, and Performance: Theoretically Revisiting Mother Clap's Molly House', in *Queer People: Negotiations and Expressions of Homosexuality, 1700–1800*, ed. Chris Mounsey and Caroline Gonda (Lewisburg, PA, 2007), 99–113; Declan Kavanagh, *Effeminate Years: Literature, Politics, and Aesthetics in Mid-Eighteenth Century Britain* (Lewisburg, PA, 2017), xvi–xxii. In their overview of the state of the field, Caroline Gonda and Chris Mounsey argue that both essentialist and social constructionist approaches have their strengths, and 'neither, on its own, encompasses all the subtleties needed for the analysis of homosexuality': 'Queer People: An Introduction', in *Queer People*, ed. Mounsey and Gonda, 9–37, at 11.

[54] Kavanagh, *Effeminate Years*, passim. Also see Sally O'Driscoll, 'The Molly and the Fop: Untangling Effeminacy in the Eighteenth Century', in *Developments in the Histories of Sexualities: In Search of the Normal, 1600–1800*, ed. Chris Mounsey (Lewisburg, PA, 2013), 145–72, and William Gibson and Joanne Begiato, *Sex and the Church in the Long Eighteenth Century* (London and New York, 2017), 206–10.

[55] Helen Berry, *The Castrato and his Wife* (Oxford, 2011), 83–4.

Given the 'tolerance and recognition' afforded the marriage in social circles, Berry has argued that new doctrines of romantic love could 'open up a variety of possible relationships' which were accommodated in society, 'ahead of the Church, the State, and the legal establishment in reforming marriage laws'.[56] Romantic relationships between same-sex couples are beyond the scope of this book. However, as an era of rapidly changing attitudes to love, marriage, and sex, the eighteenth century provides the ideal period in which to consider how romantic love and sexual relationships were understood and enacted between men and women, how they conducted their courtships with the aim of becoming husband and wife, and what it meant to them when these relationships faltered before the altar. To put it another way, what did it mean to marry in Georgian England?

The women studied in this book married at an average age of 23, compared to men at an average age of 29.[57] These figures broadly reflect research in population studies, which has placed the average age of marriage at 24 for women and 26 for men. While there is not sufficient data here to reliably chart variations within this sample, demographers have shown that age at marriage varied according to social rank, with most noblemen waiting until their early thirties to marry. Couples also married earlier as the century progressed, with the average age at marriage falling by 2.1 years for men and 2.5 years for women between 1710 and 1829.[58] This study therefore rediscovers the emotional lives of men and women at a particular moment in the life cycle. Ever since Platonic philosophies of love, love was 'born to hate old age' and seen to reside 'with young people'.[59] This view persisted through the eighteenth century, with Mary Wollstonecraft writing in 1792 that 'Youth is the season for love in both sexes', after which 'thoughtless enjoyment' and 'sensation' were replaced by greater 'reflection'.[60] Nonetheless, these lofty ideals about young love could be tempered in practice, as remarriage remained common, with historians estimating that 7.9 per cent of women getting married by 1740 had previously been widowed, and around 15 per cent of eighteenth-century weddings overall having at least one party remarrying.[61] Two out of sixty of the courtships in

---

[56] Ibid., 158, 217–18. On the flexibility of marriage in practice, also see Patricia Crawford and Sara Mendelson, 'Sexual Identities in Early Modern England: The Marriage of Two Women in 1680', *Gender and History* 7.3 (1995): 362–77; Fraser Easton, 'Gender's Two Bodies: Women Warriors, Female Husbands and Plebeian Life', *Past & Present* 180 (2003): 131–74; Helen Berry, 'Queering the History of Marriage: The Social Recognition of a Castrato Husband in Eighteenth-Century Britain', *History Workshop Journal* 74.1 (2012): 27–50.

[57] The exact figures are 23.46 and 29.28. These are based upon fifty-two individuals for whom data is available, and exclude those marrying for the second or third time.

[58] The figure drops from 27.3 in 1710–19 to 25.2 in 1820–9 for men, and from 26.3 in 1710–19 to 23.8 in 1820–9 for women. This had important consequences for fertility rates, as the average bride was of childbearing age for more than two extra years by the end of the era. E. A. Wrigley, R. S. Davies, J. E. Oeppen, and R. S. Schofield, *English Population History from Family Reconstitution 1580–1837* (Cambridge, 1997), 134–9, esp. Table 5.3. For mean age at first marriage in noble families, see T. H. Hollingsworth, 'The Demography of the British Peerage', Supplement to *Population Studies* 18.2 (1964): 11.

[59] The Speech of Agathon in Plato's *Symposium* (c.380 BC), in *The Philosophy of (Erotic) Love*, ed. Solomon and Higgins, 21.

[60] Mary Wollstonecraft, *A Vindication of the Rights of Woman* (London, 1792), 51.

[61] This represents a significant fall from the seventeenth century, when around twenty-five per cent of marriages involved at least one party remarrying. Wrigley et al., *English Population History*, 164.

Appendix 1 represented a man or woman's second or third marriage, while sixteen of the ninety breach of promise cases in Appendix 2 involved a widow or widower as either plaintiff or defendant.[62]

The duration of courtship could vary from a few weeks to several years. At one extreme, the fifteen-year-old Isabella Eccleston ran off in 'hasty youth' to marry her coachman in 1725.[63] At the other, the wheelwright Jedediah Strutt intermittently courted the domestic servant Elizabeth Woollat for seven years. Jedediah and Elizabeth's son Joseph (1765–1844) later repeated their pattern by investing seven years in his courtship of Isabella Douglas. Letters suggest that the average period was between one and four years. Nonetheless, it can be difficult to isolate when a courtship began based on love letters as sources, due to the widespread destruction of missives. While the poet Eleanor Anne Porden likely met the explorer John Franklin (1786–1847) after visiting HMS *Alexander* and *Isabella* in Deptford in 1818—inspiring her heroic poem 'The Arctic Expeditions'—the couple's earliest surviving letters are dated three years later in 1821.[64] Moreover, substantial collections of letters rich in evidence for historians generally survive for couples conducting more protracted courtships, leading individuals to correspond at length during extended periods of separation. As Eleanor teased John during his voyage to Canada in May 1821, 'like gunpowder plot and May day, your letters come but once a year'.[65]

Courtship did not take place in a vacuum, with family and friends playing a key role in the making of a match. As Martin Ingram has found in his work on the church courts in Elizabethan and early Stuart England, marriage required the 'multilateral consent' of friends and family members.[66] They could act as 'facilitators and prompters' to secure or improve an engagement, or could even end it altogether. David Cressy suggests that their primary role was at either end of the process, initially screening promising (and less promising) suitors, and later drawing up contracts once a couple was engaged to marry.[67] The couples studied in this book conducted their courtships under general familial oversight—women shared suitors' love letters with friends, mothers, and aunts; fathers could keep men courting their daughters at arm's length until a fortune was secure, and make their sons reconsider, defer, or terminate an incongruous match. Joan Perkin has characterized the process as 'a sort of willing drift into a suitable alliance'.[68] This book reveals that family and friends also provided an important source of practical and

---

[62] The vicar's widow Elizabeth Leathes (née Reading) married her second husband Edward Peach in 1790, while the banker and brewer Francis Cobb married his third wife Charlotte Mary Curwen in 1805.

[63] Model letter of apology by Richard How I, for Isabella Everard (née Eccleston) to copy and send to her parents, 6 September 1726, HW86/17, BAS.

[64] John Franklin named the Porden Islands in the Canadian Arctic Archipelago after Eleanor during his voyage to Canada between 1819 and 1822. Henry Duff Traill, *The Life of Sir John Franklin* (Cambridge, [1896] 2012).

[65] Eleanor Anne Porden to John Franklin, 23 May 1821, D3311/8/1/12, DRO.

[66] Martin Ingram, *Church Courts, Sex and Marriage in England, 1570–1640* (Cambridge, 1990), 136.

[67] Cressy, *Birth, Marriage and Death*, 257.

[68] Joan Perkin, *Women and Marriage in Nineteenth-Century England* (London, 2002), 60.

emotional support during the breakdown of a relationship. It remained extremely rare for couples to elope and disregard parental wishes altogether, as with the rector Edward Leathes and reverend's daughter Elizabeth Reading, who escaped to London in 1774 to marry by licence, aided by their friends, and Betsy's aunt and uncle Catherine and William Nelson.

This book endeavours to move away from the oppositional categories of marrying for love *or* status, individual choice *or* the interests of kin, which repeatedly set the terms for debate in histories of marriage and the family. As post-revisionist scholarship in the last twenty years has made clear, individuals at the time were well aware that a balance was to be struck between the two. Rather, it aims to explore the full range of emotions experienced by ordinary men and women engaging in courtship, as expressed in text and object. Given the 'affective turn' in recent historical scholarship, the time is ripe for doing so. As Katie Barclay recently declared, 'marriage is back on the historical agenda.'[69] This book returns marriage to the agenda by forging new links between histories of courtship, emotions, and the material world. In seeking to draw an emotional map of courtship, I ask, how did couples conceptualize and convey their emotions in words and objects? How did they negotiate this potentially fraught period in the life cycle? Such a study helps us to understand what it really meant to engage in courtship in eighteenth-century England, from the perspective of lovers themselves.

LOVE IN OBJECTS

Material objects from letters to locks of hair held a central place in rituals of courtship, and were used to negotiate, cement, and publicize a match. The material culture of courtship has received sustained attention from scholars of sixteenth- and seventeenth-century England.[70] In particular, Diana O'Hara has outlined how the meaning of a particular gift was determined by the object itself, its symbolic and economic value, the occasion of giving, and the intentions of the giver.[71] In a society often dependent upon non-literate forms of communication, the exchange of gifts was a crucial form of language and an important socially recognized custom. Their purpose during courtship was publicly to 'conduct the parties through these vulnerable times', from its early stages to a formal betrothal, and finally a

---

[69] Katie Barclay, 'Marriage', in *Early Modern Emotions: An Introduction*, ed. Susan Broomhall (London and New York, 2017), 217–20, at 219.

[70] See Peter Rushton, 'The Testament of Gifts: Marriage Tokens and Disputed Contracts in North-East England, 1560–1630', *Folk Life* 24.1 (1985): 25–31; Laura Gowing, *Domestic Dangers: Women, Words and Sex in Early Modern London* (Oxford, 1996), 159–64; O'Hara, *Courtship and Constraint*, 57–98; Loreen Giese, *Courtships, Marriage Customs, and Shakespeare's Comedies* (New York, 2006), 81–157; Sarah Anne Bendall, 'To Write a Distick upon It: Busks and the Language of Courtship and Sexual Desire in Sixteenth- and Seventeenth-Century England', *Gender and History* 26 (2014): 199–222; Sarah Ann Robin, 'Pictures, Posies and Promises: Love and the Object: The English in the Seventeenth Century' (unpublished PhD thesis, Lancaster University, 2016).

[71] O'Hara, *Courtship and Constraint*, 57. On the changing symbolism of objects, also see Juana Green, 'The Sempster's Wares: Merchandising and Marrying in *The Fair Maid of the Exchange* (1607)', *Renaissance Quarterly* 53.4 (2000): 1084–118.

post-contractual period culminating in a church wedding.[72] The comparative neglect of eighteenth-century rituals is an oversight rectified in this book. Amanda Vickery recognized the sentimental value of gifts in *The Gentleman's Daughter* (1998), presenting items such as letters, hair-work rings, purses, and ruffles as objects 'rich with memory', particularly when women invested time in crafting gifts by hand.[73] Love tokens played a vital role in preserving the identity of the giver, and acted as an important site of memory for the recipient.

As argued in the following chapters, objects also played a fundamental role in creating and affirming feelings of love. Following the art historian Louise Purbrick, this book treats gifts as 'acts of love', which expressed 'the significance of a person that cannot be contained in words; their exchange creates attachments, acknowledges and affirms the extent of a family; they are the cause of tears of sadness and joy'.[74] The book uses the emerging field of emotions and material culture to demonstrate the fundamental role played by objects in eliciting and concretizing the experience of love. It argues that emotions are not only shaped through words, but can be prompted by particular objects, whether a love letter, purse, or portrait miniature.[75] This analysis provides us with a broader understanding of courting practices, to include those who may not have engaged in epistolary culture, but who built their relationships through sending and receiving valentines, smelling fragrant posies, and gazing upon hair-work gifts.

In considering how rituals of courtship shape experiences of love, I agree with Monique Scheer's influential theory of emotions as a kind of practice. As part of the 'nexus of doings and sayings' involved in courtship, words, gestures, and sensory engagement with objects were crucial in 'mobilizing' particular emotions. For courting couples, touching, smelling, and gazing at love tokens worked 'to evoke feelings where there are none, to focus diffuse arousals and give them an intelligible shape'. In this way, courtship 'is not just a behaviour but has performative effects on the constitution of feelings and the (gendered) self'.[76] Love is thus something that we *do* through particular socially and historically determined rituals. Here, we might usefully adapt the Duc de la Rochefoucauld's maxim—to also include bodily movement—that 'Love, like fire, subsists by continual motion.'[77] As in Bourdieu's concept of *habitus*, conceptualizing how people inhabit their social worlds, a lover's interaction with objects is guided by embodied practices that have been 'internalized as a second nature'.[78] Just as emotions change over time, the rituals used to produce these emotions are rooted in a particular moment.

---

[72] O'Hara, *Courtship and Constraint*, 63–4, 75.   [73] Vickery, *The Gentleman's Daughter*, 21–3.

[74] Louise Purbrick, 'I Love Giving Presents: The Emotion of Material Culture', in *Love Objects: Emotion, Design, and Material Culture*, ed. Anna Moran and Sorcha O'Brien (London, 2014), 9–20, at 19.

[75] For an introduction to the study of emotions and material culture, see Stephanie Downes, Sally Holloway, and Sarah Randles, eds., *Feeling Things: Objects and Emotions through History* (Oxford, 2018), esp. Ch. 1, 'A Feeling for Things: Past and Present', 8–26.

[76] Scheer, 'Are Emotions a Kind of Practice?' esp. 209–12.

[77] François de La Rochefoucauld, *Maxims and Moral Reflections* (Edinburgh, [1665] 1798), 57.

[78] Pierre Bourdieu, *The Logic of Practice* (Stanford, CA, [1980] 1990), 56.

Affect theory has gained increasing traction among historians, anthropologists, philosophers, psychologists, and cultural theorists seeking to understand the affective relationship between people and things. Affect can be defined as a kind of intensity or arousal that precedes conscious thought. As Jo Labanyi explains, it is 'the body's response to stimuli at a precognitive and prelinguistic level'.[79] Sara Ahmed has used affect theory to consider how particular goods are designated 'objects of happiness'. Certain items such as love tokens 'become happy *for us*, if we imagine they will bring happiness *to us*'. In this way, objects are 'sticky' as they garner positive value as they are exchanged, becoming viewed as causes of happiness, as 'happiness means' or 'happiness pointers'.[80] We can see the role of such 'sticky' objects in producing feelings of love between courting couples. One letter from the Justice of the Peace Anthony Hamond to Mary Ann Musters in 1828 described how:

> I am not yet to set [sic] down to write to my dearest Mary Ann as I am horribly out of Temper I know nothing that is so likely to cure me as writing to you indeed I already begin to feel the good Effects of this remedy.[81]

The sending and receipt of letters and tokens thus 'pointed' individuals toward happiness, and worked to produce feelings of love. Anthony believed that a letter to Mary Ann would improve his mood, imbuing the letter in advance with positive affect. Once he began to write, the letter pointed him toward happiness.

In using objects to analyse the emotional experience of courtship, this book adopts what Bernard Herman has termed an 'object-driven' approach to material culture. This approach involves using objects—and textual accounts of objects—to reveal the values and beliefs of the people who created, exchanged, and interacted with them. As previously noted, I aim to reconnect objects with their social, cultural, and emotional contexts through a process of 'thick description'.[82] This book also makes use of Jules David Prown's 'object-centred' methodology in interpreting objects as 'artistic fictions' that 'materialize belief'.[83] Through unravelling the particular fictions of handkerchiefs, hair, gloves, rings, and snuffboxes as cultural artefacts, the language of objects provides invaluable evidence for this book of how 'culture speaks its mind'.[84]

[79] Jo Labanyi, 'Doing Things: Emotion, Affect, and Materiality', *Journal of Spanish Cultural Studies* 11.3–4 (2010): 223–33, at 224.

[80] Sara Ahmed, 'Happy Objects', in *The Affect Theory Reader*, ed. Melissa Gregg and Gregory J. Seigworth (Durham, NC and London, 2010), 29–51. Also see Sara Ahmed, *The Cultural Politics of Emotion*, second edition (Edinburgh, 2004), esp. 218–25.

[81] Hamond to Musters, undated (c.1828), HMN 5/95/3, NRO.

[82] Bernard L. Herman, *The Stolen House* (London, 1992), 3–4.

[83] Jules David Prown, *Art as Evidence: Writings on Art and Material Culture* (New Haven, CT and London, 2001), 220–34.

[84] Ibid., 237. Here, Prown distinguishes between the 'hard material culturist' who 'focuses on the reality of the object itself' and the 'soft material culturist' who aims to 'discover underlying cultural beliefs'. This research falls into the latter category.

THE PRESENT STUDY

This book rediscovers the emotional and material dimensions of courtship in Georgian England using the words and objects selected by couples to negotiate their relationships. The first two chapters consider formulations of love in words. Chapter 1 rediscovers the 'script' shaping romantic language in the eighteenth century. As the social psychologist Lubomir Lamy argues, love 'is first and foremost a *story*', with individuals following a '*script*' for love that describes how a romantic relationship should normally unfold'.[85] The chapter provides a thematic overview of the various religious, physical, and literary tropes shaping the language of love. It sets out the wider framework that guided the language used by lovers in Georgian England, and how they conceived and navigated—and therefore experienced—love itself.

After fleshing out this broader framework, I look more closely at the role of love letters in navigating courtship. Chapter 2 considers how letters worked to move a relationship forward, and facilitate greater emotional intimacy between writers. The chapter evaluates the role of the love letter on the path to matrimony using the correspondences of eight couples of varied social rank. Letter-writing is presented as a distinct stage of courtship, during which couples negotiated, tested, and cemented a marital bond. Men and women adopted particular gendered strategies, with women demonstrating their virtue, modesty, and self-doubt to suitors, who in return emphasized their sincerity, and—with increasing frequency over the century—rhapsodized about their depth of feeling. Engagement to marry was not a single moment but a lengthy process, becoming more assured as greater numbers of letters were exchanged. The chapter demonstrates the emotional value of missives as 'thoughts' or 'favours' sent by loved ones, which were treated as treasured possessions and praised as sources of pleasure that could even transcend death itself.

The following two chapters examine love in objects. Chapter 3 uses sensory interaction with love tokens to explore the process of falling in love. It brings together gifts typically selected by courting men, such as garters, rings, and stay busks, with those characteristically chosen by women, such as violets and hairwork tokens, plus letters, locks of hair, silhouettes, and miniature portraits given by both sexes. The chapter reveals how highly ritualized ways of gazing at, touching, and smelling these items both created and expedited the experience of love. In the absence of a lover, the power of imagination could make pictures 'grow the more finish'd, and acquire a greater Resemblance', while letters could fire the passions 'as if the Persons themselves were present'.[86] By considering how individuals collected and interacted with gifts, the chapter responds to Monique Scheer's call for historians of the emotions to think 'harder about what people are *doing*' by looking at the 'bodies and artifacts of the past'.[87]

---

[85] Lubomir Lamy, 'Beyond Emotion: Love as an Encounter of Myth and Drive', *Emotion Review* 8.2 (2016): 97–107, at 103.

[86] *Letters of Abelard and Héloïse. To which is prefix'd, A Particular Account of their Lives, Amours, and Misfortunes. Extracted chiefly from Monsieur Bayle. Translated from the French,* fourth edition (London, 1722), Letter II, Heloise to Abelard, 105.

[87] Scheer, 'Are Emotions a Kind of Practice?' 217.

Once I have established the role of letters and tokens in facilitating the experience of love, Chapter 4 reveals what was *new* to the period, from porcelain snuffboxes, glass signets, and watch papers printed with romantic motifs to the increasingly elaborate laced and embossed valentine cards sold by printers, booksellers, and stationers shops. The eighteenth century is presented as an important transitional period in the modernization and commercialization of romantic customs. After Hardwicke's Marriage Act of 1753 required marriages to take place at church in a single legal event—precluding suits in the church courts to compel the performance of a marriage contract—courting couples exchanged an ever-diversifying range of new consumer goods as romantic gifts.[88] A growing number and variety of novelty items such as printed handkerchiefs were designed specifically as valentine souvenirs, as Valentine's Day developed into a love industry. The chapter explores how love was packaged and sold to consumers in new ways, and the consequences of this shift for the rituals and experiences of romantic love.

Yet as men and women engaging in courtship were well aware, romantic relationships did not always result in matrimony. The final two chapters of this book analyse the language and rituals of romantic breakdown. Chapter 5 examines the cultural codes of romantic suffering. The chapter begins by analysing how men and women engaging in troubled relationships conceptualized their emotional turmoil using the language of the heart. It considers the cultural influence of archetypal heroines such as Armida, Queen Dido, and Ophelia, as women's suffering from love assumed an increasingly dominant role in popular culture from mid-century. The cult of sensibility transformed women in love into objects of sympathy, whose misfortunes were caused by their tender and feeling hearts. This redefinition of gender roles transformed the suicidal lover from a female to a male figure—exemplified by Goethe's Werther—with eighteenth-century men committing heroic acts of passion whilst their sweethearts languished away. The chapter closes by tracing the disintegration of relationships through objects. It reveals how it was imperative for lovers to return letters and romantic gifts with the utmost urgency in order formally to terminate an engagement.

The final chapter analyses the legal consequences of broken relationships using ninety breach of promise cases under the common law. It unpicks the nature of the suit including the verdicts, gender balance, damages awarded, age, occupation, and social status of plaintiffs and defendants. While women brought 81.8 per cent of cases, they were also more likely to win. Most plaintiffs and defendants were 'decent' members of the middling sort: their status 'was not very elevated; but it was respectable'.[89] I show how the action changed in response to the emotional

---

[88] The provisions of the Act became law on 25 March 1754. It required a valid marriage to be preceded by the calling of the banns on three consecutive Sundays, or the purchase of a costly wedding licence from the Archbishop of Canterbury. It applied to all Anglican, Catholic, Presbyterian, Baptist, and Independent ceremonies, only exempting Jewish and Quaker weddings. For a comprehensive overview, see Rebecca Probert, *Marriage Law and Practice in the Long Eighteenth Century* (Cambridge, 2009), 232-5, 314–39.

[89] *Simpson vs. Timperon, Morning Post*, 10 March 1828, 17857, British Newspapers 1600–1900: https://www.connectedhistories.org/resources/bu/

shifts outlined in the previous chapter, as by the 1790s romantic hurt was presented in court as a uniquely female grievance. Cases increasingly came to rely upon demonstrating the hurt feelings of spurned lovers, where a man was not thought to suffer 'the like disparagement as when it happens to a female'.[90] Finally, the chapter reveals how objects such as love letters, wedding licences, wedding clothes, and furniture for the marital home were crucial in securing a victory in court, by providing material evidence of proximity to marriage.

The Game of Love in Georgian England concludes by outlining how courting practices actively cultivated particular feelings, and sets out the wider significance of these findings for the history of emotions. Rituals of falling in and out of love have important consequences for our understanding of how men and women navigated social relationships in words and objects, and of the performative effects of these rituals in the constitution and navigation of feeling.

---

[90] *Leeds vs. Cooke and Wife, Morning Post*, 2 March 1803, Issue 10736.

1

The Language of Love

To LOVE *v. a.* [lufian, Saxon.][1]

1. To regard with passionate affection, as that of one sex to the other.

Good shepherd, tell this youth what 'tis to *love*. – It is to be made all of sighs and tears; It is to be made all of faith and service; It is to be all made of fantasy, All made of passion, and all made of wishes [...]

Shakespeare. As you like it.

2. To regard with the affection of a friend.

None but his brethren he, and sisters, knew, Whom the kind youth prefer'd to me, And much above myself I *lov'd* them too.

Cowley.

3. To regard with parental tenderness.

He that loveth me shall be *loved* of my father, and I will *love* him, and will manifest myself to him.

John xiv. 21.

4. To be pleased with.

Fish used to salt water delight more in fresh: we see that salmons and smelts *love* to get into rivers, though against the stream.

Bacon's Natural History N°. 703.

5. To regard with reverent unwillingness to offend.

Love the Lord thy God with all thine heart.

Deuteronomy. vi. 5.

In 1755, the first edition of Samuel Johnson's *Dictionary of the English Language* provided five separate definitions of the verb 'To LOVE', covering diverse themes from passionate affection to friendship, and parental tenderness. The most common sense of the word is cited first, leading to the more unusual.[2] These divergent ideas illustrate the inherent contradictions in the term that existed contemporaneously

---

[1] 'To Love' in Samuel Johnson, *A Dictionary of the English Language: In Which the Words are Deduced from their Originals, and Illustrated in their Different Significations by Examples from the Best Writers*, first edition (London, 1755), Vol. II, 73. For the sake of brevity, only the first quotation used to illustrate each term is repeated here.

[2] Johnson aimed to 'show by what gradations of intermediate sense [each word] has passed from its primitive to its remote and accidental signification, so that every foregoing explanation should tend to that which follows, and the series be regularly concatenated from the first notion to the last': *Dictionary*, Vol. I, 7.

in the eighteenth century. Whilst love was a Godly principle given to and from the Lord, it was also a sexualized term for passion and desire. Likewise, love was both the guiding principle of parental affection and the objectification of a loved one. The pervasive concept manifested itself in scores of other terms describing objects such as a 'loveknot', 'lovetoy', and 'loveletter'. It also foretold the inherent dangers of romantic love, such as falling prey to the 'lovetrick' of a 'lovemonger' and becoming 'lovelorn' and 'lovesick'. As Shakespeare wrote in *As You Like It*, the passionate affection uniting men and women was 'all made of fantasy...and all made of wishes', as individuals embraced or jettisoned particular romantic tropes to describe, intensify, and give shape to their emotions.

This chapter outlines how understandings of love among courting couples were contingent upon particular religious, medical, and literary developments. It argues that the expression of love relied upon appropriately adapting, reusing, and engaging with a number of devices that were shared between writers and recipients. As the social psychologist Lubomir Lamy recently noted, the 'meaning we give to our core affect is forever changing according to the information that we are given', with society offering lovers a 'script' to inform their experience.[3] The centrality of culture to emotional experience has long been realized by psychologists and neurologists; as Oliver Sacks famously wrote, 'culture tunes our neurons.' Our reliance on culture in formulating emotion means that our nervous systems 'need culture as much as they need chemicals. Without language and culture, we are like headless monsters.'[4] Philosophers such as Peter Goldie have similarly argued that our way of thinking about love is undoubtedly 'shaped by our environment'.[5] By examining the language used by lovers, we can consider how eighteenth-century couples conceptualized, formulated, and expressed their emotions. Taking this further—following William Reddy's pioneering work on 'emotives'—such expressions intensified, modulated, and even created the experience of love. The 'emotion words' chosen by lovers thus had 'a direct impact' on the feelings they referred to.[6]

The chapter is divided into three thematic sections, each focusing upon one guiding principle of romantic love in eighteenth-century England. The first section uses love letters to explore the founding doctrines of Christian love in the Bible, the Book of Common Prayer, and *Paradise Lost*, considering denominational differences between Anglican, Unitarian, and Quaker letters. The second looks at changes in physical understandings of love from the humours to the nerves, including new philosophies of the 'chemistry' and 'electricity' of attraction. Finally, the third section examines archetypal couples such as Troilus and Cressida invoked in love letters, plus new tropes disseminated through epistolary, romantic, and gothic fiction. These diverse ideas in religion, medicine, science, and literature influenced the expectations and experiences of courting couples by determining the signs, symptoms, and conventions of romantic love in Georgian England.

---

[3] Lamy, 'Beyond Emotion', 99.

[4] David Howes, 'Culture Tunes Our Neurons', in *Empire of the Senses: The Sensual Culture Reader*, ed. David Howes (Oxford, 2005), 22.

[5] Peter Goldie, 'Love for a Reason', *Emotion Review* 2.1 (2010): 61–7, at 62.

[6] Reddy, *Navigation of Feeling*, 103–7.

In reconstructing the passion, affection, and reverence that comprised romantic love, the chapter uses evidence from eighteen different courtships alongside excerpts from religious tracts, medical treatises, dictionaries, novels, plays, poems, and ballads. Key questions include, how did the expression of romantic love evolve over the long eighteenth century? How did religious beliefs shape romantic language? How did the language of love adapt to new medical and scientific discoveries? Who were the archetypal couples in fiction? What purpose did this language serve for courting couples? These help us to conceptualize how lovers situated themselves—and crafted their relationships—within wider romantic culture. The literary theorist Roland Barthes wrote that the 'amorous subject cannot write his love story himself'.[7] So how did eighteenth-century couples compose their love stories?

RELIGIOUS LOVE

The first part of this chapter analyses how particular religious doctrines and denominational beliefs shaped conceptions of romantic love. Certain writers specified the two books sitting before them as they composed their love letters: the Bible and prayer book.[8] The Bible was distributed throughout all levels of society, inextricably linking romantic and biblical notions of love. It was one of the most influential books of the early modern period, and had a vast readership, increasingly becoming the focus of preliminary education in the eighteenth century. Copies were distributed by groups such as the Society for Promoting Christian Knowledge and the Bible Society.[9] After discoursing 'on Religion' with her friend Sally Sheppard in 1760, the tailor's daughter Sarah Hurst wondered how there could be 'so astonishing a thing in the World as an Atheist'. Two years later, she gave 'thanks to the supream Being for making my Harry mine'.[10] The Unitarian John Eccles (d. 1780) was equally convinced of the celestial nature of love, proclaiming, "Tis an inexpressible power, that moves all the faculties of the soul . . . 'tis a celestial spark . . . 'tis the finishing stroke of heaven, the polish of existence.'[11] Numerous phrases in courtship letters were directly inspired by biblical passages, with the banker and brewer Francis Cobb (1759–1831) noting in 1805, 'Grace, Mercy & Peace be with you, My Dearest Love—thanks to a kind God for the Mercies of this day.'[12] Such language can be found throughout the King James Bible, with Timothy and Titus each praying for 'Grace, mercy and peace, from God our Father and Jesus Christ our Lord.'[13] These lovers used celestial language to characterize love as a heavenly force, even obliquely transferring passages from the Bible to their own letters.

[7] Roland Barthes, *A Lover's Discourse: Fragments*, trans. Richard Howard (London, [1977] 2002), 93.

[8] Anthony Hamond to Mary Ann Musters, undated (*c.*1828–30), HMN/5/95/1, NRO.

[9] See Scott Mandelbrote, 'The English Bible and its Readers in the Eighteenth Century', in *Books and their Readers in Eighteenth-Century England*, Vol. II, *New Essays*, ed. Isabel Rivers (London and New York, 2003), 35–78, esp. 46–50.

[10] Diary of Sarah Hurst, 23 March 1760, MS 3543 and 3 June 1762, MS 3545, HM.

[11] Eccles to Hays, Letter XXXIX, in Wedd, ed., *Love-Letters of Mary Hays*, 78.

[12] Francis Cobb to Charlotte Mary Curwen, 28 January 1805, EK/U1453/C287/4, Kent History and Library Centre, Maidstone (subsequently KHLC).

[13] For example Timothy 1:1, 2:1, and Titus 1:4, The Bible, Authorized King James Version (subsequently KJV).

Christian couples rooted their letters in biblical doctrines to debate the virtuous or selfish nature of humanity. The Unitarian lovers James Nicholson (1718–73) and Elizabeth Seddon (1721–91) used debates about human nature as the founding doctrine of their courtship between 1738 and 1740. As Elizabeth argued in December 1738, 'with regard to moral virtues we are in a Great measure free agents...I think no moral virtues will bring us to Heaven, tho' there is no attaining Heaven without them.'[14] Such theological issues provided a stimulating subject for discussion, with Elizabeth reminding James that 'it is your turn to propose the next To pick.'[15] The political philosopher Thomas Hobbes famously argued that virtue was solely a matter of private will and that humans were essentially selfish and sensual. Adam's mortality was brought about by his first sin, while Jesus 'hath satisfied for the Sins of all that believe in him; and therefore recovered to all Believers, that eternal Life, which was lost by the Sin of Adam'.[16] In contrast, moralists such as Francis Hutcheson, Joseph Butler, and Anthony Cooper, third Earl of Shaftesbury argued that humans were naturally virtuous.[17] Such debates were discussed at length by nonconformist couples such as Elizabeth and James, allowing them to gauge their compatibility before marriage. These written discussions ceased immediately after their union on 11 October 1740, as they had served their purpose in encouraging intellectual exchange between the couple. Through providing a fertile ground for debate, discussion of religious maxims facilitated the development of a mutual bond on the road to matrimony.

The Bible shaped individual conceptions of love using the relationships of particular couples.[18] The Old Testament told the inspiring stories of the beautiful Rebecca and her betrothal to Isaac, which she considered 'the most happy event of her life'. Eighteenth-century texts advised readers that 'every one entering on that state, ought to have chiefly in their eye...such principles and dispositions as Rebecca had received from a regular and godly education.'[19] Naomi was also blissfully happy with her husband Elimelech: 'in marriage she has sacrificed her all, conscience excepted, to the will and power of her husband, and now looks up to him as her

---

[14] Elizabeth Seddon to James Nicholson, 2 December 1738, GBB133 Eng. MS 1041/9 (Box 1), John Rylands Library, Manchester (subsequently JRL).

[15] Ibid., 7 August 1738, GBB 133 Eng. MS 1041/3.

[16] 'Of a Christian Commonwealth', from *Leviathan* in *The moral and political works of Thomas Hobbes of Malmesbury* (London, 1750), 296, 302. For later Hobbesian thinkers such as Benedict de Spinoza and Pierre Bayle, see Isabel Rivers, *Reason, Grace and Sentiment: A Study of the Language of Religion and Ethics in England 1660–1780* (Cambridge, 2000), Vol. II, 14, 16, 20–2, 64, 96, 197, 245–6.

[17] See *An inquiry into the original of our ideas of beauty and virtue* (London, [1725] 1738) and *An essay on the nature and conduct of the passions and affections* (London, [1728] 1730). John Wesley argued that Hutcheson's position was particularly dangerous as he made morality independent of God. See Rivers, *Reason, Grace and Sentiment*, Vol. I, 230–1, and Thomas Dixon, *From Passions to Emotions: The Creation of a Secular Psychological Category* (Cambridge, 2003), 69–70. See also Anthony Ashley Cooper, third Earl of Shaftesbury, *Characteristicks of men, manners, opinions, times* (London, [1711] 1732), Vol. II, esp. 175–6, and Joseph Butler, *The analogy of religion, natural and revealed, to the constitution and course of nature* (London, 1736), esp. 57.

[18] For the deliberate shift towards matrimonial lexicon in early modern Bible translations, see Naomi Tadmor, 'Women and Wives: The Language of Marriage in Early Modern English Biblical Translations', *History Workshop Journal* 62.1 (2006): 1–27.

[19] John Baird, *Dissertations, chronological, historical, and critical, on all the books of the Old Testament* (London, 1778), Dissertation XXII, 331–3.

earthly all... they are no longer twain but one flesh.'[20] Publications on the 'Happiness of Kissing' utilized a kiss between Rachel and Jacob in Genesis to represent 'the Power of Love'. The kiss provided 'an Introduction to a stricter Intimacy, which terminated in a happy Marriage'.[21] Further popular couples were Naomi's daughter-in-law Ruth and the generous Boaz, who were the subjects of numerous contemporary plays and poems such as Thomas Haweis' *Ruth. A Sacred Oratorio* (1778) and *Ruth, or, The fair Moabitess* (1810). The relationship between the three provided a model of the kindness of God, as his disciples looked after one another; 'So Ruth to Naomi, Boaz to Ruth.'[22]

Couples such as Adam and Eve paradoxically represented both the joys of love and dangers of deception. The Bedfordshire gentleman Samuel Whitbread II harnessed Adam's dialogue with the Angel Raphael to conceptualize his feelings for Elizabeth Grey, describing how 'when I hear from thee I seem in Heaven / & thy words / Bring to their sweetness no satiety.'[23] The tale was dramatized in Book IX of John Milton's *Paradise Lost* (1667) and republished annually in the eighteenth century as 'the sale increased double the number every year.'[24] Milton's epic had a profound effect on romantic love through the intimate relationship he created between Adam and Eve. Adam praised how 'we are one, / One flesh; to lose thee were to lose myself', while Eve replied 'O glorious trial of exceeding love... One heart, one soul in both.'[25] The wheelwright Jedediah Strutt referenced Milton in his courtship letters to Elizabeth Woollat, conceptualizing his garden as Adam's 'Nuptial Bower' and using the lush 'Sweets' of Eden to anticipate the 'pleasures of Bliss and Love'.[26] Milton also explored the subject of 'man's disobedience, and the loss thereupon of Paradise', explaining the role of Satan disguised as the serpent in man's downfall.[27] Spurned lovers such as Richard Law of Marylebone were inspired by Eve's disobedience, writing to Jane Townley in 1816 that 'you were once pleasant to me as the blooming Maid of Paradise, till you was deceived by the serpent, and perswaded [*sic*] to change your angelic form.'[28] The tale provided a rich vocabulary of love and deception, with Samuel, Jedediah, and Richard neglecting to name the book they quoted from explicitly, instead presuming the recipient's complicity in the shared language of love.

The Book of Common Prayer used to conduct Anglican ceremonies provided devout writers with a guidebook of pious lexicon to express their emotions. The Margate banker and brewer Francis Cobb and his sweetheart Charlotte Mary Curwen regularly referred to themselves as 'your Unworthy Man', 'his unworthy servant', and 'this unworthy Handmaid, & servant' in their letters.[29] Such phrases

---

[20] John MacGowan, *Discourses on the Book of Ruth* (London, 1781), 20.

[21] *A desertation wherein the meaning, duty and happiness of kissing are explained, from Genesis* (London, 1780), 7–8.

[22] MacGowan, *Discourses*, Sermon VI, 116.

[23] Samuel Whitbread II to Elizabeth Grey, Spa, 11 September 1787, W1/6577, No. 31, BAS.

[24] John Milton, *Paradise Lost. A Poem, In Twelve Books* (London, [1667] 1788), preface.

[25] Ibid., Book IX, 245.

[26] Jed. Strutt to Woollat, Blackwell, 25 June 1755, D5303/4/6, DRO.

[27] Milton, *Paradise Lost*, Book I, 14.

[28] Richard Law to Jane Townley, Doncaster, 10 May 1816, Add MS 47796, f. 1r, BL.

[29] Cobb to Curwen, 1 August 1805, EK/U1453/C287/5, and Curwen to Cobb, 13 December 1805, EK/U1453/C2/A/9, KHLC.

mirrored the general thanksgiving 'Almighty God, Father of all mercies, we, thine unworthy servants, do give thee most humble thanks for all thy goodness to us.'[30] The couple also discussed psalms they had read, with Charlotte asking Francis to 'inform me [of] the verses of the Psalms you used to repeat in a morning when the Lord favored us by being together in his presence, I admired them very much.' These include Psalm XXXIV, 'The Hosts of God encamp around / Deliv'rance he affords to all / O make but Trial of his Love.' The notion of a 'trial' was frequently employed during courtship letters, where lovers prayed 'for support under this my great trial'.[31] Nonetheless, this did not mean that all self-professed Anglicans drew upon godly discourses in their letters, as only a select number who were particularly devout chose to do so. On the whole, it was more common for women to draw upon religious language in their missives, as this allowed them to emphasize their piety to their prospective husbands.

Quaker couples located their love in the soul, which was the place of communion between man and God. As the flour merchant Thomas Kirton (1709–57) wrote to Olive Lloyd (1707–75) in 1734, his sentiments 'respecting thee' acted 'on my Soul'.[32] Quaker writers also characterized marriage as a union of minds or spirits, with the minister's niece Betty Fothergill (1752–1809) noting in her diary in 1770 that separation 'could not dis Joint [*sic*] the union of minds which is the seat of Intellectual love'.[33] The merchant and ship-owner William Rathbone III similarly urged his future daughter-in-law Hannah Reynolds in 1786 to make 'a religious influence...the foundation of the union of your spirits'.[34] Quaker emphasis upon marriage as the 'Seed of God' reflects the expectation that individuals would marry within the Society of Friends.[35] The importance of maintaining the pure and godly foundations of marriage was reinforced in texts such as William Smith's *Joyful Tidings to the Begotten of God in All* (1663) which was repeatedly republished throughout the eighteenth century. Quaker couples intertwined the languages of love and Quakerism to eschew the physicality of love, locating their emotions in the soul while using their letters to construct a spiritual and intellectual union before marriage.

Courtship letters by nonconformist women could be more assertive than letters by their Anglican counterparts, due to a greater emphasis upon female education and the prominent role of female ministers, preachers, and missionaries.[36]

---

[30] *Abridgement of the Book of Common Prayer, and administration of the Sacraments* (London, 1773), 35.

[31] Curwen to Cobb, January 1805, EK/U1453/C287/2, KHLC.

[32] Thomas Kirton to Olive Lloyd, 14 August 1734, TEMP MSS 210/2/96, Library of the Society of Friends, London (subsequently LSF).

[33] Diary of Betty Fothergill, 8 February 1770 (Fifth Day), MS. Vol. 5, 51/1, p. 27, LSF.

[34] William Rathbone III to Hannah Reynolds, 8th 7th month 1786, RP. III. 1. 253, Liverpool University Library, Liverpool (subsequently LUL).

[35] Moses West's *A Treatise Concerning Marriage. Wherein the Unlawfulness of Mixt-Marriages is Laid Open*, was republished in 1732, 1735, 1736, 1761, and 1780. On Quaker marriage practices, see Edward H. Milligan, *Quaker Marriage* (Kendal, 1994) and on distinctive features of Quaker letter-writing, see Susan Whyman, *The Pen and the People: English Letter Writers 1660–1800* (Oxford, 2009), 144–54.

[36] Quakers paid assiduous attention to their children's schooling, educating them in Quaker ways and enabling them to use written texts as devotional aids. All Quaker ministers were expected to be able to read the Bible, while reading and writing were vital for their spiritual development. Women

The Quaker Betty Fothergill saw the ironmonger Alexander Chorley as her 'Pheonax' [*sic*], hoping that he would 'allways love me allways be gratefull allways be complasant'. However, when one letter in 1769 convinced her that he was just 'like the rest', she wrote to instruct him on how to improve his faults:

> I ventured to give him some advice upon a few things I had observd [*sic*] with respect to himself – they where [*sic*] slight errors which I knew he Cou'd easily Correct – & as acting the part of a real Friend I thought it my place to remark them. which I did in the manner my real regard suggested & not with the acrimony of a severe Critict…

However, Betty was surprised to find her advice coolly received:

> how was I mistaken in my Congectures when instead of tender acknowledgements I recieved [*sic*] a few Cool thanks & several accusations of want of affection & in short an air of Coldness… it shockd me to see such spirit of mistaken pride, which I plainly saw Was the source.[37]

Betty's Quakerism and education had made her confident in expressing her views on decorous behaviour; when Alexander later apologized for his harsh words, Betty noted the pleasure she felt at his flexibility.[38] She was determined not to follow the example of the 'poor women' of her acquaintance who had been 'cajoled by degrees to lose their liberty' during courtship, until they had 'nothing to do but quietly submit'.[39] Betty was particularly critical of Alexander's sinful pride. Pride was a popular topic in letters between nonconformist couples, with James Nicholson and Elizabeth Seddon repeatedly condemning 'that Cursed bitter root of pride'.[40] As Betty's uncle Samuel (1715–72) advised a young woman shortly before her marriage, 'Pride is its own punishment; fly from it as from a contagion which it strangely resembles: it infects and corrupts the soul.'[41]

While devout couples were brought together by their shared beliefs, certain writers in the late eighteenth century came to view romantic love as a religion in its own right.[42] Men such as Captain Richard Dixon described a complete inability to *exist* without their sweethearts, writing that 'I am now convinc'd you are inseparably connected with my existence—without you Life would be burthensome and distressing.'[43] Total absorption in love reached its peak in the first decades of the nineteenth century; the Romantic poet John Keats described how 'My love has

---

were allowed to practise as ministers from the founding of Quakerism *c.*1652, while a small minority also published theological texts. See Rebecca Larson, *Daughters of the Light: Quaker Women Preaching and Prophesying in the Colonies and Abroad 1700–1775* (London, 1999), esp. 82–5 on literacy, and Christine Trevett, *Quaker Women Prophets in England and Wales 1650–1700* (Ceredigion, 2000).

[37] Diary of Betty Fothergill, December 1769, MS. Vol. 5, 51/1, LSF.
[38] Ibid., 4 December 1769 (Second Day).   [39] Ibid., 21 December 1769 (Fifth Day).
[40] Seddon to Nicholson, 24 July 1738, MS 1041/2, JRL.
[41] Transcript of a letter from Samuel Fothergill to a young woman, in R. Hingston Fox, *Dr John Fothergill and his Friends* (London, 1919), Appendix C, 415.
[42] Karen Lystra has argued that in nineteenth-century America, romantic love 'contributed to the displacement of God by the lover as the central symbol of ultimate significance', as romantic relationships became 'more powerful and meaningful' than religious loyalties. See Karen Lystra, *Searching the Heart: Women, Men, and Romantic Love in Nineteenth-Century America* (New York and Oxford, 1989), 8.
[43] Richard Dixon to Esther Maria Cranmer, 7 May 1782, 8215/7, Surrey History Centre, Woking (subsequently SHC).

made me selfish. I cannot exist without you. I am forgetful of everything but seeing you again—my Life seems to stop there—I see no further. You have absorbed me.'[44] For the Justice of the Peace Anthony Hamond, life without his sweetheart would 'not be worth having'.[45] These new discourses illustrate transformations in the lexical expression of love, as the beloved woman was elevated above life itself. Yet while such men deified their sweethearts, the individual absorbed in love was consistently depicted as a female figure. Figure 1.1 depicts a young woman languishing in a chair; in idolizing the material artefacts of love she turns her back on Christianity, and the closed Bible and crucifix behind her. The caption misquotes Shakespeare's *Two Gentlemen of Verona*—' "For thee I pray, for thee I sigh and weep" '—and transforms the idolatrous lover from a man to a woman.[46] The girl's sinful behaviour reveals how romantic love could pose a threat to religion, as her 'devotions' defy the love of God. The image demonstrates how absorption in love was disparaged as a female preoccupation, despite primarily appearing in letters by men.

Impassioned men such as John Eccles used courtship letters to conceptualize the physicality of their love. As John wrote to the novelist Mary Hays in August 1779, 'Will he no more with eager haste, / Fly from the world to my embrace? / This hand, will he not softly press? / These lips, will he no more caress?'[47] Such language was mirrored in the Bible, which portrayed romantic love as an all-encompassing physical force, particularly in the Song of Songs. The book created numerous connections between love, wine, fruit, honey, and fire that provided an early model for the expression of passion. Passages such as 'O my spouse, drop as the honeycomb: honey and milk are under thy tongue' transformed the unrefined substance of milk into a natural carrier of love.[48] Milk was later adopted as a symbol of constancy in Mary Wollstonecraft's letters to the explorer Gilbert Imlay, describing his fickleness as 'milk and water affection'.[49] While milk represented unblemished love, Imlay's affection had been sadly watered down. Solomon's Song provided readers with a vast range of amorous metaphors for describing love's passion:

> Thy lips are like a thread of scarlet, and thy speech is comely: thy temples are like a piece of a pomegranate within thy locks.[50]

> Let him kiss me with the kisses of his mouth: for thy love is better than wine.[51]

> Many waters cannot quench love, neither can the floods drown it: if a man would give all the substance of his house for love, it would utterly be contemned.[52]

---

[44] Keats to Brawne, postmark 13 October 1819, Letter VII, in Forman, ed., *Letters of John Keats to Fanny Brawne* (London, 1878), 35–6.

[45] Hamond to Musters, undated (1828–30), HMN 5/95/2, NRO.

[46] While trying to seduce Silvia in Act IV, Scene II, Proteus declares, 'Vouchsafe me yet your picture for my love, the picture that is hanging in your chamber: To that I'll speak, to that I'll sigh and weep': *The Two Gentlemen of Verona* (1589–93). I am grateful to Katie Barclay for attributing this quotation.

[47] 'A Poem to Miss Hays', 31 August 1779, Letter XXXII in Wedd, ed., *Love-Letters of Mary Hays*, 68.

[48] Solomon's Song 4:11, KJV.

[49] The Promised Land was also described as 'a land flowing with milk and honey' in Exodus 3:8, KJV. Ingpen, ed., *Love Letters of Mary Wollstonecraft*, Letter VI, December 1793, 11. This is almost forty years before the *Oxford English Dictionary* records the first use of the phrase. See 'milk-and-water, v.', *Oxford English Dictionary* (online) (subsequently *OEDO*): http://www.oed.com/view/Entry/2341 65?rskey=MdusMw&result=2&isAdvanced=false.

[50] Solomon's Song 5:3, KJV.   [51] Solomon's Song 1:2, KJV.

[52] Solomon's Song 8:7, KJV.

Fig. 1.1. R. J. Lane after G. S. Newton, *A Girl at Her Devotions*, London, 1824, lithograph, image 24.5 cm × 20.5 cm, Wellcome Collection, London, 672767i, CC BY 4.0.

Eighteenth-century letter-writers such as John Eccles and Mary Wollstonecraft selected different metaphors such as milk and water in describing their affection. However, the continuing emphasis upon the hands, lips, and physical embraces of the lover reveal the continued influence of the Song of Songs in expressing the immediacy of desire.

PHYSICAL LOVE

The second part of this chapter examines physical understandings of love, beginning with the 'great luminary of medicine' Galen of Pergamum. Galen's works on circulation and the heart constituted an authoritative source of medical knowledge until the emergence of physicians such as William Harvey in the seventeenth century. As one anatomist noted in 1754:

> Galen has supplied to us the common fountains from whence the physiology of the human body has been taught, for near fifteen ages after him, down even to the times of Harvey... he is still a very deserving and professed anatomist, the last of the Greeks, the most eminent of all the ancients.[53]

Galen was a student of both Hippocrates and Plato, and from his arrival in Rome in AD 162 he was able to treat senators for disorders such as lovesickness by cooling their overheated humours.[54] He rejected Aristotle's view that the heart was the controlling organ of the body, arguing that it mirrored the tripartite division of heaven, sky, and earth—between the head, the breast, and the lower body.[55] Within this system there were four elements or 'humours'—blood, yellow bile (choler), phlegm, and black bile (melancholy). While blood was hot and moist like air, yellow bile was hot and dry like fire, phlegm was cold and moist like water, and black bile was cold and dry like earth.[56] In his treatise *De Temperamentis* (*On Mixtures*) Galen argued that the 'well-balanced' body should have a perfect mixture of hot, cold, dry, and wet; deviations from this model caused imbalance, illness, and extreme displays of particular emotions such as anger or melancholy.[57]

The central consequence of Galen's model for love was that men and women were thought to have different emotional tendencies, determined by the balance of their humours. Whilst men were thought to be generally hot-natured, women were seen as cold-natured.[58] As he argued in *De Usu Partium* (*On the Usefulness of the Parts of the Body*) this was because 'it was better for the female to be made colder so that she cannot disperse all the nutriment she concocts', creating the perfect environment in which a foetus could grow.[59] The preponderance of water in women's physical make-up made them more prone to tears and sudden irrational rages, whilst their greater passivity made them more subject to emotional extremes such as hysteria and lovesickness. This reflected Aristotle's theory that men possessed

---

[53] Albrecht von Haller, *Dr Albert Haller's physiology; being a course of lectures upon the visceral anatomy and vital oeconomy of human bodies* (London, 1754), Vol. I, xxxv–xxxvi.

[54] Christopher Gill, Tim Whitmarsh, and John Wilkins, 'Introduction', in *Galen and the World of Knowledge*, ed. Christopher Gill, Tim Whitmarsh, and John Wilkins (Cambridge, 2009), 4–5.

[55] Fay Bound Alberti, *Matters of the Heart: History, Medicine, and Emotion* (Oxford, 2010), 18–19.

[56] Ibid., 18. See R. J. Hankinson, 'Philosophy of Nature', in *The Cambridge Companion to Galen*, ed. R. J. Hankinson (Cambridge, 2008), 210–41, at 219.

[57] Galen, *De Temperamentis* (*On Mixtures*), Book I, in P. N. Singer, *Galen: Selected Works* (Oxford, 1997), 202–31.

[58] Galen, *Ars Medica* (*The Art of Medicine*), in Singer, *Galen*, 361.

[59] Galen, *De Usu Partium* (*On the Usefulness of the Parts of the Body*), trans. Margaret Tallmadge May (Ithaca, NY, 1968), 631.

more heat than women, whose bodies retained more moisture.[60] The connection between women's wet physical make-up and hysteria was a key legacy of Galenism, and was still evident in eighteenth-century notions of female melancholy and the 'vapours'. Samuel Johnson attributed 'the *vapours* to which the other sex are so often subject' to women's 'diseased nerves', associated with melancholy, spleen, and hypochondrial maladies.[61]

During the early modern period, the work of René Descartes was instrumental in reorienting scientific study to focus upon the mind, replacing Galen's humoural model with a mechanistic notion of the human body.[62] Certain aspects of Cartesian thinking reflected older notions of the 'animal spirits' utilized by Galen.[63] In his *L'Homme* (*Treatise of Man*) of *c.*1637, Descartes argued that 'animal spirits' retained the speed that the heat of the heart had given them, but ceased 'to have the form of blood' and became more like 'a wind or a very subtle flame'.[64] His crucial intervention was to reinstate the mind as the central means of perceiving particular emotions, introducing a new system involving the 'nerves', 'spirits', and 'brain'. Descartes' work meant that love ceased to be seen as a physical entity embedded in the heart, but led to a nervous result in the body when it was perceived by the mind. In his final book *Les Passions de l'âme* (*The Passions of the Soul*) in 1649, Descartes described how upon viewing a loved one,

> the impression this thought forms in the brain guides the animal spirits via the sixth pair of nerves toward the muscles around the intestines and ... toward the heart; and that, being driven there with greater force than [the blood] in other parts of the body, it enters [the heart] in greater abundance.[65]

The central Cartesian legacy for eighteenth-century love was the prioritizing of the mind as the key means of processing one's emotions, which subsequently caused a physical response in the body. Writers eagerly took up this notion of love as a 'passion of the soul'. The poet Judith Cowper described her love in an unsent letter as 'so strong, so soft a Passion' in 1723, and her suitor Captain Martin Madan as 'thou Kindest Truest, Only Charmer of my Soul!'[66]

Scientific advances generated new ways for individuals to conceptualize their feelings, such as by describing the 'chemistry' and 'electricity' of their attachment.

---

[60] See Fay Bound Alberti, 'Emotions in the Early Modern Medical Tradition', in *Medicine, Emotion and Disease, 1700–1950*, ed. Fay Bound Alberti (Basingstoke, 2006), 3–4, and Robert L. Martensen, *The Brain Takes Shape: An Early History* (Oxford, 2004), esp. 153–74.

[61] 'Vapour' [in the plural] in Johnson, *Dictionary*, Vol. II, 1011.

[62] For his research into the pineal gland as the seat of the soul, see René Descartes, *Treatise of Man*, trans. Thomas Steel Hall (Cambridge, [1662] 1972). Although this text was written before 1637, it was not published in Latin until 1662, and the original French until 1664.

[63] Galen cited Herophilus' use of 'psychic pneuma' in coining the term 'animal spirits'. See Edwin Clarke and Charles Donald O'Malley, *The Human Brain and Spinal Cord* (Berkeley, CA, 1968), 144, 147.

[64] Descartes, *Treatise of Man*, 21, 28. When these spirits were 'abundant' they made humans prone to generosity, liberality, and love, whereas when they were 'lacking' they excited malice, timidity, inconstancy, tardiness, and ruthlessness, 72–3. Also see René Descartes, *The Passions of the Soul*, trans. Stephen Voss (Cambridge, [1649] 1989), 25–7.

[65] Descartes, *Passions of the Soul*, Article 102, 74.

[66] Cowper to Madan, Hertingfordbury, 1723, MS Eng. Lett. c. 284, f. 2, BLO.

The term 'chemistry' was first used to denote an 'instinctual attraction or rapport between two or more people' in 1656.[67] The discovery of static electricity by William Gilbert in the seventeenth century likewise gave rise to a language of 'electricity' and love.[68] The term was first used in a figurative sense to mean 'a feeling of excitement' by Edmund Burke in 1796.[69] In Mary Hays' novel *Memoirs of Emma Courtney* (1796), the heroine's discovery that she could move to London, and breathe 'the same air' as her idol Augustus, 'electrified' her heart.[70] These scientific discourses demonstrate how the lexical innovations of particular discoveries filtered into public consciousness, providing innovative new ways for lovers to formulate their emotions.

The evolution of diseases such as lovesickness reveals the interrelationship between love, science, and medicine. Suffering from love was historically the domain of troubadours, who declared that 'to love truly and not to suffer—would make me in my own eyes a cheat.'[71] Lovesickness increasingly came to be defined as a female condition during the Renaissance, becoming exclusively female by the eighteenth century. This affected how the disease itself was construed. It historically consisted of two stages: a hot, moist, and sanguine stage characterized by fiery passion, and a cold, dry, and melancholy stage evidenced by fear and sorrow.[72] However, by the eighteenth century lovesickness had shed its fiery stage, and the only remaining symptoms were the tears, fainting, meekness, melancholy, and languishing of the second stage. These reflect the feminizing of lovesickness, plus the growing influence of nervous debilities in the evolution of the disease. Nervous illnesses were thought to begin with 'a general debility; languour, and depression of spirits...a pale sunk countenance; vertigo, or slight head-ach; disturbed sleep'. A patient became 'unable to sit out of bed' and lay 'in a kind of stupor'. Nervous maladies and lovesickness shared similar causes, namely youth, 'depressing passions', and a 'sedentary life'. Those under thirty were seen as particularly vulnerable, clearly isolating courting women as a high-risk group.[73] In 1748, the heiress Elizabeth Jeffreys was twenty-four years old and was convinced that her 'great weakness...proceeded from Love', making it impossible for her to show the 'least grain' of fortitude without diminishing her love for the barrister Charles Pratt. Elizabeth thus embraced her suffering as clear proof of her attachment, noting with satisfaction that 'I am, as every body observes grown very Grave.'[74]

Love letters were seen to present a particular threat to the disposition of vulnerable young women; one short epistle could leave Elizabeth Jeffreys in excessively

---

[67] 'Chemistry, *n.*', *OEDO*: http://www.oed.com.ezproxy01.rhul.ac.uk/view/Entry/31274?redirectedFrom=chemistry#eid.

[68] See William Gilbert, *De Magnete* (*On the Magnet*) (London, 1600).

[69] 'Electricity, *n.*', *OEDO*: http://www.oed.com.ezproxy01.rhul.ac.uk/view/Entry/60259?redirectedFrom=electricity#eid.

[70] Mary Hays, *Memoirs of Emma Courtney* (Oxford, [1796] 2009), 92.

[71] Giraut de Borneil, 'Can creis la fresca fueil'els rams', in *The Cansos and Sirventes of the Troubadour Giraut de Borneil: A Critical Edition*, ed. Ruth Sharman (Cambridge, 1989), 166.

[72] Lesel Dawson, *Lovesickness and Gender in Early Modern English Literature* (Oxford, 2008), 3, 20–1.

[73] John Gregory, *Elements of the practice of physic* (Edinburgh, 1772), 41–2.

[74] Jeffreys to Pratt, 28 February 1748, U840/C9/11, and 2 March 1748, U840/C9/12, KHLC.

Fig. 1.2. *Love Sick: The Doctor Puzzled*, undated (*c.*1820), lithograph with watercolour, Wellcome Collection, London, 11202i, CC BY 4.0.

low spirits, 'crying almost all morning'.[75] The direct correlation between love letters and lovesickness is dramatized in the lithograph *Love Sick: The Doctor Puzzled* (Figure 1.2) where a perplexed older doctor takes the pulse of a languid young woman.[76] Her glazed eyes, drooping head, and pale lily-white skin contrast with

---

[75] Ibid., 6 August 1748, U840/C9/16, KHLC.
[76] Other copies of this lithograph have been dated to *c.*1820. See *Love Sick: The Doctor Puzzled*, Francis A. Countway Library of Medicine, Harvard, olvwork383585.

the ruddy cheeks of the standing doctor. As she slumps in an armchair with a dazed expression on her face, her mischievous maid secretly slips a love letter into her hand. The print enjoyed such lasting popularity that it was parodied almost fifty years later, with a humorous reversal of gender roles as female physicians take the pulse of a languishing man.[77] It testifies to the power of letters in fuelling the experience of love, and the cultural construction of women in love as both physically and mentally weak.

While languishing from lovesickness was a feminine malady, men could legitimately share the sighing, sleeplessness, and dreaming which remained defining physical symptoms of love. *The Dictionary of Love* presented 'sighs' as 'useful interjections in the love-language' which lessened 'the pain of pronouncing those dreadful decisive words, *I love you*'.[78] Ballads dramatized how one sailor 'sigh'd & cast his Eyes below' while thinking of his sweetheart, while a man courting a nobleman's daughter 'found by her sighs and languishing eyes' that she loved him.[79] Lovers often used written sighs to denote an emotional interlude in letters and diaries. The Quaker Betty Fothergill recorded her lover's activities in her diary 'with an accompanying sigh', describing how 'Sighs woud force thier [*sic*] way...Tho I knew AC was too far of[f] to recieve [*sic*] them.'[80] The Bedfordshire gentleman Samuel Whitbread II repeatedly heaved a 'painful sigh' in his letters to Elizabeth Grey, compared to his 'sigh of pleasure' when thinking of her.[81] Furthermore, the Quaker banker and poet Paul Moon James regularly sighed in his love poems to Olivia Lloyd, describing how 'I smiled to mark thy gentle breast, / Soft trembling to the sigh of mine.'[82]

Sighing, trembling lovers also described experiencing visions of their beloved. In 1759, the tailor's daughter Sarah Hurst wrote a paean to Henry Smith that 'sleeping or waking he alone employs my thoughts.' Henry appeared frequently in her dreams, prompting her to muse 'how perplexing are these Chimeras of the Brain.' While dreaming, Sarah could hear Henry 'talk & feel his caresses, sweet delusion, but I wake & it fleets away'.[83] While Sarah's fantasies were described in the relative privacy of her journal, certain men boldly described their dreams in love letters. The apothecary John Lovell wrote to Sarah Harvey in 1757 dramatizing how 'My Imagination frequently conducts me into your Presence when I am asleep, and the visionary Interview awakes me presently. I regret each Time that it is not real.' On some occasions he 'felt so strong an Impression on my Mind that it seem'd as if you had been personally present with me'.[84] While the symptoms of

---

[77] 'Punch, or the London Charivari: Lady-Physicians', 23 December 1865, *Punch*, Vol. 49, 248.

[78] 'Sighs', in *The Dictionary of Love. In which is contained, The Explanation of most of the Terms used in that Language* (London, 1753), 203–4.

[79] Ballad by John Gay in misc. poems on love and marriage by Princess Amelia, 1744, LWL Mss Vol. 14, Lewis Walpole Library, Farmington, CT (subsequently LWL); 'The LADY's Garland', 1763–75, Roxburghe Collection, C. 20.f. 9. (320–1), English Broadside Ballad Archive (subsequently EBBA).

[80] Diary of Fothergill, 8 February 1770 (Fifth Day), MS. Vol. 5, 51/1, 26–7, LSF.

[81] Whitbread II to Grey, Thun, 1 August 1787, W1/6567, No. 21, BAS.

[82] James, 'To Olivia Lloyd', undated (pre-1808), TEMP MSS 403/9/19/1/1/15, LSF.

[83] Diary of Hurst, 27 January 1759, 28 September 1759, and 12 November 1759, MS 3542, HM.

[84] John Lovell to Sarah Harvey, Bath, 28 August 1757, 161/102/2, WSA.

love could be shared by men, lovesickness remained exclusively a female malady. The disease involved an extension of these ailments, as sighing, languishing women were consumed by their fantasies to sink into a prolonged languor.

LITERARY LOVE

The enduring impact of classical poetry meant that certain phrases used by eighteenth-century lovers had routinely been employed for centuries before. New editions of *Ars Amatoria* (*The Art of Love*) by the Roman poet Ovid claimed that his advice could 'with very little force of imagination, be made applicable to love affairs of the present day'.[85] Young men were advised to use their linguistic flair to flatter 'hollow' women into marriage: 'By flatteries we prevail on woman-kind, / As hollow banks by streams are undermin'd.'[86] Katharina Volk has argued that the *Ars Amatoria* is really about 'the art of the love affair': *amor* is something to be learnt by following Ovid's 'simple steps'.[87] The success of flattery in courtship was a historical variable, with suitors in the later eighteenth and early nineteenth centuries placing increasing emphasis upon the *avoidance* of flattery. When the politician Henry Goulburn wrote a love poem to his sweetheart Jane Montagu in 1811, he deliberately eschewed flattering her physical features, promising, 'I will not say that thou art fair, / Nor praise the lustre of thine eye... But when I sing, my theme shall be / The matchless beauty of thy mind.'[88] Compared to his advice for men, Ovid's recommendations for courting women were more superficial. Tips included dressing to emphasize their best features, adopting a feminine poise, and generally being well turned-out for when a man made his advances.[89] The paradoxical nature of Ovid's advice reveals the unambiguous dichotomy between male activity and female passivity amid the hunt or battlefield of courtship.

Ovid's guide laid the foundation for texts such as Andreas Capellanus' *De Arte Honeste Amandi* (*The Art of Courtly Love*), known as *De Amore* (*c*.1185). The text presented love as a kind of suffering, based on fear of either failing to attain, or losing, the object of your love. Love was a mutable and unstable bondage that kept heroic men in captivity.[90] These narratives lingered into the early eighteenth century, with one writer presenting himself as a 'Heroique Man' ensnared by the 'Magick Charms' of love.[91] By the 1730s, such modes of expression had fallen out of fashion. When the Quaker flour merchant Thomas Kirton wrote to his future wife Olive Lloyd in 1734, he recognized that

---

[85] 'Notes on Ovid's Art of Love' in Ovid, *The Art of Love* (London, 1813), 275.

[86] Ovid, *Art of Love*, 26.

[87] Katharina Volk, 'Ovid on Love as a Cultural Construct', in *The Art of Love: Bimillennial Essays on Ovid's Ars Amatoria and Remedia Amoris*, ed. Roy Gibson, Steven Green, and Alison Sharrock (Oxford, 2006), 235–51.

[88] Henry Goulburn to Jane Montagu, 1811, 304/D/Box 2, SHC.

[89] Ovid, *Art of Love*, 66–76.

[90] Louis Mackey, 'Eros into Logos: The Rhetoric of Courtly Love', in *The Philosophy of (Erotic) Love*, ed. Solomon and Higgins, 336–51.

[91] Oroondates to Statira (Mrs Ann Webb), undated (early eighteenth century), FRE 5412, East Sussex Record Office, Brighton (subsequently ESRO).

I know Heroick Love, and Friendship are things out of Fashion, and thought fit only for Knights Errant, and to Love with discretion, or in plain English, to try for advancement thereby, is the most generally rec^d Notion: But I condemn their low Ideas, 'Tis thy Noble mind, as well as comely Personage, I so much admire.[92]

While Thomas was writing, he was aware that he was subverting fashionable conventions. Nonetheless, this did not stop him from using chivalric language anyway, demonstrating how individuals adopted or rejected particular tropes as they pleased. Heroic knights and angelic maids enjoyed a renaissance in the late 1770s and 1780s, supporting Mark Girouard's notion of a 'Return to Camelot' in British art, architecture, and literature from *c.*1788.[93] The resurgence may have been inspired by Gothic novels such as Horace Walpole's *The Castle of Otranto* (1764). Fifteen years after the novel's publication in 1779, John Eccles praised Mary Hays as 'A maid of pure, angelic mind'.[94] In return, she praised his knightly qualities, as 'the guard of my honor [*sic*] and character'.[95] Contemporary obsession with chivalry inspired Walter Scott's best-selling poem 'The Lay of the Last Minstrel' in 1802, ensuring the continuing domination of chivalrous knights and fair maidens in perpetuating the ennobling power of love.

Lovers such as Troilus and Cressida were invoked by writers to encapsulate the torment of unfaithful love. The couple had been widely known from the twelfth century, where Troilus was a Greek warrior rather than a lover in histories of the Trojan War.[96] The novelist Mary Hays dramatically likened herself to Cressida in 1779, writing that 'If I am false, or swerve from truth and love...To stab the heart of perjury in maids, / Let it be said, "false as Maria Hays".' As Cressida proclaimed, 'Yea, let them say, to stick the heart of falsehood, / As false as Cressid.'[97] The romantic poet John Keats also empathized with Troilus' predicament in 1819, describing how his 'greatest torment' was that Fanny Brawne was 'a little inclined to the Cressid', as he was constantly fearful of her infidelity.[98] The romance of 'Troilus and Criseida' and her affair with the warrior Diomede was the subject of Giovanni Boccaccio's poem 'Il Filostrato' in the early fourteenth century, inspiring Geoffrey Chaucer's *Troilus and Criseyde* (*c.*1381–6) and William Shakespeare's *Troilus and Cressida* (1602), which subsequently became the most popular version of the tale. By adopting these characters in their love letters, Mary and John simultaneously demonstrated their learning whilst articulating complex emotional states. They may have used guides such as *The Beauties of Shakespeare* to select the most emotive passages, which recommended the description of Cressida's

---

[92] Kirton to Lloyd, 14 August 1734, TEMP MSS 210/2/96, LSF.

[93] Mark Girouard, *The Return to Camelot: Chivalry and the English Gentleman* (London, 1981), esp. 16–38.

[94] Eccles to Hays, 31 August 1779, Letter XXXII, in Wedd, ed., *Love-Letters of Mary Hays*, 67.

[95] Hays quoted in a letter from Eccles, Letter XLI, ibid., 80.

[96] See Geoffrey Chaucer, *Troilus and Criseyde*, ed. Barry Windeatt (London, [*c.*1381–6] 2003), xvi.

[97] Ibid., Act III, Scene 2, 75; Hays to Eccles, 11 October 1779, Letter LXVI, in Wedd, ed., *Love-Letters of Mary Hays*, 128.

[98] Keats to Brawne, undated, *c.*February 1820, Letter XII, in Forman, ed., *Letters of John Keats*, 47–8.

falsehood as chosen by Mary Hays as a fitting 'Protestation of Love'.[99] Through using these figures to understand the changing dynamics of their relationships, writers applied the drama and deceit of courtly love to their own lives.

Shakespeare's plays enjoyed renewed popularity during the eighteenth century, with *Romeo and Juliet* becoming the apogee of tragic love. Public interest reached its peak with the creation of John Boydell's Shakespeare Gallery on Pall Mall in 1792. The star-crossed lovers were invoked in newspaper reports of breach of promise trials as the epitome of doomed romance, dramatizing how Juliet waited 'at the tomb of Capulet, lamenting her lost Romeo'.[100] Writers such as John Keats referenced Romeo in their love letters, who confirmed the image of the impetuous suitor 'going off in warm blood' in pursuit of love. Keats and his brother George each endeavoured to read a passage from Shakespeare every Sunday morning at ten o' clock.[101] He also cited passages from *The Tempest* in his love letters, such as '"I cry to dream again."'[102] Such usages were typical of professional writers, who repeatedly referenced luminaries such as Shakespeare in conceptualizing their romantic struggles. As Keats wrote to Fanny Brawne *c.*1819–20, 'What would Rousseau have said at seeing our little correspondence!...I don't care much—I would sooner have Shakespeare's opinion about the matter.'[103]

At this point in his relationship, Keats had been reading Rousseau's famous adaptation of the romance of the philosopher Peter Abelard and his gifted young pupil Héloïse. Abelard was a theologian, musician, and poet, and master of the cathedral school at Notre Dame in Paris. He seduced his talented student Héloïse, who soon became pregnant with their child. Héloïse's uncle Fulbert forced the couple to marry in secret, before ordering Abelard's castration to punish his reckless behaviour.[104] The tale had a profound impact upon eighteenth-century couples, with John Hughes' translated paraphrase of their letters in 1714 inspiring Alexander Pope's poem 'Eloisa to Abelard' in 1717. The poem brought to life the emotional power of Abelard's letters when read by Héloïse:

> SOON as thy letters, trembling, I unclose,
> That well-known name awakens all my woes.
> Oh name for ever sad! for ever dear!
> Still breath'd in sighs, still usher'd with a tear.[105]

Pope's poem revelled in romanticism and increased the public's appetite for France's most famous couple, whose letters were already published in eleven new editions

---

[99] *The Beauties of Shakespeare Selected from his Plays and Poems* (Dublin, 1783), 137.

[100] *Morning Post and Gazetteer*, 19 June 1801, 10237.

[101] John Keats to George and Georgiana Keats, 18 December 1828, in Grant F. Scott, ed., *Selected Letters of John Keats* (Cambridge, MA and London, 2002), 216.

[102] Keats to Brawne, undated, and 19 October 1819, Letters IX, XXXI, in Forman, ed., *Letters of John Keats*, 38, 83–4.

[103] Keats to Brawne, Letter XXVIII, ibid., 77–8.

[104] Keats to Brawne, Letter XXVIII, 3 July 1819, Letter I, ibid., 3. See Constant J. Mews, *Abelard and Heloise* (Oxford, 2005).

[105] Alexander Pope, 'Eloisa to Abelard', in Alexander Pope, *A collection of Essays, Epistles and Odes* (London, 1758), 124. The letters are also quoted in Mary Hays' *Memoirs of Emma Courtney*, 71.

by 1773. Rousseau's *Julie, ou la nouvelle Héloïse* (1761) made an apt romantic gift, with Mary Wollstonecraft sending William Godwin the last volume in 1796 'to remind you, when you write to me in <u>verse</u>, not to chuse the easiest task, my perfections; but to dwell on your own feelings—that is to say, give me a bird's-eye-view of your heart.'[106] Mary's letters reveal her hope that the *New Héloïse* would help William to actualize his feelings. The tailor's daughter Sarah Hurst was equally moved by Rousseau's novel in 1761, praising how 'the tenderness of these letters pierces my very soul.' Sarah's identification with the heroine was encouraged by her own fraught romance with Henry Smith, writing that 'none who have not experienc'd the enthusiasm of love can relish their beauties.' She mused that 'much ought to be imitated & much avoided; one sees in Eloisa, a hapless victim to youthfull [*sic*] folly called love & the false step it caus'd her to make.'[107] While readers identified with the romances of literary couples, these also provided a pertinent warning of the potential dangers of romantic love.

The eighteenth century witnessed the birth of the epistolary novel, prioritizing the role of letter-writing in the formation of a person's identity and actualization of their emotions.[108] Samuel Richardson's *Pamela* (1740) presented letters as vehicles for a person's innermost thoughts, with Pamela recording and developing her feelings for Mr B in letters to her parents. The letters provide a vehicle for the novel's power struggles, and are hidden under a rosebush by Pamela in an attempt to conceal them from Mr B. Pamela's parcel is later discovered by Mrs Jewkes and given straight to him, causing Pamela great angst that 'he will see all my private Thoughts of him, and all my Secrets.'[109] The seizure of her letters displays Mr B's power over Pamela, as her voyeuristic master, suitor, and superior. The novel developed the notion of women as virtuous, chaste, modest, and sincere, whereas Richardson's male characters were governed by their strong passions.[110] These drove them to impetuous acts such as kidnap, as committed by Lovelace in *Clarissa* (1747–8) and Pollexfen in *The History of Sir Charles Grandison* (1753–4).

In Richardson's *Clarissa*, the sheer volume of letters means that they '*replace* the narrated events; it is the act of writing them that forms the action of the novel'.[111] Like the concealment and seizure of Pamela's missives, control over Clarissa's letters is used as a means of power, with the heroine's family confiscating her pens and ink

[106] Wollstonecraft to Godwin, 1 July 1796, No. 1, MS Abinger c40, fols. 1–2, BLO. For the impact and popularity of the text, see Robert Darnton, *The Great Cat Massacre and Other Episodes in French Cultural History* (London, 1985), 225–49.

[107] Diary of Hurst, 18 and 28 November 1761, MS 3544, HM.

[108] Robert Adams Day has found that 200 out of every 500 works published between 1660 and 1740 (40 per cent) used an epistolary structure. See Adams Day, *Told in Letters: Epistolary Fiction before Richardson* (Ann Arbor, MI, 1966), 2.

[109] Samuel Richardson, *Pamela; or, Virtue Rewarded* (Oxford, [1740] 2001), 226–8.

[110] For the key doctrines of sentimentalism presented in *Pamela*, see Reddy, *Navigation of Feeling*, 157–8. For an in-depth analysis of the novel's publication and reception, see Thomas Keymer and Peter Sabor, *Pamela in the Marketplace: Literary Controversy and Print Culture in Eighteenth-Century Britain and Ireland* (Cambridge, 2005).

[111] John Preston, '*Les Liaisons Dangereuses*: Epistolary Narrative and Moral Discovery', *French Studies* 24.1 (1970): 23–36, at 24. For readers' reception of the text, see Thomas Keymer, *Richardson's Clarissa and the Eighteenth-Century Reader* (Cambridge, 1992).

in an attempt to isolate her and force her to marry the boorish Roger Solmes. Richardson's Clarissa was the victim of love, with her kidnap and isolation causing a slow, painful decline and eventual death. Her symptoms included frailty, fainting fits, 'dimmed' eyesight, and tremors in her limbs. The author broke down the gradual onslaught of her illness for readers:

> Who would have thought that... I should be so long a dying!—But see how by little and little it has come to this. I was first taken off from the power of *walking*: then I took a *coach*—a coach grew too violent an exercise: then I took a *chair*... Next, I was unable to go to *church*; then to go *up* or *down stairs*; now hardly can move from one *room* to *another*... My *eyes* begin to fail me, so that at times I cannot see to read distinctly; and now I can hardly *write* or hold a pen.[112]

Clarissa's untimely death left Richardson inundated with letters from critics demanding that the novel end happily, as with Pamela's marriage to Mr B. However, he insisted that Clarissa's death provided a Christian model of how to live and die which would be rewarded in heaven.[113] As with notions of female passivity disseminated in courtly romances, Richardson's novels played a guiding role in propagating the view of women as victims of love, whereas the sexually voracious man was a 'beast of prey'.[114]

The climax of sensibility in the closing decades of the century revelled in weeping emotional lovers such as the protagonists of Goethe's *The Sorrows of Young Werther* (1774) and Mary Hays' *Memoirs of Emma Courtney* (1796).[115] The heroine of Hays' novel recognised the impact of romances such as Rousseau's *New Héloïse* in feeding her sensibility, as her school friends 'procured for me romances from a neighbouring library, which at every interval of leisure I perused with inconceivable avidity'.[116] Emma spent a large proportion of the novel crying:

> After the rude stare of curiosity... was gratified, I was left to sob alone.[117]
>
> I wept, I suffered my tears to flow unrestrained.[118]
>
> I burst into tears – I could not help it.[119]
>
> I endeavoured in vain to repress its sensations, and burst into a flood of tears.[120]

The novel was shaped by Mary's own tragic romance with John Eccles between 1779 and 1780, where she described how 'The tears which flow from reading a

---

[112] Samuel Richardson, *Clarissa, or The History of a Young Lady* (London, [1747–8] 1985), L464, Belford to Lovelace, 1336–7.

[113] Jocelyn Harris, 'Introduction', in *Samuel Richardson's Published Commentary on Clarissa 1747–65*, ed. Thomas Keymer (London, 1998), Vol. I, xviii–xix.

[114] Richardson, *Clarissa*, L317, Howe to Clarissa, 1016.

[115] On the literature of sensibility, see Susan Manning, 'Sensibility', in *The Cambridge Companion to English Literature 1740–1830*, ed. Thomas Keymer and Jon Mee (Cambridge, 2004), 80–99; Ute Frevert, *Emotions in History—Lost and Found* (Budapest and New York, 2011), 108–12; and Julie Ellison, 'Sensibility', in *A Handbook of Romanticism Studies*, ed. Joel Faflak and Julia M. Wright (Chichester, 2016), 37–54. On weeping, see Thomas Dixon, *Weeping Britannia: Portrait of a Nation in Tears* (Oxford, 2015), esp. Chs. 6–8.

[116] Hays, *Memoirs of Emma Courtney*, 20, 25: 'In the course of my researches, the Heloise of Rousseau fell into my hands.—Ah! with what transport, with what enthusiasm, did I peruse this dangerous, enchanting, work!'

[117] Ibid., 16.   [118] Ibid., 32.   [119] Ibid., 36.   [120] Ibid., 40.

tragical tale are not unpleasing, they soften while they distress.—Sensibility, be thou ever mine!'[121] Such language was by no means confined to literary women, with the Quaker banker and poet Paul Moon James also declaring sensibility to be 'Love's best advocate' in 1806.[122] Mary and Paul's letters demonstrate how new idioms in literature were eagerly adopted by courting couples to characterize the intensity of their emotions, as the script for love came to prioritize natural and spontaneous displays of feeling.

The heroines of Jane Austen's novels were each in ardent pursuit of falling and being 'in love', with Julia Bertram 'quite ready to be fallen in love with' and Marianne Dashwood 'so desperately in love' that she was 'quite an altered creature'.[123] The word 'love' appeared seventy-six times in *Sense and Sensibility* (1811), ninety-two times in *Pride and Prejudice* (1813), and 124 times in *Mansfield Park* (1814). On this criterion alone, Austen's novels outweighed even Goethe's *Sorrows of Young Werther* (at sixty-one) and Radcliffe's *Romance of the Forest* (at seventy-five).[124] The popularity of these romantic tales demonstrates the immense influence of literature in raising the expectations of courting couples and helping particular linguistic strategies to flourish. David Perkins argues that in their daily lives, 'the Romantics heard poetry more than most of us do', encouraging a climate of romantic idealism, as individuals read poetry aloud with family and friends.[125] Nonetheless as Amanda Vickery reminds us, 'new idioms do not necessarily connote new behaviour' since 'hope and experience are different creatures'.[126] Henry William Bunbury's *A Tale of Love* (Figure 1.3) was published in 1786 during the first flourish of Romanticism. It encapsulates the escapism of romantic tales, as a group in Tudor and Elizabethan costume gather on a balcony to hear a love story. The story in question dramatizes the execution of a young Jacobite officer on what should have been his wedding day, causing his fiancée to die from grief. The seated group engage their 'tender hearts' by heaving a sigh and shedding a tear over the lovers' fate, and indulging their own romantic fantasies.[127]

Literary heroines fuelled the idea that love was a female preoccupation, when in reality most romantic poetry was written by men. The men studied throughout this book repeatedly quoted poetry to demonstrate their education and convey their passion with literary flair. The Derbyshire cotton-trader Joseph Strutt selected a dramatic passage from James Thomson's 'Winter' (1726) in his love letters to

---

[121] Hays to Eccles, 21 November 1779, Letter CI in Wedd, ed., *Love-Letters of Mary Hays*, 176. For further examples, see letters from Wollstonecraft to Imlay, esp. Letter IV, Paris, September 1793 and Letter XI, Paris, January 1794 in Ingpen, ed., *Love Letters of Mary Wollstonecraft*, 8, 22–3.

[122] James to Lloyd, 29 June 1806, TEMP MSS 493/9/19/1/3, LSF.

[123] Jane Austen, *Sense and Sensibility* (London, [1811] 2000), 134, and *Mansfield Park* (London, [1814] 2007), 33.

[124] Based on a keyword search for 'love' using Literature Online: https://www.proquest.com/products-services/literature_online.html. Figures taken from original editions where possible.

[125] David Perkins, 'How the Romantics Recited Poetry', *Studies in English Literature, 1500–1900* 31.4 (1991): 655–71, at 656.

[126] Vickery, *The Gentleman's Daughter*, 41. Also see Schneid Lewis, *In the Family Way*, 17–20, 30–1.

[127] William Shenstone, 'Jemmy Dawson, A Ballad; written about the Time of his Execution, in the Year 1745', in *The Works in Verse and Prose, of William Shenstone, Esq.* (London, 1764), 185–8.

Fig. 1.3. James Bretherton after Henry William Bunbury, *A Tale of Love*, London, 1786, stipple engraving and etching, 45.6 cm × 37.1 cm, British Museum, London, 1917, 1208.2411. © The Trustees of the British Museum, All Rights Reserved.

evoke life as a 'scene of toil'.[128] The Bedfordshire gentleman Samuel Whitbread II chose Edward Young's melancholic 'Night Thoughts' (1742–5) to conceptualize his love for Elizabeth Grey, changing Young's 'Think'st thou the theme intoxicates

[128] Jos. Strutt to Douglas, 18 December 1787, MS 3101/C/E/4/8/9, Library of Birmingham (subsequently LOB).

my song' to 'Think'st thou the Theme intoxicates my Pen.'[129] He also adapted Oliver Goldsmith's *The Traveller; or, A Prospect of Society* (1764), replacing the word 'brother' with 'Bessy': 'My heart untravelled fondly turns to thee / Still to my Bessy turns with ceaseless pain / & drags at each remove a lengthening Chain.' Goldsmith's prose was selected as 'a Quotation that is truly descriptive of my Feeling', allowing Samuel to express his romantic agony in the style of fashionable new authors.[130] Neither Joseph nor Samuel named their source, flattering the recipient by presuming their knowledge of the author.

A significant proportion of courting men composed their own original poetry. In 1757, the Quaker gentleman Richard How II wrote 'a verse compos'd on the death of a Lady's Lapdog' during the breakdown of his relationship with Elizabeth Johnson. He eulogized, 'Mourn all ye Nymphs, the fatal Loss deplore, Tho frdshps Lost to be regain'd no more', writing, 'whether sufficiently expressive let others judge'.[131] Educated gentlemen such as Richard would have been familiar with a range of classical authors. He may have been inspired by the Roman poet Catullus' popular lament on the death of his lover's sparrow, which also began 'Mourn and wail, O ye Venuses and Cupids!'[132] The London gentleman John Eccles (1779), Derbyshire cotton-trader Joseph Strutt (1786), Quaker banker Paul Moon James (1808), and politician Henry Goulburn (1811) also composed original poetry for their sweethearts, illuminating the continuing role of romantic verse as a key vehicle for masculine wooing.[133] It enabled men to set themselves apart from competing suitors by showcasing their education and refinement, as in Ovid's *Art of Love*, reinforcing our view of courtship as a decidedly masculine pursuit.

Given the prevalence of conduct literature in society as a whole, it is highly likely that writers would have been aware of prescribed forms of expression in published letter-writing guides. *Academies of Complement* were popularized during the seventeenth century, with practically minded *Secretaries* appearing c.1687, *Letter-Writers* c.1750, and *Arts of Correspondence* c.1790.[134] Manuals were cheaper than novels, costing just one shilling in London until the 1790s, when they rose to two shillings.[135] Manuals for love letters formed a distinct genre, and were repeatedly reissued under the belief that there were 'no kinds of epistolary writing requiring so much attention as those relating to Love and Marriage'.[136] Others such as Reverend Thomas Cooke's *The Universal Letter-Writer; or, New Art of Polite Correspondence* (1788) contained entire sections dedicated to 'Love, Courtship,

---

[129] Whitbread II to Grey, Bordeaux, 16 June 1787, W1/6555, No. 10, BAS.

[130] Ibid., Clarges Street, 6 May 1787, W1/6546, No. 1, BAS.

[131] How II to Johnson, c.1757, HW87/224, BAS.

[132] Catullus, Song 3, in Dorothea Wender, *Roman Poetry: From the Republic to the Silver Age* (Carbondale and Edwardsville, IL, 1991), 6.

[133] Eccles to Hays, 31 August 1779, Letter XXXII, in Wedd, ed., *Love-Letters of Mary Hays*, 68; Jos. Strutt to Douglas, 25 January 1786, MS 3101/C/E/4/8/1, LOB; James to Lloyd, undated (pre-1808), TEMP MSS 403/9/19/1/1, 2, 15, 19, LSF; Goulburn to Montagu, 1811, 304/D/Box 2, SHC.

[134] Eve Tavor Bannet, *British and American Letter Manuals, 1680–1810*, Vol. I, *Academies of Complement, 1680–1806* (London, 2008), xix.

[135] Eve Tavor Bannet, *Empire of Letters: Letter Manuals and Transatlantic Correspondence, 1680–1820* (Cambridge, 2009), xi, 12.

[136] *The New lover's instructor; or, Whole art of Courtship* (London, c.1780), 6.

and Marriage'.[137] Awareness of these conventions was vital, with the poet Eleanor Anne Porden threatening to send the explorer John Franklin a second-hand copy of *The Complete Letter Writer* during their courtship in December 1822. This was only partly in jest; the text was intended 'for your especial use' after John dared to send his literary lover a number of lacklustre letters which were overtly factual, concise, and uninspiring. Eleanor complained, 'you are glad to fling the pens in the fire, and seek amusement in any other form—nevertheless I must confess you have a little disappointed me.'[138]

These 'template' letters reinforced traditional gender roles during courtship, as men made their first gallant addresses, which were received by women with caution and surprise. Such guides were not used as direct templates by actual couples, but broadly tie-in with the general themes of romantic culture. *The Art of Courtship; or the School of Love* (c.1775) listed three pages of 'Witty and ingenious Sentences' for men to use during courtship:

> You walk in artificial Clouds, and bathe your Lips in sweet Dalliances.
>
> Report could never have got a sweeter Air to fly in than your Breath.
>
> Not the Mountain Ice congeal'd to Crystal, is more bright than you.
>
> The Sun never met the Summer with more Joy.[139]

The purpose of these phrases was to help potential suitors impress women with their knowledge of romantic conventions. Such phrases were designed to entertain readers with their sparkling wit, and perhaps inspire flights of fancy of their own. The extravagant metaphors in *The Art of Courtship* strongly reflect the language used by men in the late eighteenth and early nineteenth centuries, influenced by the emergence of Romanticism. The Yorkshire bridle-maker John Fawdington drew liberally upon ambient metaphors in his letters to Jane Jefferson in 1787, proclaiming, 'Many a time have I wander'd alone in the Fields by Moonlight & in my usual Romantic Way whisper'd to the Passing Breaze a tender tale...thou art all my Riches and all my Hope.'[140] Similarly, the Quaker banker Paul Moon James wrote numerous poems to his sweetheart likening her to a 'beauteous flow'r' and their love to an 'opening bud'.[141] The dramatic metaphors used in these letters demonstrate how men's romantic language had become particularly prone to hyperbole towards the end of our period, drawing upon natural metaphors that were well-known among literate lovers.

---

[137] Thomas Cooke, *The Universal Letter-Writer; Or, New Art of Polite Correspondence* (London, 1788), 61–99.

[138] Porden to Franklin, Hastings, 18 December 1822, D3311/8/1/10, DRO.

[139] *The Art of Courtship; or the School of Love* (London, c.1775), 14–16.

[140] John Fawdington to Jane Jefferson, 3 March 1787, Z. 640/7, North Yorkshire Record Office, Northallerton (subsequently NYRO).

[141] 'To Olivia Lloyd', undated (pre-1808), and 2 November 1807, TEMP MSS 403/9/19/1/15, 19, LSF.

CONCLUSION

This chapter has presented the language of love as a learned style crafted within a number of historically specific frameworks. Discourses of love enabled couples to elucidate their feelings, determine their compatibility, chart the changing status of their relationship, and build a closer emotional bond in pursuit of matrimony. For particularly devout lovers, texts such as the Bible and Book of Common Prayer provided a fruitful means of developing a connection through theological debate. In Quaker letters, writers eschewed physical declarations to locate their emotions in the soul. While certain writers used *Paradise Lost* to formulate romantic resentment, others utilized the same text to declare their love, adapting the verse to their own purposes. A person's mood determined the literature they chose; jealous or insecure writers might select Shakespeare's *Troilus and Cressida*, while the melancholic could opt for Young's 'Night Thoughts'. Citing these texts was a mark of education and refinement, and they were frequently quoted without explicitly naming the source, flattering the recipient by presuming their shared knowledge of romantic tropes.

The overarching principle of these sources is that courtship was a man's game, as suitors assumed the character of chivalrous knights and hot-blooded heroes to underscore their masculinity. It is remarkable just how many eighteenth-century men put pen to paper in penning original poems for their sweethearts. These included a wide range of suitors across class boundaries from manufacturers to politicians. In contrast, only spirited women such as the poet Judith Cowper penned lines in return. While it is possible that further women wrote love poems during courtship that they subsequently destroyed, it would be impossible for historians to know with any certainty due to the lack of surviving manuscripts. Women such as Elizabeth Teft, Martha Fowke Sansom, and Ann Yearsley certainly published love poetry during this period, but you would not know it from consulting courtship letters.[142] While men in epistolary, sentimental, romantic, and Gothic fiction were constructed as being in hot pursuit of love, women were depicted languishing from fainting fits and nervous tremors caused by their emotions. While the pursuit of love was definably male, suffering from love had become explicitly female.

Romantic love was shaped by a number of quintessential couples in fiction: Adam and Eve, Romeo and Juliet, Troilus and Cressida, Abelard and Héloïse, Pamela and Mr B, Clarissa and Lovelace, Werther and Charlotte, Elizabeth Bennet and Mr Darcy. These figures were repeatedly referenced in courtship letters, enabling couples to apply the drama and deceit of romantic tales to their own lives. At the beginning of this chapter, Shakespeare characterized love as 'all made of

---

[142] See Paula R. Backscheider, *Eighteenth-Century Women Poets and Their Poetry: Inventing Agency, Inventing Genre* (Baltimore, MD, 2005), and Paula R. Backscheider and Catherine E. Ingrassia, eds, *British Women Poets of the Long Eighteenth Century: An Anthology* (Baltimore, MD, 2009), esp. Section C, 'Love Poems', 359–90.

fantasy'. During the eighteenth century, writers such as Rousseau argued that love 'creates for itself another universe'.[143] As we have seen, within this universe, the script for love was subject to continual change. The next chapter of this book presents the exchange of love letters as a distinct stage of courtship, revealing the efficacy of the letter in encouraging the development of intimacy, and moving a relationship forward.

[143] Jean-Jacques Rousseau, *Eloisa: or, a Series of Original Letters* (Dublin, 1766), Vol. I, xx.

2

Love Letters

When the gentlewoman Judith Cowper (1702–81), daughter of Justice Spencer Cowper, sat down to write a love letter in 1723, she longed for a space to rationalize her feelings for the handsome Martin Madan (1700–56), a Captain in the Coldstream Guards. In her letter, Judith rhapsodized about Martin's desirability, wit, sincerity, and unaffected love for her. Her feelings were 'so infinitly [*sic*] above all ye Low Ideas I have hitherto conceiv'd of Love, that I Want a new name, to Express ye Warmth, ye freindship [*sic*], ye admiration, ye shore then Love with wch I am yours...I abandon my self intirely to ye soft, ye Irrisistable passion you first made me Know.'[1] After using the missive to give shape to her feelings, on the reverse Judith wrote the lines 'never to be sent'. Yet she still opted to write a love letter rather than an entry in her diary, as the genre provided an important space that could be appropriated by lovers to articulate romantic emotions within set parameters. The letter provided an invaluable material space for Judith to shape her growing affection for her dashing suitor, facilitating and expediting the experience of love.

Love letters provided a direct way to create emotional intimacy between two individuals who were sometimes hundreds of miles apart. The exchange of missives allowed courting couples to gain 'a more intimate knowledge of each other's feelings and sentiments' which could even surpass an equal number of personal meetings.[2] Letter-writing thus engendered an emotional bond between a couple, forming an important stage of courtship in its own right. Writers were keen to affirm when they had officially begun exchanging love letters, as this marked the beginning of a formal relationship. As Mary Wollstonecraft wrote to William Godwin in 1796, 'I like your last—may I call it love letter? Better than the first.'[3] In this way, love letters played a guiding role on the path to matrimony, and were highly valued and carefully preserved, making them one of the key surviving genres of eighteenth-century letters. Letters were exchanged in their hundreds as a relationship progressed, usually coming to an end once a couple moved into the marital home. For those living in closer proximity, the role of letter-writing in facilitating greater familiarity and knowledge of a person's character might be substituted for conversing, exchanging gifts, taking tea, dining together, strolling through public

---

[1] Cowper to Madan, 1723, unsent, MS Eng. Lett. c. 284, f. 3, BLO.
[2] Porden to Franklin, Hastings, 18 December 1822, typescript of lost original, D3311/8/1/21, DRO.
[3] Wollstonecraft to Godwin, 17 August 1796, MS Abinger c. 40, f. 21, BLO.

Fig. 2.1. *A Receipt for Courtship*, London, 1805, hand-coloured engraving, British Cartoon Prints Collection, Prints and Photographs Division, Library of Congress, Washington, DC, 20540 USA, LC-USZC4-4741.

walks, gardens, and fairs, attending assemblies and plays, and sitting up late talking. Nonetheless, many couples elected to correspond anyway despite living in close quarters, using letters to arrange rendezvous, explain any behaviour lest it be misjudged, and repeat or intensify declarations made in person. As Carol Houlihan Flynn writes, 'Love declared on paper means far more than love declared orally.'[4]

The role of letters as vessels for romantic love was ridiculed in the engraving *A Receipt for Courtship* in 1805 (Figure 2.1), where a gallant gentleman offers a love letter to a seated woman and she tentatively accepts it. The letter is held cautiously between their fingers and thumbs, granting it the status of a precious artefact as it passes between them. The text satirizes the role of letters in orchestrating their relationship, through 'Two or three messages sent in a day' and 'Two or three love letters writ all in rhymes'. It cruelly concludes that 'Two or three months keeping strict to these rules /Can never fail making a couple of fools'. The print presents love letters as material proof of love, with the letter representing a receipt for a man's affections. This was certainly the view of Lord Edgcumbe and his family when his

---

[4] Carol Houlihan Flynn, *Samuel Richardson: A Man of Letters* (Princeton, NJ, [1982] 2014), 259.

'best beloved' son Richard (1716–61) began courting Lady Diana West (1731–66), youngest daughter of the 'odious' Lord De La Warr in 1750. The family were outraged at Richard's behaviour, believing that the promiscuous De La Warr daughters would 'fuck <u>with any body</u>'. Their main concern was whether the couple were exchanging love letters, begging 'to know whether you are sure there is a Correspondence still kept up; Sir from That, & what Engagements may be therein taken, arise at my Fears'.[5] The exchange of love letters was therefore a sure sign of a forthcoming engagement, and made an attachment between a couple infinitely more difficult to end. As one suitor wrote to a 'Lovely Girl' in 1775, 'If I am so happy as to receive a Billet from your fair hand, by the bearer of this;—I have a proposal to make to you.'[6]

This chapter draws upon substantial collections of love letters in provincial archives to present letter-writing as a distinct stage of courtship. The exchange of missives was an emotionally fraught period for both men and women, and was fundamentally important in fostering, gauging, and testing a romantic bond. The chapter first explores how love letters were written and crafted, before examining how men and women used their letters in different ways as vehicles for stressing gendered virtues such as sincerity, virtue, or modesty. The final section sets out the emotional value of letters for couples, which were pored over, touched, and kissed to deepen an emotional connection. The chapter reveals the role of love letters in navigating courtship and facilitating a couple's growing intimacy, outlining how writers worked within epistolary conventions to formulate, intensify, and declare their emotions.

The chapter utilizes a detailed analysis of eight relationships distributed across the Georgian era. These include Captain Martin Madan and the poet Judith Cowper (*m.* 1723), the linen merchant James Nicholson and Elizabeth Seddon (*m.* 1740), surgeon George Gibbs and Ann Vicary (*m.* 1747), wheelwright Jedediah Strutt and Elizabeth Woollat (*m.* 1755), M. P. Isaac Martin Rebow and Mary Martin (m. 1772), cotton-trader Joseph Strutt and Isabella Douglas (*m.* 1793), brewer Francis Cobb and Charlotte Mary Curwen (*m.* 1805), and finally the army ensign Robert Garrett and Charlotte Bentinck (*m.* 1814). The relationships encompass regions from Devon to Derbyshire and religious denominations from Anglicans to Dissenters. They have intentionally been drawn from a wide social spectrum, to demonstrate how love letters coursed through society at different levels. The men worked as wheelwrights, surgeons, bankers, brewers, soldiers, and Members of Parliament, while the women were domestic servants, poets, gentlewomen, and members of the aristocracy. Priority has been given to sources featuring both sides of a correspondence, or those with corroborating evidence such as memoirs, and family and business letters. These are complemented by proposals of marriage, novels, conduct literature, dictionaries, newspaper reports, and contemporary prints, to provide further evidence about the languages and customs of romantic love.

---

[5] Henry Fox to Charles Hanbury Williams, 25 September–6 October 1750, CHW10902/52, fols. 55–8, LWL.

[6] Copy of love letter from 'G. M. L', 1775, FEL 616, 554 × 1, NRO.

WRITING THE LOVE LETTER

Courtship letters brim with declarations of impatience and apprehension, as writers utilized epistolary conventions to craft a heightened emotional state of tension and agitation. Both courting men and women were expected to 'pay their tribute of anxiety' in writing.[7] These accounts of the suspense and anxiety of awaiting letters helped to create a reciprocal emotional bond between a couple. In 1723, Captain Martin Madan implored Judith Cowper, 'you Promis'd me an answer last night, I depend upon y^r Promise.'[8] The Exeter surgeon George Gibbs described waiting for letters in the 1740s 'with the utmost impatience'.[9] When desperate for news on whether Ann Vicary's father approved of their union, George hoped 'that I may be deliverd of this Suspence; which I hate of all things in the World'.[10] The following decade, the domestic servant Elizabeth Woollat pleaded with Jedediah Strutt at her letter's close, 'shant I hear from you soon.'[11] Love letters written by professional scribes likewise implored recipients to 'banish the must [sic] intolerable suspence' from a lover's breast.[12] Professed desperation for a response can also be found in written proposals of marriage, where men described enduring 'that torture of suspense', waiting 'anxiously by most anxiously for a reply to the present'.[13] Accounts of the anxiety of awaiting letters were used to reveal a writer's commitment to a correspondence—and by extension a relationship—through reinforcing the high value of the letters they received.

Lovers demonstrated their dependability by promising never to disappoint one another by failing to write. Individuals regularly claimed to pen their letters by seizing the 'first moment I've had to myself'.[14] When the banker and brewer Francis Cobb travelled to Rochester in August 1805, he wrote to Charlotte Mary Curwen as soon as he arrived, in order to prove his commitment. He began his epistle by describing how, 'That you may not in any wise be disappointed, My Dearest Love, I will begin here, at Rochester, while they are preparing me a little Eggd wine with a Toast.'[15] His letter suggested that Francis was committed to his beloved, and would not miss the smallest opportunity to correspond with her. Charlotte was equally keen to meet her obligations to her suitor, writing on 4 October 1805 that 'you will not be uneasy if you should not hear from me, on the regular appointed days...you may depend upon me, my dear Love, not to disappoint you if I can help it.'[16] Love letters thus bound courting couples together

---

[7] 'Anxiety', in *The Dictionary of Love*, 25. Cf. 'Agitation', 21–2.

[8] Madan to Cowper, undated (*c*.1723), MS Eng. Lett. c. 284, f. 7v, BLO.

[9] Gibbs to Vicary, 1740s, MS/11021/1/25, LMA.

[10] Ibid., June 1740s, MS/11021/1.

[11] Wollat to Jed. Strutt, April 1755, D5303/4/3, DRO.

[12] Copy of a love letter by the scribe J. Johnston for the merchant William Calder, 28 February 1813, Valentines (uncatalogued), Box 1, John Johnson Collection, Oxford (subsequently JJC), BLO.

[13] Thomas Cobb to Miss Torre, Margate, 10 May 1827, R/U11/C39, KHLC.

[14] Madan to Cowper, undated (*c*.1723), MS Eng. Lett. c. 284, f. 28r, BLO.

[15] Cobb to Curwen, Canterbury, 1 August 1805, EK/U1453/C287/5, Bundle A, KHLC.

[16] Curwen to Cobb, Fenstanton, 4 October 1805, EK/U1453/C287/8, Bundle A, KHLC.

emotionally by providing a material vessel for the anxiety, suspense, and care through which they proved their commitment and built a relationship.

Over the eighteenth century, writers increasingly narrated the melodrama of catching and receiving particular posts. With the greater regularity and reliability of deliveries, writers evidently knew when a specific post was due, and crafted their letters accordingly.[17] The gentlewoman Mary Martin (*c.*1751–1804) portrayed the precise timing of writing to catch the post as a source of great anxiety. Characterizing the production of love letters as a pressurized experience allowed Mary to emphasize her devotion by presenting it as a trial that she had to endure in order to communicate with her lover. The catching of the post thus became a challenge that she was willing to overcome for love. On 3 January 1772, she described how 'I was forc'd to scratch off as fast as I cou'd make my Pen go, & of Course cou'd not attempt to Read y least bit of it over.'[18] Mary used a similar strategy throughout her correspondence with Isaac Rebow. On 23 June 1772, she dramatized the theatrical scenario of keeping the postman waiting 'till his Patience was quite Exhausted, & he hurried me so, that I knew not what I did', causing her to leave 'three Blank sides' of expensive paper. Worst of all, Mary recorded that the melodrama of catching the last post had 'given me a <u>Wrinkle</u>'.[19] Couples parted by the Atlantic similarly penned hasty notes under pressure if they heard of a ship sailing. As the soldier Robert Garrett wrote from Lisbon in 1811, he could not let the opportunity pass, but had 'little time so can not write much'. Robert recognized 'What nonsense I am writing', but the act of writing itself—and his professed haste—was sufficient to convey his devotion.[20]

Many writers were complicit in the practice of circulating their love letters among family and friends, even sending unsealed missives to be inspected before they reached the recipient.[21] Figure 2.2 depicts two fashionably dressed women strolling in the garden of a country house while discussing a love letter one has received. Far from keeping her romantic exploits a secret, the recipient is eager to discuss them with a friend, even bringing a letter along to show her. The sharing of love letters naturally changed the purpose of the letter, having an inevitable effect upon the way writers expressed themselves. As Rosemary O'Day has argued, the writer of a letter was taking up a position and presenting a particular image of themselves to the recipient. The image they chose to project would have been

---

[17] Whyman, *The Pen and the People*, 58–9.

[18] Mary Martin to Isaac Rebow, 3 January 1772, A12691, Box 1, Vol. II, f. 183, Essex Record Office, Chelmsford (subsequently ERO).

[19] Ibid., 23 June 1772, A12691/16, Box 1, Vol. II, f. 229, ERO.

[20] Robert Garrett to Charlotte Bentinck, 26 April 1811, R/U888/C11/7, KHLC. On the rhythms of sending letters across the Atlantic, see Sarah Pearsall, *Atlantic Families: Lives and Letters in the Later Eighteenth Century* (Oxford, 2008), 38–42.

[21] The apothecary John Lovell's letters to Sarah Harvey were sent unsealed to allow her aunt to read them first, 'in great Hopes that it may effectually dissipate all her Doubts concerning me', Bath, 9 July 1757, 161/101, WSA. On the circulation of letters, see Martyn Lyons, 'Love Letters and Writing Practices: On *Écritures Intimes* in the Nineteenth Century', *Journal of Family History* 24.2 (1999): 232–9 at 234, 236; Eustace, '"The cornerstone of a copious work"', 517–8, 529–31; Barclay, *Love, Intimacy and Power*, 28–9.

THE LOVE LETTER.

Fig. 2.2. *The Love Letter*, London, 1785, etching with roulette, plate mark 35.2 cm × 25.2 cm, 785.10.11.01. Courtesy of the Lewis Walpole Library, Yale University.

shaped by their intended audience, be it one individual or their entire family.[22] Whilst arranging their wedding in 1805, Charlotte Mary Curwen read Francis Cobb's letters aloud to her Aunt Barber to convince her of his 'tenderness', as 'Aunt B' worried that Francis would keep Charlotte from her as a companion. Charlotte gleefully reported back that 'though she made no remarks, I evidently saw, that she was very much pleased at what you had written.'[23] The sharing of his letters prompted Francis to write lengthy descriptions of Aunt Barber's virtues that appear to be directly addressed to her:

> I have a real regard for your Aunt, independent of my Connexion [*sic*] with you, and that I shall certainly have a great pleasure, as far as in me lies, in Contributing, and Contriving for her happiness and comfort – and you may therefore, assure her, as from my own lips, that I shall be truly glad to see her with you, whenever the Lords time may be, that I shall be favord in making you my wife... you owe her, more than you will Ever be able to make her returns.[24]

While Francis and Charlotte were happy to share certain sentiments with Aunt Barber, others were more closely guarded and deliberately withheld from their letters. On 2 October 1805 Charlotte described how 'I have so much which I could talk about which I cannot write', entreating him to come and visit her in person.[25] Six years later, Charlotte Bentinck circulated Robert Garrett's letters around their family and friends until many of them fell to pieces.[26] While Robert was the son of an army Captain, Charlotte was the daughter of Lord Edward Charles Cavendish-Bentinck, and granddaughter of the Duke of Portland. Knowing that Charlotte's family disapproved of their relationship, Robert used his letters to ingratiate himself to them, jesting that 'Your mother I dare say is as funny & full of her drole remarks as ever.'[27] These couples recognized that love letters would be perused by wider individuals than the named recipient, using this to their advantage by reading or sending carefully constructed missives to chosen family members. Letters helped to advance a courtship by acting to quell any doubts about a man's character, proving the suitability of a match to a woman's family.

CRAFTING THE LOVE LETTER

The ideal love letter was clearly structured, neatly presented on good quality paper, and ran to several pages in length, followed by a series of postscripts. Yet while writers may have been aware of certain rules, this does not mean they were followed. After spending the day planting hyacinths in 1772, the gentlewoman Mary Martin joked, 'Don't fancy now from y pretty steady Hand I write, & y eveness

---

[22] Rosemary O'Day, 'Tudor and Stuart Women: Their Lives through their Letters', in *Early Modern Women's Letter Writing, 1450–1700*, ed. James Daybell (Basingstoke, 2001), 127–42, at 129.
[23] Curwen to Cobb, Fenstanton, 7 October 1805, EK/U1453/C2/3, Bundle A, KHLC.
[24] Cobb to Curwen, 25 October 1805, EK/U1453/C287/10, Bundle A, KHLC.
[25] Curwen to Cobb, Fenstanton, 2 October 1805, EK/U1453/C287/6, Bundle A, KHLC.
[26] Introduction to R/U888/C14, KHLC.
[27] Garrett to Bentinck, Camp near Alfayates, Portugal, 10 June 1812, R/U888/C11/30, KHLC.

[*sic*] of y Lines, that I was a little Tipsy last Night...y <u>Digging</u>, &c. &c. has made my Hands, Arms, & Shoulders, so immoderately stiff, that I really can hardly move them at all to Day.' Later in the same letter, Mary noted that 'Since I wrote y foregoing my Sister has added to y steadiness of my Hand prodigiously, for she has Frighten'd me almost out of my Senses by taking some of her Stuff (as she Calls it)', making her 'so Extremely Ill' that Mary thought she would have to call a physician.[28] In 1805, the brewer Francis Cobb also described feeling self-conscious about dropping a large blot of ink on to the page where he intended to compose a love letter. Nonetheless he decided to use it anyway, informing Charlotte that 'I have made a sad blot My Charley 'ere I begin, but that shall not prevent my using the paper.'[29] Writers thus deviated from the model love letter depending upon their day-to-day activities, plus the physical and material realities of writing. While a blot of ink or haphazard presentation may have departed from the recommended style, these features made love letters more visceral by providing an imprint of a writer's identity and mood at the moment of writing.

Love letters were expected to be extensive enough to prove a writer's sincerity. They also had to be worth the financial outlay, as unless missives came prepaid, recipients were responsible for paying for the letters they received. Leaving blank paper at the bottom of a page was a particularly heinous crime—not to mention an expensive one—as writers had the space but not the sentiments to complete their missive.[30] The surgeon George Gibbs was often compelled to apologize 'for the clean Paper that I shall leave at the Bottom of my Letter' to reassure Ann Vicary of his sincerity. He generally endeavoured not to conclude his missives 'till all my Paper is fill'd up'.[31] The most desirable approach was that adopted by the gentlewoman Mary Martin, whose letters increased significantly in length throughout her protracted courtship with her cousin Isaac Rebow. Her longest in 1772 was a verbose eleven pages long, with Mary jesting that he should forgive her for the 'curious <u>short</u> Epistle'.[32] She consistently used up to three postscripts, creating the impression that she was unable to tear herself away from the page.[33] Mary's earlier omission of three blank sides of paper had become an affectionate joke between the couple, and after her eleven-page letter followed by three postscripts in 1772 she quipped, 'Well I do think you will not Talk any more of y Three Blank sides, for fear I shou'd send you a whole Quire of Paper next time, wrote full.'[34] In love letters, an entire page of postscripts was by no means unusual. A particularly

[28] Martin to Rebow, 18 February 1772, A12691/7, Box 1, ff. 201–3, Vol. II, ERO.

[29] Cobb to Curwen, 28 January 1805, EK/U1453/C287/4, Bundle A, KHLC.

[30] From 1711, a single sheet cost 3*d.* to post eighty miles, rising sharply to 3*d.* for fifteen miles and 4*d.* for thirty miles by the end of the century. On postage rates, see Whyman, *The Pen and the People*, 53, 63.

[31] Gibbs to Vicary, Exeter, 21 June 1746, MS/11021/1/21, 7 and 9 July 1746, MS11012/1/26–7, LMA.

[32] Martin to Rebow, 23 June 1772, A12691, Box 1, Vol. II, f. 238, ERO.

[33] See Fay Bound, 'Writing the Self? Love and the Letter in England, *c.*1660–*c.*1760', *Literature & History* 11.1 (2002): 1–19, at 9, and Lyons, 'Love Letters', 235–6.

[34] Martin to Rebow, 23 June 1772, A12691, Box 1, Vol. II, f. 239, ERO.

loquacious writer was entitled to thanks 'for writing so much', as this represented time invested in the recipient, and a relationship.[35]

Writers made fastidious efforts to keep their love letters neat and well presented, and poorly presented missives were liable to being transcribed anew.[36] Individuals aimed to craft their letters in the neatest hand possible, as a tribute to the recipient. However, this ideal style was not always obtainable, with deviations in the appearance of letters revealing a writer's mood and situation at the time of writing.[37] Writers purchased the best quality paper they could afford, with numerous writers using the most expensive paper with gilt edges. The finest gilt-edged paper was made by the Dutch, which even surpassed luxury French writing paper.[38] While there is no clear-cut difference, gentlewomen such as Mary Martin generally utilized smoother and whiter paper than domestic servants such as Elizabeth Woollat, as illustrated in Figures 2.3 and 2.4. The authors of love letters were clearly aware of the variable quality of their paper and how this was perceived by recipients. They apologized when their presentation fell below usual standards, with Mary Martin proclaiming 'hang y Paper, & y Pens, for y former is so full of Hairs, & y latter so bad, that I cannot write y least Decent to Night.'[39] Other writers complained of the low quality paper available while away from home, lamenting from Cornwall that 'You may guess, my dearest Love, the barbarity of this Country where I am at present by yᶜ Colour of yᶜ Paper.'[40]

Love letters were deeply individual items, and a person's handwriting had the power to evoke a strong emotional response. The handwriting of the domestic servant Elizabeth Woollat was painstakingly produced in a heavy hand, with each letter standing separate from the next. The words combine to form unsteady lines, with a surplus of ink where she replenished her quill or went over a character again (Figure 2.3). The care she took in constructing her letters demonstrated her affection and desire to improve to Jedediah Strutt. In contrast, the handwriting of the gentlewoman Mary Martin flowed evenly across the page in orderly straight lines. Each word was confidently italicized and embellished, using decorative flourishes to adorn the letters 'y' and 'd' (Figure 2.4). Mary's ornamented style acted as a symbol of her literacy, education, and ease at writing. Handwriting directly reflected an individual's personality, acting as an extension of the self.[41] The brewer Francis Cobb viewed his handwriting as a sign of his own mortality after the death of his three wives, reporting in February 1831 that 'By the good hand of my God

---

[35] See Curwen to Cobb, Fenstanton, 2 October 1805, EK/U1453/C287/6, Bundle A, KHLC, and Porden to Franklin, 22 May 1822, with a separate page of postscripts, D3311/8/1/14 (ii), DRO.

[36] See Lovell to Harvey, Bath, 4 December 1756, 161/102/2, WSA.

[37] Eleanor Anne Porden's letters to John Franklin are littered with crossings out, such as one missive written from Berners Street on 22 May 1822, D3311/8/1/14 (i), DRO. The changes appear to have been designed to improve her language, as the word 'alarm' was replaced with 'terror', 'speculations' was replaced with 'disquisitions', and 'fury' was replaced with 'vengeance'.

[38] Dena Goodman, *Becoming a Woman in the Age of Letters* (Ithaca, NY and London, 2009), 194–7.

[39] Martin to Rebow, 1 January 1772, A12691, Box 1, Vol. II, f. 179, ERO.

[40] Pratt to Jeffreys, Liskeard, 25 July 1745, U840/C/1/2, KHLC.

[41] On the 'precious' status of handwriting, see Whyman, *The Pen and the People*, 88, and Bound, 'Writing the Self?', 10.

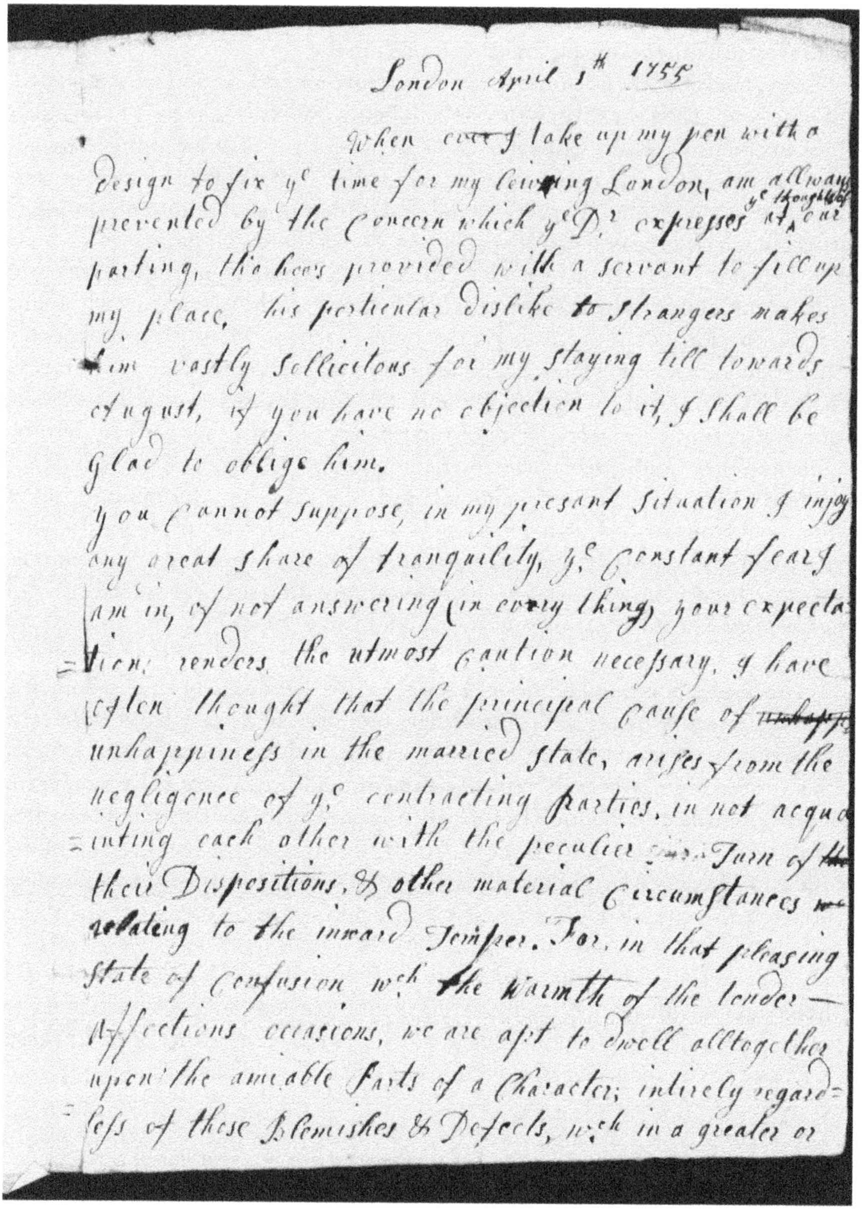

London April 1st 1755

When ever I take up my pen with a
design to fix ye time for my leaving London, am allways
prevented by the concern which yr Dr expresses at our
parting, tho hees provided with a servant to fill up
my place, his perticular dislike to strangers makes
him vastly sollicitous for my staying till towards
August, if you have no objection to it, I shall be
glad to oblige him.

You cannot suppose, in my present situation I enjoy
any great share of tranquility, ye constant fears
am in, of not answering (in every thing) your expectations, renders the utmost caution necessary, I have
often thought that the principal cause of
unhappiness in the married state, arises from the
negligence of ye contracting parties, in not acqua-
inting each other with the peculier Turn of
their Dispositions, & other material Circumstances
relateing to the inward Temper. For, in that pleasing
state of confusion wch the Warmth of the tender —
Affections occasions, we are apt to dwell alltogether
upon the amiable parts of a Character; intirely regard-
less of those Blemishes & Defects, wch in a greater or

Fig. 2.3. Letter from Elizabeth Woollat to Jedediah Strutt, London, April 1755, Derbyshire Record Office, Matlock, D5303/4/3.

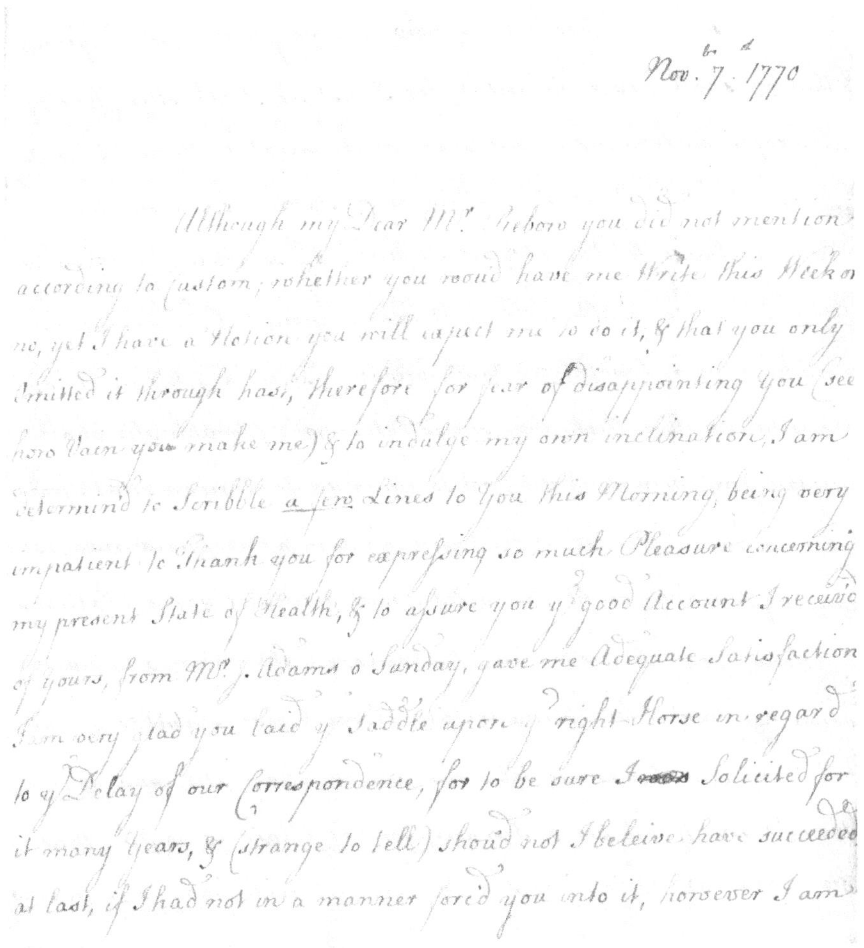
Nov. 7th: 1770

Although my Dear Mr. Rebow you did not mention according to Custom; whether you woud have me Write this Week or no, yet I have a Notion you will expect me to do it, & that you only Omitted it through hast, therefore for fear of disappointing you (see how Vain you make me) & to indulge my own inclination, I am determin'd to Scribble a few Lines to You this Morning, being very impatient to Thank you for expressing so much Pleasure concerning my present State of Health, & to assure you ye good Account I receive of yours, from Mr. J. Adams o Sunday, gave me Adequate Satisfaction I am very glad you laid ye Saddle upon ye right Horse in regard to ye Delay of our Correspondence, for to be sure I Solicited for it many Years, & (strange to tell) shoud not I beleive have succeeded at last, if I had not in a manner forc'd you into it, however I am

Fig. 2.4. Letter from Mary Martin to Isaac Rebow, Essex, 7 November 1770, Mary Martin Rebow Papers, Manuscripts, Archives, and Special Collections, Washington State University Libraries, Pullman, WA, WSU MASC Cage 134.

upon me, I am still spared, and have the opportunity of again shewing my handwriting here at the commencement of the month in which it pleased the Lord to give me birth.'[42]

Letters of couples such as the domestic servant Elizabeth Woollat and wheelwright Jedediah Strutt studied in this chapter reveal how romantic lexicon was adopted and adapted by a broad swathe of writers. Having said this, the self-conscious and crafted nature of the language of love made rural suitors subject to derision in popular culture. *The Gentleman's Magazine* delighted in printing

[42] William Francis Cobb, *Memoir of the Late Francis Cobb, Esq. of Margate* (Maidstone, 1835), 90.

'Singular and Extraordinary' pieces ridiculing rural lovers. In 1743, it reproduced an 'Authentic Copy' of a love letter from a 'Welchman' to his sixty-year-old sweetheart in Bristol. This Welsh troubadour tried in vain to adopt the language of heroic love, describing how 'none but you can give Plasture to cure the Wound, that you made in my Hart', and sitting 'at your Feet…to crave your favour'.[43] Such chivalric language had fallen out of use in the 1720s, revealing his futile attempts to keep up with romantic fashions. In 1746, the magazine printed an exchange between a farmer and his sweetheart entitled 'Exmoor Courtship, Or, A Suitoring Discourse, in the Devonshire Dialect and Mode'. This second example used phonetic spelling to present the pair as coarse yokels. The protagonist Margery Vagwell complained that her over-amorous suitor had 'a creem'd ma yearms, and a'morst a burst ma neck' with his sexual advances, and would not stop 'a grabbling o' wone's tetties'. The farmer threatened to beat his competitors into submission, giving them 'a whapper, and a wherret, and a whisterpoop too'.[44] Compared to the unfashionable Welshman, the Devonshire couple were derided as uncouth country folk. Yet while rural lovers were ridiculed as out of touch in print culture, the writers of varying social rank studied throughout this book reveal that a diverse range of couples engaged in romantic correspondence, utilizing widely recognized romantic lexicon. The Derbyshire courtship of Elizabeth and Jedediah in the 1740s and 1750s provides an equivalent example of this rural couple, as he was the son of a small farmer and maltster. Yet Jedediah's letters demonstrate in-depth knowledge of romantic modes of expression. Because writers drew upon a widely recognized vocabulary of love—as outlined in Chapter 1—their regional 'accent' was occulted in order to write as a lover.

The volume of surviving love letters changes markedly over time. Extant letters are particularly scarce in the first half of the eighteenth century, where collections often contain only a single letter, or small number of missives. Only two letters survive between Judith Cowper and Martin Madan in 1723 before Martin was breathing 'the very sentiments of my soul' on to her outstretched hand, and proclaiming himself 'entirely yours'.[45] It may be that the couple exchanged fewer missives, or that their movement in court circles led Judith to destroy their letters more assiduously. Letters were preserved in far greater numbers from mid-century, with a boom in romantic epistles in the 1780s. The upsurge may have been because of the spread of literacy, the popularity of revelatory epistolary novels such as *Pamela* (1740) and *Julie, ou la nouvelle Héloïse* (1761), or the rise of romanticism inspiring increasing numbers of lovers to write. The language of love also became more accessible, as writers turned away from the 'Continual growing Pain' bemoaned by troubadours at the turn of the century.[46] Moreover, love letters came to be viewed as sentimental objects that were worth preserving, particularly among early Victorians such as the children of Joseph Strutt and Isabella Douglas, and

[43] *Gentleman's Magazine*, March 1743, Vol. 13, 150. Archive issues available at http://onlinebooks.library.upenn.edu/webbin/serial?id=gentlemans.
[44] Ibid., June 1746, Vol. 16, 297–300, at 298.
[45] Madan to Cowper, undated (*c.*1723), MS Eng. Lett. c. 284, f. 6r, BLO.
[46] Oroondates to Statira (Mrs Ann Webb), undated (early eighteenth century), FRE 5418, ESRO.

Charlotte Mary Curwen and Francis Cobb, who courted in the late eighteenth and early nineteenth centuries.

The love letter was a highly versatile genre, with the distinguishing features of missives changing in light of wider fashions for courtly love, sensibility, and romanticism. Susan Whyman has outlined how people came to write 'more naturally' to one another as the century progressed, as 'the epistolary balance between self-expression and controlled use of norms tipped towards more freedom'.[47] Changing mores are clearly evident in how courting couples addressed one another. One courtly letter to an 'Inestimable madam' from 1717 eulogizes about her 'polite, amiable, acute, and facetious, illustrious, immaculate, person', invoking the writer's agony on three occasions without once mentioning the word love.[48] In the 1730s, the linen merchant James Nicholson and gentleman's daughter Elizabeth Seddon adopted the Latin pseudonyms 'Lucius' (Light) and 'Honoria' (Honour) in their missives, concluding as 'sincere friends' to embody the honourable foundations of their courtship. The nature of the love letter changed markedly to become more familiar and intimate in the second half of the century. While Sarah Pearsall has argued that courtly language 'remained in some force in courtship letters', the missives studied here do not bear out this conclusion.[49] From mid-century, the obedient and honourable lover became primarily affectionate and loving, with men increasingly stating their love explicitly at a letter's close. In 1755, the wheelwright Jedediah Strutt concluded his epistles by vowing 'that I Love you and that I am yours'.[50] This more openly affectionate style persisted into the first decades of the nineteenth century. In the 1810s, the soldier Robert Garrett concluded his letters to his 'poor love' Charlotte Bentinck by sending his 'very, very best love to you'.[51] In the wake of the cult of sensibility and romanticism, the love letter had adopted a more intimate emotional lexicon that came to value direct and repeated avowals of love by men before matrimony.

The tenor of epistles also changed over the course of a relationship, as love letters recorded and reinforced a couple's growing commitment. How can we ascertain when a couple considered themselves engaged to marry? The moment of engagement is one of the silences in the historical record, partly due to the ritual destruction of letters. Nicole Eustace has argued that couples in British America were 'considered engaged once they were "published"', that is once they had announced to the world their intentions'.[52] We can see this in the letters of Judith Cowper and Martin Madan, as the pair openly discussed sending an emissary to Judith's father to seek formal approval for the match in 1723, after which their nuptials were 'intirely

---

[47] Whyman, *The Pen and the People*, 22.

[48] Copy of a love letter from Mr J. Gallant to Mrs Mann (later Mrs Sibbs), 19 July 1717, WKC7/450/10, NRO. Also see proposal of marriage by Edward Hall in 1713, where he promised 'Madam fear nothing all shall be plain & you shall Have fair Dealing from your intended spouse', HW86, BAS.

[49] Pearsall, *Atlantic Families*, 97.

[50] Jed. Strutt to Woollat, Blackwell, April 1755, D5303/4/4, DRO.

[51] Garrett to Bentinck, Lisbon, 26 April 1811, R/U888/C11/7, KHLC.

[52] Eustace, '"The cornerstone of a copious work"', 530.

settl'd'.[53] Most writers remained far more coy. The surgeon George Gibbs first mentioned searching for a marital home in his eighth surviving letter to Ann Vicary in 1744.[54] By his eleventh surviving letter George was making frequent social visits to the Vicary household.[55] By his sixteenth letter on 5 July 1745 George was bold enough to *hint* at marriage in 'anticipating that which, I hope, is yet to come'.[56] Nonetheless, a formal engagement was seldom discussed explicitly in writing. Two years into his relationship with Charlotte Bentinck in 1813, the soldier Robert Garrett professed himself tired of courting—'I think we have had enough of that to satisfy us'—and hoped that once he returned, he and Charlotte would set about 'changing our conditions as the country people call it'.[57] George and Robert were thus emboldened to allude to marriage more confidently as their courtships progressed towards the altar. However, notions of an engagement or marriage were rarely discussed in explicit terms due to the sharing of letters and the perceived risks of a failed relationship for a woman's reputation.

GENDERING THE LOVE LETTER

Men and women used their letters in different ways in order to move a relationship forward. Due to men's traditional role as the instigators of courtship, one of the key tropes of men's love letters was their sincerity. Men throughout the eighteenth century were keen to emphasize the honesty, sincerity, and openness of their suit, assuring women that their affection was 'grounded upon the truest foundation of sincere affection' and was 'not to be diminished with any dishonour'.[58] In 1723, Captain Martin Madan mounted his courtship on a foundation of 'honour, & sincerity', in which Judith Cowper 'plac'd every Hope I can possibly Entertain of Future Happiness'.[59] In the 1740s, the surgeon George Gibbs was proud to declare that 'I have behaved with all the Openness & Sincerity from the Beginning of this affair, which I think it demands.'[60] Later in 1787, the cotton-trader Joseph Strutt declared that 'I love sincerity & seldom speak or write what I do not mean.'[61] Such overwhelming emphasis was placed upon sincerity because courtship was a momentous period in the build up to marriage, causing female anxiety about dishonest lovers who could potentially break an engagement and damage their reputation.

---

[53] Cowper to Madan, undated (c.1723), MS Eng. Lett. c. 284, f. 16r, BLO.
[54] Gibbs to Vicary, 10 [–] 1744, MS 11021/1/8, LMA.
[55] Ibid., Exeter, 29 October 1744, MS 11021/1/11, LMA.
[56] Ibid., Exeter, 5 July 1745, MS 11021/1/16, LMA.
[57] Garrett to Bentinck, Castelo Melhor, Portugal, 27 March 1813, R/U888/C11/43, KHLC.
[58] 'JH' to Catherine Wood, January 1763, D/SEN 5/5/1/9/1/1, Cumbria Record Office, Carlisle (subsequently CRO).
[59] Madan to Cowper, undated (c.1723), MS Eng. Lett. c. 284, f. 6r, and Cowper to Madan, undated (c.1723), c. 284, f. 9r, BLO.
[60] Gibbs to Vicary, 1740s, MS/11021/1/1, LMA.
[61] Jos. Strutt to Douglas, Derby, 23 November 1787, MS 3101/C/E/4/8/8, LOB.

Once a correspondence had been established for a number of years, men could use their letters to discuss their professional activities at length with their future wives. In the third year of his courtship with Ann Vicary *c*.1746, the surgeon George Gibbs regaled Ann with tales of disputes at the Exeter County Hospital 'to determine whether the number of Surgeons is to be reduced to three; or whether it shall remain in ye Choice of the Committee either to let the matter rest where it is at present, or to recommend a fourth Surgeon to the General Court in any future Times when they think proper'.[62] Two years into his courtship with Charlotte Bentinck, the soldier Robert Garrett provided her with detailed accounts of military manoeuvres to distribute amongst his family. This designated Charlotte a key conduit of news about Robert's fortunes. On 21 July 1813 Robert dramatized the Siege of Pamplona:

> Genl O'Donnell with about 14,000 Spaniards relieved the 3^d & 4th divisions in blockading Pamplona. During the time we were there we kept the garrison in very good order not allowing them to come out to cut the corn, even under cover of the guns of the Town. They tried it four or five times but always found it to be a losing game, that at last they desisted.[63]

These detailed descriptions of a man's line of work demonstrate how the dynamics of a correspondence shifted over time. Several years into their courtships, George and Robert used their letters to inform women about their daily routines, the progress of their careers, and their prospects for the future.[64] When talking at length about the routines of work, a man consciously informed a woman that he was a success professionally, also making her his confidante, foreshadowing her role as his wife.

Throughout the period of courtship, men's love letters were largely unconstrained by conventions of modesty, allowing them to ruminate at length about the nature of love. Unlike Judith Cowper's unsent letter used to open this chapter, men's musings about love made their way successfully through the post. The second surviving letter from George Gibbs to Ann Vicary on 8 September 1744 was a lengthy manifesto of 'serious Reflections' about love. He described how:

> There is my Dear, a certain Pleasure that attends over the anxieties of a reasonable & undissembled Passion, which I shoud think but ill exchanged for those trifling amusements which the World generally make their Happiness to depend on...indeed if a man be necessarily affected by the Judgment he passes on his own Conduct, this Reflection must undoubtedly give him some Satisfaction.[65]

These reflections allowed George to portray himself as a reasonable man of solid judgement and exemplary conduct. They also showcased his intellect and thoughtful nature to his future wife—particularly as her social status was more elevated

---

[62] Gibbs to Vicary, Exeter, June, 1740s, MS11021/1/25, LMA. Also see MS11021/1/17 and 21.

[63] Garrett to Bentinck, Camp near Roncesvalles, Spain, 21 July 1813, R/U888/C11/56, KHLC.

[64] For a further example, see letters from Charles Pratt to Elizabeth Jeffreys, where he dramatized life on the court circuit, describing how 'I must descend again to ye business of ye Circuit & prepare to Go into Court for ye Trumpet sounds & I am in ye first Cause wch is an assault & Battery': Pratt to Jeffreys, 7 July 1749, U840/C/1/20, KHLC.

[65] Gibbs to Vicary, Exeter, 8 September 1744, MS 11021/1/2, LMA.

than his own. The wheelwright Jedediah Strutt was equally reflective in his letters to Elizabeth Woollat *c*.1755. He mused that 'Love has long since been ~~the~~ my darling passion tho' it was not till lately that I had any taste for Connubial pleasures...[it] is the subject of all my thoughts...at present I know of nothing worthy the name of Love that is not intended that way.'[66] These extracts underscore the purpose of courtship letters in providing men with a space to rationalize their thoughts about love and marriage, presenting themselves as intellectually capable and sincere to their sweethearts.

In contrast, women's letters were more reserved about their emotions, restricting their access to the 'power inherent in the act of loving'.[67] Female virtue was one of the pillars of conduct literature, with John Gregory praising how 'conscious virtue' could 'awe the most shameless and abandoned of men' and John Moir arguing that 'the most splendid accomplishments are...eligible only as auxiliaries to virtue.'[68] Suitors repeatedly impressed the critical importance of virtue upon women. In a letter to Elizabeth Seddon in 1738, the linen merchant James Nicholson outlined how the ideal 'friend' should exhibit 'Constancy and faithfulness, knowledge & Discretion, a Chearfull Wenness [*sic*] of Temper, together with a Continued series of virtuous actions...[friendship] absolutely refuses any Commerce with vice, & it is virtue alone y^r begins & improves it'.[69] The letter acted as a thinly veiled manifesto for his expectations in a future wife. The cotton-trader Joseph Strutt was equally keen to impress the importance of virtue upon his fiancée Isabella Douglas in 1788, arguing that 'If I have inforced Virtue strongly, I have not inforced it too much—the word has a comprehensive meaning.' He encouraged her to 'listen' to the instruction of virtue, '& you will be sure to meet the reward it will bestow—Innocence, Modesty, Truth & Happiness.'[70]

Women's courtship letters were defined by their modesty and the exhibition of self-doubt, even when the author was a proficient writer. As early as the sixteenth century, female writers used modesty as a rhetorical strategy to project an image of self-improvement and vulnerability.[71] Modesty remained a dominating theme of women's love letters throughout the eighteenth century. Judith Cowper was an accomplished poet, and correspondent of Alexander Pope. Nonetheless, *c*.1723 she asked Martin Madan to 'find some Excuse for all ye very silly things you have heard me say, & seen me write, I should not send this were I to read it over again...whenever you see me next, don't mention it.'[72] In a similar vein, the

[66] Jed. Strutt to Woollat, Blackwell, 28 June (*c*.1755), D5303/4/6, DRO.

[67] Katie Barclay and Rosalind Carr, 'Women, Love and Power in Enlightenment Scotland', *Women's History Review* 27.2 (2018), 176–98, at 181. Cf. Ruth Yeazell, *Fictions of Modesty: Women and Courtship in the English Novel* (Chicago, IL, 1984).

[68] John Gregory, *A Father's Legacy to his Daughters* (London, 1774), 35–6, and John Moir, *Female Tuition; or, An Address to Mothers, on the Education of Daughters*, second edition (London, 1786), 244.

[69] Nicholson to Seddon, Liverpool, 23 June 1738, 920 NIC/6/1/1, Liverpool Record Office, Liverpool (subsequently LIRO).

[70] Jos. Strutt to Douglas, 12 October 1788, MS 3101/C/E/4/8/13, LOB.

[71] See James Daybell, 'Female Literacy and the Social Conventions of Women's Letter-Writing in England, 1540–1603', in *Early Modern Women's Letter Writing*, ed. Daybell, 59–76, at 62, 66.

[72] Cowper to Madan, undated (*c*.1723), MS Eng. Lett. c. 284, f. 8v, BLO.

gentleman's daughter Elizabeth Seddon repeatedly emphasized her unworthiness in letters to James Nicholson in 1738. During their ongoing debate about human nature in January, she admitted that the topic 'requires a more Eloquent pen than Mine to Set it forth'. Elizabeth reminded James of her humility in July, where she described how 'to Define this Irregular Passion in all its parts...requires a wiser head to do it'. Later in November she owned 'I have proposed what I am very incapable of solveing', maintaining James' dominance in intellectual matters.[73] Modesty extended across the social spectrum: the domestic servant Elizabeth Woollat took a similarly deferential tone in her humble letters to Jedediah Strutt before their marriage in 1755, describing how 'I write to you more for my own sake then [*sic*] yours; less to make you thinke I write well, then [*sic*] to learn from you to write better.'[74] By emphasizing the need to improve her writing skills, Elizabeth presented herself as modest and self-effacing to her admirer. Her desire to learn was realized during their exchanges, as her epistolary literacy improved remarkably over the years. By 1755 she was using noticeably longer words such as 'Disconcerted', 'Inferiority', and 'Consciousness', and her spelling had improved enormously.[75] Conventions of female modesty persisted throughout the century; Elizabeth's son Joseph Strutt described the ideal pose as a 'bashful Modesty' in 1787, which he had 'so often & so strongly recommended' to his sweetheart Isabella.[76]

In contrast to men's emotionally expressive letters, women's epistles were more guarded. John Gregory warned female readers that 'men will complain of your reserve. They will assure you that a franker behaviour would make you more amiable.'[77] The surgeon George Gibbs had done exactly that in 1744, complaining to Ann Vicary that 'we are to be convinc'd of your Importance by being kept at a Distance, & treated with a contemptuous kind of Reserve.'[78] Ann had initially been hesitant to begin a romantic correspondence with George, as this confirmed that they would soon be engaged. When she finally acquiesced, he praised how 'you cant imagine how much you have obliged me by this Indulgence, & as you have at last broke thro' those little Objections which you had conceived to such a

---

[73] Seddon to Nicholson, Liverpool, 27 January, 24 July, and 18 November 1738, GBB 133 Eng. MS 1041/1, 2 and 8 (Box 1), JRL.

[74] Wollat to Jed. Strutt, undated (pre-1755), D5303/1/2 (iii), DRO. In what may be a fragment of the same letter she continues, 'I have wrote this letter in such a hurry y^t I dare say you cant reed [*sic*] it, and I emagin [*sic*] you think to your self I wish I never had, had it, and I realy am in debate with my self wheather [*sic*] I shoud sent it or not', D5303/1/2 (i).

[75] See Woollat to Jed. Strutt, London, 15 February 1755, D5303/4/2, DRO. The gentlewoman Mary Martin wrote polished and neat letters to her suitor Isaac Rebow, who praised her for her 'Knack of Epistolizing', 1 July 1772, A12691, Box 1, Vol. II, f. 242, ERO. However, she still repeatedly described her desire to improve, noting, 'O! what wou'd I give that I cou'd properly express my Sentiments on y Occasion...I am every Day, more & more sensible, that I have not "y Pen of a ready Writer", therefore must Content myself, with Assuring you, it is my fervent Wish, & shall be my most earnest Study, & I think (see how Vain you make me) I shall in all probability succeed': 5 May 1772, A12691, Box 1, f. 212, Vol. II.

[76] Jos. Strutt to Douglas, Derby, 7 October 1787, MS3101/C/E/4/8/7, LOB. Richard Dixon adopted a similar tone in letters to Maria Cranmer in 1782, praising how 'You are a good Girl and always think and act with propriety', Buxton, 7 May 1782, 8215/7, SHC.

[77] Gregory, *A Father's Legacy*, 36.

[78] Gibbs to Vicary, 22 September 1744, MS/11021/1/3, LMA.

Correspondence, I may hope you will not refuse to give me the Pleasure of hearing from you oftener than at first you proposed.'[79] Several women showed further reticence, claiming to be fearful of disappointing their suitors. The domestic servant Elizabeth Woollat expressed her concern at falling below Jedediah Strutt's expectations in a future wife. As she wrote in 1755 (displayed in Figure 2.3):

> you Cannot suppose, in my present [*sic*] situation I injoy any great share of tranquility, ye Constant fear I am in, of not answering (in every thing) your expectation renders the utmost caution necessary, I have often thought that the principal Cause of unhap-piness in the married state, arises from the negligence of ye contracting parties, in not acquainting each other with the peculier [*sic*] Turn of their Dispositions.[80]

Elizabeth may have felt genuine fear at the challenge of impressing a man she admired, or this may have provided an additional way to demonstrate her modesty and self-doubt to her future husband.[81] Women's reluctance to enter into the domain of romantic correspondence was reflected in their letters, which were more cautious, hesitant, and emotionally guarded than men's.

One further stance recommended by John Gregory was religious devotion, arguing that 'men consider your religion as one of their principal securities for that female virtue in which they are most interested.'[82] However, this approach was not adopted by all women, with only extremely pious women such as the Unitarian Elizabeth Seddon and Anglican Charlotte Mary Curwen allowing religious dis-courses to dominate their letters. Debating Christian maxims enabled these women to demonstrate their intellectual capabilities by discussing theological issues with their suitors. As Elizabeth noted in 1738, 'we may consider that true virtue and Practical religion never so flourishes in the Christian world as in that part that is under Persicution [*sic*]; which *in my opinion* shows that it is the plenty of spiritual food we injuy that Surfits [*sic*] us.'[83] Religious zeal could also provide a source of power for women looking to cement their place in a new home. This was especially true for women such as Charlotte, whose suitor Francis Cobb had been married twice before. In 1805, she challenged him that if he did not allow her to educate his children with a bias agreeable to her views, she could not see their relationship progressing any further: 'I shall teach them the prayer book: as I believe it to be according to the scriptures, & if we are not agreed upon this point, my hands are tied therefore how can my affections be enlarged.'[84] Francis himself was deeply

---

[79] Ibid., Exeter, 1740s, MS/11021/1/17, LMA.

[80] Woollat to Jed. Strutt, London, 5 April 1755, D5303/4/3, DRO.

[81] An additional example is provided by Isabella Douglas, who described how 'I am fearful I tres-pass on your time & patience', quoted in a letter from Jos. Strutt to Douglas, Derby, 18 December 1787, MS 3101/C/E/4/8/9, LOB.

[82] Gregory, *A Father's Legacy*, 23. Also see Wetenhall Wilkes, *A Letter of Genteel and Moral Advice to a Young Lady...* (Dublin, 1741), 38–61, 68–70; *The Lady's Preceptor. Or, a Letter to a Young Lady of Distinction upon Politeness...* (London, 1743), 5–6; Moir, *Female Tuition*, esp. 258.

[83] Seddon to Nicholson, Liverpool, 28 September 1738, GB 133 Eng. MS 1041/6 (Box 1), JRL. My italics.

[84] Curwen to Cobb, 12 July 1805, EK/U1453/C2/1, Bundle A, KHLC.

religious, making Charlotte's piousness a powerful tool in determining the dynamics of their new household.

Charlotte's challenge to Francis' authority demonstrates how courting women could wield a significant degree of power, delaying their marriage by asking 'for another half year to consider the matter'.[85] In her study of nineteenth-century America, Karen Lystra has argued that courting women frequently orchestrated 'at least one dramatic emotional crisis' to test their suitors' love.[86] The letters studied in this chapter reveal that women's emotional testing was a persistent feature of courtship throughout the eighteenth century. These rituals of testing grant women significantly more autonomy than historians such as Katie Barclay have allowed in arguing that elite Scottish women 'were not allowed to express emotion, until they finally accepted a proposal of marriage'.[87] In 1723, Judith Cowper tested Martin Madan by seeing whether he would eschew the opera for her, without having to ask him directly. When he failed the test and went oblivious to the opera, she questioned, 'How is it Possible for me to fancy you as Sencire [*sic*] as I would have you, w^n an opera, nay one you did not Like, could make you Leave me?' Judith retorted that 'I would not have left you', and demanded that Martin 'write to me in the morn^g & Let me know whether you continue to Love me or not.'[88] Her stunned lover responded, 'surely you was not in earnest... am I then become insipid to you? can you change thus soon?'[89] Martin evidently paid penance for his error, and the couple were married on 7 December 1723. A similar rite of passage is evident in the courtship of the cotton-trader Joseph Strutt and Isabella Douglas. Two years into their courtship in May 1788, Isabella wrote to Joseph casting 'doubts & suspicions' over their relationship, and accusing him of neglect. Joseph retorted that 'if my love for you is lessened by time or by absence, it is not true love', and promised that 'in my thoughts you are always uppermost, & of my Heart the Mistress.'[90] Isabella orchestrated a whole series of crises to ensure that Joseph's love was secure—in 1789 she reportedly spread rumours with her friends that he had 'basely & wickedly' deserted her, in order to force him to reaffirm his commitment to marry.[91] These examples demonstrate the degree of power that women could wield during courtship. The crises created by Judith, Isabella, and Charlotte were a useful strategy in enabling them to discover the intensity of their suitors' devotion, reminding them that a woman's love was not to be taken for granted.

VALUING THE LOVE LETTER

Love letters were gifts exchanged by lovers, retaining the essence of the individuals who gave them. As the anthropologist Marcel Mauss has argued, 'Even when

---

[85] Ibid., 12 July 1805, EK/U1453/C2/1, Bundle A, KHLC.
[86] Lystra, *Searching the Heart*, 157.   [87] Barclay, *Love, Intimacy and Power*, 91.
[88] Cowper to Madan, 1723, MS Eng. Lett. c. 284, ff. 26–7, BLO.
[89] Madan to Cowper, 1723, MS Eng. Lett. c. 284, f. 29v, BLO.
[90] Jos. Strutt to Douglas, Derby, 5 May 1788, MS 3101/C/E/4/8/11, LOB.
[91] Ibid., Derby, 7 January 1789, MS 3101/C/E/4/8/16, LOB.

abandoned by the giver, it still forms a part of him. Through it he has a hold over the recipient.'[92] Elizabeth Seddon kept her letters from James Nicholson under lock and key, guarding them 'more carefully than any treasure I have'.[93] Before his marriage in 1755, the Derbyshire wheelwright Jedediah Strutt made a direct correlation between his letters and 'thoughts', pondering that 'if every thought for you had been a Letter, Millions perhaps wou'd not Comprize the sum.'[94] Others repeatedly described their letters as 'favours', as if sent as a token by the writer.[95] The soldier Robert Garrett revealed his emotional investment in Charlotte Bentinck's letters in 1811 by describing them as 'so valuable a dear treasure', reminding her that 'nothing gives me greater delight, it is the only substitute I have...for not being with you.'[96] Lovers treated their letters as treasured possessions, claiming to read them over on a regular basis. In 1787, Joseph Strutt purported to have read one epistle from Isabella Douglas 'over & over again, nay I have read it so often that I can almost repeat it'.[97] Since sources such as diaries do not mention whether lovers actually reread their letters ad infinitum, we cannot know if they did so on a regular basis, or if the rereading of letters provided a fitting epistolary device with which to express a writer's love.

The intrinsic value of love letters imbued them with the power to transcend death, and individuals frequently wrote love letters to be read posthumously in case some accident should befall them. The Bedfordshire gentleman Samuel Whitbread II wrote a letter to his sweetheart Elizabeth Grey should he die during his Grand Tour, promising, 'If ever You receive this letter, which I hope will not be the case, You will with it receive all the letters that You will have written to me.'[98] The act of returning her letters ensured that she would be provided with a physical comfort after his death, as their love letters provided both an embodiment of their relationship, and of Samuel himself. Women such as Francis Cobb's second wife Mary (*née* Blackburn) (1773–1802) took similar precautions should they die during childbirth. Mary's letters allowed her affection to transcend death and provide Francis with a way to rekindle their love as a means of comfort. In a letter written seven years before her death in 1802, she praised how, 'A happier life, I verily believe, none ever knew. Your tenderness to me has been beyond example...I love you to my very heart, and have experienced all I could wish from you to make my life happy.'[99] The eternal value of love letters was captured in visual culture, in works such as Jean-Baptiste Greuze's *Le Tendre Ressouvenir* (*Tender Memory*)

[92] Marcel Mauss, *The Gift: Forms and Functions of Exchange in Archaic Societies*, trans. Ian Cunnison (London, [1954] 1970), 9.

[93] Seddon to Nicholson, Liverpool, 18 November 1738, GB 133 Eng. MS 1041/8, Box 1, JRL.

[94] Jed. Strutt to Woollat, undated (pre-1755), D5303/1/1, DRO.

[95] Seddon to Nicholson, Liverpool, 7 August, 17 October, and 18 November 1738, GB133 Eng. MS 1041/3, 7–8 (Box 1), JRL. Martin to Rebow, 18 September 1768, A12691, Box 1, Vol. I, f. 10, and 27 April 1772, A12691, Vol. II, f. 210, ERO.

[96] Garrett to Bentinck, Malhada Sorda, Portugal, 20 May 1811, R/U888/C11/8, and near Ciudad Rodrigo, Spain, 16 August 1811, R/U888/C11/13, KHLC.

[97] Jos. Strutt to Douglas, Derby, 7 October 1787, MS 3101/C/E/4/8/7, LOB.

[98] Whitbread II to Grey, Clarges Street, 6 May 1787, W1/6613, No. 30, BAS.

[99] See transcript of Mary's letters in Cobb, *Memoir*, 42–5.

(1762–3). The oil painting depicts a young widow seated next to an open box of her husband's letters—which have clearly been rifled through—while clutching at several pages in her hand. She immerses herself in her husband's missives while touching a marble bust of his face, which gazes down upon her. The ritual of touching and rereading letters allows the woman to indulge in loving memories and resurrect her husband's identity in order to assuage her grief.[100]

Courting men describe carrying love letters around in their pockets, touching and kissing them as symbolic substitutes for women. While women may have done the same, the fetishistic connotations of kissing letters prevented them from acknowledging this in writing. Sigmund Freud argued that the use of objects as a symbolic substitute was a form of sexual fetishism which was 'habitually present in normal love, especially in those stages of it in which the normal sexual aim seems unattainable or its fulfilment prevented'.[101] Captain Martin Madan fantasized about walking paths trod by his sweetheart in 1723: 'There will I clasp ye Phantom, pull out the letter you've so often ask'd for, & kiss it to its native white.'[102] Others used letters to provide a symbolic 'portal' between them and their sweethearts by placing them on or near their bodies while they were asleep. The romantic poet John Keats slept with Fanny Brawne's letters between his legs and under his pillow as a way to be closer to her in 1820. He also promised to 'kiss your name and mine where your Lips have been—Lips! why should a poor prisoner as I am talk about such things?'[103] The physicality of these rapturous declarations is typical of early nineteenth-century love letters, especially those produced by Romantic poets such as Keats. The kissing of love letters marked the fetishization of the letter as an object because of its connection with a lover, in turn becoming a direct substitute for them.[104] Such behaviour was enshrined in sentimental novels, which utilized men's kissing of letters as a sign of their infatuation. In Frances Burney's *Evelina* (1778), Lord Orville kissed the letter consenting to his marriage to the novel's heroine, while a besotted Werther wrote to Charlotte in Goethe's *Sorrows of Young Werther* (1774) that he 'quickly raised your letter to my lips' after reading it.[105]

Love letters were repeatedly praised as a source of emotional enjoyment, eliciting feelings of cheer, happiness, and joy, and a sense of comfort and gratification. In the 1740s, the surgeon George Gibbs described how he experienced 'no Pleasure, to be compared wth that which thy Letters give me'.[106] Similarly in 1772, the

---

[100] Jean-Baptiste Greuze, *Le Tendre Ressouvenir*, France, 1762–3, oil on canvas, 40 × 32 cm, P454, Wallace Collection, London.

[101] Sigmund Freud, *On Sexuality: Three Essays on the Theory of Sexuality and Other Works*, ed. Angela Richards, trans. James Strachey (London, 1977), Vol. 7, 65–8, at 66. Also Tim Dant, 'Fetishism and the Social Value of Objects', *Sociological Review* 44. 3 (1996): 495–516.

[102] Madan to Cowper, 13 October 1723, MS Eng. Lett c. 284/2, f. 4r, BLO.

[103] Keats to Brawne, 1820, Letters XII and XXII, in Forman, ed., *Letters of John Keats*, 48, 65.

[104] Sarah Hurst recorded a strange incident of her aunt requesting to kiss courtship letters from Henry Smith; 'Mrs Wicker comes & desires to kiss my Harrys letter, I consent but think it a little odd': Diary of Hurst, 20 October 1759, MS 3542, HM.

[105] Johann Wolfgang von Goethe, *The Sorrows of Young Werther* (Oxford, [1774] 2012), 26 July 1771, Book 1, 29, and Frances Burney, *Evelina, or The History of a Young Lady's Entrance into the World* (Cambridge, [1778] 1996), 259.

[106] Gibbs to Vicary, 1740s, MS/11021/1/1, LMA.

gentlewoman Mary Martin praised the 'most infinite Satisfaction' of receiving Isaac Rebow's letters, which 'gave me more Pleasure, than I can find Words to Express'.[107] The joy of communicating your love—and finding it returned—was a source of immense satisfaction, making the heart 'a seal of happiness' with 'comfort within & warmth & Heavenly sunshine without'.[108] The composition of love letters was doubly enjoyable for writers due to the pleasure they brought to recipients. Suitors enjoyed 'no Pleasure equal to that which arises from contributing to thy Satisfaction; Coud [sic] I therefore be so cruel... to refuse thee such a Trifle as a Letter?'[109] Charlotte Mary Curwen was also cheered to know that her letters pleased Francis Cobb in 1805, describing how 'I feel much pleasur [sic] in being obliged to write to you this morning, & more particularly so, as I flatter myself, my letter will not be altogether unwelcome.'[110] The emotional value of love letters as material sources of comfort and satisfaction was therefore mutually constituted with the importance granted to missives by recipients.

The high emotional value of love letters made them a powerful force in exacerbating or alleviating the agitation of love. The overwhelming emotional consequences of receiving a love letter were dramatized in Jane Austen's *Persuasion* (1818) where Anne Elliot receives a letter from Captain Wentworth declaring his unwavering love:

> Such a letter was not soon to be recovered from. Half an hour's solitude and reflection might have tranquilized her; but the ten minutes only which now passed before she was interrupted, with all the restraints of her situation, could do nothing towards tranquillity. Every moment rather brought fresh agitation. It was overpowering happiness.[111]

The novel emphasized the importance of self-reflection in coping with the 'overpowering' impact of receiving letters. The sensation was not always pleasurable, with Charlotte Mary Curwen describing how her suitor's doubts about their relationship had caused 'palpitations' of mind and body and she was 'obliged to take brandy before I could hold my pen at all, to write'.[112] Nonetheless, love letters also provided a balm or 'cordial' for this agitation, diffusing a 'placid serenity' to writers' spirits.[113] On 2 October 1805, Charlotte praised how love letters had provided 'a cordial to my spirits, & I think I got some good from it'.[114] Two weeks later she again celebrated their medicinal properties as 'a cordial to my dejected mind'.[115] Whilst doubting letters could cause immense agitation, reassuring letters possessed important 'healing powers' in lifting depressed spirits and calming the mind.

---

[107] Martin to Rebow, 5 May 1772, A12691, Box 1, Vol. II, f. 212 and 1 July 1772, A12691, Box 1, Vol. II, f. 242, ERO.

[108] Robert Lloyd to Hannah Hart, March 1804, TEMP MSS 210/3/222, LSF.

[109] Gibbs to Vicary, Exeter, 5 July 1746, MS/11021/1/23, LMA.

[110] Curwen to Cobb, January 1805, EK/U1453/C287/2, Bundle A, KHLC.

[111] Jane Austen, *Persuasion* (London, [1818] 2008), 199.

[112] Curwen to Cobb, 18 October 1805, EK/U1453/C2/5, Bundle A, KHLC.

[113] Hays to Eccles, 9 August 1779, in Wedd, ed., *Love-Letters of Mary Hays*, 41.

[114] Curwen to Cobb, Fenstanton, 2 October 1805, EK/U1453/C287/6, Bundle A, KHLC.

[115] Ibid., Fenstanton, 18 October 1805, EK/U1453/C2/5, Bundle A, KHLC.

Other forms of correspondence had the same therapeutic qualities, acting as a means of catharsis and self-justification.[116]

CONCLUSION

This chapter has presented the exchange of love letters as a distinct stage of courtship, which was fundamental to the forming, securing, and testing of a romantic bond. Writers across the social spectrum used their missives to create an emotional attachment before marriage by describing the anxiety of catching the post, the suspense of waiting for a delivery, and the dejection when promised letters failed to arrive. To correspond was to build a commitment before matrimony. The sharing of letters helped to quell any familial doubts, particularly for men such as Robert Garrett courting women of a more elevated status. These men used their letters to showcase their sincerity, affability, and intellectual capability to their sweethearts, and their families.

Love letters enabled courting couples to assess one another's disposition in anticipation of a happy marriage, and endeavour to meet the expectations of a future husband or wife. As one woman concluded a particularly frank assessment of her own virtues and shortcomings in 1755, 'These I take to be the distinguishing parts of my Character.'[117] Many men utilized their letters as a means of instruction to impress the importance of virtue upon their sweethearts. In turn, women tested the lengths their suitors would go to in order to prove their love. While corresponding did not signify a formal engagement, it certainly foreshadowed an impending marriage. In this sense, engagement was not a single moment but a lengthy process, becoming more assured as greater numbers of letters were exchanged. Nonetheless, it was incredibly rare for an engagement to be explicitly discussed in writing, in order to guard against potential broken relationships. As Richard Edgcumbe's panicked family wrote at the outset of this chapter, a failed courtship of an unsuitable bride could 'stick to Him through Life' and leave him 'queer & nasty till He dys'.[118]

The genre changed over the Georgian era as the language of romantic love became more informal and emotionally expressive. At the start of the eighteenth century, suffering suitors heroically declared their romantic agonies, before coming to craft their letters 'in plain English'.[119] In light of the natural and spontaneous feeling celebrated by the cult of sensibility, letters became markedly more familiar as overt protestations of love were granted new importance in the formation of a relationship. The dynamics of a correspondence also shifted during courtship itself, with men entering into lengthy descriptions of work, and women staging a number of dramatic emotional crises in the later stages of a relationship.

[116] James Daybell, 'Introduction', in *Early Modern Women's Letter Writing*, ed. Daybell, 8; Leonie Hannan, *Women of Letters: Gender, Writing and the Life of the Mind in Early Modern England* (Manchester, 2016), 169.

[117] Woollat to Jed. Strutt, April 1755, 5303/4/3, DRO.

[118] Fox to Hanbury Williams, 16–27 October 1750, CHW10902/52, fols. 59–62, LWL.

[119] Kirton to Lloyd, Rimpton, 14 August 1734, TEMP MSS 210/2/96, LSF.

The feature that unites all of the lovers studied in this chapter was the immense value that they placed upon their letters as treasured possessions and embodiments of the absent sender. Touching and kissing love letters, and keeping them close to the body, provided a vital means of creating emotional intimacy between courting couples. Sensory interaction with romantic gifts played an essential role in producing and strengthening feelings of love, as revealed in the next chapter.

3

Love Tokens

When the Harrow-educated army ensign Robert Garrett (1794–1869) began wooing the granddaughter of the Duke of Portland Charlotte Bentinck (1789–1819) in 1811, he charmed her with a variety of exotic tokens acquired during his time abroad. While serving in Spain and Portugal during the Peninsular Campaign he sent her an almanac and 'a little box of trifles' including some buttons, two bottles of jasmine, and the 'neatest & most genteel' ring he could find of Portuguese manufacture. He was disappointed with the 'silly' ring, 'every thing they make being so vulgar', and was frustrated at not being able to find the sheet music and Spanish castanets she desired. Charlotte responded to these exotic presents with domestic gifts, sending him a violet, an English flower denoting faithful love, and a handmade purse and white hair-work handkerchief to demonstrate her esteem and domestic skill.[1] Charlotte's mother also gave him a ring, an important symbolic gift signifying that Charlotte and Robert would soon be wed. Even after a horse bit his ring finger, Robert determinedly bent the ring back into shape, and continued to wear it. When the 'poor old ring' finally broke apart, he took to carrying it around in a purse that Charlotte had knitted for him, in order to maintain the intimate emotional bond that they had built through objects.[2]

As this chapter will show, the exchange and use of romantic gifts provided a key way for courting couples to negotiate the path to matrimony. Material objects determined how people related to one another by providing a key means of conceptualizing and processing their emotions. They also played a vital role in preserving the identity of the giver, acting as an important site of memory for the recipient. Ulinka Rublack has argued that humans create 'a sense of being' through 'creative exchange with the material world'. We 'relate' to objects 'emotionally' and 'think that they represent our tastes, values, wishes, and spirituality, our connection with others and to our past'.[3] Clara Tuite has presented love in particular as a 'complex multimedia event', where the tokens exchanged by lovers represent 'intricate material nestings' of their relationship.[4] The study of material culture therefore

---

[1] 'A lover had, fond as the kissing breeze / That woos in spring the purple violet; / Faithful as holy truth; and as sincere': John Bidlake, *The sea: a poem. In two books* (London, 1796), 54.

[2] Garrett to Bentinck, Malhada Sorda, 20 May 1811, R/U888/C11/8; near Ciudad Rodrigo, 16 August 1811, R/U888/C11/13; Camp between Rueda and For de Sillas, 9 July 1812, R/U888/C11/32, KHLC.

[3] Ulinka Rublack, *Dressing Up: Cultural Identity in Renaissance Europe* (Oxford, 2010), 3.

[4] Clara Tuite, 'Tainted Love and Romantic Literary Celebrity', *English Literary History* 74.1 (2007): 59–88, at 62.

provides historians with a way to access the emotional lives, subjectivity, and identity of individuals in history. The selection of gifts formed part of a creative process where lovers chose particular symbolic objects and often went on to personalize them with engravings, embroidery, and amorous messages. Such objects could then be touched, smelled, and gazed upon to encourage the development of love.

Contemporary letters evince a deep awareness of the emotional power of objects, far beyond their financial value. Anthropologists such as Marcel Mauss have long argued that objects possess personalities of their own, and 'have values which are emotional as well as material; indeed in some cases the values are entirely emotional'. Mauss argues that the emotional value of the gift lies in the motives for exchange, for friendship or love, as 'to give something is to give a part of oneself...while to receive something is to receive a part of someone's spiritual essence.'[5] Annette B. Weiner has coined the term 'inalienable possessions', which contain many similar qualities to love tokens. Such objects 'are imbued with the intrinsic and ineffable identities of their owners which are not easy to give away. Ideally they are kept from one generation to the next.'[6] More recently, Daniel Miller analysed the possessions accumulated by the inhabitants of a single London street. The items assembled by each person were seen to 'store and possess, take in and breathe out the emotions with which they have been associated'. Items such as a borrowed dress, a gravestone, and a hand-woven bedcover do not only 'represent' particular feelings, but mediate, transfer, and share emotions between people.[7]

How exactly did objects acquire this emotional charge? For psychologists and neuroscientists such as Lisa Feldman Barrett, it is affect that 'leads us to believe that objects and people in the world are inherently negative or positive'. We therefore 'experience affect as a property of an object...rather than as our own experience'.[8] In unconsciously imbuing an object with positive or pleasant affect, and designating it a love token, we therefore experience it as a conduit to romantic emotions when used in a particular way. We then attribute these pleasant qualities to the object itself, as capable of inspiring feelings of love. As Feldman Barrett writes, 'You are truly an architect of your own experience. Believing is feeling.'[9]

This chapter is divided into three sections, and is structured around the key rituals of gazing at, touching, and smelling love tokens. At its heart are two essential questions: first, which gifts did courting men and women exchange and why? Second, how did these gifts work to move a relationship forward both practically and emotionally? In other words, what did they *do* to foster a romantic bond? In endeavouring to answer these questions, I investigate how items were purchased

---

[5] Mauss, *The Gift*, 10, 63.

[6] Annette B. Weiner, *Inalienable Possessions: The Paradox of Keeping-While-Giving* (Oxford, 1992), 6, 151.

[7] Daniel Miller, *The Comfort of Things* (Cambridge, 2008), 38.

[8] Lisa Feldman Barrett, *How Emotions are Made: The Secret Life of the Brain* (London, 2017), 75.

[9] Put another way, 'you feel what your brain believes. Affect primarily comes from prediction': Feldman Barrett, *How Emotions are Made*, 78.

or produced, how much they would have cost, how objects varied according to the social status of couples, which particular items were given by men and women, at which stage of courtship they were exchanged, their metaphorical and symbolic meanings, and which objects were particularly weighted towards matrimony. Ultimately, the chapter aims to reveal the vital role of objects in producing, negotiating, and intensifying feelings of love.

The chapter draws upon objects mentioned by couples in courtship letters alongside extant objects held in museum collections, sold by auction houses, described in poetry, ballads, songs, and novels, and depicted in paintings and print. This multi-layered approach is necessitated as it is incredibly rare for the precise items described in love letters to survive, while the objects collected by museums have often lost details of the men and women who gave and received them. As emphasized in the recent volume *Tangible Things*, material objects 'do not exist entirely independently of texts', but regularly combine both words and material evidence for scholars to examine.[10] Joanne Begiato has further noted that 'evidence of handling, wear and tear, rubbing, and polishing often only exist in descriptive or narrativised form', requiring historians 'to deploy social history techniques to build a contextual picture of practice'.[11] This chapter builds such a picture by examining how objects acquired and conveyed meaning both through inscribed messages, their design and material properties, and the ways in which they were given, received, and used by lovers.

Our relationship with things assumed a key role in Enlightenment thought, with philosophers granting sensory interaction with objects an important place in the workings of the human mind. John Locke's *Essay Concerning Human Understanding* (1689) argued that humans are born *tabula rasa*, with the mind as a blank slate or white sheet of paper 'void of all Characters'. The senses then 'let in' certain ideas to 'furnish the yet empty Cabinet'. It is by interacting with objects that our senses '*convey into the Mind*, several distinct *Perceptions* of things', which we reflect upon in order to supply the mind with ideas.[12] G. J. Barker-Benfield has traced the evolution of this new 'nervous system of sensational psychology' over the century, and its popularization at the pulpit, in periodicals, poetry, and sentimental fiction.[13] Love too was a sensory experience. For the French writer Stendhal, the 'birth of love' awakened all of a person's senses. To love was 'to enjoy seeing, touching, and sensing with all the senses, as closely as possible, a lovable object which loves in return'.[14]

---

[10] Laurel Thatcher Ulrich, Ivan Gaskell, Sara J. Schechner, and Sarah Anne Carter, *Tangible Things: Making History through Objects* (Oxford, 2015), 5.

[11] Joanne Begiato, 'Moving Objects: Emotional Transformation, Tangibility, and Time-Travel', in *Feeling Things*, ed. Downes, Holloway, and Randles, 229–42, at 237.

[12] John Locke, *An Essay Concerning Humane Understanding. In Four Books* (London, 1690), Book I, 8; Book II, 37.

[13] G. J. Barker-Benfield, *The Culture of Sensibility: Sex and Society in Eighteenth-Century Britain* (Chicago, IL and London, 1992), 6.

[14] Stendhal, *On Love*, in *The Philosophy of (Erotic) Love*, ed. Solomon and Higgins, 135.

GAZING

Francesco Bartolozzi's engraving *The Mirror of Love* (1788) depicts a reclining woman gazing intently into a mirror held by a hovering cherub. A plump Cupid sleeps before her, with his hand resting lightly on his bow, and his feet on a quiver of arrows. The woman's gaze anticipates her being wounded by Cupid's arrow of love (Figure 3.1). Bartolozzi's engraving is after the Italian painter Giovanni Battista Cipriani's *The Genius of Modesty preventing Love Unveiling Beauty*, where the woman is Venus herself. Venus' gaze embodies Platonic notions of love as aroused by gazing upon beauty, in pursuit of knowledge: 'the lover is turned to the great sea of beauty, and, gazing upon this, he gives birth to many gloriously beautiful ideas and theories, in unstinting love of wisdom.'[15] Notions of love inspired by gazing on beauty lingered into the eighteenth century, with one soldier writing to a lady from Horse Guards barracks in 1765 that the sight of her 'Conquering Eyes' had captured his heart. He described himself as being entranced by her 'Perfection',

Fig. 3.1. Francesco Bartolozzi after Giovanni Battista Cipriani, *The Mirror of Love*, Britain, 1788, stipple engraving, image 14.6 cm × 17.5 cm, Yale Centre for British Art, Paul Mellon Collection, B1978.43.564.

---

[15] Plato's *Symposium*, in *The Philosophy of (Erotic) Love*, ed. Solomon and Higgins, 25–6.

believing that 'nothing less Beautiful than <u>yourself</u>, cou'd have given me any Concern.'[16]

A lover's gaze remained a component part of falling in love, making the eye a vitally important part of the body in transmitting a person's feelings. Courting couples described their eyes as the keys to their hearts, with the poet Judith Cowper writing to Martin Madan in 1723 that 'my Heart is in my Eyes.'[17] Fifteen years later, the heiress Elizabeth Jeffreys wrote to Charles Pratt that her eyes revealed 'the trouble of my Heart, they are, as you have told me often, very tell tale'.[18] A lover's gaze was a key component of romantic novels, where men and women were continually directing a loaded 'look' or 'glance' toward their beloved. As Jean-Paul Sartre has argued, to look upon another is a personal project whereby we transcend that person, utilize them, and designate them the object of our love. In short, 'The beloved is *a look*.'[19] In Maria Edgeworth's *Belinda* (1801), the heroine imagined that her future husband Clarence Hervey used 'all the eloquence of eyes' to declare wordlessly 'I *adore you*, Belinda.'[20] To gaze upon a person was to designate them an object of love, and to convey the hidden desires of the heart through the eyes.

Gazing upon a portrait of a beloved provided courting couples with a way to create and intensify feelings of love. The types of portrait available varied according to social rank. A silhouette was the most affordable option as it could be created in a single sitting, and cost as little as a penny. Miniatures in ink were more expensive, with one London artist charging nine shillings for a portrait executed at his home in 1746. Painted miniatures were more again, at around three guineas, rising tenfold for renowned artists such as Richard Cosway, official Painter to the Prince of Wales.[21] William Ward's mezzotint *The Pledge of Love* (1788) depicts a fashionable gentlewoman seated beneath a tree, with her legs crossed, holding a folded love letter in her hand (Figure 3.2). Alone by the riverbank, she is completely absorbed in the process of looking at a miniature suspended on a ribbon around her neck. The inscription reads:

> The lovely Fair with rapture views
> This token of their love
> Then all her promises renews
> And hopes he'll constant prove.

Lovers were expected to gaze at silhouettes and miniature portraits at length while remembering their beloved's physical qualities, imagining the 'rapture' of being

[16] James Nelthorpe to Abigail Way, New Bond Street or the Horse Guards, London, March 1765, SPK 1/3/2, ESRO.

[17] Cowper to Madan, 1723, MS Eng. Lett. c. 284, f. 27r, BLO.

[18] Jeffreys to Pratt, 28 February 1748, U840/C9/11, KHLC.

[19] Jean-Paul Sartre, *Being and Nothingness: An Essay on Phenomenological Ontology*, trans. Hazel E. Barnes (London and New York, [1943] 2003), 393. Italics in original.

[20] Maria Edgeworth, *Belinda* (Oxford, [1801] 2008), 15.

[21] Stephen Lloyd, ' "Perfect Likeness": An Introduction to the Portrait Miniature', in Julie Aronson and Marjorie E. Wieseman, eds, *Perfect Likeness: European and American Portrait Miniatures from the Cincinnati Art Museum* (New Haven, CT, 2006), 17–31, at 23, and Catalogue no. 74, 'James Ferguson, *A Young Gentleman, c.*1750', 174.

THE PLEDGE OF LOVE.

Fig. 3.2. William Ward after George Morland, *The Pledge of Love*, London, 1788, mezzo-tint, 38 cm × 27.5 cm, British Museum, London, 1873,0510.2630. © The Trustees of the British Museum, All Rights Reserved.

with them, and renewing the 'promises' which brought them together. In the first volume of his novel *In Search of Lost Time*, Marcel Proust wrote that there was 'much to be said' for the Celtic belief that lost souls were 'held captive' within inanimate objects. As soon as we gain possession of these objects, the dead 'start and tremble, they call us by our name, and as soon as we have recognised them the spell is broken'. The sensations created by gazing at objects, and making a pledge of love, enabled lovers to access the 'soul' of the absent, allowing loved ones to 'return to share [their] life'.[22]

The romantic gaze enabled men and women to animate momentarily the lifeless ink or paint before them, in order to summon an absent lover. As Héloïse had written to her tutor Abelard, 'By a peculiar Power, Love can make [your picture] seem Life it self, which as soon as the lov'd Object returns, is nothing but a little Canvas and dead Colours.'[23] Her words were regularly echoed in the letters and diaries of courting couples. In 1723, Captain Martin Madan wrote that he had 'gaz'd my soul away' looking at Judith Cowper's 'Beautifull Image', helping to form a romantic connection while they were apart.[24] The tailor's daughter Sarah Hurst exchanged silhouettes with Captain Henry Smith in 1759, noting in her diary that 'I oft gaze on his lifeless Image.' Sarah was so moved by gazing at Henry's portrait that it inspired her to write some verses, working to intensify her feelings before Henry returned from sea.[25] While courting the politician Henry Goulburn in 1811, Jane Montagu found his portrait 'my greatest comfort'. Jane wished that it 'would look at me, as the original would do', with his 'benevolent' and 'smiling' face. Like Héloïse, Jane found that Henry's image bore a particular resemblance to him 'when you are not by'—the greater the distance, the better the likeness.[26] These extracts suggest that portraits were gazed at in hopes of enlivening the sitter in their absence, serving to foster loving feelings as a tangible connection to a loved one. The emotional power held by these images swiftly came to an end once a lover returned, to become 'dead colours' once more.

Gazing upon an object could even be a more powerful ritual than the continuing presence of a loved one, especially in the romantic cultivation of absence. Absence, after all, was the opening entry in *The Dictionary of Love*, which bemoaned how lovers turned themselves into martyrs using the 'trite hyperboles of hours being months, months years, and years whole ages, in their kalendar'.[27] In *A Lover's Discourse*, Roland Barthes sets out how the 'fiction' of absence operates by transforming the separation of lovers 'into an ordeal of abandonment'.[28] Such fictions of absence were crafted in material culture, with posy rings and patch boxes

---

[22] Marcel Proust, *In Search of Lost Time*, Vol. I, *Swann's Way*, trans. C. K. Scott Moncrieff and Terence Kilmartin (New York, 1992), 59–60.

[23] *Letters of Abelard and Héloïse*, Letter II, Héloïse to Abelard, 105.

[24] Madan to Cowper, 13 October 1723, MS Eng. Lett. c. 284, f. 4r, BLO.

[25] Diary of Hurst, 3 April 1759 and 16 September 1759, MS 3542, HM.

[26] Montagu to Goulburn, 14 October 1813, 304/A4/Box 1, No. 2, SHC. As Héloïse wrote, 'we are much fonder of the Pictures of those we love, when they are at a great Distance, that [*sic*] when they are near to us. It seems to me as if the farther they are removed, their Pictures grow the more finish'd, and acquire a greater Resemblance': Letter II, 105.

[27] 'Absence', in *The Dictionary of Love*, 12–13.   [28] Barthes, *A Lover's Discourse*, 13–17.

inscribed with mottoes such as 'Tho absent not forgotten', 'Present in Absence', and 'In Absence be True', representing the ordeal of remaining loyal during periods of separation.[29] By gazing upon love tokens in highly ritualized ways during periods of absence, lovers could reflect both on a relationship, and on themselves. As the psychoanalyst Jacques Lacan famously put it, the gaze does not just look, '*it also shows*'.[30] The writer Mary Hays' suitor John Eccles equated this realization with sight in 1779, writing 'I was blind before, but now I see. Absence has taught me that you are invaluable, a jewel of inestimable worth.'[31]

Of course, periods of absence were not always positive and revelatory, and could also generate feelings of anxiety, dejection, distress, unease, pain, and sorrow. As Barthes writes, 'Sometimes the metonymic object is a presence (engendering joy); sometimes it is an absence (engendering distress).'[32] While separated from Judith Cowper in the 1720s, Captain Martin Madan instructed her to 'look on y[r] Finger' at a ring 'that may be a means, of remembring [*sic*] me, & then you'll pitty my absence'.[33] This process of looking closely at an object with the intention of remembering and consciously *missing* a lover indulged anxious feelings in times of separation, in order to build a stronger attachment. Love and suffering were two sides of the same coin. As the wheelwright Jedediah Strutt mused *c*.1748, 'pleasure, and pain' were 'two Consistant attendants on humane natture', and 'which may be the same thing, happiness and Misery, Joy and Sorrow, Love and hatred'.[34] Indulging in the misery of absence worked to intensify a person's attachment, in hope of their eventual happiness.

By the closing decades of the century, couples could even exchange painted eyes as tokens. Lovers' eyes gazed longingly out of eye miniatures, sometimes accompanied by hair, an eyebrow, or tear, surrounded by precious stones such as pearls, diamonds, or rubies. These miniature portraits were most commonly set into brooches or rings, but also appeared on pendants and pins, and inside étuis, trinket boxes, and watch fobs. Painted eyes also played a parallel role in mourning rituals, harnessing different motifs such as snakes to represent eternal life.[35] Eye miniatures enabled lovers to gaze surreptitiously at one another's eyes, joined by the secret of whom they were looking at. From the 1780s, they grew in popularity as fashionable love tokens for both men and women, especially between 1790 and 1810, testifying to the fleeting fashions for new consumer objects. Figure 3.3 is an eye miniature by an anonymous British artist, set into a gold brooch. The eye cries

---

[29] Gold posy ring with inscription 'IN x ABSENCE x BE x TREV x', seventeenth or eighteenth century, 1961,1202.375, Victoria & Albert Museum, London (subsequently V&A); silver gilt posy ring with French inscription 'PRESENT EN ABSENCE', seventeenth or eighteenth century, AF.1365, V&A; enamel patch box painted with the motto 'Tho absent not forgotten', Bilston, *c*.1790, NK5004. G7 B46 1790 Flat, Yale Centre for British Art, Yale University.

[30] Jacques Lacan, *The Four Fundamental Concepts of Psycho-Analysis*, ed. Jacques-Alain Miller, trans. Alan Sheridan (London, 1977), 75. Italics in original.

[31] Eccles to Hays, 2 August 1779, in Wedd, ed., *Love-Letters of Mary Hays*, 30.

[32] Barthes, *A Lover's Discourse*, 173.

[33] Madan to Cowper, undated (*c*.1723), MS Eng. Lett. c. 284, f. 19v, BLO.

[34] Jed. Strutt to Woollat, *c*.1748, D5303/1/1, DRO.

[35] See Graham C. Boettcher, ed., *The Look of Love: Eye Miniatures from the Skier Collection* (London, 2012), esp. Catalogue of the Exhibition, 83–195.

Fig. 3.3. Eye miniature painted in watercolour on ivory, set with pearls and crying diamond tears, England, *c*.1790–1820. © Victoria & Albert Museum, London, P.56-1977.

tears of diamonds, representing the sorrow of separation, with the combination of diamonds and pearls proclaiming the purity of virtuous love.[36] The eye does not look directly at the viewer, but averts its gaze, suggesting that the female sitter was either absorbed in her own emotions, or was too modest to stare brazenly at the recipient. It provides evidence of what Marcia Pointon terms the 'gazing game' surrounding portrait-objects, where individuals were obliged to hold an object in their hand, 'focus intently', and think deeply in order to grasp the item's true meaning.[37] By gazing intently and sending longing looks at miniatures, the eye provided a way for love to enter the body.

Further romantic gifts such as love spoons could also look out at their owners. Love spoons originated in Wales in the later seventeenth century, also extending to the west of England. One spoon dated *c*.1810 features two bright blue glass eyes under clear mica panels. The wide eyes gaze at the owner, and towards the couple's future life together. The eyes may also have functioned like the two inset mirrors, to avert the evil eye.[38] More unusual gifts featured not a lover's eyes, but their lips. As Pointon writes, this 'explicitly controlled splitting of the body into its various elements' facilitates the process of conjuring 'single memories and fragments of the lost object'.[39] One bracelet dated *c*.1820 features moist pink lips painted in watercolour on ivory, hidden inside a gold locket. The space around the lips could readily have been painted with the rest of the sitter's face, but instead shows only the blank ivory, suggesting the lips are emerging from a dream or reverie. The lips bear a faint smile, as if imagining the pleasure and frustration of the individual secretly

[36] On the manifold connotations of diamonds and pearls, see Marcia Pointon, *Brilliant Effects: A Cultural History of Gem Stones & Jewellery* (New Haven, CT and London, 2009), 43–4, 86–9, 107–24.

[37] Marcia Pointon, ' "Surrounded with Brilliants": Miniature Portraits in Eighteenth-Century England', *The Art Bulletin* 83.1 (2001): 48–71, at 63, 68.

[38] Welsh treen love spoon with inset 'eyes', *c*.1810, Sale 5686, Lot 298, 'Christie's Interiors— Masters & Makers', 9 March 2010; Edward H. Pinto, *Treen and Other Wooden Bygones: An Encyclopaedia and Social History* (London: G. Bell & Sons, 1969), 159–63.

[39] Pointon, *Brilliant Effects*, 301.

gazing at the lips, but unable to kiss them, or see the sender in their entirety.[40] To gaze at a loved one's lips meant to imagine their touch, and the delight of physically being together. When worn around a lover's wrist, the bracelet brought together the lips of the sender with the body of the recipient, to ensure that a loved one remained present, even in absence.

TOUCHING

Gifts were sanctified by the touch of a loved one, and either symbolically or literally formed part of the human body. The act of touching objects imbued them with a particular emotional power that could transcend life on earth. Goethe's sentimental hero Werther asked to be buried in his blue frockcoat and buff-yellow waistcoat because his love Charlotte had 'touched them and thereby made them holy'.[41] Concealed in his pocket was a red ribbon that she had worn on her breast the first time they met, which he had begged to have and kissed 'a thousand times'.[42] Now it was to be buried with him to lie with his body eternally, and literally become a part of it. As Barthes notes, 'Every object touched by the loved being's body becomes part of that body, and the subject eagerly attaches himself to it.'[43] The category of 'touching' is used here to refer to objects worn touching the body, such as garters, stay busks, gloves, and rings, objects such as hair that were literally taken from it, and the ritualized act of touching, caressing, and kissing these items.

Garters were practical gifts used to hold up a woman's stockings, but were also physically suggestive of the inside of her leg. Surviving examples are inscribed with a couple's initials and romantic verses comparing the touch of a garter to 'Kissing When Two Lovers Meet'.[44] The bluestocking Elizabeth Montagu witnessed courting couples purchasing garters on her visit to the Northfleet fair in Kent *c*.1740, describing how 'in one booth were nymphs and swains buying garters with amorous poesies; some only with the humble request, "when these you see, remember me" others a poetical and more familiar "be true to me as I'm to thee".'[45] The wearing of garters emblazoned with the message 'remember me' would have encouraged a woman to think of her suitor when undressing, and associate him with the bare skin beneath her petticoats. As the very 'surface' of the body, the skin provides our 'interface with things', against which love objects are held, touched, and tied.[46] Worn at this interface, the erotic overtones of garters made them a

---

[40] Gold bracelet with watercolour on ivory miniature of a lover's lips, c.1820, Rowan and Rowan Antiques, London: https://www.rowanandrowan.com/sub-rosa-lovers-lips/.

[41] Goethe, *Sorrows of Young Werther*, 110.

[42] Ibid., 47.   [43] Barthes, *A Lover's Discourse*, 173.

[44] Knitted cotton garters bound with blue silk satin, inscribed VE C 98, England (probably), 1798, T.196&A–1964, V&A; woven silk garters, inscribed 'AS KISSING WHEN TWO LOVERS MEET', England, 1700–29, T.42–1955, V&A.

[45] Elizabeth Montagu to Margaret Cavendish, Duchess of Portland, *c*.1740, MSS MO 295, Huntington Library, California.

[46] Brian Massumi, 'The Autonomy of Affect', *Cultural Critique* 31 (1995): 83–109, at 85.

particularly intimate gift, used to keep the memory of a relationship alive, subsuming the identity of giver and gift into a single object. Many women would also have used ribbons received as fairings to tie their stockings below the knee, continuing to provide a source of erotic identification with a lover.

Stay busks were a further intimate gift worn touching the female body. They had been a 'favourite gift' since the introduction of bodies to women's dress in the sixteenth century and were particularly popular in less affluent rural areas.[47] While sailors popularly crafted scrimshaw busks from whalebone, most were typically made from wood, particularly fruitwood, boxwood, sycamore, or beech. Busks exchanged as love tokens were personally carved by men, providing a smaller parallel to lovers carving their initials and the dates of their relationship into trees.[48] Sarah Anne Bendall has presented the 'rigid busk' as a 'phallic object' standing in place of the virile male lover, inserted down the front of a woman's stays, pressing against her breasts at the top, and groin at the bottom. A busk inscribed with a man's initials represented an 'act of possession', inscribed 'on the woman herself; claiming her body as his from afar'.[49] Like garters, busks were worn as concealed objects known only to the wearer, adding to their erotic connotations. They were frequently carved with hearts to symbolize the fusing of two souls in one: worn near a woman's heart, and warmed by her body. Some even had secret compartments at the back to store a lock of a man's hair, literally bringing two bodies together.[50]

Decorative gloves given from men to women were suggestive of the ancient ritual of winning a lady's hand. The symbolism of gloves arose from their association with handfast (where betrothal was completed by a handclasp) or the challenge of the gauntlet.[51] Diana O'Hara has found that the glove was the most common textile exchanged during courtship in sixteenth-century Canterbury, which was given thirty-seven times out of a total of 403 transactions.[52] Gloves could be purchased from haberdashers, milliners, fairs, and street-sellers who also sold gifts such as ribbons.[53] During his Grand Tour in 1787, Samuel Whitbread II promised to send his sweetheart Elizabeth Grey 'some Gloves...for which Montpellier is famous, that you may remember the Town'.[54] A lady's hand was symbolic of her affections as a whole, with Samuel desiring Elizabeth to tell the whole world the 'destination of your Hand' nine days before their wedding in 1788.[55] In 1794, the protagonist of the poem *Lines Sent to a Young Lady, With a Pair of Gloves, on*

[47] Gillis, *For Better, For Worse*, 31; Bendall, 'To Write a Distick upon It', 199.

[48] See *Classical scene of lovers carving their initials on a tree trunk*, eighteenth century, France, etching and engraving, 2003.2354.80/P.A., Bowes Museum; S. Lover, *A young woman picks a rose while her companion carves dates in the trunk of the tree*, engraving, V0039001, Wellcome Images.

[49] Bendall, 'To Write a Distick upon It', 205–6, 209–10.

[50] Owen Evan-Thomas, *Domestic Utensils of Wood, 16th to 19th Century* (London, 1932), 130. Chip-carved sycamore staybusk with sliding compartment, 1769, Wales or West Country, Call-me-naïve Antiques: http://www.call-me-naive.com/folk-art/very-rare-chip-carved-documentary-stay-busk-with-sliding-compartment-dated-1769/.

[51] O'Hara, *Courtship and Constraint*, 84.   [52] Ibid., 69.

[53] Therle Hughes, *English Domestic Needlework 1660–1860* (London, 1961), 208.

[54] Whitbread II to Grey, Montpellier, 3 July 1787, W1/6561, BAS.

[55] Ibid., London, 17 January 1788, W1/6608, BAS.

St. Valentine's Day sent his love rival a glove to initiate a duel for the lady Delia, demonstrating its symbolic power:

> Brimful of anger, not of love,
> The champion sends his foe a glove;
> But I that have a double share
> Of the soft passion – send a pair.[56]

The glove was therefore a morally imbued gift, and a symbol of winning over a lady's affections. The romantic symbolism of gloves continued into the early nineteenth century, with printed kid leather gloves produced in Spain becoming fashionable consumer objects for women across Europe and North America, often printed with images of loving couples, Venus, and Cupid.[57]

The most symbolically important gift adorning a lady's hand was the ring, which served as a mark of ownership, and a visible advertisement of her engaged or married status. Wedding rings were only worn by women, and were not popularized for men until the mid-twentieth century.[58] While rings remained a constant part of romantic rituals, their designs changed over time. Restoration-style 'fede' rings comprised of clasped hands faded in popularity in the early eighteenth century, while pearl rings were displaced by diamonds in its second half.[59] Before her marriage to the gentleman Samuel Whitbread II in 1788, Elizabeth Grey wore a ring he had given her as a public declaration of their love. Samuel wrote to her in 1787 to ask, 'pray does the Pearl Ring maintain it's [*sic*] rightful place. I trust it does.'[60] At the highest social level, men such as John Spencer (1734–83), great-grandson and heir of Sarah, Duchess of Marlborough, could afford to lavish their future wives with expensive jewel-encrusted rings. His sweetheart Georgiana Poyntz (1737–1814) described how during an excursion to Wimbledon Park in 1755,

> [H]e gave me a ring for a keep sake it is a very Pretty one...in the Middle is a ruby round that a row of small Brilliants & round that another row of small rubys There is a Motto round the ring & another motto engraved upon the Back part of the setting in small letters which I shew to no lady...The Motto round the Ring is <u>Mon</u> <u>Coeur</u> <u>est</u> <u>tout</u> <u>a</u> <u>Toi</u> the other is <u>Gardez</u> <u>le</u> <u>tien</u> <u>pour</u> <u>moi</u>.

John's family were ambivalent about his choice of bride, and he left England soon after for the Continent, returning to marry when he came of age. His intention to marry Georgiana was confirmed by the exchange of the ring in the presence of her family, with the motto privately reassuring Georgiana that she had his heart. It provided a material point of contact between the couple during their separation,

---

[56] *The political farrago: being a miscellaneous assemblage of epigrams and other jeux d'espirit* (London, 1794), Vol. II, 48.

[57] See, for example, women's kid gloves printed with Cupid riding a dolphin, Spain, *c.*1825–50, 43.1981a–b, Museum of Fine Arts, Boston, MA.

[58] Cressy, *Birth, Marriage and Death*, 343; Vicki Howard, 'A "Real Man's Ring": Gender and the Invention of Tradition', *Journal of Social History* 36.4 (2003): 837–56.

[59] See Pointon, *Brilliant Effects*, 36, 86, 88–9, 107–24.

[60] Whitbread II to Grey, London, 31 December 1787, W1/6601, BAS.

with John making Georgiana 'promise not to open it till I came to London'.[61] Rings have remained the central emblem of the betrothed couple until the present day, showing remarkable continuity in the face of legal and cultural changes. English folk traditions such as placing the wedding ring upon the fourth finger of the left hand have continued unchanged, deriving from the belief that 'a certain vein...runs from thence as far as the heart.'[62]

While gifts such as garters, gloves, stay busks, and rings were worn touching a woman's body, symbolizing the leg, hand, or heart, the exchange of hair allowed individuals literally to give part of the body that would outlast their human lives. Hair was perceived as an eternal gift, which acted as a symbol of immortal love and affection. The enduring power of hair was perpetuated in the poetry of John Donne, where skeletons of a 'loving couple' wear a 'bracelet of bright hair' in their grave.[63] It appeared in eighteenth-century songs such as 'The Token' in 1794, where a sailor named Jack carries a piece of broken gold, braided hair and a snuff-box from his sweetheart.[64] The symbolic properties of hair made it the second item in addition to rings which guaranteed marriage. This view was disseminated in novels; in Maria Edgeworth's *Belinda* (1801), the heroine resolved that Clarence Hervey was evidently 'attached to another' after a lock of hair fell from a letter in his pocket.[65] Similarly, in Jane Austen's *Sense and Sensibility* (1811) Margaret Dashwood was sure that Willoughby and Marianne would 'be married very soon, for he has got a lock of her hair'.[66] Locks of hair were repeatedly sent as tokens enclosed in courtship letters. From May to September 1787, the gentleman Samuel Whitbread II was sent on an enforced Grand Tour by his father, to reconsider his attachment to Elizabeth Grey. The two intensified their romance through the continual exchange of letters and tokens throughout Samuel's trip. When he returned, they exchanged several instalments of hair in their letters to confirm their impending marriage, with Samuel promising to 'not desire any more hair, nor quite thin your flowing locks'.[67] These material fragments—part of a man or woman's 'flowing locks'—possessed a special efficacy as part of the living body of the lover.

Hair was regularly woven into braids and plaits to create delicate hair-work jewellery, with the rector's daughter Elizabeth Reading receiving a ring with her suitor's initials set in hair in 1772, and Samuel Whitbread II commissioning a new pair of buttons with Elizabeth Grey's hair and initials set into the back in 1787.[68] It is likely that most pieces were commissioned from professionals, as manuals of

---

[61] Georgiana Poyntz to Theadora Cowper, 1755, Althorp collection, Add MS 75691, f. 2, BL.

[62] Cressy, *Birth, Marriage and Death*, 342.

[63] John Donne, 'The Relic', in *A complete edition of the poets of Great Britain* (London, 1792), Vol. IV, 37. Hair was also used in Donne's poem 'The Funeral' (*c.*1635), ibid., 36.

[64] *The Hampshire Syren: or, Songster's Miscellany* (Southampton, 1794), 12–13.

[65] Edgeworth, *Belinda*, 139.

[66] Austen, *Sense and Sensibility*, 43–4. Also see passages on lockets containing hair or made from plaited hair given as love tokens in Georgiana Cavendish, *The Sylph*, third edition (London, 1779), Vol. I, Letter IX, 101 and Vol. II, Letter XXVII, 42–3.

[67] Whitbread II to Grey, London, 29 November 1787, W1/6586, No. 3, and 4 January 1788, W1/6603, No. 20, BAS.

[68] Reading to Leathes, 25 October 1772, BOL 2/4/16, NRO; Whitbread II to Grey, 29 November 1787, W1/6586, No. 3, and 4 January 1788, W1/6603, No. 20, BAS.

Fig. 3.4. Enamelled gold ring set with watercolour on ivory silhouette, and panel of woven hair behind glass, England or France, *c.*1780, 2.2 cm (H) × 2.1 cm (W) × 1.9 cm (D). © Victoria & Albert Museum, London, M.174-1962.

instruction did not appear until the 1840s and 1850s.[69] Such tokens allowed individuals to carry a fragment of the absent lover touching their own body, in the form of buttons, rings, lockets, pins, and watch chains. The ring in Figure 3.4 features a watercolour silhouette of a woman on ivory, framed by the emotive declaration 'JE CHERIS JUSQU'A SON OMBRE' ('I cherish even her shadow'). On the reverse is a plaited lock of the woman's hair behind glass, to be worn touching the owner's ring finger. Such silhouettes were introduced in the 1770s as a cheaper alternative to portrait miniatures, making hair-work tokens featuring portraits accessible to less wealthy individuals.[70] The example here was either created as a love token, or *in memoriam*. It depicts a woman in profile, surrounded by the instruction or exhortation to cherish her, even as a 'shadow'. The shadowy silhouette stands in for the absent woman, enabling the owner of the ring to indulge in fond memories in order to reaffirm their attachment.

The immense value of love objects was said to resemble that of holy relics such as the four nails or true cross, as they were revered as treasures by their owners. Samuel Johnson conflated religious and secular relics in his definition of the term in 1755, as 'That which is kept in memory of another, with a kind of religious veneration.'[71] In 1791, a commentary of rituals surrounding holy reliquaries in Mecca was published, including a silver case containing a black stone reported to

[69] Manuals include W. Martin, *The Hair Worker's Manual* (London, *c.*1840s) and W. Halford and C. Young, *A Jewellers' Book of Patterns in Hair Work* (London, *c.*1850).
[70] Clare Phillips, *Jewels & Jewellery* (London, 2008), 67.
[71] 'Relick', in Johnson, *Dictionary*, Vol. II, 537.

have fallen to earth with Adam. The reliquary was 'exceedingly respected, and piously kissed by all devout pilgrims', just as letters and tokens were kissed as a 'sacred Chalice' by lovers.[72] While relics provided a bridge between heaven and earth, love tokens acted as a means of contact between absent loved ones. The Romantic poet Lord Byron recognized these parallels in his poem 'The Pledge of Love' in 1806:

> This band, which bound thy yellow hair,
> Is mine, sweet girl! thy pledge of love;
> It claims my warmest, dearest care,
> Like relics left of saints above.[73]

As Byron's paean on a velvet hair tie suggests, almost any object could be transformed into a romantic relic if adopted by a lover into their collection. In Jane Austen's *Emma* (1816), Harriet Smith curates a sad collection of discarded fragments touched by Mr Elton, which she stores in a decorated wooden box wrapped in silver paper and labelled 'Most precious treasures'. Harriet's relics included a 'small piece of court plaister' cut from a segment used to dress a cut to Mr Elton's finger, and 'the end of an old pencil...without any lead'. The value of the plaster lay in the fact it was touched by Mr Elton, who passed it to Harriet by hand. She 'could not help making a treasure of it' and so 'put it by never to be used, and looked at it now and then as a great treat'.[74]

Courting couples repeatedly described reading and writing letters while touching gifts such as portraits and locks of hair. This ritualized process served to create feelings of love during prolonged periods of separation. As Sara Ahmed has argued, once objects have been 'judged to bring happiness', they come in use as 'happiness-means, as what we might do, or what we might have, to reach happiness'.[75] Each of the objects described in this chapter represents something we might have, or might use, to achieve the feeling of being in love. While a portrait provided a material embodiment of the absent, a lock of hair literally formed part of a lover's body. In the 1780s, Captain Richard Dixon signed off his love letters by kissing a portrait of his sweetheart 'with rapture'. He wished 'God bless you' and drank to her health, as if the portrait was Maria herself.[76] The Justice of the Peace Anthony Hamond described the process of reading letters from Mary Ann Musters *c.*1828: 'If I am cold and wet I do not open them [until I] am comfortably settled in the great chair I am writing in & then I devour them, I am sure I shall wear out that dear Lock of hair If I stay much longer from you.' He also described how

---

[72] 'Alâi Ibn Abi Bakr, Burhan al-Dâin, al-Marghâinanâi, *The hedàya, or guide; a commentary on the Mussulman laws*, trans. Charles Hamilton (London, 1791), Vol. I, lviii; Keats to Brawne, undated (*c.*1 March 1820), Letter XXII, in Forman, ed., *Letters of John Keats*, 65.

[73] Byron, 'The Pledge of Love', in *The Poetical Love-Token. By the editor of the 'Forget-Me-Not'* (London, 1850), 2.

[74] Jane Austen, *Emma* (Oxford, [1816] 2003), 265–6. A court plaister was a dressing made from silk or cotton, isinglass, and glycerine, which was cut to size and moistened in order to stick.

[75] Ahmed, *Cultural Politics of Emotion*, 219.

[76] Richard Dixon to Maria Cranmer, Buxton, 7 May 1782, 8215/7, and undated (1780s), 8215/8, SHC.

Fig. 3.5. Isaac Cruikshank, *The Illustrious Lover or the D. of Cumberland done over*, London, 1804, etching with watercolour, Wellcome Collection, London, 12198i, CC BY 4.0.

'I will read a chapter [of the Bible] say a prayer for my dear Mary Ann kiss her dear lock of hair and wish [*sic*] good night…and will also give her a little advice not to fidget herself & to take a quiet ride every day.'[77] These extracts suggest that writers touched and kissed tokens to create the sensation that they were together, allowing the tactile distance between them to be bridged.

The assortment of tokens amassed by lovers was continually touched, kissed, and smelled to deepen a romantic connection, creating new forms of behaviour among individuals who surrounded themselves with romantic gifts. By enveloping ourselves with highly valued objects, we create a 'near sphere' or 'horizon of likes' comprising carefully chosen things that we wish 'to have, touch, taste, hear, feel, see' around us, which then 'take up residence within our bodily horizon'.[78] The particular materiality of love tokens engenders these rituals, as small portable and (often) durable objects that can readily be manipulated, worn, held, and moved by humans, in order to move ourselves. The ritualized process of handling love tokens is satirized in Isaac Cruikshank's etching *The Illustrious Lover* (Figure 3.5). It ridicules the Duke of Cumberland, who isolates himself with a chest full of 'Keepsakes' to celebrate his love for Mrs Powell. His distracted monologue describes how

[77] Anthony Hamond to Mary Ann Musters, HMN 5/95/1 and 5/95/4, undated (*c.*1828), NRO.
[78] Ahmed, 'Happy Objects', 32.

I talk in my sleep, in short I act the part of a Fool – O the dear Plant. the dear the ever dear Pink cotton – my Charmer, my dearest dear, my adored my Celestial, I have Invoked Cupid, Mercury, Mars, Saturn, Venus, & all the Deites to Santion [*sic*] our heaven born love.

The etching hints at the important role of sweet scents in hastening the development of love, with barley sugar, sugar plums, comfits, and candy sitting atop the love letters on the table. Similarly, the Duke declares that 'I shall adore the Paper, the Ink, the very grease of your hand, which like a Dog I can by Instinct smell.' He holds a red ribbon belonging to Mrs Powell to his mouth—like Goethe's Werther— using its scent to fuel his fantasies. The primacy of the ribbon also underlines the Duke's effeminacy, as ribbons would usually have been given as fairings from men to women. The most outwardly masculine feature of this ritual is his arousal, as the phallic watering can in his lap spouts water all over the plant on the table, fuelling his desire. He pants, 'O that lovely loose dress—allways [*sic*] be loose…I shall never forget what I then saw.' It reinforces the haptic power of assembled objects in stirring loving thoughts, acting as material sites of romantic emotion.

SMELLING

What was the sweet scent of love? In Jane Austen's *Persuasion* (1818), Anne Elliot's burgeoning love for Captain Wentworth is 'almost enough to spread purification and perfume all the way'.[79] As historians of the senses have argued, smells are able to 'affect us on a physical, psychological and social level' and 'evoke strong emotional responses'.[80] Smells have a powerful role in summoning emotionally charged memories of people, places, and moments in our past. The philosopher Michel Serres argues that once a particular blend of scents is manifest, 'a whole world rushes in', leaving us 'dazzled, ecstatically, by our proximity to this overabundant memory'. Love in particular 'perfumes our lives, aromas resurrecting encounters in all their splendour'.[81] The scent of love tokens was not mentioned by couples in writing as frequently as the rituals of gazing upon and touching gifts. Nonetheless, when combined with the types of objects selected for exchange and discourses on the fragrant perfume of love in wider culture, these reflections can provide us with unique insights into the role of smelling in engendering a romantic bond.

Love was particularly evoked by fragrant smells, which were associated with virtuous femininity. As Elizabeth Foyster notes in relation to early modern Scotland, 'Desirable women smelt sweet', as in Robert Burns' appraisal of love as 'a red, red, rose'. In contrast, lustful women such as adulteresses, fornicators, and

---

[79] Austen, *Persuasion*, 155.
[80] Constance Classen, David Howes, and Anthony Synnott, *Aroma: The Cultural History of Smell* (London, 1994), 1.
[81] Michel Serres, *The Five Senses: A Philosophy of Mingled Bodies*, trans. Margaret Sankey and Peter Cowley (London, [1985] 2016), 171–2.

prostitutes carried 'the foul smell of venereal disease'.[82] The most virtuous woman of all—Samuel Richardson's heroine Pamela—saw her virtue rewarded when she married her master Mr B at the novel's climax. Her new husband rhapsodized that 'all Nature, methinks, blooms around me, when I have my *Pamela* by my Side.' He went on to sing Pamela a song praising how 'all the Beauties of the Year / Diffuse their Odors at your Feet, / Who give to ev'ry Flow'r its Sweet.'[83] Part of Pamela's desirability was the purity and uncorrupted nature of her sweet smell, akin to a bed of flowers after the rain.

Love tokens were often particularly odiferous objects such as flowers, perfume, scented gloves, baskets of fruit, nutmeg graters, and *bonbonnières* for storing confectionary. Under the seven-part system set out by Carl Linnaeus and his student Andreas Wåhlin in *Odores Medicamentorum* (1752), these scents would broadly have been classified as aromatic (like bay leaves), fragrant (like saffron, jasmine, and polianthus flowers), or ambrosial (like musk and civet).[84] Pleasantly scented love tokens could be particularly effective gifts by associating loved ones with particular smells. In Edgeworth's *Belinda* (1801), Clarence Hervey is associated with the otto of roses that suffuses his perfumed letters.[85] In 1811, the soldier Robert Garrett sent Charlotte Bentinck two bottles of jasmine as a gift, an exotic plant originating in India and Southeast Asia that was known for its sweet floral fragrance.[86] Jasmine was cultivated in the East and West Indies, and had been a popular component of English perfumes since the seventeenth century. Charlotte may have used the jasmine as perfume, or to scent potpourri to disseminate the scent throughout her home.[87] Fashionable potpourri vases were produced by manufacturers such as Wedgwood, painted with exotic motifs such as Chinese flowers.[88] Charlotte would subsequently have associated the floral scent of jasmine with her lover, with the immediacy of the fragrance transporting something of Robert from Lisbon to be with her in Ramsgate.

Perfume bottles could be crafted from expensive materials such as gold or porcelain, with more affordable versions made from opaque glass or enamels. Such bottles were frequently painted with amorous mottoes in French, the language of

---

[82] Elizabeth Foyster, 'Sensory Experiences: Smells, Sounds and Touch', in *A History of Everyday Life in Scotland, 1600 to 1800*, ed. Elizabeth Foyster and Christopher Whatley (Edinburgh, 2010), 217–33, at 227.

[83] Richardson, *Pamela*, 494–5.

[84] Richard Pulteney, *A General View of the Writings of Linnaeus* (London, 1781), 254–5. *Odores Medicamentorum* is frequently attributed solely to Linnaeus, but was actually a dissertation by his student Andreas Wåhlin. These dissertations were 'joint products' between Linnaeus and his students, which according to custom defended the ideas of the former. See the Original Linnaean Dissertations Database at the Hunt Institute for Botanical Documentation: http://huntbot.org/linndiss/linndiss/intro.

[85] Edgeworth, *Belinda*, 281–2.

[86] Garrett to Bentinck, Lisbon, 26 April 1811, R/U888/C11/7, KHLC; Ghillean Prance and Mark Nesbitt, eds, *The Cultural History of Plants* (New York and London, 2012), 246.

[87] Holly Duggan, *The Ephemeral History of Perfume: Scent and Sense in Early Modern England* (Baltimore, MD, 2011), 155, 164–7.

[88] See caneware potpourri vase and cover, Wedgwood, Etruria, *c.*1790, 34 cm (H) × 23 cm (W), C.75&A–1986, V&A; bone china potpourri vase, Ridgway & Sons, Hanley, 1808–13, 16.5 cm (H) × 15.2 cm (W), 2520–1901, V&A; black basalt stoneware potpourri vase painted with Chinese flowers, Wedgwood, Staffordshire, *c.*1810–20, 20.7 cm (H) × 22.8 cm (W), CIRC.312–1963, V&A.

Fig. 3.6. Enamel on copper scent bottle with base inscribed 'PENSEZ A MOY' [*sic*], Bilston, 1765–70, 9.4 cm (H). © *Wolverhampton Art Gallery*, BI448, http://blackcountry-history.org/.

love and romance. Surviving examples depict two cherubs holding a fountain upon their backs, inscribed 'FONTAINE DAMOUR' ('Fountain of Love'), and two lovebirds wrapped in a loveknot reading 'PRENES [*sic*] LES POUR MODELES' ('Take them as examples').[89] The scent bottle in Figure 3.6 was produced in Bilston in the West Midlands, which had a thriving trade in diminutive enamel tokens between *c.*1760 and 1790. Such objects had fallen out of fashion by 1830.[90] Like most early examples, this bottle was hand-painted. It has a *repoussé* design of two lovers following one another through a floral landscape around the stem. The base is painted with a sprig of gold flowers and the text 'Think on Me' in French. Like these two intertwined lovers, individuals were encouraged to use the transporting properties of scent to reflect on a relationship. Individuals filled their personalized bottles at perfumeries with scents that had been 'mixed especially', in order to scent letters, handkerchiefs, and gloves as fragrant emissaries of their love.[91]

[89] Fountain of love scent bottle, Chelsea Porcelain Manufactory, pre-1754, soft-paste porcelain, 1971.75.22a, b; Love birds scent bottle, Staffordshire, enamel on copper, 1760–5, 64.101.809a, b, Metropolitan Museum of Art, New York (subsequently MET). The fountain of love was a popular romantic motif and also appears in paintings by Jean-Honoré Fragonard.

[90] Tom Cope, *Bilston Enamels of the Eighteenth Century*, Black Country Society: http://www.historywebsite.co.uk/Museum/metalware/bilston.htm.

[91] Jonathan Reinarz, *Past Scents: Historical Perspectives on Smell* (Urbana, IL, 2014), 71.

Flowers historically provided a symbol of love. Flora was the Roman goddess of flowers and was particularly associated with spring, the season for romance. In her perpetually blooming garden, she scattered seeds in order to 'bring colour to the monochrome earth'.[92] One mariner in the early eighteenth century styled himself 'Oroondates' after the Prince of Scythia in the French romance *Cassandra* (1642–50), while his sweetheart Mrs Ann Webb of Rye was the beautiful Princess Statira. Oroondates conceived of flowers as a sweet-scented embodiment of his love, writing that he had hoped to 'have presented Statira with a nosegay' that morning, but in their place offered her a poem about beautifully perfumed flowers. He declared, 'Go Virgin flowers your Early sweetness pay / Salute y lovely nymph that's Queen of May.' Oroondates compared his sweetheart to Flora, praising how her 'fragrant breath will fill you wth perfume'.[93] Popular songs similarly described young men promising their sweethearts flowers; in 'O Dear What can the Matter be', Johnny brought his lover 'a delicate basket of posies', a 'garland of lillies' [*sic*], and a 'garland of roses' from the fair as a pledge of his esteem.[94]

Nosegays were small fragrant bunches of flowers typically worn on the front of a woman's bodice, exchanged both as gifts of love and friendship. In 1769, the writer Elizabeth Carter wrote to her friend Elizabeth Montagu thanking her for a nosegay presented as a parting gift. She 'contented myself with kissing the roses and myrtles because they had belonged to you, and by this pleasure solaced myself, to the great surprize of John, who, I dare say, often wondered what charm the flowers possessed'.[95] The sweet-smelling flowers embodied her absent friend, with the ritual of kissing the nosegay providing a source of pleasure and a tribute to their friendship. Nosegays also provided affordable romantic gifts, whether picked by hand or purchased from street-sellers. In Laurence Sterne's *A Sentimental Journey* (1768), the servant La Fleur presents a bouquet to his lover, but is devastated to discover that she has subsequently re-gifted it to another man.[96] In 1781, the young watchmaker's apprentice Boys Errburrill waited outside the home of the peruke-maker's daughter Ann Collet in order to present her with a nosegay. After Ann put the nosegay in water, the two went for a walk, and sat up by the fire until late.[97] The print *Love in a Village* depicts a young suitor offering a woman a sprig of red roses as a romantic gift (Figure 3.7). The scene is taken from the ballad opera of the same name, where a young man and woman of fortune each run away and

---

[92] John Ayto, ed., *Brewer's Dictionary of Phrase and Fable*, seventeenth edition (London, 2007), 527; Jack Tresidder, ed., *The Complete Dictionary of Symbols in Myth, Art and Literature* (London, 2004), 187–8.

[93] Oroondates to Statira, undated (early eighteenth century), FRE 5416, ESRO.

[94] 'O Dear what can the matter be', in *The Golden Glove's Garland, Containing a Choice Collection of New Songs* (Newcastle, *c.*1785), 6.

[95] Elizabeth Carter to Elizabeth Montagu, 1 October 1769, in *Letters from Mrs Elizabeth Carter to Mrs Montagu* (1817), Vol. 2, British and Irish Women's Letters and Diaries (subsequently BIWLD): https://alexanderstreet.com/products/british-and-irish-womens-letters-and-diaries.

[96] Laurence Sterne, *A Sentimental Journey through France and Italy* (Dublin, 1768), 93–4.

[97] Ann was subsequently a witness for the defence at Boys' trial for a highway robbery committed the same evening. He was found guilty and sentenced to death, but was later pardoned. See Trial of Boys Errburrill and William Ives for highway robbery, 30 May 1781, t17810530-25, Old Bailey Online (subsequently OBO).

LOVE IN A VILLAGE.

Fig. 3.7. *Love in a Village*, London, 1784, 35 cm (H) × 25 cm (W), hand-coloured mezzo-tint, British Museum, London, 2010, 7081.1265. © The Trustees of the British Museum, All Rights Reserved.

disguise themselves as a gardener and chambermaid respectively, in order to avoid a marriage arranged by their parents. The two then fall in love in their new country guises. The fragrant roses symbolize both the allure and dangers of romantic love; they cut the suitor's fingers as he picks them from the rose bush, exclaiming 'Psha; rot these roses, how they prick one's fingers.'[98]

The symbolic and cultural meanings of particular blooms enhanced their emotional value for courting couples, determining the ability of the flowers to convey particular sentiments. Roses were thought to have miraculously blossomed from the prayers of a 'fayre Mayden' in Bethlehem, and were associated with the peerless Virgin Mary. Violets were also important Christian symbols, emblematic of modesty, humility, faithful love, and truth, making them an appropriate gift selected by courting women.[99] In 1812, Charlotte Bentinck sent a pressed blue violet to her suitor Robert Garrett while he was camped between Rueda and Tordesillas in Spain. Violets were a native English flower, literally providing a piece of England for Robert to keep while he was abroad. He praised it as a 'very applicable' gift which 'accords with the sincerest sentiments of <u>my</u> heart & I flatter myself it does also with the dear object of my affections'.[100] In carrying part of Charlotte's identity, and emblematizing her fidelity and true love, the flower deepened the couple's intimacy while they were apart. Pressed flowers sent in letters could also be kissed upon sending and receipt, as a means of transporting a kiss between lovers by post.[101] Beverly Seaton has argued that the fragrance of flowers was central to their symbolism, with violets carrying a sweet floral scent that was indicative of virtue.[102]

The arresting scent of love letters was equally important in creating and intensifying an emotional bond, as epistles could transport the distinctive aroma of writers and their surroundings. As Serres asserts, 'as far as the nose is concerned, the emanations of whomever we have loved remain.'[103] In 1813, Robert Garrett wrote from Spain that Charlotte Bentinck's 'dear letters smell so nice and sweet that I fancy myself at Ramsgate again when I put them to my poor nose'.[104] Robert's account demonstrates the transporting properties of scent, as the 'sweet' smell of her letters made him feel instantly at home. The ability of love letters to take on a person's smell was dramatized in Elizabeth Gaskell's *Cranford* (1853), where a bundle of letters from the 1770s create 'a faint, pleasant smell of Tonquin beans in the room. I had always noticed this scent about any of the things which had belonged to her mother; and many of the letters were addressed to her—yellow

---

[98] *Love in a Village; A Comic Opera. As it is Performed at the Theatre Royal in Covent-Garden*, ninth edition (London, 1764), Act I, Scene III, 8.

[99] Ayto, ed., *Brewer's Dictionary of Phrase and Fable*, 1190; Beverly Seaton, *The Language of Flowers: A History* (Charlottesville, VA, 1995), 44.

[100] Garrett to Bentinck, Camp between Rueda and For de Sillas, 9 July 1812, R/U888/C11/32, KHLC.

[101] Ina Lindblom, 'The Botany of Friendship and Love', *Scandinavian Journal of History* 41.3 (2016): 410–26, at 415–16.

[102] Seaton, *Language of Flowers*, 44, 55.   [103] Serres, *The Five Senses*, 172.

[104] Garrett to Bentinck, Camp near Villa de Don Diego, 3 June 1813, R/U888/C11/51, KHLC.

bundles of love-letters, sixty or seventy years old.'[105] Gifts such as letters were invested with additional emotional value as they carried these scented 'emanations' of their writers—whether the sweet smell of Ramsgate or vanilla-scented tonka beans—which acted to resurrect powerful memories of beloved people and places.

CONCLUSION

This chapter has revealed how sensory interaction with gifts provided a way to produce feelings of love and intensify an emotional bond. Meditating upon tokens stimulated loving thoughts of the absent and encouraged the development of intimacy. As the Bedfordshire gentleman Samuel Whitbread II wrote to Elizabeth Grey in 1787, 'the more I think upon the more amiable I find you, & the more I love you.'[106] Samuel sent boxes full of trinkets to his sweetheart, including earrings from Paris and gloves from Montpellier, recognizing, 'I cannot find Words that keep pace with my feelings.'[107] Objects provided a means of doing so, and were continually touched, kissed, smelled, gazed upon, conversed with, carried around, and used as vehicles to strengthen a couple's attachment.

Items such as gloves, rings, and stay busks did not necessarily possess any essential qualities as love tokens, other than their symbolic association with matrimony. Certain objects such as earrings, buttons, and bottles of jasmine lacked these same social and cultural meanings. As Jane Austen joked in *Emma*, even a plaster or the end of an old pencil could be tokens of love. Rather, these objects were designated conduits for creating and affirming feelings of love by the ways in which they were collected, preserved, and used by couples, in a similar way to religious relics. Relics were also small objects designed to be carried around, touched, and kissed, and were also frequently parts of the body such as tooth and bone. Alexandra Walsham has argued that relics are created 'as a consequence of the beliefs and practices that accumulate around them. They are the products and confections of the cultures that engender and reverence them. The making of them is both a social and a cognitive process.'[108] To this I would add a sensory process, as love tokens are distinguished as precious relics by the particular ways in which they are *used* by couples.

The exchange of gifts introduced new ways of behaving for courting couples, as their behaviour was mediated through the persona of the lover. It was this private practice of obsessing over love tokens which undeniably marked a person as being 'in love', as cruelly satirized in Cruikshank's *Illustrious Lover*. The most devout worshipper at the Temple of Hymen was Goethe's Werther, who knelt before a bunch of flowers given by his love Charlotte overnight as 'holy and visible signs' of

---

[105] Elizabeth Gaskell, *Cranford* (New York, 1853), 90. Tonquin beans are now known as tonka beans, the seeds of the *dipteryx odorata* tree.

[106] Whitbread II to Grey, Francfort, 31 August 1787, No. 28, W1/6574, BAS.

[107] Ibid., 23 June 1787, No. 12, W1/6557, BAS.

[108] Alexandra Walsham, 'Introduction: Relics and Remains', in 'Relics and Remains', ed. Alexandra Walsham, *Past & Present Supplement* 5 (2010), 9–36, at 14.

divine grace.[109] In *c.*1828, the Justice of the Peace Anthony Hamond was delighted to have 'got rid of' his sister for the journey from London to see his sweetheart Mary Ann Musters at Colwick Hall in Nottingham, as he liked 'to be alone in my carriage as I can then indulge in the most agreable [*sic*] reveries', having 'bought the essential ring' for their wedding.[110]

While a range of objects could be called upon to produce romantic emotions, the items selected by couples changed over the course of the century, augmenting traditional gifts such as garters and locks of hair with an assortment of consumer objects such as books, sheet music, watch papers, and valentine cards. The next chapter of this book turns from the ritualized use of objects to the items themselves, to ask, what was new?

---

[109] Goethe, *Sorrows of Young Werther*, 105.
[110] Hamond to Musters, Grosvenor Place, London, *c.*1828, 5/95/5, NRO.

4

The Marketplace of Love

Francesco Bartolozzi's engraving of a *Market of Love* from 1793 depicts a group of young women in classical dress selecting Cupids from a makeshift pen (Figure 4.1). One of the Cupids crouches within the pen, clutching an arrow to wound the women's hearts, making them vulnerable to love. In the background, a woman carries her new winged companion home on her shoulder. The group are quite literally shopping for love, typifying the celebration of romantic ideals in visual culture. This chapter explores how romantic customs evolved over the Georgian era, to form a new marketplace of love. The celebration of romantic love coincided with a boom in luxury goods and the rise of shopping as a leisure activity. In this climate, love could be packaged and sold to consumers through a range of new objects. Products such as enamel toys, epistolary gifts, souvenirs, and printed valentine cards heralded the increasing commercialization of the economy of love. The celebrated engraver Bartolozzi had a role to play in this transition, designing, drawing, and engraving two valentines *c.*1800, depicting an 'Endless Knot of Love' and 'Sailor's Farewell'. The scenes were printed in black and white on single sheets of paper, and could be purchased by couples from printers, booksellers, and stationers for a few pence each, and sent as a valentine.[1]

The eighteenth century saw an expanding range of goods, and a growing number and variety of shops where consumers could buy them. Broad streets 'lined with shop windows' and new walking routes for window-shopping were created to facilitate polite consumption in towns.[2] Over the course of the century, shops increased in size, and came to dominate exclusive shopping areas such as the Royal Exchange and St James's in London. Shops provided fashionable spaces to engage in polite sociability while browsing the latest luxury goods displayed in shop windows, ensconced in glass cases, nestled in decorative boxes, and presented on shelves lined with velvet. In the grandest establishments, candlesticks, sconces, high ceilings, neoclassical pillars, and glazed windows combined to create an atmosphere of light and space.[3] Helen Berry has described shops 'aimed at the

---

[1] Francesco Bartolozzi, 'The Endless Knot of Love', *c.*1800, Valentines (uncatalogued), Box 2, JJC, BLO; Bartolozzi, 'Sailor's Farewell', *c.*1800, OB1996.9, The Postal Museum, London (subsequently TPM); The trial of William Stephens for theft on 15 February 1827 valued twelve valentines at 3 shillings, or 3 pence each, t18270215-30, OBO.

[2] Peter McNeil and Giorgio Riello, 'Luxury and Fashion in the Long Eighteenth Century', in *Treasured Possessions from the Renaissance to the Enlightenment*, ed. Victoria Avery, Melissa Calaresu, and Mary Laven (Cambridge, 2015), 153–61, at 157.

[3] Serena Dyer, 'Shopping, Spectacle & the Senses', *History Today* 65.3 (2015): 30–6; Jon Stobart, 'Shopping Streets as Social Space: Leisure, Consumerism and Improvement in an Eighteenth-Century

Fig. 4.1. Francesco Bartolozzi, *Market of Love*, Britain, 1793, line engraving, Yale Centre for British Art, Paul Mellon Collection, B1978.43.565.

middling and upper sorts' as 'crucial features of the urban landscape', as 'venues for the interaction of social relationships, leisure and commerce'.[4] The growth of towns drove the increasing specialization of both shops and consumer goods, providing a space for individuals to discover the latest objects à la mode and craft their identity, reputation, and social status.[5]

Neil McKendrick famously called the upsurge in consumer demand a 'consumer revolution', characterized by 'such a convulsion of getting and spending, such an eruption of new prosperity, and such an explosion of new production and marketing techniques, that a greater proportion of the population than in any previous society in human history was able to enjoy the pleasures of buying consumer goods'. This so-called 'orgy of spending' was said to be driven by the rich,

---

County Town', *Urban History* 25.1 (1998): 3–21, at 17–19; Claire Walsh, 'Shop Design and the Display of Goods in Eighteenth-Century London', *Journal of Design History* 8.3 (1995): 157–76, at 160–7.

[4] Helen Berry, 'Polite Consumption: Shopping in Eighteenth-Century England', *Transactions of the Royal Historical Society* 12 (2002): 375–94, at 377.

[5] Frank Trentmann, *Empire of Things: How We Became a World of Consumers, from the Fifteenth Century to the Twenty-First* (London, 2016), 93–4.

then emulated by the middling ranks.[6] However, historians have since disputed the timing and intensity of the 'eruption' or 'explosion' described by McKendrick, questioning whether or not it was sufficient to constitute a 'revolution', and challenging the notion that consumers were motivated by the desire to emulate their social superiors.[7] What we can say with greater certainty is that—continuing the trend from the seventeenth century—the middling sorts enjoyed greater wealth, bigger living spaces, and more of a number and variety of consumer goods.[8] The labouring poor also enjoyed greater access to consumer durables (such as watches) and semi-durables (such as clothing and furniture). John Styles has shown how plebeian men and women of courting age 'enjoyed disposable incomes sufficient to acquire petty luxuries', particularly fashionable clothing, which could be deployed as 'a sign of sexual maturity, an emblem of material self advancement, a means of sexual attraction' and 'a currency in sexual competition'.[9]

Consumer objects were eagerly taken up by courting couples and exchanged as romantic gifts. How did couples invest these objects with emotional meaning? As the social anthropologist Arjun Appadurai notes, commodities in the marketplace are by nature standardized, identical, and available for anyone to purchase for a set price. The issue in commoditized societies is 'how to create human relations in a world where all things are potentially in the market or on the market'. To some extent, consumer objects acquire value simply by being sent as a gift: ' "standard" objects quickly become *my* gift, the thing you gave me, and so on.'[10] And yet handmade objects are widely taken to possess a particular emotional power, representing 'time, labour and affection made concrete'.[11] While handmade items are literally shaped by the touch of their creator, the standard features of industrially produced objects are pre-determined by their design.[12] As the pace of industrialization accelerated over the eighteenth century, many consumer objects given as gifts were still made in part or in whole by hand—the hands of furriers, jewellers, printers, potters—but not the hands of the sender. Joanne Begiato has called on historians of emotions to consider how people 'create relationships with objects of all kinds', not only handmade or artisanal products. If 'the unique end product of hand-crafting carries more emotional freight', then scholars studying

[6] Neil McKendrick, 'The Consumer Revolution of Eighteenth-Century England', in Neil McKendrick, John Brewer, and J. H. Plumb, *The Birth of a Consumer Society: The Commercialization of Eighteenth-Century England* (London, 1983), 9–33, at 9–11.

[7] For a particularly influential critique, see John Styles, 'Manufacturing, Consumption and Design in Eighteenth-Century England', in *Consumption and the World of Goods*, ed. John Brewer and Roy Porter (London and New York, 1994), 527–54, and for an overview of changing debates, see Maxine Berg, *Luxury and Pleasure in Eighteenth-Century Britain* (Oxford, 2005), 9–13.

[8] Styles, 'Manufacturing, Consumption and Design', 537.

[9] Styles, 'Custom or Consumption? Plebeian Fashion in Eighteenth-Century England', in *Luxury in the Eighteenth Century: Debates, Desires and Delectable Goods*, ed. Maxine Berg and Elizabeth Eger (Basingstoke, 2003), 103–15, at 111, 113.

[10] Arjun Appadurai, 'The Thing Itself', *Public Culture* 18.1 (2006): 15–21, at 19–20. Italics in original.

[11] Vickery, *The Gentleman's Daughter*, 188.

[12] Gillo Dorfles, 'The Man-Made Object', in *The Man-Made Object*, ed. Gyorgy Kepes (New York, 1966), 1–8, at 1.

machine-made goods must explore the different ways in which these objects acquired affective value.[13] This chapter responds to this call by exploring the affective meanings of the new world of goods.

The chapter draws upon extant objects in archives, auction houses, and museums, alongside ballads, courtship letters, diaries, newspaper reports, novels, poems, plays, and trade cards. It is divided into two parts. The first examines new types of popular gifts exchanged by courting couples in Georgian England, such as fashionable printed cottons, muslins and furs, sheet music, books, toys, and epistolary goods. The second traces the evolution of Valentine's Day over the long eighteenth century, from hand-drawn puzzles to printed and embossed lace paper cards. The chapter asks, how did courtship evolve alongside the new world of goods? What did these objects offer courting couples? How were consumer objects invested with emotional value? Overall, it charts the increasing mechanization, commercialization, and modernization of the economy of courtship over the long eighteenth century, and the new ways in which consumer goods could be harnessed as objects of emotion.

CONSUMING LOVE

Men and women engaging in courtship in Georgian England had a wealth of consumer goods at their fingertips. The new types of goods selected by couples could be novelties (such as toys, watch papers, and souvenir handkerchiefs), configure status (such as pianos, sheet music, exotic textiles, and furs) or have more serious educational value (such as history books). These objects provided couples with an increasing range of individualized ways in which to express their love, show their investment in a relationship, and demonstrate their character as a prospective spouse. Maxine Berg has set out how luxury goods 'deployed quality, art, and style together with invention, mechanism, imitation, and novelty', in order to provide consumers with 'delight, comfort and convenience, utility, the agreeable'.[14] A gentleman might reasonably send a woman he was courting a basket of fruit, joints of meat, flowers, sheet music, books, a seal matrix, a perfume bottle, a ring, earrings, a necklace, and a portrait miniature. This was considered money well spent as a tangible investment in a relationship, and the fusing of two souls into one; as the barrister Charles Pratt wrote to the heiress Elizabeth Jeffreys in 1749, 'how can my money be so well employed, as when it is bestowed upon my second self.'[15]

Many of the gifts selected by courting men were representative of the global trade in luxuries with Asia and the Americas. Fine muslins were the most expensive cotton textiles, and had been imported by East India Companies since the seventeenth century, particularly from the province of Dhaka in Bengal.[16] In 1761, Captain Henry Smith gave his sweetheart Sarah Hurst two pieces of delicate Indian muslin as a gift—one to fashion into a petticoat and negligée, and another to accessorize her outfits with fashionable muslin aprons and ruffles.[17] These translucent muslins imported from Asia were highly valued as objects of 'wonder' and 'sensuality'. From at least the 1770s, British manufacturers sought to produce high-quality muslins and calicoes to rival these exotic imports.[18] Joseph Strutt and his family owned several cotton and calico-spinning mills throughout Derbyshire, enabling Joseph to shower his sweetheart Isabella Douglas with textile gifts. In 1792, he sent her 'twenty one yards of fine & beautiful Callicoe' to make three gowns—two for Isabella and one for her sisters. He hoped they would 'all like them & long wear them with health & pleasure'.[19] Joseph was able to supplement his calico with a range of associated objects, including a knitting machine, several bundles of cotton, and 'the best tassels & Rings I could possibly procure in Silver'.[20] Both Henry's and Joseph's gifts were luxury goods representing a significant financial outlay. As a cotton-trader, Joseph managed to go one step further with the range of textiles he could procure. Both men sent these fabrics as romantic gifts in the final year of their courtship, when the expenditure represented an investment in the women who would soon become their wives.

Luxury goods such as furs could provide gentlemen with a way to underscore their status to their prospective wives, foregrounding the situation in which they could expect to live once married. The English had sourced pelts from North America since the mid-seventeenth century—including beaver, fox, lynx, marten, mink, muskrat, and otter—enjoying a monopoly over Hudson Bay after the signing of the Treaty of Utrecht in 1713.[21] Items 'in the Fur Line' were then made to order by furriers back in England for high prices.[22] Married men purchased fur accessories such as tippets for their wives, and courting men accordingly followed suit.[23] In 1760, Captain Henry Smith purchased some marten skins for Sarah Hurst, which she had made into a fashionable muff and tippet worth six guineas (more than £850 in today's money).[24] The Bedfordshire gentleman Samuel Whitbread II similarly ordered some sables for Elizabeth Grey upon returning from his Grand Tour

---

[16] Maxine Berg, '"The Merest Shadows of a Commodity": Indian Muslins for European Markets 1750–1800', in *Goods from the East, 1600–1800: Trading Eurasia*, ed. Maxine Berg, with Felicia Gottmann, Hanna Hodacs, and Chris Nierstrasz (Basingstoke, 2015), 119–34.

[17] Diary of Hurst, 10 May 1761, MS3544, HM.

[18] Berg, '"The Merest Shadows of a Commodity"', 120, 129–30.

[19] Jos. Strutt to Douglas, Derby, 3 January 1792, MS3101/C/E/4/8/30, LOB.

[20] Ibid., 9 March 1792, MS3101/C/E/4/8/31.

[21] Arthur J. Ray, *Indians in the Fur Trade: Their Role as Trappers, Hunters and Middlemen in the Lands Southwest of Hudson Bay, 1660–1870* (Toronto, 1974), 51; Ann M. Carlos and Frank D. Lewis, 'The Economic History of the Fur Trade: 1670 to 1870' (2008): https://eh.net/encyclopedia/the-economic-history-of-the-fur-trade-1670-to-1870/.

[22] Draft trade card of Joseph Butter, fur manufacturer, London, Heal, 65.4, BM.

[23] Margot Finn, 'Men's Things: Masculine Possession in the Consumer Revolution', *Social History* 25.2 (2000): 133–55, at 147.

[24] Diary of Hurst, 22 November 1760, MS3543, HM. Real-price cost calculated using https://www.measuringworth.com/.

in 1787, to be fashioned into a muff. After his sister Mary told him 'no such furs are to be bought', Samuel wrote to his love 'Tanto meglio say I' ('all the better'), 'J'ai choisi l'<u>unique</u>, [pour] qu'elle porte les uniques' ('I choose the unique, so that she wears the unique'). In the end, he was delighted at how handsome the muff appeared, as a material manifestation of his good taste, social standing, and ability to provide Elizabeth with all the trappings of fashionable society.[25] The uniqueness of Samuel's gift was important to him, as it was emblematic of the strength of his attachment and the lengths to which he would go to provide for his future wife.

A further costly gift for moneyed suitors was a pianoforte, which gradually eclipsed the harpsichord as the genteel instrument of choice over the course of the century. The famed piano manufacturer Broadwood was established in London in 1728, producing around 400 square pianos a year by the 1790s, and ceasing the production of harpsichords altogether by 1793.[26] Small square pianofortes were designed for the houses of the middling sorts, and could be moved from room to room to facilitate domestic sociability and provide a vehicle for showcasing feminine taste and accomplishment. A Broadwood piano cost around twenty guineas (£21) in 1780, plus a further guinea to deliver, falling to £18 in total a generation later.[27] There was a resulting demand for sheet music, with the number of shops selling music in London skyrocketing from twelve in 1750, to thirty by 1794, and 150 by 1824.[28] Nonetheless, printed music remained costly, and so thrifty individuals often continued copying notes out by hand. In Jane Austen's *Emma* (1816), Frank Churchill sends Jane Fairfax a Broadwood pianoforte as a gift during their secret engagement. The orphaned Jane was 'mistress of music', but had never had 'even the pitifullest old spinet in the world, to amuse herself with', making it a particularly thoughtful present. The inclusion of some Irish melodies alongside the piano showed it to be 'thoroughly from the heart. Nothing hastily done; nothing incomplete.'[29] For Frank, the value of his gift lay in the careful planning and thought that underpinned it (the irony being that it was particularly thoughtless to send a piano to a woman you were secretly engaged to, who lacked a home of her own). While serving in Portugal during the Peninsular Campaign in 1812, the soldier Robert Garrett promised to send some music to his sweetheart Charlotte Bentinck, which the regiment's bandmaster had copied out at his request.[30] The gift showed a particular effort to amuse and entertain Charlotte in his absence, and bring something of Portugal home to her in Ramsgate.

Books were another gift signifying the steady rise in paper products. Books allowed lovers to gauge one another's reactions to particular texts, and share their own reading preferences. A person's favourite books also revealed their education, disposition, and world view. Courting couples did more than simply exchange

---

[25] Whitbread II to Grey, 29 November 1787, W1/6586, BAS.

[26] Tim Blanning, *The Triumph of Music: Composers, Musicians and their Audiences, 1700 to the Present* (London, 2008), 178–9.

[27] Ibid., 181.

[28] Arthur Loesser, *Men, Women and Pianos* (New York, 1954), 251–2.

[29] Austen, *Emma*, 169.

[30] Garrett to Bentinck, Camp near Alfayates, Portugal, 10 June 1812, R/U888/C11/30, KHLC.

romances; they had a varied diet of books encompassing biography, education, history, geography, and politics. The selection of texts available became ever more diverse, as the number of published titles 'mushroomed' from the late 1740s until the century's close, growing by more than 2 per cent each year.[31] The catalogue of one bookseller in a county town in 1785 listed more than 5,000 titles and 20,000 volumes for consumers to choose among.[32] The Derbyshire cotton-trader Joseph Strutt regularly sent history books to his sweetheart Isabella Douglas in an effort to improve her intellectual capabilities before marriage. He made sure to read texts such as the Greek historian Plutarch's celebrated *Lives* and Oliver Goldsmith's *History of Rome* (1769) before sending them to Isabella, highlighting 'a few sentiments that exactly meet my Ideas—I have marked two, which all who think at all must surely approve'.[33] The exchange of personally marked books allowed Joseph to impress upon Isabella the ideas that were most important to him. Joseph repeatedly stressed that the 'improvement of your mind at this time is of the most serious importance', cautioning Isabella that it would only be her 'own fault' if she did not 'employ them to a useful purpose'.[34] While this may appear rather draconian, Joseph was also showing his support for Isabella's professed desire to make progress 'in Historical Reading'. She wanted 'to proceed in it 'till I have a pretty clear Idea of all nations in general, & of our own in particular'. Joseph thus sent a range of books to encourage her desire for education, pledging that 'any other book or any thing else you want do not scruple one moment to ask me for, if it can be procured you shall have it.'[35]

Isabella was active in the process of exchange, sending Joseph several books over their protracted courtship. She was free to do so as books could also be exchanged between friends and family members, and did not have the same status in the hierarchy of gifts as objects such as rings or hair, which publicly announced that marriage was imminent. In 1786, she sent Joseph her 'favourite' Plutarch (the fifth volume of *Lives*) and asked him to procure the sixth when possible. She also described her reaction to controversial political texts such as Thomas Paine's seditious *Rights of Man* (1791) and *Thoughts on the Peace* (1783), which she had been 'highly gratified' reading.[36] Isabella's interests extended from history and politics to geography. In 1791, she recommended an 'interesting & entertaining' book on the Pelew Islands by George Keate and an English translation of the explorer François Le Vaillant's *New Travels into the Interior Parts of Africa* for 'the pleasing account it gives of the natives of that savage country'. These continual exchanges did not come cheap, with popular novels in smaller octavo or duodecimo formats usually costing

---

[31] James Raven, 'The Book Trades', in *Books and their Readers*, Vol. 2, ed. Rivers, 2.

[32] Stobart, 'Shopping Streets as Social Space', 12.

[33] Jos. Strutt to Douglas, Derby, 5 May 1788, MS 3101/C/E/4/8/11, LOB. For a further example, see letters from Whitbread II to Grey, where he advised her to 'look at my Marks': Bordeaux, 16 June 1787, W1/6555, No. 10, BAS.

[34] Jos. Strutt to Douglas, Sandy Brook, 10 August 1789, MS 3101/C/E/4/8/18, LOB.

[35] Douglas to Jos. Strutt, Sandy Brook, 19 December 1791, MS3101/C/E/5/15/9; Jos. Strutt to Douglas, Derby, 16 November 1790, MS 3101/C/E/4/8/21, LOB.

[36] Douglas to Jos. Strutt, Sandy Brook, 19 December 1791, MS 3101/C/E/5/16/9, LOB.

around two to three shillings per volume, rising to ten to twelve shillings for 'more serious works' in larger quarto or folio size. Coupled with the general rise in book prices in the second half of the eighteenth century, it is no wonder that Joseph and Isabella took such great care of the books they exchanged, even keeping the protective covers on to 'prevent their being rubbed'.[37] It transpires Joseph did purchase Keate's *Account of the Pelew Islands* (1788), as recommended by Isabella. It can be found in an inventory of more than one hundred books later bequeathed to their daughter, suggesting that the book retained its emotional value long after it had been read.[38]

Literate lovers could also purchase inkwells, paper, and seals to aid the creation of their love letters. Dena Goodman has analysed the exchange of gifts such as heart-shaped inkwells as 'tokens of love or friendship' between French correspondents, arguing that they worked 'to remind the woman of the man to whom she is supposed to be writing'.[39] Small ephemeral items such as signets were used to set hot wax to seal a person's letters. They could be personalized by adding a bust of the sender, their initials, or pertinent symbolic images. Their specificity suggests that certain seals may solely have been used in the creation of love letters, helping to formulate a shared bond between a couple. One soft-paste porcelain seal from 1752–4 presents Cupid forging hearts as a blacksmith, with his hammer poised to fall on a red heart positioned on the anvil. The phrase 'IL EST POUR VOUS' ('It is for you') is painted around the die, with 'JE LES UNIT' ('I unite them') on the matrix itself.[40] Both the seal as a romantic gift and the letters it imprinted worked to increase a couple's intimacy. As the gentlewoman Mary Martin wrote to her suitor Isaac Rebow in 1771, 'Pray take notice of my seal & tell me how you like it.' Her seal featured the motto 'VIVONS UNIS' ('Let's Live United'), declaring her feelings for Isaac in wax, circumventing the need to write them by hand.[41] Porcelain and moulded glass seals presented as gifts were durable and lightweight keepsakes that could be kept in pockets, or hooked onto ribbons and carried around. Extant glass signets depict two hearts above the Altar of Love to signify a loving marriage[42] and a faithful dog pausing to look up below the message 'TOUJOURS FIDELE' ('Always Faithful') (Figure 4.2). Like books, signets were practical and portable gifts that could be collected by individuals as part of an ever-diversifying assortment of love tokens.

Over the century, small trinkets and their accompanying accessories boomed in popularity, and were sent by both courting men and women as love tokens. These

[37] Ibid., Sandy Brook, 10 February 1791, MS 3101/C/E/5/16/6, LOB; David Allan, *A Nation of Readers: The Lending Library in Georgian England* (London, 2008), 45.

[38] 'Inventory & Valuation of Pictures, Busts, Books, Prints, Wines, Household Goods and Furniture, Horses & Carriage &c bequeathed to Mrs Galton under the Will of the Late Joseph Strutt Es^{re} deced', 1844, D3772/EL2/2/3, DRO.

[39] Goodman, *Becoming a Woman in the Age of Letters*, 183.

[40] Chelsea Porcelain seal depicting Cupid forging hearts, 1752–4, 007616, Steppes Hill Farm Antiques Ltd.

[41] Martin to Rebow, 15 October 1771, A12691, Box 1, Vol. I, f. 144, ERO.

[42] Blue moulded glass signet depicting the 'Altar of Love', Birmingham, 1750–1850, 1998F571, Birmingham Museums and Art Gallery.

Fig. 4.2. Purple glass signet (seal matrix) inscribed 'TOUJOURS FIDELE' ('Always Faithful'), Birmingham, 1750–1800, 1.7 cm (H) × 1.3 cm (W) × 0.6 cm (D), 1934F103.10. © Birmingham Museums Trust.

petty commodities were miniature in scale but perfect in design.[43] Just as the language of love readily evolved in tandem with social and cultural shifts, so did its material culture. Fashionable 'toys' were novelty objects such as buckles, buttons, decorative boxes (for storing patches, snuff, and implements for writing, knitting, and sewing), fans, perfume bottles, porcelain, and watches. Such trifles could be purchased at auction, and from china shops, toy shops, jewellers, booksellers, and stationers. By 1797, York boasted three toy dealers, which ranked among the ten shops with the highest income in town.[44] Toymen often combined several trades, with Richard Adey of Warwick styling himself as a toyman, hairdresser, and perfumer, and George Ragsdale of London operating as a toyman, jeweller, and goldsmith. While the former sold scented soaps, perfumes, and combs, the latter sold decorative boxes and watches.[45] Toys were popularly exchanged as gifts between friends, family members, and courting couples, with one shopper returning from Tunbridge Wells in 1748 having bought 'every one in the family something' for under four shillings apiece.[46] Toys were not restricted to social elites, but could be purchased by the aspiring middle classes and occasionally the lower orders of society.[47] The cost varied greatly according to the materials used, with a pair of

[43] Kathryn Jones, 'The "Irresistible Tide of Luxury"', in *The First Georgians: Art & Monarchy 1714–1760*, ed. Desmond Shawe-Taylor (London, 2014), 394–439, at 396.

[44] Lorna H. Mui and Hoh-Cheung Mui, *Shops and Shopkeeping in Eighteenth-Century England* (London, 1989), Table 22, 123, and Table 24, 129.

[45] Trade card of Richard Adey, 1743–1845, E.197–1943, V&A; bill head of George Ragsdale, 1768, E.215–1943, V&A.

[46] Jeffreys to Pratt, 25 August 1748, U840/C9/22, KHLC; Letter from Elizabeth Sheridan Lefanu to Alicia Sheridan Lefanu, 15 June 1785, in *Betsy Sheridan's Journal: Letters from Sheridan's Sister, 1784–6 and 1788–90*; Diary of Frances Burney, 15 July 1788, in *Diary and Letters of Madame D'Arblay*, ed. Charlotte Frances Barrett, Vol. 4, BIWLD.

[47] McNeil and Riello, 'Luxury and Fashion', 160.

paste shoe buckles costing around £6 and a gold snuffbox set with diamonds and rubies an exorbitant £46.[48]

Many such romantic trinkets were designed specifically with lovers in mind. Marius Kwint has argued that ceramic souvenirs were highly valued for their durability, offering 'the immutability and constancy to which the ideals of kinship aspired'.[49] Of course, ceramic objects were only durable if suitably protected, with specially designed velvet-lined shagreen carrying cases to protect treasured items from wear and tear costing up to ten guineas each.[50] The Chelsea Porcelain Manufactory was likely established around 1745 by the Huguenot silversmith Nicholas Sprimont (1713–71), following the success of European manufactories in Meissen (est. 1710) and Vincennes (est. 1740). Whole series of Chelsea toys were produced using master moulds made from wax and lead, providing the wealthiest consumers with an extensive choice of goods.[51] Romantic inscriptions were taken from the objects they adorned, such as a patch box resembling a basket of fruit with the inscription 'L'amour les a Cueilli pour la plus Belle' ('Love Picked them for the Most Beautiful').[52] These small luxury items were associated with the 'Frenchifying' of English customs. They were typically decorated with inscriptions in French, which had an international reputation as the language of flirtation, courtship, and love, propagated by texts such as *The Dictionary of Love* (first published in French in 1741 and translated into English in 1753).[53] Popular phrases included:

Je suis votre captive	I am your captive
Gage de mon amour	Pledge of my love
Imitez Nous	Imitate Us
Pour L'Honneur et L'Amour	For Honour and Love
Je Blesse Mais J'Attache	I Wound but I Attach

These standard romantic phrases were repeated widely on toys, homemade valentines, and embossed paper designed for lovers. Chelsea toys printed with these ubiquitous mottoes represented valuable gifts for wealthy consumers as a result of the company's aristocratic and royal patronage, rivalling the best luxury goods Europe had to offer.

---

[48] Jones, 'The "Irresistible Tide of Luxury"', 433.

[49] Marius Kwint, 'Material Memories: A History of the Souvenir', *Tate: The Art Magazine* (1998), 45–9, at 48.

[50] Scent bottle with shagreen carrying case, 1752–8, in John Cecil Austin, *Chelsea Porcelain at Williamsburg* (Williamsburg, VA, 1977), 108–9; Jones, 'The "Irresistible Tide of Luxury"', 436.

[51] Austin, *Chelsea Porcelain at Williamsburg*, 110.

[52] Chelsea Porcelain bonbonnière in the form of a basket of fruit, London, c.1759–69, 3.5 cm (H) × 5.1 cm (L), 414:275–1885, V&A.

[53] As far afield as Russia, readers learned the language of love using translations of texts such as Paul Tallement's *Voyage to the Island of Love* (trans. French to Russian in 1730) and *The Dictionary of Love* (trans. French to Russian in 1768). Victor Zhivov, 'Love à la mode: Russian Words and French Sources', in *French and Russian in Imperial Russia*, ed. Derek Offord, Lara Ryazanova-Clarke, Vladislav Rjéoutski, and Gesine Argent (Edinburgh, 2015), Vol. II, 214–41, at 214–15. Jean-François Dreux du Radier's *Dictionnaire d'Amour* was partially translated from French into English and substantially updated in 1753 by John Cleland, author of the infamous pornographic novel *Fanny Hill: Memoirs of a Woman of Pleasure* (1748).

Fig. 4.3. Printed watch paper titled 'Matrimony', late eighteenth to early nineteenth century, featuring a colour scene of a couple gazing toward a church, and handwritten dedication on the reverse, 5.57 cm (D), British Museum, London, 1958, 1006.2533. © The Trustees of the British Museum, All Rights Reserved.

Pocket watches first emerged in the later seventeenth century and 'quickly became a coveted possession of every social class'.[54] A watch-paper was a circular piece of paper, linen, or silk around five centimeters in diameter, used from the mid-eighteenth century to protect the glass of pocket watches. Paper discs could be cut from magazines, printed silk versions purchased from shops, and embroidered examples handmade by women.[55] Handwritten dedications on the reverse were used to enhance their emotional value. The example in Figure 4.3 celebrates the ideal of marriage for love, and is printed with a couple gazing out towards a church. The reverse is inscribed 'except [*sic*] this trifle from A friend whose love for the[e] will never end.' In 1759, the tailor's daughter Sarah Hurst sent a 'vastly pretty' watch-paper to Captain Henry Smith, created for the pair by Sarah's friend Miss Pigott, sister of the local curate. The paper depicted Henry being crowned by Cupid with a chaplet of roses, next to Mars crowned by a laurel wreath, and a poem about love and glory.[56] Such keepsakes were by no means confined to courtship and could also be exchanged as tokens of friendship. The purpose of such small trifles was not obligation akin to a ring or lock of hair, but novelty and fun.

Snuff was first consumed in Britain towards the end of the seventeenth century, and was associated with the aristocracy and court of Charles II. The practice

---

[54] Jan de Vries, *The Industrious Revolution: Consumer Behaviour and the Household Economy, 1650 to the Present* (Cambridge, 2008), 2.

[55] See printed silk watch-paper 'To a Friend', 1958,1006.2633.225, BM; 'New Emblematical Watch Print', in *Lady's Pocket Magazine*, published by Harrison & Co, 1796, Banks, 132.200, BM; embroidered linen watch-paper with paper backing, decorated with flowers, hearts, and motto 'Love the Giver', 1958,1006.2549, BM; hand-coloured engraving or hand-drawn watch paper with the Lord's Prayer inside a heart and wreath of flowers, 1825, E.562–1937, V&A.

[56] Diary of Hurst, 10 January 1759 and 5 February 1759, MS3542, HM.

became more widespread after a fleet of Spanish ships loaded with snuff was captured in 1702, and this exotic luxury surged onto the British market. Snuff was an 'ambrosial dust' made from ground tobacco blended with flavours such as ginger, musk, orange, rose, and pepper, with one day's supply carried by users in snuffboxes.[57] Snuffboxes were exchanged by both sexes as tokens of love and friendship. Designs multiplied from the carved wood and tortoiseshell of the previous century to porcelain, papier-mâché, and, for the wealthiest consumers, agate, rock crystal, ivory, silver, and gold. Emily Friedman has emphasized the seductive power of snuff taking, presenting the snuffbox as a foreign object 'at once fascinating, attractive, and filled with mischief'.[58] Surviving boxes feature scenes of courtship, seduction, and elopement, and even secret compartments with rotating erotic scenes.[59] One gold-mounted ivory snuffbox carved in Dieppe *c.*1750 contains a miniature portrait of John Spencer in enamel on copper, painted in London in 1753–5 by the renowned Swiss portraitist Jean-Étienne Liotard. Liotard painted a matching portrait of John's future wife Georgiana Poyntz in 1754, probably to celebrate their betrothal. This exquisite item may have been intended as a gift for Georgiana before their wedding the following year.[60] Ivory aside, snuffboxes were also exchanged by the gentry and middling sorts. In the 1770s, the writer Mary Hays sent a snuffbox to her suitor John Eccles as a courtship gift. Such was the box's emotional value that he later bequeathed it to his youngest sister in his will, as an object rendered 'of inestimable worth by the giver'.[61] Boxes could be invested with additional affective value by inscriptions recording the sender, recipient, and date of the gift, and by portrait miniatures either gazing out from the lid, or hidden inside for the owner's eyes only.

Souvenir handkerchiefs first emerged in the seventeenth century, becoming one of the most common commemorative items in the eighteenth. Unlike smaller examples designed for sneezing into, and wiping the face and hands after taking snuff, these large designs were purely decorative.[62] Handkerchiefs were traditional romantic gifts, recalling the 'favours' given from ladies to knights to display on their helmets during jousts, with women working handkerchiefs as love tokens that could be woven with hair.[63] A series of technological innovations in the second half of the eighteenth century enabled the printing of complex large-scale designs

---

[57] Emily C. Friedman, *Reading Smell in Eighteenth-Century Fiction* (Lanham, MD, 2016), 26, 40.

[58] Ibid., 44–6.

[59] Painted enamel snuffbox depicting lovers in a landscape, Birmingham, 1758–60, BI417, Black Country History (subsequently BCH); George II Erotic Automaton Snuffbox Set, James Cox, London, *c.*1770, Sale 1361, Lot 26, Christie's, New York; George III Stobawasser papier-mâché snuffbox cover, *c.*1790, SA474929, Blackwood Antiques; Japanned snuffbox titled 'Running away', *c.*1830–40, LP81, BCH; Snuffbox with amorous scene titled 'La va-t-il', *c.*1825–75, LP124, BCH.

[60] Ivory gold-mounted snuffbox inset with miniature by Jean Étienne Liotard, London and Dieppe, 1750–5, LOAN: GILBERT.408–2008, V&A.

[61] 'Mr Eccles' Will', 24 November 1779, in Wedd, ed., *Love-Letters of Mary Hays*, 203.

[62] Dawn Hoskin, 'Considerations on a Handkerchief', 16 December 2013: http://www.vam.ac.uk/blog/creating-new-europe-1600-1800-galleries/considerations-handkerchief.

[63] Humphrey Senhouse III to Catherine Wood, 27 September 1768, D/SEN 5/5/1/9/1/5, CRO; Garrett to Bentinck, 16 August 1811, R/U888/C11/13, KHLC.

Fig. 4.4. Souvenir printed cotton handkerchief 'Valentine's Day, or the 14th of Febr[y]', England(?), *c.*1793, 61 cm × 67 cm, Courtesy of The Lewis Walpole Library, Yale University.

in intricate detail. Wood-block printing gave way to copper-plate printing in the 1750s, followed by rotary printing using engraved cylinders in the 1780s. The productivity of a roller was at least twenty times that of a wooden block, enabling manufacturers to produce large runs of high-quality identical designs.[64] The sizeable souvenir handkerchief in Figure 4.4 is titled 'Valentine's Day, or the 14th of Febr[y]', printed with scenes of courtship in madder red ink. The central ribbon declares, 'Accept my Heart for I have thine, I chuse You for my VALENTINE.' The owner has embroidered 'EB 1793' in white thread onto the left side, in order to claim ownership of this consumer object and commemorate the moment she received the gift. It testifies to the growing prominence of Valentine's Day as a commercial ritual, as new novelty objects were produced for the enjoyment and pleasure of a wider range of consumers.

[64] Giorgio Riello, 'Asian Knowledge and the Development of Calico Printing in Europe in the Seventeenth and Eighteenth Centuries', *Journal of Global History* 5 (2010): 1–28, at 23–4.

VALENTINE'S DAY

Valentine's Day was a staple celebration on the eighteenth-century calendar, marked by traditional folk rituals, and—increasingly—new more commercial customs. The evening before Valentine's Day, groups of young people would gather to 'draw Lots' to determine their valentine, which was 'look'd upon as a good Omen of their being Man and Wife afterwards'. Valentine lotteries were said to be a common 'rural Tradition' in 'the youthful Part of the World', with couples remaining 'valentines' from 14 February until Easter Day.[65] The French traveller Henri Misson (*c*.1650–1722) described both men and women drawing billets, meaning that 'each has two Valentines: but the Man sticks faster to the Valentine that is fallen to him.' Billets and romantic verse were then displayed upon a couple's bosoms or sleeves for several days, with this 'little Sport' often ending 'in Love'.[66] The rare folded-paper valentine in Figure 4.5 was created *c*.1750 as part of a valentine lottery. The handwritten rhyme on the sixth heart (lower centre) reads, 'As grapes grow on the Vine / By lot you came my Valentine / But if you take it in Disdain / I pray return it back again.'[67]

For most of the century, valentine gifts were anonymous poems, rhymes, or puzzles designed or copied out by lovers. The sending of poetic mottoes can be dated to the 1660s, when the diarist Samuel Pepys did 'first observe the fashion'.[68] As argued in Chapter 1 of this book, citing and writing poetry constituted a key vehicle for eighteenth-century men to woo their sweethearts. One true lovers' knot from 'J.E.' to a 'Fair Lady' in 1729 copied out a labyrinthine puzzle about love's criss-crossing, reading 'A cros begins Loves cris cros row loves not without a cros or two a duble cros begins this [k]not Love without crosses merits not.'[69] This same rhyme with no beginning or end featured among the 'Fancies and Fantasticks' in *Witt's Recreations* (1640), republished in seven new editions as *Recreation for Ingenious Head-peeces* (1643–83).[70] Around this puzzle, 'J.E.' drew eight numbered hearts containing romantic rhymes, such as 'Witt wealth and Beauty all do well But constant Love doth farr Excell.' Again, these can be found etched inside posy rings and printed in books of epigrams, which flourished as a genre during the seventeenth century.[71]

The sharing of homemade acrostics, riddles, and puzzles was a standard part of courting behaviour, which was steadily incorporated into the Valentine's Day

---

[65] Henry Bourne, *Antiquitates Vulgares, or the Antiquities of the Common People* (Newcastle, 1725), 174–5.

[66] *The Frighted West-Country Man's Garland* (London, *c*.1705), 9–10; *M. Misson's Memoirs and Observations in his Travels over England* (London, 1719), 330–1.

[67] For a similar valentine of folded hearts probably created for a lottery, see card by David Bursell, *c*.1797, DDX114/8, East Riding Archives.

[68] Henry B. Wheatley, ed., *The Diary of Samuel Pepys M.A. F.R.S.* (London, 1893), 16 February 1667.

[69] Photocopy of valentine from J.E. to a 'Fair Lady', 1729, 2M37/608, HRO.

[70] George Watson, ed., *The New Cambridge Bibliography of English Literature* (Cambridge, 1974), Vol. I, 1010.

[71] William Winstanley, *The new help to discourse or, Wit, mirth, and jollity* (London, 1680), 202; Diana Scarisbrick, *Historic Rings: Four Thousand Years of Craftsmanship* (Tokyo, 2004), 99–103.

Fig. 4.5. Folded heart-shaped valentine created as part of a lottery, *c.*1750, Cornwall Record Office, Truro, X54/1.

repertoire. In 1757, Captain Henry Smith of the Marine Corps sent the tailor's daughter Sarah Hurst a hand-drawn acrostic of her name.[72] Women could also take part in creating puzzles, with Elizabeth Grey sending a riddle to the Bedfordshire gentleman Samuel Whitbread II in 1787, for him to unravel during his Grand Tour. Samuel pledged to 'keep it most charily', asking Elizabeth not to 'blame my stupidity' that he had taken so long to solve it. Nonetheless, Samuel understood the meaning of the riddle in encouraging him to think on her, pledging 'believe me, You cannot be thinking of me at any time that I am not thinking upon You.'[73] The creation of romantic puzzles showed particular time and effort

---

[72] Diary of Hurst, 1757, MS3542, HM. Also see 'An Acrostick on the Amiable Miss Carus, Beckhead, Kirkby Lonsdale Westmorland', 18th–19th century, WDBIG/1/113, Cumbria Record Office, Kendal.

[73] Whitbread II to Grey, 31 August 1787, W1/6574, BAS.

dedicated to entertaining a loved one, while solving these puzzles required a reciprocal investment. One twisting true lovers' knot sent from John Thomas of
Kempley Court in Gloucestershire to his future wife Elizabeth *c*.1780 extended to
more than 300 words in length, 'Crossing winding turning in and out, and neaver
ceasing turning round a bought.' John gave Elizabeth a set time to decipher his
puzzle, asking whether 'in half an hour' she could make out the meaning of his
knot (true love).[74] The winding poem about mutual love and marriage resembles
the printed verse on the souvenir handkerchief in Figure 4.4, which winds in
hearts and circles around the central image, revealing how traditional customs
were gradually integrated into the period's growing consumer culture. By
c.1800, the 'Endless Knot of Love' had found its way into print after being
engraved by Bartolozzi, signifying the increasing commercialization of the
romantic economy.

   As Valentine's Day progressively became part of print culture, valentine writers
emerged as a new genre, reproducing romantic dialogues, poems, songs, country
dances, short stories, and excerpts from plays to instruct and entertain.[75] They
were generally fifty to eighty pages in length, costing only sixpence to purchase.
Valentine writers were similar in style to letter-writing guides, which printed fictional correspondences between courting couples for the enjoyment of readers.[76]
Unlike letter-writing guides, there is evidence that valentine writers were used as
direct models by men and women, who copied chosen poems out verbatim onto
valentine cards.[77] Valentine writers form part of the broader celebration of
romantic love in the second half of the eighteenth century. The frontispiece to
Every Lady's Own Valentine Writer (1794) depicted a scene from Thomas Holcroft's
comedy *The Road to Ruin* (1792) where young Sophia Freelove receives a paper
valentine baked into a plum cake, which she had told her suitor Mr Dornton was
the custom in Gloucestershire. Hence customs that had previously been part of
folklore and customary gifting practices found their way into print. The story
of Valentine's Day is also the story of print, and of the manufacturing and sale of
decorated paper.

   The gradual and uneven transition from personally to professionally produced
valentines began in the second half of the eighteenth century, when new types of
printed papers and cards were sold to consumers across Europe at low cost. Novelty
printed writing paper could be purchased in Austria, Germany, Italy, and France,
with individuals reporting back from Paris that ladies were 'writing on paper of

---

[74] True love knot from John Thomas of Kempley Court to his future wife Elizabeth, Gloucestershire,
c.1780, E.767–1985, V&A.
   [75] See *The Complete Valentine Writer: Or, The Young Men and Maidens Best Assistant* (London,
1780?), *The New English Valentine Writer, Or The High Road to Love; for Both Sexes* (London, 1784),
and *Every Lady's Own Valentine Writer, in Prose and Verse, for the Year 1794* (London, 1794).
   [76] *Every Lady's Own Valentine Writer* for 1798 recommended *The Whole Art of Courtship*, *Every
Lady's Own Fortune Teller*, and *The Letter Writer, or every Lady's own Secretary* as further reading, 31.
   [77] One printed valentine in the John Johnson Collection features a handwritten poem copied from
Richardson's New London Fashionable Gentleman's Valentine Writer (1828), Valentines (uncatalogued), Box 1,
JJC, BLO.

every colour, with inks of every colour'.[78] The British ambassador in Dresden Charles Hanbury Williams (1708–59) wrote that the French were 'a very silly People in triffles [*sic*] but a very wise one in Essentials', and accordingly purchased a new decorated paper called 'Papier a La Dauphine' in 1748 to share with his daughters. A picture of a gentlewoman in the top left corner replaced the opening address 'Madam' and her footman at the bottom right the closing address 'servant'.[79] In France, *cartes d'amitiés* ('friendship cards') were exchanged between lovers, friends, and family members, particularly to mark the New Year. In Austria and Germany, *freundschaftskarten* were printed on card from mid-century, with decorative borders evolving into more elaborate illustrations.[80] These developments are indicative of a much broader shift in the economy of letter-writing. As Dena Goodman has argued in her study of the epistolary paraphernalia purchased by Frenchwomen, decorated paper represented 'part of the expansion of the consumer economy through the creation, invention, importation and marketing of new and existing goods as novel, fashionable and useful'.[81]

In a related development in the commercialization of writing practices, engraved 'writing blanks' or 'school pieces' with colourful borders surged in popularity from *c.*1780 to *c.*1820. Like valentines, they were sold by the sheet for special occasions such as Lady Day, Midsummer, Michaelmas, and Christmas. Colour designs included *Emblems for the Improvement of Youth* (1784), *Pilgrim's Progress* (1784), and *Shakespeare's Seven Ages* (1797), to be completed by children in their best handwriting and presented to their parents as tokens of duty and affection.[82] Novelty papers were also produced for the covers and endpapers of books, which were marbled, coloured, and gilded for decorative effect.[83] Bookbinders, booksellers, newsagents, papermakers, printers, publishers, and stationers across the country purchased marbled papers at around one pence per sheet, and either sold them on to consumers or used the paper to create tasteful paper inkpots, decorate brass inkstands, and line small boxes and letter-cases.[84] The development of a domestic paper industry was a source of national pride, as collecting and processing rags employed 'a vast many people', driving advances in manufacturing and revealing the increasing perfection of the arts.[85] Guides such as Robert Dossie's *Handmaid*

---

[78] Louis Racine to his daughter Mme de Neuville de Saint-Héry, Paris, 4 October 1746, cited in Goodman, *Becoming a Woman in the Age of Letters*, 187; Frank Staff, *The Valentine and its Origins* (London, 1969), 40.

[79] Charles Hanbury Williams to his daughters Charlotte and Fanny, Dresden, 30 June 1748, MSS Vol. 181, 11391, CHW 81–7, LWL.

[80] Staff, *The Valentine and its Origins*, 27–9, 56.

[81] Goodman, *Becoming a Woman in the Age of Letters*, 162.

[82] JJC Educational Folder 4: Engraved Writing Blanks, BLO; *Carington Bowles's New and Enlarged Catalogue of Useful and Accurate Maps, Charts and Plans; Prints, Writing Books* (London, 1784), 156; Julie Anne Lambert, *A Nation of Shopkeepers: Trade Ephemera from 1654 to the 1860s in the John Johnson Collection* (Oxford, 2001).

[83] See Geoffrey Wakeman, *English Marbled Papers: A Documentary History* (Loughborough, 1978); Richard J. Wolfe, *Marbled Paper, its History, Techniques and Patterns* (Philadelphia, PA, 1989); Tanya Schmoller, *A Yorkshire Source of Decorated Paper in the Eighteenth Century* (Sheffield, 2003).

[84] Schmoller, *A Yorkshire Source of Decorated Paper*, 21, 27.

[85] 'Paper: Remarks', *The Universal Dictionary of Trade and Commerce* (London, 1774), Vol. II, 416.

to the Arts (1758) advised manufacturers how to gild paper and stain it a rainbow of hues using verdigris (green), turmeric (yellow), indigo (blue), and privet berries (purple).[86]

In this climate of innovation and experimentation, with a variety of colour designs being printed on an ever-expanding range of paper goods, it is no wonder that Valentine's Day—with its profusion of paper—gradually became part of the consumer economy. The earliest printed valentine card with an accompanying date was produced in 1797 by John Fairburn, who ran a family bookshop on Minories in London from 1795 to 1810. The century had witnessed a steady increase in the proportion of booksellers and stationers' shops, with only one reporting bankruptcy in London in 1748, rising to ten by 1770 (representing 4.3 per cent of shops in total); corresponding figures in the provinces were three and eight for the same dates, respectively (2.8 per cent in total).[87] London was the epicentre of the book trade: by 1823, 8.5 per cent of shops in London were booksellers and stationers, compared to 6.5 per cent of shops in Bristol, 5.6 per cent in Norwich, and 3.6 per cent in Manchester.[88] Fairburn's shop sold a wide selection of chapbooks, maps, prints, pamphlets, political tracts, songs, cards, and valentine writers. His valentine cards each repeat the same standard rhyme about a 'design…to be your Valentine', and are printed with ribbons, cupids holding garlands of flowers, kissing doves, burning torches of love, the altar of love, hearts shot through with arrows, and ostensibly every other symbol in the romantic repertoire. Customers could choose between cards printed with different central images, whether a young woman picking flowers outside a country cottage or the goddess plenty seated on a grassy knoll. The card in Figure 4.6 was sent to Mr Brown of Kent Road in London from his 'well wisher' Catherine Mossday, requesting that he visit on Sunday as she had 'something particular to say' to him. To enhance its appeal to consumers, the card features ten roundels of lace paper circling the main image, each with a pink flower cut into the centre.

The emergence of printed cards sold by booksellers, stationers, and paper manufacturers resulted in an immense increase in the volume of cards purchased and sent by lovers. *The Times* reported that on Valentine's Day 1804,

> the Twopenny Post had such an extraordinary influx of letters, with Valentines inclosed, that the Postmen, although assisted by a number of supernumeraries, could not get through their deliveries in the regular time. At the receiving house, in New-street, Covent-Garden, near 1000 Valentines were put into the box.[89]

In total, it was reported that 60,000 letters were sent, rising to 80,000 the following year.[90] As Leigh Eric Schmidt argues, the valentine 'had become a commercial product, a piece of merchandise marketed and consumed'. This shift is reflected in

---

[86] Robert Dossie, *The Handmaid to the Arts* (London, 1758): 'Of gilding paper, and vellum or parchment', 390–8, 'Of staining paper, or parchment, of various colours', 445–7.
[87] Mui and Mui, *Shops and Shopkeeping*, Table 6, 63.
[88] Ibid., Table 7, 69.   [89] *The Times*, 15 February 1804, 5496.
[90] *The Ipswich Journal*, 23 February 1805.

Fig. 4.6. Hand-coloured printed valentine card published 12 January 1797 by John Fairburn, 146 Minories, London, 1797, 25.5 cm (L) × 19.5 cm (W). © York Museums Trust (York Castle Museum), DA 2324.

the changing etymology of the term. In the seventeenth and eighteenth centuries, a 'valentine' meant a sweetheart or suitor. As 'Oroondates' wrote to his 'Statira' around the turn of the century, it was 'She that with a good morrow and salute I might inoffenceively [*sic*] nominate Valentine', hoping she would 'accept me and approve my choice'.[91] However, by the early nineteenth century the word meant predominantly 'an object of exchange...for which one went shopping'.[92]

Who were the people sending and receiving these cards? Valentines provide such a valuable insight into romantic customs in Georgian England because they crossed the boundaries between town and country. Valentine's Day in popular culture was fashioned as a ritual for 'country lasses with their swains', with pastoral imagery dominated by idealized country cottages, wooded groves, birds, flowers, shepherds, and shepherdesses.[93] Paintings such as George Morland's cottage-door scene *Johnny Going to the Fair* were reissued as popular engravings, with the new title *Valentine's Day* (1787) to celebrate simple rural pursuits uncorrupted by civilization. Yet valentines were not only the preserve of rural couples; they were also sent between growing industrial cities such as Manchester, Liverpool, and London. These represented England's three most populous urban centres by 1801, with a combined population of more than 1.1 million, up from just over 589,000 a hundred years earlier.[94] It may be that as more people moved to towns and cities, they took traditional rituals such as Valentine's Day celebrations with them. At the same time, during a period of escalating enclosure, urbanization, and industrialization, the celebration tapped into an idealized image of simple and honest life in rural England that increasingly found itself under threat.

As well as spanning town and country, the sending and receipt of valentines united rich and poor. Verses in valentine writers primarily addressed the lower sorts, with fictional letters exchanged between women working in service (laundry maids, lady's maids, dairy maids, and cooks), in trade (milliners, mantuamakers, and oyster sellers), and labourers (bricklayers, blacksmiths, cutlers, masons, tanners, thatchers, and wheelwrights).[95] To some extent this image was accurate: valentines certainly enabled couples with lower levels of epistolary literacy to participate in romantic culture. Many of the handwritten inscriptions on printed cards were penned by those who seem unlikely to stretch to a full love letter. The printed card in Figure 4.7 features the handwritten message 'Last Night i dreimt a drem i realy thot it twos tru i soll somboddy all by my bed sid...i rely thot it twos you.'[96] And yet cards also survive by members of the middling sort and gentry such as the Derbyshire schoolmaster William Spencer (1790–1866), the naval officer R. Pitt, the writer and philanthropist Elizabeth Cobbold (1765–1824) of Cliff House in Ipswich, and the young John Lovell (1761–1837) of Cole Park in Wiltshire.[97]

[91] Oroondates to Statira (Mrs Ann Webb), undated (early eighteenth century), FRE 5412, ESRO.

[92] Leigh Eric Schmidt, 'The Fashioning of a Modern Holiday: St. Valentine's Day, 1840–1870', *Winterthur Portfolio* 28.4 (1993), 209–45, at 215.

[93] *Every Lady's Own Valentine Writer* for 1794, 4.

[94] Peter Borsay, ed., *The Eighteenth-Century Town: A Reader in English Urban History 1688–1820* (New York and London, 2014), Table 1, 42.

[95] Based on letters printed in *The Complete Valentine Writer* and *The New English Valentine Writer*.

[96] Hand-coloured printed valentine card with lady stealing arrows from a sleeping Cupid, *c*.1820, OB1996.85, TPM.

[97] Acrostic valentine from William Spencer to Harriet Holmes, 1811–14, E.1207–1925, V&A; watercolour valentine from R. Pitt in Brixham to his wife Anne in Ilfracombe, *c*.1805, Nancy Rosin Collection; valentines created by Elizabeth Cobbold, published as *Cliff's Valentines* (Ipswich, 1813); cut-paper valentine made by John Lovell for 'ES' and 'PHL' (probably his brother Peter Harvey Lovell), 1778, 161/133, WSA.

Fig. 4.7. Hand-coloured printed valentine card of a woman stealing a sleeping Cupid's arrows, *c.*1820, 20 cm (H) × 25 cm (W). © Royal Mail Group Ltd, Courtesy of The Postal Museum, London, OB1996.85.

Like the image of Valentine's Day as a rural preoccupation, the celebration's association with plebeian men and women granted it an image of artless naïveté, even as it progressively evolved into a commercial event.

Lithographic printing (literally 'printing on stone') was invented in Germany *c.*1798 by the Bavarian actor, playwright, and amateur printer Alois Senefelder (1771–1834). Lithography was a planographic (flat) printing technique, utilizing a chemical process, as greasy ink was used to mark a smooth surface—ideally a polished limestone.[98] Senefelder had been searching for an economical means of copying music, with transfer lithography facilitating the popularization of sheet music as a romantic gift in the early nineteenth century. It was also essential to the commercialization of valentines, with retailers eagerly adopting the new method to print short-runs of romantic illustrations at low cost.[99] The German bookseller Rudolph Ackermann set up a lithographic press in London in 1817, publishing an English translation of Senefelder's instructional manual *A Complete Course of Lithography* in 1819. Ackermann praised the advantages of lithography in 'the multiplication of copies', enabling printers to produce 'identical facsimiles' of particular images.[100] Valentines in the 1820s were often printed in black and white using lithography and hand-coloured by retailers. Since the pen and ink designs were drawn straight onto the limestone, they were easy to alter, add to, or wipe clean, meaning that the same floral borders could be repurposed alongside new images and romantic verse, providing ever-greater choice for consumers.[101]

Lovers frequently wrote their own messages on top of these printed cards, suggesting the paper on its own was not sufficient. This practice of adding personalized inscriptions to consumer objects reflects Michel de Certeau's notion that '[e]veryday life invents itself by *poaching* in countless ways on the property of others.' People create their identities through '*ways of using*' commercial products.[102] Writing over a consumer object such as a printed valentine card actively changed the meaning of the object, through the addition of handwriting and personal sentiments that made the card unique to the sender. For de Certeau, these practices represent a form of resistance to wider structures of power and authority. Individuals create a personal 'bricolage' or 'collage' by 'reusing and recombining' particular materials: the meaning of the object changes, coming to derive from its new use.[103] And yet the handwritten inscriptions on valentine cards were rarely original. Rather, individuals copied additional traditional verses over the standard message provided on the card itself. Printed cards therefore provided a means of creating a multi-layered pastiche or bricolage of romantic messages. The imprint of a writer's hand, and the particular poems they chose to reproduce, worked to make the valentine personal and emotionally valuable. This tradition continued in greetings cards over

---

[98] The printing areas are covered with grease, while the blank areas are moistened with water. Once ink is applied to the printing surface it clings to the greasy areas, but is repelled by the damp ones. See Susan Lambert, *Prints: Art and Techniques* (London, 2001), 70–82, and Michael Twyman, *Lithography 1800–1850* (London, 1970), 68–9. For a detailed explanation, see Henry Trivick, *Autolithography: The Technique* (London, 1960).

[99] Maurice Rickards and Michael Twyman, *The Encyclopedia of Ephemera* (London, 2000), 151; James Mosley, 'The Technologies of Print', in *The Oxford Companion to the Book*, ed. Michael F. Suarez and H. R. Woudhuysen (Oxford, 2010), Vol. I, 98.

[100] Joseph Pennell, *Royal Society of Arts. Cantor Lectures on Artistic Lithography* (London, 1914), 9.

[101] Twyman, *Lithography*, 128–9: 'The surface was merely scraped away and, providing this was not done too deeply, it could be drawn on again with the pen or brush.'

[102] Michel de Certeau, *The Practice of Everyday Life* (Berkeley and Los Angeles, CA, [1984] 2011), Vol. I, xii–xiii.

[103] Michel de Certeau, *Culture in the Plural*, trans. Tom Conley (Minneapolis, MN and London, [1974] 1997), 49.

the nineteenth and twentieth centuries, where senders commonly underlined key words in printed poems, in order to highlight the most important sentiments.[104]

As Valentine's Day boomed as a love industry, manufacturers created elaborate new designs to draw in consumers, such as 'flower cage' cards—also termed 'cobweb', 'beehive', and 'birdcage' cards—which were especially popular between *c.*1815 and *c.*1830. A circle of paper was hand painted with naturalistic designs of flowers, birds, butterflies, doves, and country cottages, and cut in a lattice pattern. A string in the centre of the lattice could then be lifted to form a domed 'cage', revealing a hidden image. The latticed circle was then affixed to paper decorated with hand-painted borders, embossed love poems, and romantic motifs. Manufacturers included H. Dobbs and Co, who began trading as stationers, engravers, and fancy paper manufacturers at 8 New Bridge Street in Blackfriars in 1803, and were later appointed ornamental stationers to the king.[105] Flower cages patented by Dobbs include a rose (*c.*1813–16), a cherub in a rose (1816), and parrot tulip and moss rose (1819), all affixed to paper embossed by the paper manufacturers Pine, Smith & Allnutt, later Smith & Allnutt, of Loose in Kent.[106] Such items were painstakingly designed and assembled by manufacturers, and purchased by lovers for their novelty, the quality of the workmanship, and fashionable design.

Embossed paper borders and ornamental lace paper added to the luxurious feel of valentines as desirable consumer objects. As the cultural theorist Barry Shank has argued, these features together offered 'delicacy, refinement, and complexity' to consumers.[107] The first English patent for producing embossed paper was granted to the Birmingham die-engraver and coin manufacturer John Gregory Hancock in 1796. (Embossing is a form of relief printing, where a design is impressed into paper blind [without ink].[108] The technique involves putting pressure onto paper placed on an engraved metal die, thus requiring higher-quality paper that can withstand the additional force.[109]) Embossed paper featured declarations of love in French such as 'Je Blesse Mais J'Attache' ('I wound but I attach'), mimicking inscriptions on porcelain toys. Embossed harps, violins, and frolicking cupids clearly demarcated these items as tokens of love.[110] Producers also experimented with lace paper, where sections of the paper were perforated, as in the roundels framing John Fairburn's printed valentine card in Figure 4.6. One early example postmarked

---

[104] Barry Shank, *A Token of My Affection: Greeting Cards and American Business Culture* (New York and Chichester, 2004), 236.

[105] Embossed draft trade card of 'Dobbs and Company', Heal, 111.52, BM; embossed draft trade card of 'Henry Dobbs', 1760–1818, D,2.423, BM; embossed draft trade card of 'Henry Dobbs', 1760–1818, D,2.588, BM; embossed draft trade card for the 'Patent Paper Manufactory' at No. 8 New Bridge Street, D,2.484, BM.

[106] Flower cage card of a rose marked 'Dobb's Patent', 1813–16, A28549/53, Museum of London; flower cage card of a cupid in a rose, watermarked Smith & Allnutt, 1816, 1981.1136.529, MET; flower cage of a parrot tulip and moss rose, marked 'Dobbs Patent', paper watermarked Smith & Allnutt, 1819, 1981.1136.525, MET.

[107] Shank, *A Token of My Affection*, 57.

[108] The technique is also known by the French term *gaufrage*. See Lambert, *Prints*, 37.

[109] Staff, *The Valentine and its Origins*, 42; Shank, *A Token of My Affection*, 56.

[110] Embossed valentine stamped 'Dobb's patent', 1814, E.1534–1929, V&A; embossed flower cage card, *c.*1820, OB1995.28, TPM.

1802 uses a lace paper border to frame a print of Bartolozzi's *The Marriage of Cupid and Psyche* (1789–90), enhancing the artistic merit of the valentine as an aesthetically beautiful consumer object.[111]

The story of Valentine's Day over the long eighteenth century is not simply a linear narrative of change; the increasing popularity of valentines designed and produced by manufacturers also encouraged a concomitant boom in homemade cards. Schmidt has argued that 'exposure to new commercial products sparked an imaginative engagement with unwonted rituals and a proliferation, even an invention, of a new artefact—the homemade valentine.'[112] I argue here that homemade valentines did not represent the invention of new artefacts, but rather a reinvigoration of traditions dating back to the mid-eighteenth century. These homemade tokens repeated romantic verse such as 'if you take it in disdain I pray return it back again' first used in valentines at least seventy years earlier.[113] In 1811–14, the schoolmaster William Spencer sent his future wife Harriet Holmes a hand-drawn acrostic poem spelling out her name in elaborate gothic calligraphy. Above is a watercolour of the goddess plenty (as in Figure 4.6), and below a young woman (perhaps intended to represent Harriet) carving a poem about friendship in stone.[114] As this chapter has shown, the exchange of homemade acrostics was a standard part of the material culture of courtship in Georgian England. As in the new types of gifts studied in the first part of this chapter, the overarching shift was towards more goods, and more choice, for lovers as consumers.

CONCLUSION

This chapter has presented the long eighteenth century as an important transitional period in the modernization and commercialization of romantic customs. The era saw the emergence of new consumer objects exchanged by courting couples, including Indian muslins, printed sheet music, watch-papers, and porcelain toys such as patch boxes. It also witnessed the uneven spread of literacy, fuelling the popularity of books and epistolary paraphernalia as romantic gifts. However, this is not to say that older customs were swept away, as gifts such as letters, locks of hair, and rings maintained their symbolic and emotional power to bind a couple together. Rather, these traditional gifts were augmented with new consumer objects and souvenirs specifically designed with lovers in mind. The printed valentine was part of a new economy of love, where courting couples could choose among an ever-greater selection of goods. Like Bartolozzi's engraving described at the beginning of this chapter, love had become a booming marketplace, where gilded, painted, and latticed gifts provided couples with fashionable new ways to formulate their emotions and declare their love.

---

[111] Staff, *The Valentine and its Origins*, Fig. 32, 36.

[112] Schmidt, 'The Fashioning of a Modern Holiday', 218.

[113] Folded heart-shaped valentine created as part of a lottery, *c.*1750, X54/1, Cornwall Record Office, Truro; unfinished puzzle purse, *c.*1820, HMU 1/1/3, ESRO.

[114] Acrostic valentine from Spencer to Holmes, 1811–14, E.1206–1935, V&A.

Consumer objects clearly made emotionally valuable gifts, which were regularly exchanged by courting couples as romantic offerings. How did these objects accrue emotional value? Objects could be rendered particularly meaningful gifts by their high cost and status as exotic luxury goods (like furs or Indian muslins). They might be valued for their exquisite craftsmanship (by makers such as H. Dobbs & Co or the Chelsea Porcelain Manufactory). Gifts often drew upon the symbolic imagery of romantic love, reproducing images of hearts, flowers, lovebirds, cherubs, cupids, churches, faithful dogs, country cottages, and lovers in bucolic scenery. Consumer objects sent as gifts might be particularly thoughtful (to encourage the recipient's passion for reading, writing, or knitting). They might take on new meanings as one smaller component of a wide-ranging assortment of fashionable goods sent as love tokens.

Such objects held particular value if they had been adapted or modified by senders in some way, in order to render them unique. Items such as snuffboxes could be personalized using inset portraits, initials, and the dates of exchange. Books took on new meanings as gifts through carefully chosen sections underlined by hand, while watch papers and printed valentines could be embellished with hand-written inscriptions. These interventions by the buyer or sender transformed generic objects into gifts that were quite literally one of a kind. As new cultures of consumption generated new types of romantic gift, lovers adapted these objects in innovative ways in order to appropriate them as tokens of love. Returning to Arjun Appadurai's work on commodities discussed at the beginning of this chapter, a card may be generic, but once it bears the mark of my hand, and has been inscribed with personally chosen messages, its meaning is transformed as *my* card.

Valentines often mused in symbol and verse on the wounds caused by love, which could ensnare, enchain, cut, pierce, and break the heart. Many examples, like the token created for a lottery in Figure 4.5, literally came in the form of fragile paper hearts to be unfurled by recipients. Each of the men and women studied in this book was acutely aware of the possibility that a loved one might reject their advances and disdain their precious gifts. Moreover, the emotional meanings of love tokens once accepted did not last forever, but changed markedly once a relationship came to an end. Many courtships in Georgian England did not conclude at the altar, but in drooping spirits and distraction, chasing the 'nauseous letters' and tokens once sent in pursuit of matrimony.[115] It is to the end of courtship, and the torment of love, that this book now turns.

---

[115] William Bell to Catherine 'Kitty' Williamson, London, 28 December 1743, M/10/3/3, BAS.

5

Romantic Suffering

Heart-ach. *n. s.* [*heart* and *ach.*] Sorrow; pang; anguish of mind.

Heart-break. *n. s.* [*heart* and *break.*] Overpowering sorrow.

Heart-burned. *adj.* [*heart* and *burn.*] Having the heart inflamed.

Heart-rending. *adj.* Killing with anguish.

Heart-sick. *adj.* 1. Pained in mind.

                2. Mortally ill; hurt in the constitution.

Heart-sore. *n. s.* Struck with sorrow.

Heart-wounded. *adj.* Filled with passion of love or grief.

When Samuel Johnson published the first edition of his *Dictionary of the English Language* in 1755, it contained twenty-four separate terms prefixed with the word 'heart', extending over three columns of his book. The dictionary featured adjectives such as 'heart-rending' and 'heart-wounded' to describe being consumed by love, grief, and anguish, and nouns such as 'heart-sore' to characterize those who were 'Struck with sorrow'. A striking number of terms involved the torment of love, imagined through emotive words such as 'heart-robbing' and 'heart-burned'.[1] The anguished terminology of heartbreak was almost granted the same precedence as love itself. The pervasive presence of the language and archetypes of the broken-hearted demonstrates the contemporary obsession with tormented lovers and their sick, sore, wounded, and breaking hearts.

Courting couples were painfully aware that matrimony was by no means a fait accompli, with a significant proportion of relationships stalling before they reached the altar. In the aftermath of a failed relationship, unmarried women routinely retrieved and destroyed their love letters in order to protect their reputation and erase the memory of romantic hurt. Letters of the women Anne Louisa Dalling (*c.*1784–1853) and Lady Elizabeth Grey (1798–1880), studied in this chapter, were both destroyed. Thankfully for historians, precious letters have survived from Anne and Elizabeth's suitors, siblings, and parents. Mary Berry (1763–1852) never married after her unsuccessful courtship and opted not to destroy her missives, but 'sealed up' the correspondence to reread four decades later, in the belief that 'some feelings, in some minds are indelible.'[2] These letters are analysed alongside substantial cultural commentary found in conduct literature, medical treatises, criminal trials, novels, poems, ballads, songs, plays, and prints.

[1] Johnson, *Dictionary*, Vol. I, 1025–6.
[2] Note by Mary Berry, October 1844, Add MS 37727, f. 193r, BL.

Nine troubled courtships form the heart of this chapter. After battling familial opposition for a decade, Captain Henry Smith (1723–94) secretly married the tailor's daughter Sarah Hurst by licence in 1762, while the Reverend Edward Leathes (1747–88) eloped with the rector's daughter Elizabeth Reading (1748–1815) in 1774. The Reverend Charles Powlett and vicar's daughter Anne Temple managed to overcome parental objections to marry in 1796, once Charles had secured an income of £400 per year. The remaining six couples engaged in fraught and ultimately unsuccessful relationships; after the death of Edward Leathes in 1788, Elizabeth married her childhood sweetheart Edward Peach (d. 1805) in 1790, only to separate four years later. Mary Berry was deserted by her fiancé Lieutenant-General Charles O'Hara (*c.*1740–1802) in 1796, while Anne Louisa Dalling's fiancé Sir Gilbert Stirling (*c.*1779–1843) 'disappeared' in 1805 just hours before their wedding. Jane Townley ceased contact with her admirer Richard Law as she devoted herself to the prophetess Joanna Southcott (1750–1814), causing him to pursue her angrily between 1807 and 1822. Charlotte Lambourne repeatedly turned down the surgeon John Dewey (b. *c.* 1788) between 1809 and 1816, as she was his senior and possessed no fortune. Unfortunately for John, his protestations that this was a 'fortunate circumstance' went unheeded.[3] Finally, John Kerr, Earl of Ancram (1794–1841) was forced to break off his engagement to Lady Elizabeth Grey in 1823 after his father declared his opposition to the match.

This chapter represents the first dedicated study of tortuous and terminated courtships in Georgian England. It is divided into five sections. The first explores how courting couples conceptualized their romantic suffering using the language of the heart. The second presents Armida, Queen Dido, and Ophelia as archetypal victims of love in popular culture. The third and fourth sections trace an important emotional shift from the mid-eighteenth century, where women in the popular imagination wasted away from love due to their tender and feeling hearts, and men became associated with the violent masculinized act of suicide. The final section charts the breakdown of courtships through the return of letters and tokens. The chapter asks, how did courting couples understand and enact romantic suffering? How were relationships deconstructed in words and objects? What were the anticipated and actual consequences when courtship went wrong?

BREAKING THE HEART

Men and women navigating the ecstasy and dejection of courtship conceptualized their emotional states using the language of the heart, which was presented as wounded, dying, and breaking from the high passions of love. Hearts in love did not suddenly break, but went through a number of distinct phases. These began when the heart was cut or pierced by love, pulling on the heartstrings once a person was

---

[3] Copy of letter from Dewey to Lambourne, Letter book, undated (*c.*June 1811), 32M77/F/C30, f. 16, HRO.

consumed with feeling. Continued suffering from love resulted in disease or damage to the heart, which had been left vulnerable to attack. The final stage of lovers' distress was the breaking or death of the heart, which represented the ultimate sign of romantic suffering.

The initial damage to a lover's heart was caused by a metaphorical weapon such as an arrow, dart, or dagger which was said to cut, prick, or pierce the organ. The injuries caused by these pointed weapons signified the beginning of love whilst also foreshadowing the heart's destruction. As an anonymous butler wrote to a housekeeper in the same residence in Norfolk *c.*1830, 'there is a chain of love / Fast in the middle of my heart / I have stricken a Fatal dart / From whence fresh showers of blood did flow.'[4] The symbolism of the wounded heart was shaped by competing religious and classical discourses, centring on the spear which pierced the heart of Jesus and the arrows fired by Venus' son Cupid, which inspired love in unsuspecting individuals. Troubadours signalled the beginning of love by declaring that 'I have an arrow in my heart.'[5] Heroines such as Dido were metaphorically transformed into deers pierced by the arrows of love. Virgil's *Æneid* used the metaphor to characterize Dido falling in love, wandering 'all through the city in her misery, / Raving mad, / like a doe pierced by an arrow / Deep in the woods of Crete...as she runs all through the Dictaean forest / The lethal shaft clings to her flank.'[6] The unfortunate 'Bess of Bedlam' was also wounded by venomous arrows, decrying 'How sharp's the pointed arrow / which flew at my poor breast!'[7]

Once the initial wound had been made to a lover's heart, they were vulnerable to becoming diseased or plagued by love. Ballads such as 'Phillida Flouts Me' (*c.*1600) likened love to a fatal plague, wailing 'Oh what a Plague is Love / I cannot bear it.' The ballad remained popular throughout the eighteenth century, and was republished in numerous poetic compendiums.[8] The embittered suitor Richard Law described his heart as 'plagued' by the actions of his intended Jane Townley in November 1817, cruelly addressing her as 'thou inveterate Plague of my heart'.[9] Richard's furious epistles reveal that his anger stemmed from being forced to remain a bachelor despite having found a perfectly suitable wife. He spitefully ranted, 'come come dont puff yourself up about your Virginity, it is through such proud insolent conceited Nuns as you, That many a brave and proper man goes Wifeless and Childless to the Grave.'[10]

[4] Copy of letter from a butler to a housekeeer, watermark 1830, BUL 13/5, 619 × 5, NRO.

[5] Sordello (*c.*1200–*c.*70), 'Tant m'abellis lo terminis novels', in Eric Jager, *The Book of the Heart* (London, 2000), 69.

[6] Virgil, *Æneid* (29–19 BC), Book IV, 79.

[7] *Captain Wedderburn's courtship to Lord Roslin's daughter. to which is added, Bess of Bedlam* (Glasgow, 1780), 7.

[8] See, for example, George Ellis, *Specimens of the early English poets* (London, 1790), 317–20 and *The poetical epitome* (London, 1791 and 1792), 414–5.

[9] Law to Townley, 13 November 1817, Add MS 47796, f. 48r, BL.

[10] Ibid., Marylebone, 1816, Add MS 47796, f. 3r, BL.

For women such as the tailor's daughter Sarah Hurst, the trauma of love was enough to 'rend my Heart strings to part'.[11] Such terminology was part of the legacy of ancient conceptions of anatomy, where the tendons or nerves were thought to brace and sustain the heart.[12] As the dissenting minister Abraham Taylor preached in his treatise of 1730, when 'our heartstrings break, if we rely on Christ by faith, we may have abundant support'.[13] The heart's 'strings' rose to new prominence under the culture of sensibility, with the heart conceived of as a musical instrument with strings that vibrated with feeling. Heartstrings provided evidence of a person's delicate sensibility and the exquisite sensitivity of their nerves.[14] Richardson's heroine Pamela used a psalm to describe the struggle to protect her virtue, which left her 'Heart strings almost broke'.[15] The heart's 'strings' were seen to throb, burst, or break from the high passions of love. In *As you like it, a poem, addressed to a friend* (1785), the muse experienced 'Her heartstrings throbbing' while the protagonist of 'Quashiba's Return' (1791) described how 'my heartstrings were rent into twain' as Quashiba had wronged him.[16] Sarah Hurst's description of the parting strings of her heart was thus an indication of her emotional sensitivity, indicating the fragility of her heart in coping with her faltering relationship.

The final stage of a lover's sorrow was the breaking or death of the heart, which only happened when lovers believed they would part for good. When Sarah Hurst feared that her suitor would never return from sea in 1759, she wrote 'my fears hourly increase on his account, my heart dies within me.'[17] Sarah may have been influenced by the book of Samuel in the Old Testament, where the foolish Nabal's 'heart died within him' as he was avenged by God.[18] The expression may also have arisen from ballads such as 'Phillida Flouts Me', where the hero described how love 'so Torments my mind / that my heart faileth'.[19] The breaking of the heart was such a serious occurrence that many ballads were dedicated to the *possibility* that it might break, with one man who 'thought that my Heart would been broken' when he witnessed his sweetheart marrying another, and an additional suitor whose heart was 'ready to break', but not actually doing so. The same discourse was used in the letters of the reverend's daughter Elizabeth Reading in 1772, after Elizabeth's father insisted she break off her courtship with Edward Leathes following reports of his bad character. The next day, an exculpatory letter from Edward provided a 'healing Balm' to her 'almost broken heart'.[20] The important terms here were

[11] Diary of Hurst, 29 April 1759, MS 3542, HM.

[12] 'Heart-strings, *n.*', *OEDO*, http://www.oed.com/view/Entry/85134?redirectedFrom=heartstrings.

[13] Abraham Taylor, *A practical treatise of saving faith* (London, 1730), 318.

[14] Ann Jessie van Sant, *Eighteenth-Century Sensibility and the Novel: The Senses in Social Context* (Cambridge, 2004), 9–12.

[15] Richardson, *Pamela*, 141.

[16] *As you like it, a poem, addressed to a friend* (London, 1785), 10; 'Quashiba's Return', in *The attic miscellany; and characteristic mirror of men and things* (London, 1791), 416–17.

[17] Diary of Hurst, 24 September 1759, MS3542, HM.   [18] Samuel 1:25, 1:37, KJV.

[19] 'Phillida Flouts Me', in misc. poems on love and marriage by Princess Amelia, MSS Vol. 14, LWL.

[20] 'THE FORLORN LOVER', *c.*1730–69, C.20, f.9 (324–5), EBBA; 'Sweet WILLIAM of Plymouth', *c.*1736–63, C.20, f.9 (332–3), EBBA; Reading to Leathes, 4 November 1772, BOL 2/4/18, NRO.

'thought', 'almost', and 'ready', as these texts hinted at heartbreak in order to reveal the severity of a lover's troubles.

While eighteenth-century hearts were frequently wounded or broken, they were rarely described to be 'aching'. The most famous description of 'heartache' was created by Shakespeare, where Hamlet describes 'The Heart-ache and the thousand natural shocks...To sleep? perchance to dream; ay, there's the rub.'[21] The aching heart was mentioned in passing by the tailor's daughter Sarah Hurst in August 1759, as she wondered 'how many thousand heartachs [*sic*] do we experience to one satisfaction.' These 'heartaches' referred to the difficulties of selecting a spouse, after her friend Miss Pigott expressed her determination to marry.[22] However, when conceptualizing her changing emotional state, Sarah preferred to describe 'a palpitation' and 'tumult' in her heart, which caused a violent pain in her 'side'.[23] Lieutenant-General Charles O'Hara made a similar formulation in 1795, promising to 'sooth' [*sic*] Mary Berry's 'throbbing breast'.[24] Whilst a 'heartache' denoted a particular difficulty encountered by a couple, their emotional troubles were thus conceptualized as a 'tumult', 'throbbing', and 'pain'. This distinction was reflected in printed texts in the late eighteenth century, where heartache could be caused by any unfortunate event, not necessarily romantic strife.[25] The term only acquired its modern connotations in the early nineteenth century, when heartache came to denote a pain specifically caused by love. By the early Victorian era, the aching heart had been granted 'a priori involvement' in a vast network of cultural and literary references, simultaneously reflecting growing disquiet about 'heartsickness', murmurs, and heart disease.[26]

ARCHETYPES OF HEARTBREAK

Cultural understandings of heartbreak were shaped by archetypal heroines such as Armida, Queen Dido, and Ophelia, against which new characters such as Richardson's Olivia and Clarissa were measured. These figures achieved new prominence with the growing cultural dominance of female romantic strife towards the mid-eighteenth century. Women's death from love represents the reversal of an earlier trend, as until the Renaissance lovesickness was predominantly seen as a male illness.[27]

---

[21] *The Works of Shakespear* (London, 1725), 400.

[22] Diary of Hurst, 12 August 1759, MS 3544, HM.

[23] Ibid., October 1758, 18 January 1759, 8 February 1759, and 16 March 1759, MS 3542, HM. The sailor William Bell similarly described a 'tumult in my Breast' when he feared his sweetheart Kitty had forsaken him: 22 August 1743, M/10/3/2, BAS.

[24] Charles O'Hara to Mary Berry, Portsmouth, 31 October 1795, Add MS 37727, f. 232v, BL.

[25] For example, see the conversation about heartache between Ned Shuter and Harry Howard in *The adventures of a hackney coach* (London, 1781), 124.

[26] Kirstie Blair, '"Proved on the Pulses": Heart Disease in Victorian Culture, 1830–1860', in *Framing and Imagining Disease in Cultural History*, ed. George Rousseau, Miranda Gill, David Haycock, and Malte Herwig (Basingstoke, 2003), 285–302, at 286–7.

[27] Dawson, *Lovesickness and Gender*, 3.

These three women emerge from contemporary literary, visual, and material culture as the quintessential figures invoked to represent romantic suffering.

The dominant examples of heartbreak were re-packaged and re-presented from classical and Shakespearean texts. As the periodical *The Adventurer* complained in 1766, 'every exasperated hero must rage like ACHILLES, and every afflicted widow mourn like ANDROMACHE: an abandoned ARMIDA will make use of DIDO's execrations.'[28] Such texts provided centuries-old guidance on how a broken-hearted person should act, outlining social expectations of the deserted lover. If you did not sigh, faint, cry, and court death, could you really claim to be broken-hearted? Interpretations of particular figures changed over time, with Armida's wrath, Dido's suicide, and Ophelia's distraction reinterpreted by each generation in light of contemporary beliefs about love, femininity, masculinity, and madness.

Armida was a beautiful Princess and sorceress who fell in love with the Christian hero Rinaldo in Torquato Tasso's epic poem *Gerusalemme Liberata* (1581), set during the First Crusade. The celebrated poem was published in six new editions over the eighteenth century, inspiring Handel's opera *Rinaldo* in 1711, *Armida; A Serious Opera* in 1774, and *Rinaldo; A New Serious Opera* in 1780. The romance was also immortalized in commemorative figurines produced by the Derby and Staffordshire manufactories, to decorate the houses of the wealthy and, increasingly, the middling sorts.[29] In the tale, Armida lured Rinaldo to her enchanted island, on which she had concealed a sumptuous 'magic grove' within a labyrinth. The grove bloomed in eternal spring, with every leaf suffused with love.[30] Once inside the grove, Rinaldo became intoxicated by Armida's love magic. He was eventually rescued by his fellow soldiers—brought to his senses by their dazzling armour—and returned to war to fulfil his Christian duties.[31] The furious Armida was left deserted, summoning deities from Hell to destroy her magical palace and gardens.

While Georgian audiences praised Armida for her beauty, they disapproved of the 'strange coquetry' of her love. In contrast, the love of Princess Erminia (or Herminie) of Antioch was praised as 'a soft and agreeable tenderness'.[32] Armida thus posed a challenge to Georgian conceptions of the 'soft' and meek woman in love, due to her 'artful and violent' tendencies. Still, 'All the world' agreed that 'nothing is painted with so much art as the coquetry of Armida; and that nothing is so tender as her love, so animated, moving, and touching as her complaints.'[33] Novels such as Richardson's *Sir Charles Grandison* (1753–4) resolved these tensions by presenting Armida as a victim of her passion:

[28] John Hawkesworth, *The Adventurer* (London, 1766), Vol. II, 228–9.

[29] Porcelain figurines, Derby Porcelain Factory, 1770–84, 1959,1102.117, BM; earthenware figurines, Staffordshire, 1791–5, C.61–2001, V&A.

[30] *Jerusalem Delivered; An Heroic Poem: Translated from the Italian of Torquato Tasso, by John Hoole*, fourth edition (London, 1772), Vol. II, Book XIV, 89.

[31] *Temple spectacles! By the author of The prelateiad* (Dublin, 1789), 8; *Jerusalem Delivered*, Book XVI, 117.

[32] *Anecdotes of polite literature* (London, 1764), Vol. I, 88, 97–8; *Temple spectacles!*, 8; Hugh Blair, *Lectures on rhetoric and belles lettres*, Vol. III (London, 1785), 268–9.

[33] Hugh Blair, *Essays on Rhetoric, Abridged Chiefly From Dr. Blair's Lectures on that Science*, fourth edition (London, 1801), 298, 266; *Anecdotes of polite literature*, Vol. I, 97–8.

had Sir Charles Grandison been a man capable of taking advantage of the violence of a Lady's passion for him, the unhappy Olivia would not have scrupled, great, haughty, and noble, as she is, by birth and fortune, to have been his, without conditions… Had Sir Charles been a Rinaldo, Olivia had been an Armida.

Women in the novel expressed sympathy for 'The poor Olivia! If I see her sad and afflicted, how I shall pity her!'[34] *Rinaldo; A New Serious Opera* also emphasized Armida's feeling heart, with the sorceress beseeching the audience 'What shall I do? A disappointed love who can endure? / Such as have feeling hearts, they best can tell; The wheel, the stone, the vulture, I am sure, / Can't torture with such pain the damn'd in hell.'[35]

The plight of Queen Dido of Carthage was even more ubiquitous. Dido's tragic romance with Æneas was dramatized in the fourth book of Virgil's *Æneid* (29–19 BC), the seventh of Ovid's *Heroides* (*c.*20–13 BC), Christopher Marlowe's play *Dido, Queen of Carthage* (1594), and Henry Purcell and Nahum Tate's opera *Dido and Æneas* (1688). In the tale, Dido fell in love with the Trojan prince Æneas when his ship landed at Carthage. She was distraught when Æneas was called by the Gods to fulfil his duty in Italy, leading her to stab herself atop a funeral pyre as she could not bear to live without him. Ballads such as 'The Wandering Prince of Troy' (1763–75) dramatized her plight:

> And then the Queen with bloody knife,
> Aimd at her heart as hard as stone;
> Yet somewhat loath to lose her life,
> Unto herself did make great moan;
> And rolling on her careful bed,
> With sighs and sobs these words she said,
>
> O wretched Dido Queen, quoth she,
> I see thy end approaching near;
> For he is gone away from thee.
> Whom thou dost love and hold so dear!
> Is he then gone and passed by?
> O heart, prepare thyself to die.[36]

Eighteenth-century accounts of Dido's death emphasized her 'sighs and sobs', symptoms of love which had become requisite features of feeling under the cult of sensibility. The Georgian Dido was representative of broken-hearted women as a whole, as she suffered more from love than Æneas and was too emotionally fragile to cope with her disappointment.

Dido was invoked as the archetypal heartbroken heroine in best-selling novels such as Richardson's *Clarissa*, with the rake Lovelace asking his friend John Belford,

---

[34] Samuel Richardson, *The History of Sir Charles Grandison, In a Series of Letters*, sixth edition (London, [1753–4] 1770), 172–3.

[35] *Rinaldo; A New Serious Opera* (London, 1780), 34.

[36] 'An Excellent OLD BALLAD, entitled, / The Wandering PRINCE of TROY', London, 1763–75, C.20, f.9 (730–1), EBBA.

Dost thou not think that I am as much entitled to forgiveness on Miss Harlowe's account, as Virgil's hero was on Queen Dido's?...Should Miss Harlowe even break her heart (which Heaven forbid!) for the usage she has received...what comparison will *her* fate hold to Queen Dido's? And have I half the obligation to her that Aeneas had to the Queen of Carthage?[37]

The eighteenth-century Dido was thus comparable to Richardson's languishing heroine for falling prey to men's scheming, dying 'a victim to her love'. As the novelist Mary Hays wrote to her suitor John Eccles in 1779, 'think of the baseness, the ingratitude of Eneas, who treacherously deserted a queen, who had sacrificed her honour, her happiness, her all, for him.'[38] Richardson's vulnerable Dido stands in stark contrast to the passionate Dido of classical texts. As the Greek author Apollonius Rhodius argued, 'Dido destroys herself through disappointment; too generally experienced by mankind from the prevalence of ungoverned passion.'[39] Rhodius' account reflects the classical belief that women's physical weakness made them less able to control violent passions than men. As Faramerz Dabhoiwala has argued, this view began to change in the late seventeenth century and was 'already well advanced' with the publication of novels such as *Pamela* and *Clarissa* in the mid-eighteenth century.[40] Eighteenth-century texts also marginalized the violence of Dido's suicide, which was at odds with notions of 'tender' and 'sensitive' Georgian women. Rather, writers attributed Dido's bravery to the overtly masculine side of her personality, with Adam Alexander's *Classical Biography* (1800) reminding readers that 'Elisa was her proper name; she was called Dido from her masculine courage.'[41]

Continuing fascination with Dido inspired countless paintings and prints of the queen, including Henry Fuseli's monumental *Dido* (1781), Joshua Reynolds' *The Death of Dido* (c.1775–81), and James Gillray's satirical *Dido Forsaken* (1787) and *Dido, in Despair!* (1801), which presented the deserted Emma Hamilton as the queen. Francesco Bartolozzi's etching in Figure 5.1 depicts Dido fainting with grief atop a funeral pyre, as women weep and pray around her. The sentimentalized scene features no blood or even a fatal wound, despite the dagger sitting beneath Dido's right hand. Bartolozzi's romanticized image is reminiscent of Clarissa's deathbed scene, where the heroine lies 'fainting away' with her head sinking back on her pillow, surrounded by mourners in 'speechless sorrow'.[42] Dido's tragic love affair had an enduring presence in popular culture, and was represented in material culture through wall hangings, watch cases, and cups and saucers depicting her first meeting with Æneas.[43] In this cultural context, women navigating the emotional

---

[37] Richardson, *Clarissa*, L370, 1142.

[38] Hays to Eccles, 31 August 1779 in Wedd, ed., *Love-Letters of Mary Hays*, 66.

[39] See Apollonius Rhodius, *The Argonautic Expedition* (London, 1780), Vol. I, 128; *The Arcana of polite literature* (Dublin, 1789), 24–5.

[40] Dabhoiwala, *The Origins of Sex*, 142.

[41] Adam Alexander, *Classical Biography* (Edinburgh, 1800), 159.

[42] Richardson, *Clarissa*, L481, 1362.

[43] Embroidered wall hanging, 1710–20, T.570–1996, V&A; embossed gold pair case, c.1730, 288–1854, V&A; stoneware cup and saucer, William Turner & Co, c.1803–6, 2516&A-1901, V&A.

Fig. 5.1. Francesco Bartolozzi after Giovanni Battista Cipriani, *Dido, supported on a pyre by a woman wearing a veil and diadem, fainting with grief, a dagger at her side, an old woman standing behind to left and weeping women gathered on the right*, Britain, 1778, etching and engraving, 46.6 cm × 54.5 cm on sheet, British Museum, London, 1887,0722.173. © The Trustees of the British Museum, All Rights Reserved.

experience of courtship seized upon Dido as proof of female sensitivity to and suffering from love, and a warning to beware the guiles of deceitful men.[44]

Shakespeare's Ophelia provided a further archetype of female suffering from love, with countless songs and poems describing her heart as 'sway'd by tenderness' and 'soften'd into Love'.[45] In the sentimental novel *Reuben, or, The Suicide* (1787), the protagonist meets a farmer's daughter named Ophelia who loved a faithless man 'to distraction'. Dressed in a straw hat, she sings a 'pathetic air' about lost love.[46] John Hamilton Mortimer's etching in Figure 5.2 depicts a distracted Ophelia with a crown of weeds and flowers woven into her unruly hair. She isolates herself by half-turning her back on viewers, and is dressed in loose white robes, which subsequently pull her to her death when she falls into the brook. Elaine Showalter has presented Ophelia as the 'supremely manipulable' heroine, allowing

---

[44] See Hays to Eccles, 31 August 1779, in Wedd, ed., *Love-Letters of Mary Hays*, 66.

[45] 'Ophelia', in *Apollo's Cabinet: or the muses delight* (Liverpool, 1757), 215; *The belles of Bury, a poem* (Bury, 1779), 15–16; Lady Sophia Burrell, *Poems. Dedicated to the Right Honourable the Earl of Mansfield* (London, 1793), Vol. II, 101–2.

[46] *Reuben, or, The Suicide* (London, 1787), Vol. I, 141–8.

Fig. 5.2. John Hamilton Mortimer, *Ophelia*, Britain, 1775, etching, plate 40.4 cm × 32.7 cm, The Metropolitan Museum of Art, New York, 62.557.202.

Georgian audiences to dismiss the 'erotic and discordant elements' of her character. Instead, they chose to see her as a young, innocent, harmless, pious and beautiful victim.[47] She was variously described as 'fair', 'very pathetic', and 'poor Ophelia'.[48] While writers emphasized the intensity of Armida and Dido's passion compared to their suitors, they also described Ophelia's love as all-encompassing, whereas 'Hamlet's love forms so trifling [a] part of the piece, that it cannot be regarded in that light.'[49]

The enduring influence of Ophelia was reflected in characters such as 'Bess of Bedlam', who was 'cloath'd in her Rags and Folly', roaming the countryside 'to cure her Lovesick Melancholy'. Bess was tormented by visions of her deceased lover with 'flaming Eyes', hoping to 'lay me down and dye'. She was first immortalized

[47] Elaine Showalter, *The Female Malady: Women, Madness and English Culture, 1830–1980* (London, 1985), 10–11. Also see Helen Small, *Love's Madness: Medicine, The Novel, and Female Insanity 1800–1865* (Oxford, 1996), 8–14.
[48] 'Ophelia', in *Ancient songs, from the time of King Henry the Third, to the Revolution* (London, 1790), lxix; Robert Bage, *The fair Syrian. A novel* (Dublin, 1787), Vol. I, 149, and *his Mount Henneth; a novel* (London, 1788), Vol. I, 10.
[49] *Anecdotes of polite literature*, 53.

in song by Henry Purcell, and remained a popular figure in songs throughout the eighteenth century, rolling her eyeballs while embracing a phantasmal lover.[50] Lady Clementina della Porretta in Richardson's *Sir Charles Grandison* was similarly left 'wild and disordered' after being deserted by the novel's hero, crying and continuously looking around for him.[51] 'Crazy Kate' was a madwoman in the same mould, created by William Cowper in 1785 and depicted by Henry Fuseli in 1807. Like Ophelia, her 'entire existence' was 'defined by romantic matters', which were 'enough to unhinge her entirely'.[52] These female figures shaped popular understandings of how a disappointed lover should (and should not) behave and wider perceptions of the consequences of failed relationships for courting women.

MAIDS WHO DIED FOR LOVE

On the cover of Robert Burton's *Anatomy of Melancholy* (1621), the melancholic lover was depicted as a man. Numerous heroic suitors emerge from Restoration literature suffering in pursuit of unattainable women. In Aphra Behn's translation of 'The Land of Love' (1684), the enterprising Lysander diverts his course from the country of Content to the alluring Isle of Love. He is soon left shivering and feverish by the onset of his love for Aminta. As he travels through the villages of Inquietude, Hope, and Declaration, his callous 'conqueror' retreats to The Den of Cruelty. The fainting hero entreats readers, 'Must we eternal Martyrdom pursue? / Must we still love, and always suffer too?'[53] The vituperative tract *Love given over: or, a Satyr against the Pride, Lust and Inconstancy, &c. of Woman* (1690) told a similar tale of a hero rescued from the 'vile Slav'ry' of his love for 'Faithless *Sylvia*'.[54] By the mid-eighteenth century, the rise of sensibility meant that the reign of the troubadours was over, as suffering from love had become a uniquely female domain. As the century drew to a close, lovers' melancholy, lovesickness, and hysteria each became principally female diseases, entrenching the view that women suffered more acutely from romantic hurt.

The resurgence of lovesickness during the 1750s was attributed to women's heightened sensibility and physical frailty. The languishing lovesick woman acquired increasing notoriety in popular culture, becoming the subject of numerous poems, ballads, and novels. These identified the ailment with 'poor' or 'silly' women, such as 'Poor Peg' (1794) who was 'heart-rent by a sigh of woe' and died after her lover

---

[50] Henry Purcell, 'Bess of Bedlam', Z370 (audio recording); *A Fifth grand selection of music. As performed at the Theatre-Royal in Covent-Garden* (London, 1793), 9–11.

[51] Richardson, *Sir Charles Grandison*, 349–50.

[52] Allan Ingram with Michelle Faubert, *Cultural Constructions of Madness in Eighteenth Century Writing: Representing the Insane* (Basingstoke, 2005), 150–1.

[53] Aphra Behn, *The Land of Love. A Poem* (London, 1717), 16, 26. First published as *A Voyage to the Island of Love* in 1684, adapted from Paul Tallemant's *Le Voyage de l'isle d'Amour*.

[54] *Love given over: or, a Satyr against the Pride, Lust and Inconstancy, &c. of Woman* (London, 1690), 1.

was killed in battle.[55] Others such as 'The Lovesick Maid' (*c*.1755) could not stop sobbing and groaning after being rejected:

> O why should i commit such folly
>   or why should i so silly be.
> To set my mind and my Affections
>   upon the man that loves not me…
> Sighing, moaning, sobbing and groaning
>   sure he's ungreatful [*sic*] in every part,
> But if ever i find a man more kinder,
>   'tis him alone shall ease my heart.[56]

The poem infantilizes lovesick women by suggesting that they were naïve and governed by their affections. Similar sentiments were expressed in the epistolary novel *The history of Miss Harriot Fitzroy, and Miss Emilia Spencer* (1767) when Emilia's mother cautioned her that 'There is not, in my opinion, a more ridiculous creature in nature than a love-sick girl.' In response, Emilia 'burst into tears and left the room'. The text portrays lovesickness as a demeaning disease that women suffered from by 'nature'. It highlights the involuntary nature of their suffering, with the heartbroken Emilia exclaiming, 'What a train of vile attendants is this same love accompanied with!'[57]

As Emilia noted, once women had succumbed to lovesickness they were instantly vulnerable to a 'train' of other diseases. Female writers complained of a host of symptoms including mental agitation, disquiet, fluttering spirits, melancholy, and despondency. When Elizabeth Johnson broke off her engagement to the Bedfordshire gentleman Richard How II in 1757 after discovering he had a 'former attachment', she believed that 'It is impossible for the Human Mind to feel more distress than I am under.' Elizabeth described how 'no Heart can be more susceptible of y tenderest sensations than mine & to what Purpose but to make me unhappy!' However, she promised to 'endeavor [*sic*] to bear with resignation uncommon wretchedness'.[58] The tailor's daughter Sarah Hurst was equally distressed during her troubled courtship with Captain Henry Smith. In 1759–60, she described how the relationship had caused 'a few years spent in disquietude of Mind', leaving a 'cloud of melancholy' hanging over her which had left her mind greatly discomposed. It also caused violent headaches and fits of sickness, and she was terribly afflicted with the pain.[59] A similar account was produced by the vicar's daughter Anne Temple in 1794, writing that 'My mind is now so totally overcome that I am almost indifferent to my fate; not one ray of light is visible…I must drag on a melancholy existence at a distance from him.'[60] Four months later her situation had not improved:

---

[55] 'Poor Peg. By Mr. Dibdin', in *The Hampshire Syren*, 9–10.
[56] 'The Lovesick Maid', in *The Cautious Maid's Garland* (Bristol, *c*.1755), 4–5.
[57] *The history of Miss Harriot Fitzroy, and Miss Emilia Spencer* (Dublin, 1767), 117, 121, 123.
[58] Elizabeth Johnson to Richard How II, 22 May 1757, HW87/225, BAS.
[59] Diary of Hurst, 12 April 1759 and 25 May 1759, MS3542, 27 May 1760, MS3543, HM.
[60] Journal of Anne Temple, 29 January 1794, 72M92/5, HRO.

I never found my mind in a more uncomfortable unsettled state than it has been for this last month. Nothing amuses, nothing interests me, in short I know not what to do with myself; company only encreases [*sic*] the flutter and agitation of my spirits and yet I cannot bear to be alone, solitude makes me brood over my miseries 'till I am almost distracted. Oh! how I regret the calm serenity I once enjoyed.[61]

Female friends rallied to support others suffering from the trials of love. After Lieutenant-General Charles O'Hara broke off his engagement to Mary Berry in 1796, Mary's friend Mrs Chomeley urged her to 'rouse yourself, & do not sink under Passion & disappointment, like a common weak minded Woman!'[62] Women's descriptions of their minds as 'overcome', 'agitated', and 'weak' demonstrate how they expressed their disappointment in written form in accordance with prevailing beliefs about femininity. The symptoms they described were a requisite part of suffering from love, generated by women's perceived fragility and mental instability. A related change has been identified by Faramerz Dabhoiwala, who describes how new presumptions about sex, seduction, and the natural unchastity of men had become firmly established by the mid-eighteenth century, creating a dichotomy between 'male rapacity' and 'female passivity'.[63]

When at its most extreme, the dejection and despondency of romantic hurt could lead to hysteria, which was seen to plague 'many thousands' and even 'millions' of women.[64] The physician Charles Perry explained in 1755 how dismal passions fuelled hysteric disorders:

As women who are under the scourge and tyranny of the hysteric passion, are generally prone and subject to the more dismal irksome passions of the mind – as (for example) anger, grief, fear, despondency, &c – so those passions, and the original disease, act upon and augment each other, mutually and reciprocally.[65]

The legacy of Galenism meant that female suffering was frequently attributed to their sanguine temperaments, which made their 'sensibility, and the powers of body and mind' more 'easily excited' than men.[66] In 1784, John Aikin listed hysteria as one of eight diseases peculiar to women, which were not connected with pregnancy.[67] Over the course of the eighteenth century, the nerves were increasingly prioritized over the womb as the central cause of hysteria—weakened and debilitated by strong passions—mirroring the burgeoning role played by the nerves in the experience of lovesickness. As James Adair noted in 1772, hysteria was primarily 'a disease of the whole nervous system...as for the share the uterus has...it is often accidental'.[68]

---

    [61] Ibid., 4 May 1794, 72M92/5, HRO.
    [62] Mrs Chomeley to Berry, 20 November 1796, Add MS 37727, f. 246v, BL.
    [63] Dabhoiwala, *The Origins of Sex*, 178–9.
    [64] Charles Perry, *A mechanical account and explication of the hysteric passion, under all its various symptoms and appearances* (London, 1755), 185.
    [65] Ibid., 196.
    [66] *An account of the various systems of medicine* (London, 1788), Vol. II, 114; Perry, *A mechanical account and explication of the hysteric passion*, 191, 200.
    [67] John Aikin, *Principles of midwifery, or puerperal medicine* (Edinburgh, 1784), 54.
    [68] James Makittrick Adair, *Commentaries on the principles and practice of physic* (London, 1772), 128.

Women in love were objects of sympathy, whose misfortunes had been caused by their tender and feeling hearts. After discovering that a servant girl had fallen for her fiancé in 1772, Elizabeth Reading pitied 'the poor love stricken maiden', also expressing sympathy for a 'violently smitten...distress'd swain' in her household.[69] A similar shift took place in conceptions of madness in the late eighteenth century, when the symbolic gender of the insane shifted from the 'repulsive madman' to the 'appealing madwoman'.[70] The transformation of the suffering lover from a male to a female figure was thus part of a wider cultural shift. However, this 'degrading' change was criticized by doctors such as John Aikin, who argued in 1793 that 'shrinking timidity of mind, and excessive nicety of feeling' were 'too much encouraged under the notion of female delicacy'.[71] By the time Jane Austen's *Sense and Sensibility* was published in 1811, Marianne, Elinor, Fanny Dashwood, and Nancy Steele were each defined by their propensity for weakness, lovesickness, and hysteria. Marianne was seized by a 'death-like paleness' after receiving a letter from Willoughby, causing her sister Elinor 'such a sickness at heart as made her hardly able to hold up her head'. When they later discovered Edward Ferrars' engagement to Lucy Steele, Fanny fell into 'violent hysterics' and screamed while Nancy 'fell upon her knees, and cried bitterly'.[72]

Women were susceptible to dying from love due to their tender and feeling hearts, which were unable to cope with extreme misery. As the rector's daughter Elizabeth Reading wrote to a friend in 1774, this was not a rapid process, but a gradual 'gnawing' of gloom and despondency:

> A disappointment of this nature I look upon to be the greatest misfortune that can befal [*sic*] a young Person, it throws a gloom upon the spirits which is very rarely ever got the better of, & embitters every pleasure...It is never (like other Troubles) to be eradicated from the breast, but as a worm continually gnawing upon the very vitals.[73]

Elizabeth's letter illuminates how the disappointment of a failed romance was perceived as impossible to overcome. While writing their journals during their fraught courtships with Henry Smith and Charles Powlett, Sarah Hurst and Anne Temple both presented death as the only way to end their misery. In 1759, Sarah noted that 'Death will lay his Icy hand on this animated clay, & all my perturbations in the grave shall end', reflecting 'on the happiness of early Death, & the troubles avoided by it'.[74] In 1794, Anne also wrote in her journal that she wished 'I had found peace in the silent Grave for there alone, I fear, I shall meet with it'.[75]

By conflating their torment with the 'happy' grave, Anne and Sarah were engaging in a literary tradition dating back centuries. In Henry Fielding's *Tom Jones* (1749),

---

[69] Reading to Leathes, 25 October 1772, BOL 2/4/16, NRO.

[70] Showalter, *The Female Malady*, 8.

[71] John Aikin, *Letters from a father to his son, on various topics, relative to literature and the conduct of life* (London, 1793), 339–41.

[72] Austen, *Sense and Sensibility*, 134, 194.

[73] Reading to Elizabeth Munbee, Woodstock, 31 August 1773, BOL 2/139/1, 740 × 4, NRO.

[74] Sarah also wailed, 'Oh fatal love, what mischiefs dost thou occasion': Diary of Hurst, 18 February 1759, 16 March 1759 and 25 May 1759, MS 3542, HM.

[75] Journal of Temple, 9 June 1794, 72M92/5, HRO.

Fig. 5.3. *The Maid who Died for Love*, London, watermark 1807, etching and engraving with stipple, plate mark 22.3 cm × 27.2 cm, Courtesy of the Lewis Walpole Library, Yale University, 807.09.15.01.

Molly Seagrim 'vowed never to outlive his deserting her', creating 'the most shocking postures of death', while *The history of Miss Harriot Fitzroy* (1767) described love as a 'fatally serious' illness.[76] This was the fate of the wronged lady in *The Somersetshire Tragedy* (c.1763–75), who miscarried her child and 'in sorrow she dyd.'[77] It was also suffered by 'The Maid Who Died for Love' (1807) who was depicted languishing beneath an upturned horseshoe clutching at a willow branch (Figure 5.3). The text described how 'No more she said, but droop'd her head, / Death's curtain clos'd around her eye; / Her spirit, from its mansion fled…And breath'd its flight in one short sigh.' Physically expiring for love was crafted as a fitting way to die, as it emphasized women's emotional sensitivity. They were variously described in letters, diaries, ballads, and prints as having 'poor', 'unfortunate', 'tender', and 'sensitive' hearts which were consumed with feeling.

---

[76] Henry Fielding, *The History of Tom Jones, A Foundling* (Ware, [1749] 1999), 143; *The history of Miss Harriot Fitzroy*, 117.

[77] 'The Somersetshire TRAGEDY: / OR, THE / Wronged Lady's Lamentation, and Untimely DEATH', London, c.1763–75, C.20, f.9 (648–9), EBBA.

In contrast, men were expected to resist excessive suffering from love, as it was seen as 'unmanly' and revealed their idleness and lack of self-control. John Aikin's *Letters from a father to his son* (1793) argued that low spirits 'most easily' affected 'persons of a literary turn and sedentary profession', and could be easily prevented by '*employment, employment, employment!*'[78] Protracted suffering from low spirits therefore demonstrated that a man was idle and not employing himself suitably. Conduct books advised men not to let an unspoken 'fascination' with a woman continue for long, as this could potentially 'extinguish every active, vigorous, and manly principle of his mind'.[79] The maxim applied to both unrequited love and after a relationship had come to an end. While women languished from their romantic pain, men were expected to resist, protecting their pride and demonstrating their self-control. The chaplain Charles Powlett calmly accepted the opposition of Anne Temple's parents in 1791, recognizing that it was difficult for them to know 'the real disposition of the Man, whose happiness consists in the hopes of marrying their Daughter, Fear & Suspicion are not only natural but meritorious'.[80] Others repeatedly promised to eschew the subject, with John Kerr, Earl of Ancram pledging *c.*1823 that although his 'state of suspense' was 'most wretched…on this subject I will not say more, you must know what I feel, and to enter on it would but annoy you, and be of little relief to me'.[81]

A CUSTOM OF HANGING AND DROWNING THEMSELVES

The mid-eighteenth century saw a related shift in gendered understandings of suicides motivated by love. During the late seventeenth and early eighteenth centuries, the archetypal suicidal lover was usually a woman, who took her life when deserted or forced to marry another. Ballads include 'The Damosels Tragedy' (1685–8), where the disappointed Elinor poisons herself 'opprest with Grief and Woe'. The heroine of 'The Perjur'd Swain' (1685–8) also ended her life as 'my passion is more than I'm able to bear'. In 'A Lamentable Ballad of the Lady's Fall' (*c.*1720), a pregnant maid refuses medical help to end her infant's life, and her own, after being deserted by her suitor.[82] A similar trope is discernable in fiction. Kelly McGuire has outlined how the majority of female protagonists in Eliza Haywood's amatory works in the 1720s 'either commit suicide or seriously contemplate the act'. The combination of their physical immobility and overwhelming passion imbued female characters with a 'death drive' that acted as 'the ultimate

---

[78] Aikin, *Letters from a father to his son*, 189–90.   [79] Gregory, *A Father's Legacy*, 86–7.
[80] Charles Powlett to Anne Temple, 19 March 1791, 72M92/7/11, HRO.
[81] John Kerr, Earl of Ancram to Lady Elizabeth Grey, *c.*1823, HALIFAX/A1/4/30/1, Borthwick Institute, York (subsequently BI).
[82] 'The Damosels Tragedy: / OR, True Love in Distress', London, 1685–8, 33931; 'The Perjur'd SWAIN', 1685–8, 21726; 'An Answer to the / The Unfortunate Lady. / Who Hang'd her self in Dispair', 1675–96?, 22157; 'A Lamentable Ballad of the Lady's Fall', 31270, EBBA.

expression of desire'.[83] In Haywood's best-selling novel *Love in Excess* (1719–20), the gentleman's daughter Amena was characterized by the violence of her passion, believing that death provided the only remedy for her failed courtship of the Count D'Elmont. Her wealthy rival Alvoysa eventually married the Count, plotting revenge against his admirers and her own suicide, before accidentally running into his sword.[84]

Narratives of women's violent passion shifted in the 1730s, as novels, ballads, and wider literature came to present the suicidal lover as a male figure. As the *Universal Spectator* decried in 1732, 'these few Years' had seen 'so very many and such shocking Accounts of the Increase of *Self-murder*' whereby 'Englishmen *have a Custom of Hanging and Drowning themselves*'.[85] In his characterization of the English gentleman in 1733, the German traveller Baron de Pöllnitz (1692–1775) reported that 'A great many of 'em hang themselves purely for Love.'[86] The gendered dichotomy between female languishing and male suicide is encapsulated in the ballad 'The Oxfordshire Tragedy; or, The Death of Four Lovers' (1736–63). Like the women analysed above, the damsel mourned, sighed, turned pale, and then 'laid her down and nothing spoke / Alas! for love her heart was broke'. In contrast, her suitor committed a violent suicide with his sword as guilt 'does my worldly glory blast'.[87] While the female protagonist finally runs herself through with the same sword, it is significant that she initially expires by sighing and languishing.

The prevailing argument against such an act was that suicide was a deadly sin and a crime against God, nature, and the state.[88] Yet this did not deter despairing men such as Thomas Andrews, a journeyman whose romantic turmoil is preserved in the records of the Old Bailey. In January 1732, Andrews was preparing for his wedding day, but 'the Bride never came', instead fleeing to Newmarket. This led the disappointed groom to try and 'cut his Throat with a Razor', but he was prevented by fellow lodgers who broke down his door. After the event, he was never again 'in his right Senses'.[89] Newspapers brimmed with similar cases of men hanging or maiming themselves after being rejected by women. In 1734, a man named Aldridge was rejected by his sweetheart, returning home and attempting to hang himself. Fortunately his story has a happy ending, as he was cut down in time to recover, marrying her the following Tuesday. Others were not so lucky; on 24 August 1739, a man named Mills cut his throat and 'ript himself open from the

[83] Kelly McGuire, *Dying to be English: Suicide Narratives and National Identity, 1721–1814* (London, 2012), 23–52.

[84] Eliza Haywood, *Love in Excess; Or The Fatal Enquiry, A Novel* (London, 1719–20), Parts I & II.

[85] Anon, *Universal Spectator*, 26 August 1732, in Kelly McGuire, ed., *The History of Suicide in England, 1650–1850* (London, 2012), Vol. IV, 31–6.

[86] *The Memoirs of Charles-Lewis, Baron de Pöllnitz. Being the Observations he Made in his Late Travels from Prussia thro' Germany, Italy, France, Flanders, Holland, England, &c. In Letters to his Friend* (London, 1739), Vol. II, London, 4 May 1733, Letter LIV, 460.

[87] McGuire, ed., *The History of Suicide in England*, 315–21.

[88] Paul S. Seaver, 'Suicide and the Vicar General in London: A Mystery Solved?' in *From Sin to Insanity: Suicide in Early Modern Europe*, ed. Jeffrey R. Watt (Ithaca, NY, 2004), 25–47.

[89] Soon after, he committed burglary (a capital offence) as a 'sure way to get himself rid of the World by the Hands of another'. Trial of Thomas Andrews for burglary, 23 February 1732, t17320223-40, and Ordinary's Account, 6 March 1732, OA17320306, OBO.

Pit of his Stomach to his Navel, so that his Guts were let out' after his fiancée refused to go ahead with the wedding. Similarly on 7 January 1741, a 'handsome' young carter named Dick Priest hung himself from his bedpost in despair after being 'slighted by his Sweetheart'.[90]

While conduct literature advised men to desist from 'whining' about love, suicide provided a means of escape for wounded men who could not conform to the ideal. Male suicide was constructed in popular culture as a masculinized and heroic act of passion—as the periodical *The Connoisseur* argued in 1755, 'it is the most gallant exploit, by which our modern heroes chuse to signalize themselves.' The means of committing suicide was particularly important, as 'The poor sneaking wretch, starving in a garret, tucks himself up in his list garters; a second, crost in love, drowns himself, like a blind puppy...and a third cuts his throat with his own razor. But the man of fashion almost always dies by a pistol.'[91] The chief cause was believed to be wounded pride, with the head of a Parliamentary Committee in 1823 attributing suicides by men 'in the higher stations of life' to their 'wounded shame; the result of false pride, and the fear of some imaginary degradation'.[92] Rejected or slighted men thus chose to end their lives to protect their pride rather than risk damaging their masculinity. Such heroic suicides were dramatized in Goethe's *The Sorrows of Young Werther* (1774), where the hero shot himself with two pistols, inspiring a wave of copycat suicides across Europe, and Frances Burney's *Camilla* (1796), where Nicholas Gwigg (alias Alphonso Bellamy) forced Eugenia Tyrold to 'rescue him from suicide' by consenting to marriage.[93] The Prince of Wales used a similar tactic by threatening to take his own life to win back his mistress Mrs Fitzherbert (1756–1837), stabbing himself with his sword on 8 July 1784 and reiterating his threat whenever she attempted to leave him.[94]

The suicide of the rejected man is cruelly satirized in the etching *A Cure for Love* (1819) where the protagonist looks up to the noose beside a letter that reads, 'You old Fool if you ever trouble me again with your Stupid epistles I will expose you in the public Papers.' The man's suicide was a direct result of his embarrassment, lamenting, 'Oh! my hard Fate! Why did I trust her ever?' (Figure 5.4). The grossly overweight man resembles the stout Englishman John Bull, created by John Arbuthnot in 1712. His shabby home with bare bricks and cobwebs on the windows clearly sets him apart from the fashionable men he attempts to emulate. The

[90] *Country Journal*, 16 November 1734, *Daily Gazetteer*, 24 August 1739, and *London Daily Post and General Advertiser*, 7 January 1741, in McGuire, ed., *The History of Suicide in England*, 10, 13.

[91] *Connoisseur* (*Collected Issues*), London, 9 January 1755, Issue L. For aristocrats and gentlemen as the groups most associated with suicide for honour, see Michael MacDonald and Terence R. Murphy, *Sleepless Souls: Suicide in Early Modern England* (Oxford, 1990), 276–82.

[92] 'Pride the Chief Inducement to Suicide', in *Gentleman's Magazine* 26, London, January 1756, 28; Sir John Mackintosh's Motion Respecting the Rigour of our Criminal Laws, 21 May 1823, in *The Parliamentary Debates*, ed. T. C. Hansard (London, 1824), New Series, Vol. IX, 397–432, at 416.

[93] Goethe, *Sorrows of Young Werther*, 84–7; Frances Burney, *Camilla: or, A Picture of Youth* (Cambridge, [1796] 1999), 283–90.

[94] Valerie Irvine, *The King's Wife: George IV and Mrs Fitzherbert* (London, 2005), 36–41, 54.

Fig. 5.4. *A Cure for Love*, London, 1819, hand-coloured etching, 35 cm × 24.5 cm, British Museum, London, 1895,0617.454. © The Trustees of the British Museum, All Rights Reserved.

text uses several rhyming terms from northern dialect, with the noose referred to as a 'snickett' and the three-legged stool a 'cricket'.[95] The image is one of ridicule and failed masculinity, as the 'Stupid' overweight man attempts to imitate his fashionable superiors. Even hanging himself from the flimsy beam presents a challenge, as 'The Cricket kick'd down, let him take a fair swing / and leave all the rest of the work to the string.' In placing the abandoned suitor below the noose, the image encodes the different cultural scripts governing romantic hurt for men and women. It is telling that while some women physically wasted away from lovesickness, certain men made a conscious *choice* to end their lives. While rejected men decided to cut their throats or hang themselves, women were granted no autonomy whatsoever over whether they died or not.[96]

Men's suicide from disappointed love was frequently attributed to madness, reflecting the broader reconceptualization of suicide across Enlightenment Europe from a sin to a result of insanity.[97] On 7 April 1779 Martha Ray (1742–79), mistress of the Earl of Sandwich, was murdered in the street by the soldier-turned-clergyman James Hackman (1752–79), with the case becoming a cause célèbre in the popular press. James was in love with Martha, and—seized by a 'momentary phrensy'— shot her in the head before attempting suicide. However, his pistol shot only grazed his head, and he was hanged for murder a fortnight later.[98] The case inspired Sir Herbert Croft's epistolary novel *Love and Madness* (1780), which presented the protagonist as being inspired by the suicides of Goethe's Werther and the melancholic poet Thomas Chatterton (1752–70), who drank arsenic to kill himself aged seventeen. Croft described James' 'madness of affection' and 'mad and happy' state indulging in fantasies about making love to Martha.[99] Spurned men also described how romantic rejection had driven them mad. After being refused by his sister's friend in 1779, John Cater wished 'Tortures! Torments! Daggers, & Death to me!', wretchedly concluding 'I am not myself.'[100] In 1816, Richard Law raged with anger after Jane Townley refused to marry him, accusing her of killing him on a daily basis with her cruelty. He ranted, 'you have drove me mad you have made me run distracted, and you have bewitched me out of my wits…I will do all that a mad man unchained can do at you.'[101] However, Jane never responded to his threatening letters, leaving Richard to send fifteen years of hate mail without a single reply.

---

[95] I am grateful to Helen Berry for discussing this with me.

[96] Janet Oppenheim has made a similar point in arguing that the 'element of personal choice or responsibility' was removed from Victorian women suffering from nervous collapse. See Janet Oppenheim, *'Shattered Nerves': Doctors, Patients, and Depression in Victorian England* (Oxford, 1991), 181.

[97] See Jeffrey R. Watt's edited volume, *From Sin to Insanity*.

[98] Trial of James Hackman for murder, 4 April 1779, t17790404-3, OBO.

[99] Maximillian Novak, 'Sex, Madness, and Suicide in Sir Herbert Croft's *Love and Madness*', in *Sex and Death in Eighteenth-Century Literature*, ed. Jolene Zigarovich (Basingstoke, 2013), 165–82.

[100] John Cater to Mrs Williamson, 16 December 1779, M10/4/17, BAS.

[101] Law to Townley, Doncaster, 10 May 1816, Add MS 47796, f. 2v, BL.

RITUALS OF DISINTEGRATION

Once a man had resolved to bring a courtship to an end, he was expected to notify his sweetheart immediately, in order to avoid prolonging her pain. To not do so was to transgress the boundaries of gentlemanly behaviour, as a man could stifle love 'with far greater Ease than a Woman'.[102] As Mary Berry excoriated the faithless Charles O'Hara in 1796, 'a more immediate, a more decided & a more <u>Gentlemanlike</u> avowal of a change in your sentiments' would have 'spared me many months of cruel anxiety.' Rather than choosing to end their connection in a gentlemanlike fashion, Charles used '<u>a thousand falsehoods</u>' to conceal the fact that he had simply changed his mind.[103] His conduct breached the etiquette of courtship so acutely that friends such as John Barnes were moved to write to Mary and apologize on his behalf.[104] The men of the family also came to the aid of Anne Louisa Dalling after she was jilted by Sir Gilbert Stirling just hours before their wedding in 1805. Anne's brother William Windham wrote to Gilbert to condemn his low behaviour:

> The long continued hospitality & friendship of my Mother you have returned with treachery & ingratitude: my own friendship for you…with deceit & insult: my brother was your bosom-friend & introduced you to the family; he may perhaps learn from this lesson not readily to trust again in the appearances of sincerity. For my sister, what shall I say! She has grown up through the last two years of her childhood, countenanced & encouraged by every Act, Expression & Promise of yours that she was to be your wife.[105]

In response, Andrew Stirling replied that he had spoken to Gilbert that morning, who was 'dufily [*sic*] impressed with a sense of the impropriety of his conduct to you & your family'.[106] One week later, Gilbert described how 'There are no words Sir Windham Dalling can use that I shall have any other feeling about than regret for…my unfortunate but I cannot add culpable conduct.'[107] Men were thus expected to act decisively in order to spare women and their families from any unnecessary suffering. When they did not, they were answerable to friends and family members, who reinforced the rules they had breached and reproached their deceitful behaviour.

Whilst relationships were *made* in objects, they were also *un-made* in objects, with men granted primary responsibility for returning or destroying the physical debris of a relationship in a way that would not prove damaging to either party. Returning these items was an enormously significant act, which physically and symbolically terminated the possibility of a future marriage. In 1715, the diarist Dudley Ryder's friend Mr Whatley was left unsure about the status of his relationship

---

[102] Aeneas Sylvius, *The History of the Amours of Count Schlick, Chancellor to the Emperor Sigismund, and a Young Lady of Quality of Sienna* (London, 1708), 328.

[103] Berry to O'Hara, 27 April 1796, Add MS 37727, fols. 273r–274v, BL.

[104] Berry to John Barnes, 30 August 1796, Add MS 37727, f. 243r, BL.

[105] W. Dalling to Gilbert Stirling, Harley Street, 9 March 1805, MEA 10/110, 882 × 6, NRO.

[106] Andrew Stirling to W. Dalling, Glasgow, 20 March 1805, MEA 10/110, 882 × 6, NRO.

[107] Gilbert Stirling to W. Dalling, 28 March 1805, MEA 10/110, 882 × 6, NRO.

as his sweetheart would not commit to keeping or returning his missives. Ryder described how 'upon his still pressing her she used to tell him that it could come to nothing and that she would give him his letters, [but] she never sent them him, which made him believe he was not quite forsaken neither.'[108] By ending their romantic correspondence but not returning his letters, she left their relationship in an indeterminate state, as Mr Whatley could no longer be certain whether they were courting or not. Similarly, when Charlotte Lambourne turned down John Dewey's proposal of marriage in 1809, but requested to continue corresponding in secret as his 'truly attached Friend', she (rightly) feared that her letters continued indulging 'that passion; which will not be easily shaken off'.[109] The return of letters and tokens officially marked a couple's 'disengagement' in novels such as Jane Austen's *Sense and Sensibility* (1811), with Willoughby returning 'the letters with which I have been honoured from you, and the lock of hair which you so obligingly bestowed on me' to formally terminate his connection to Marianne.[110] The novel provides an indication of wider social practices, as readers would have recognized that the return of Marianne's letters and hair officially ended their connection.

The nobleman John Kerr, Earl of Ancram, swiftly returned Lady Elizabeth Grey's letters *c.*1823 in order to protect her reputation and symbolically end their relationship. The whole process was managed by Elizabeth's mother Mary, and John's half-sister Louisa, to minimize social gossip surrounding the affair, and spare Elizabeth any unnecessary suffering. As John wrote to Elizabeth's mother, 'It might have been some relief to me to have written to her but it would have been selfish', for 'what satisfaction could she derive' from hearing a repetition of his 'deep and devoted' affection and the obstacles preventing their marriage.[111] Both sides were deeply vexed that despite their best efforts, the romance had become the subject of gossip among people of fashion, including Lady Jersey, the Duke of Wellington, and Lord Londonderry.[112] The relationship provides rare evidence of unsuccessful engagements among the nobility, who usually took great pains to ensure that a match was a success. The decisive factor was that John had acted alone rather than consulting his father, completely ignoring the prevailing etiquette of noble courtships. John's transgression forced him to grovel to Elizabeth and her family for forgiveness, believing that 'every circumstance has united to put my conduct in its worst light.'[113] The pivotal role played by John's father in terminating the relationship, and Elizabeth's mother in managing its deconstruction, demonstrates the importance of families in curtailing a romantic match. Such strict familial oversight was especially pronounced in relationships involving the nobility, in order to preserve the reputation and social prestige of both families.

---

[108] 28 October 1715, William Matthews, ed., *The Diary of Dudley Ryder 1715–1716* (London, 1939), 125–6.
[109] Lambourne to Dewey, Southampton, 14 May 1809, 32M77/F/C7, HRO.
[110] Austen, *Sense and Sensibility*, 135.
[111] John Kerr, Earl of Ancram to Mary, Countess Grey, *c.*1823–4, HALIFAX/A1/4/30/2, BI.
[112] Louisa, Countess of Sandwich to Charlotte, *c.* April 1824, HALIFAX/A1/4/30/10, BI.
[113] Kerr to Mary, Countess Grey, 4 July 1823, HALIFAX/A1/4/30/6, BI.

Each of the writers studied in this chapter expressed concern over the social implications of ending a courtship that had become well-known in the community, with Anne Temple describing the social 'punishment' due to women guilty of 'broken vows, treachery, and perjury'.[114] Suitors were acutely aware that 'Intimacies of another nature if they are long continued, cannot be broke off without great Uneasiness.'[115] They warned one another that 'the eyes of all my friends & all my acquaintance [*sic*] are watching my every motion with respect to you.'[116] This meant that 'If I were capable of so much meanness or dishonour…as to break the engagement I have formed, without a sufficient reason, I should hold myself the most contemptible of beings, & be justly entitled to the severest censure of the World.'[117] The gentleman Edward Peach was concerned that the widow Elizabeth Leathes (*née* Reading) had changed her mind about their relationship in 1790, warning her after a particularly 'severe' letter that 'Our intended Marriage is the general subject of this Country.'[118] This cautioned Elizabeth that the match could not be broken off without potentially harming her reputation. Noblewomen had to be particularly careful not to damage their prospects for an advantageous marriage, with gossip about the romance between Lady Elizabeth Grey and the Earl of Ancram spreading like wildfire in 1823, despite attempts to keep it within their 'immediate family'. John's half-sister Louisa, Countess of Sandwich was deeply vexed that the relationship had become public knowledge despite her continued attempts to suppress it, entreating Elizabeth to 'avoid him' as much as possible 'without affectation'.[119]

The concerns expressed by these individuals are understandable, as novels and conduct books continually warned that a failed relationship could be catastrophic for a young woman's reputation. After her seduction by the rake Lovelace, Richardson's heartbroken heroine Clarissa sought refuge in death in order to expiate her faults. Similarly, the protagonist of Susanna Rowson's *Charlotte: A Tale of Truth* (1791) was alienated from her family after her seduction by a soldier, dying alone after giving birth to his child. As I argued in Chapter 2 of this book, women's courtship letters were much more guarded and reserved than men's, and deliberately eschewed overt declarations of love in order to safeguard their modesty and virtue. The 'General disadvantage' of courting women, as the chaplain Charles Powlett explained, was that they 'cannot express the freedom of Sentiment that we may'.[120] Women made use of other tactics such as avoiding suitors if they did not believe a relationship would end in matrimony. In 1755, the tailor's daughter Sarah Hurst reflected on 'the unhappy situation I have drawn myself into' with Henry Smith, as her family disapproved of his visits and tried to prevent the couple from meeting. Believing that it was 'very improbable, I can ever be his', Sarah resolved to break off their

---

[114] Journal of Temple, 9 April 1794, 72M92/5, HRO.
[115] Gibbs to Vicary, undated (1740s), MS/11021/1/1, LMA.
[116] Strutt to Douglas, 5 May 1788, MS3101/C/E/4/8/11, LOB.
[117] Ibid., 7 January 1789, MS3101/C/E/4/8/16, LOB.
[118] Edward Peach to Elizabeth Leathes, 4 November 1790, BOL 2/140/2/39, NRO.
[119] Louisa, Countess of Sandwich to Charlotte, *c.* April 1824, A1/4/30/10, BI.
[120] Powlett to Temple, 25 January 1791, 72M92/7/9, NRO.

courtship. She wrote to Henry, 'I now see the time approaching that I shall be forgot, & everything that has pass'd between us, buried in oblivion.' The couple were briefly reconciled, after which Sarah tried avoiding Henry for several days. However, they eventually met to exchange 'mutual protestations of everlasting Love' and agreed to continue their romantic correspondence.[121] The risk that a courtship might fail evidently shaped relationships in their earlier stages, increasing the significance of material gestures such as love letters and romantic gifts in navigating the uneven path to matrimony.

What became of the couples studied in this chapter? While it can be difficult to reconstruct an individual's actions after a romantic correspondence comes to a close, we do know that several of the men and women made advantageous marriages soon after their disappointment. Anne Louisa Dalling married General Robert Meade (1772–1852) in 1808, three years after she was jilted by Sir Gilbert Stirling. After his proposals of marriage to Charlotte Lambourne were repeatedly rebuffed between 1809 and 1816, the surgeon John Dewey finally found a wife in 1817, also called Charlotte. Lady Elizabeth Grey married John Crocker Bulteel (1793–1843) in 1826, three years after she was forsaken by John Kerr, Earl of Ancram. These marriages suggest that despite the inevitable emotional trauma, the reputation of these men and women had not been unduly damaged by their failed relationships.

CONCLUSION

This chapter has argued that suffering from love was redefined as a characteristically female malady from the mid-eighteenth century. The dominant archetypes of heartbreak were female figures drawn from classical and Shakespearean texts, with lovers expressing sympathy for 'poor' Armida, 'wretched' Dido, and 'pathetic' Ophelia. These tales were interpreted in a new light to present love as an overpowering passion that affected women more than men. Nonetheless, the language of heartbreak was used by both sexes, who conceptualized the emotional experience of courtship through the wounding and revival of their hearts. Such language provided lovers with a rich vocabulary to pinpoint the precise stages of romantic breakdown. The popularity of particular expressions changed over the century, with the heart's strings granted new prominence under the culture of sensibility, and heartache coming to be specifically associated with romantic pain.

The delicate physical disposition of 'unfortunate' women in love assumed a prominent role in popular culture from the 1750s, as they suffered extensively from their 'poor' and 'sensitive' hearts. This manifested itself in ballads and prints where hopeless women sighed, moaned, sobbed, groaned, and died for love. It was also reflected in courtship letters, where women wrote at length about their agitated spirits, gloom, and despondency. At worst, this led to melancholy, hysteria, madness, and death. Different cultural scripts governed the experience of romantic hurt for men, as feminine despondency was replaced with the passionate masculinized act

---

[121] Diary of Hurst, 1755, MS3542, HM.

of suicide. While women were granted no control over their romantic pain, these courageous and heroic suicides provided a way for men to protect their pride, an ideal that could prove difficult for poorer men to emulate.

Clearly, despite social pressures and warnings about the dangers of a failed relationship for a young woman's reputation, not all courtships ended at the altar. As Mary Berry wrote in 1796, 'you know, that it is no <u>unheard-of thing</u> for people to change their mind upon these occasions.'[122] Men's expected pragmatic response to the end of a relationship made it an important male duty to return a woman's letters and tokens to spare them additional suffering, before reintroducing themselves into society and resuming the search for a spouse. Men such as Sir Gilbert Stirling who had behaved dishonourably left themselves at risk of a breach of promise suit from the incensed family they left behind. As Anne Louisa Dalling's brother reproached Gilbert in 1805, 'in a moment, without a word, without a line, without a whisper in the ear of a friend to tell us any cause, within a few hours of the appointed celebration, you disappear; & at six weeks end we are still left the subject, of town-talk & the newspapers!'[123] These emotionally charged suits are the subject of the next chapter.

---

[122] Berry to Barnes, 30 August 1796, Add MS 37727, f. 243r, BL.
[123] W. Dalling to Stirling, Harley Street, 9 March 1805, MEA 10/110, 662 × 6, NRO.

6

Breach of Promise

When the gentleman Knox Ward began visiting Sarah Holt 'under the umbrage of Courtship' in 1729, he spoke 'very tenderly and affectionately to her' and repeatedly promised to make her his wife. He soothed the concerns of Sarah's mother by reassuring her that his designs were honourable, while Sarah's chambermaid witnessed 'a thousand kind and tender Expressions' between the pair. When Knox abruptly changed his mind and deserted her, Sarah sued him for breach of promise, demanding damages of £4,000. In Knox's defence, he argued that although she was 'a deserving young Lady', he never would have 'undervalued' himself to marry her as she 'had not a competent Fortune', which he believed prohibited her from receiving such a large sum. The counsel for the plaintiff justified the damages as by 'having allured and enticed her to permit him to pay Visits to her at sundry Times, upon his Protestation of an inviolable Friendship; and then making a Breach and palpable Violation of his Contract, he certainly had injured the Lady very much in her Reputation, besides giving her a great deal of Uneasiness.' Once Lord Chief Justice Raymond (1673–1733) summed up the depositions and 'delivered an impartial Charge to the Jury', they took half an hour to find for the plaintiff. Sarah was awarded half of the damages she demanded, which still added up to an immense £2,000.[1]

Breach of promise suits such as the dispute between Sarah and Knox have typically been studied in conjunction with related actions concerning marriage and sexual morality, primarily seduction. In his *Road to Divorce* (1990), Lawrence Stone argued that the moral principles underpinning breach of promise and seduction suits were the joint beliefs that 'young women were innocent and defenceless victims of the wiles and pressures of men', and that women's prospects for an advantageous marriage were irreparably damaged by their loss of chastity, something which could be compensated by monetary damages.[2] While Stone cast the civil courts as the 'guardian of public morals', Katie Barclay has more recently outlined how newspaper reports of breach of promise and seduction suits between 1780 and 1830 cast readers as 'arbiters of public morality'. Such reports worked to create a unifying 'emotional public opinion', where readers were encouraged to pity seduced women and shame elderly plaintiffs or individuals seeking to marry above their station. Whether a man serving on a jury or an individual reading a

---

[1] *The Whole Proceedings on the Tryal between Mrs Sarah Holt, and Knox Ward, Esq; upon a Promise of Marriage, On Wednesday, February 25, 1729–30* (London, 1730), 3–7.
[2] Lawrence Stone, *Road to Divorce: England 1530–1987* (Oxford, 1990), 81–3.

newspaper, 'determining morality formally became the "business" of the public, as well as the church.'[3]

To date, there has been no systematic study of breach of promise in the civil courts over the long eighteenth century, following the pioneering work of Ginger Frost, Saskia Lettmaier, and Susie Steinbach on the long nineteenth century.[4] These scholars have presented the suit as a key moment in the 'legal codification of a powerful cultural ideal: the ideal of the true woman', defined by the precepts of 'domesticity, modesty, chastity, physical frailty, passionlessness, emotionality, and child-like dependence'.[5] As we will see, new emotional norms were equally important, which determined who could legitimately suffer when a relationship came to an end. Analysing the nature of breach of promise in Georgian England therefore provides unique insights into cultural constructions of romantic love, and understandings of intimacy, emotions, and romantic hurt. Since the majority of plaintiffs were women of middling status, breach of promise suits present a valuable opportunity to analyse factors such as gender, social status, and age in contemporary conceptions of courtship. Cases also shed light on the exchange of love letters and love tokens, and the language of romantic success or failure, which have been studied in detail in the preceding chapters of this book.

This chapter is based upon a sample of ninety cases reported in thirty-eight national and provincial newspapers, pamphlets, and *English Reports* between 1717 and 1830 (see Appendix 2). Such a broad source-base is necessary as breach of promise cases were tried in courts across England, in contrast to actions for criminal conversation (crim. con.) that were restricted to London.[6] Newspaper reports are particularly valuable since only a small number of breach of promise cases were featured in law reports, the majority of which were exceptional cases under appeal.[7] 'Assize Intelligence', 'Legal Intelligence', and 'Law Reports' frequently provide precise details of the age, social status, and reputation of plaintiffs, defendants, and their families. They reveal how particular cases were perceived by contemporaries, through the approving or censorious language used to describe love, desertion, and romantic suffering. Reports illuminate community interest in cases, noting when a courtroom was especially crowded, and when the crowd was satisfied (or not) with the judge's verdict. The volume of reports also reveals when cases became a cause célèbre, capturing the attention of the daily news cycle.[8]

---

[3] Katie Barclay, 'Emotions, the Law and the Press in Britain: Seduction and Breach of Promise Suits, 1780–1830', *Journal for Eighteenth-Century Studies* 39.2 (2016): 267–84.

[4] Ginger S. Frost, *Promises Broken: Courtship, Class, and Gender in Victorian England* (Charlottesville, VA and London, 1995); Saskia Lettmaier, *Broken Engagements: The Action for Breach of Promise of Marriage and the Feminine Ideal, 1800–1940* (Oxford, 2010); Susie Steinbach, 'Promises, Promises: Not Marrying in England 1780–1920' (unpublished PhD thesis, Yale University, 1996); Susie Steinbach, 'The Melodramatic Contract: Breach of Promise and the Performance of Virtue', *Nineteenth-Century Studies* 14 (2000): 1–34; Susie Steinbach, 'From Redress to Farce: Breach of Promise Theatre in Cultural Context, 1830–1920', *Journal of Victorian Culture* 13.2 (2008): 247–76.

[5] Lettmaier, *Broken Engagements*, 57.   [6] Stone, *Road to Divorce*, 247.

[7] Lettmaier, *Broken Engagements*, 10.

[8] For example, *Chapman vs. Shaw Esq.* was reported in the *World*, *Whitehall Evening Post*, and *The Times*, while *Atcheson vs. Baker* was reported in *True Briton*, *Whitehall Evening Post*, *Evening Mail*, and *The Telegraph*.

Reporters did not simply recount the facts of cases, but incensed and inflamed readers using portrayals of respectable or promiscuous parties, roguish men, and heartbroken women.

This chapter is divided into three sections, firstly outlining the development of breach of promise under the common law, and secondly analysing the nature of the suit including the verdicts, gender balance, damages awarded, age, occupation, and social status of plaintiffs and defendants. Thirdly, it considers which objects were commonly invoked as proof of an attachment, from marriage licences to wedding gowns. The chapter asks, how did the suit change over the long eighteenth century? How did actions, verdicts, and damages vary according to gender? Which features, if any, were unique to the period? This is the first study to focus exclusively on breach of promise as a common law action across the long eighteenth century. It is also the first to prioritize the role of objects in these cases, confirming the vital importance of gifts as proof of a relationship before the community and courts of law.

NOT MERELY A SPIRITUAL MATTER

The late seventeenth century saw the common law courts gradually usurping the power of the church courts to rule on the validity of matrimonial contracts. Although individual cases can be traced as far back as the sixteenth century, the principle of breach of promise was first tested under the common law during the Interregnum.[9] In *Baker vs. Smith* (1651), the plaintiff brought an action of assumpsit after her suitor promised to pay her £1,000 if she discharged him from his promise to marry. She did so, but the money never materialized.[10] The case was repeatedly adjourned as the court was divided as to whether there was a mutual promise between the couple, and whether this represented a spiritual or temporal matter.[11] The judge provided a valuable explanation of the suit as a common law action beyond the spiritual powers of the ecclesiastical courts:

> [H]ere is a mutual promise made by both parties, and there have been divers [*sic*] actions of late times brought for this cause, and they have been adjudged good, and the engagement to marry is not meerly [*sic*] a spiritual matter, and this action is not to compel the mariage [*sic*] upon the contract, but to recover damages for not doing it, and it is like to a wager, and here is a temporal loss, and therefore a temporal action doth lie.[12]

---

[9] The church courts had been abolished by Parliament in 1646, and were reinstated after the Restoration of Charles II in 1660. See S. F. C Milsom, *Historical Foundations of the Common Law* (London, 1969), 289; Stone, *Road to Divorce*, 71, 86; Lettmaier, *Broken Engagements*, 21–3. Charles J. MacColla isolated *Palmer vs. Wilder* as the first case 'in the reign of Queen Elizabeth, when it was decided that for the value of the marriage, tender was not requisite': *Breach of Promise: Its History and Social Considerations* (London, 1879), 1.

[10] An assumpsit is '(a) a promise or contract, or in writing not sealed, founded upon a consideration; (b) an action to recover damages for breach or non-performance of such contract', *OEDO*, accessed 29 June 2018: http://www.oed.com.oxfordbrookes.idm.oclc.org/view/Entry/12047?redirect edFrom=assumpsit.

[11] *English Reports* (subsequently *ER*) 82 *ER* 723.   [12] 82 *ER* 722.

The establishment of this temporal action paved the way for cases such as *Holcroft vs. Dickenson* (1672), where the Court of Common Pleas definitively ruled that since John Dickenson 'did assume and promise' to marry Mary Holcroft 'within a fortnight', 'this hindred [*sic*] her preferment to her damage of 100 pounds.'[13] When the case was referred to the King's Bench in 1673, the judges considered whether 'Marriage being a thing of ecclesiastical conusance, the common law takes no notice of it.' However, they held 'that the action well lay; for that here is a mutual contract concerning a lawful act, and though the subject matter be spiritual yet the contract is temporal'. If there was any suit contesting the lawfulness of a marriage, this remained a matter for the ecclesiastical courts, but the reparation of temporal loss after the breach of a binding contract was firmly within the realms of the common law.

The church courts were defenceless against this infringement of their powers, as canon law provided no basis for imposing fines upon wayward lovers. Nonetheless, they continued to rule on the validity of a small number of marriage contracts, with approximately one case per decade taking place at the York Consistory Court.[14] The suit was remarkably similar in common and canon law, as cases were based upon depositions given by witnesses who were cross-examined by a judge and material objects used during, or purchased in anticipation of, a marriage ceremony.[15] The key difference was that the church courts sought to discover whether or not a couple was legally married in order to dismiss or enforce their union, whereas common law courts focused on the nature of the contract between the two parties in order to impose a fine on the defendant. Judges directed a number of plaintiffs back to the church courts to redress their grievances; *Jesson vs. Collins* (1703) saw the plaintiff contesting that a contract was *per verba de future* (in the future tense) rather than *per verba de praesenti* (in the present tense), as this would make the matter eligible for common law. However, the suit was sent straight back to the spiritual courts, as the judge ruled that 'a contract *per verba de praesenti* is a marriage...and this is not releasable.'[16] A typical suit in the church courts is exemplified by the dispute between Thomas Mascall and Ursula Watson at the York Consistory Court in 1745, which hinged upon vows exchanged in the present tense during a ceremony at the home of Ursula's uncle in 1742. Whilst Thomas alleged that they decided to 'marry themselves to each other' by reading vows out of Ursula's Common Prayer Book and exchanging a gold ring, she responded that she had taken the book out of her pocket accidentally and 'did not duely weigh or consider the Force or Efficacy' of what she was doing.[17]

---

[13] 124 *ER* 933; *Journal of the House of Lords*, Vol. 12, 1666–75, 12 February 1674, pp. 634–5: http://www.british-history.ac.uk/report.aspx?compid=12875#s4.

[14] These were *Roskell vs. Knipe* (1707–8), *Massey vs. Ogden* (1713), *Hanswell vs. Dodgshon* (1729), *Mascall vs. Watson* (1743–5), and *Connell vs. Caine* (1754–7). Heather Smith, 'Women and Marriage in the Eighteenth Century: Evidence from the Church Courts, 1730–1780' (unpublished PhD thesis, University of Bristol, 2000), 22.

[15] Witnesses' testimony was paramount in both seduction and breach of promise suits, as plaintiffs and defendants were not permitted to give evidence until 1869.

[16] 90 *ER* 1152.

[17] *Mascall vs. Watson* (1743–5), Consistory Court of York, appealed from Consistory Court of Durham, TRANS.CP.1744/5, BI.

Such cases came to an abrupt halt on 25 March 1754, as the Hardwicke Marriage Act swiftly removed the power of the church courts to enforce contracts *per verba de praesenti*, and those *per verba de futuro* after cohabitation. Steinbach has suggested that although Hardwicke's Act made it 'theoretically impossible to compel marriage on the grounds of pre-contract', breach of promise suits in the civil courts took on this role after 1754, as by imposing heavy damages on a defendant, a jury might be able to 'induce him to offer [his] hand'.[18] Legal changes subsequently prompted a shift in the focus of the church courts towards cases such as *Chevely vs. Chevely* (1770) at the London Consistory Court, which disputed a couple's commitment under the guise of restitution of conjugal rights.[19] A related change took place with the shift of crim. con. cases from the church to the civil courts in the mid-eighteenth century, which Susan Staves argues reflected a new willingness 'to understand seduction as secular rather than religious experience'.[20]

The home of breach of promise in the common law was the Court of King's Bench at Westminster Hall, which also housed the Court of Common Pleas and Court of Chancery (Figure 6.1). The King's Bench was the highest court of common law in England and Wales, holding local jurisdiction over Middlesex and Westminster. It heard over one third of the cases in Appendix 2, which were frequently referred from local courts, where the defendant had obtained a *writ of certiorari*. As in church court proceedings, indictments, informations, writs, and plea rolls were recorded in Latin until 1733.

The last quarter of the eighteenth century was pivotal in creating increasing awareness of breach of promise in the popular imagination. The phrase 'breach of contract' was first mentioned in the *Universal Spectator and Weekly Journal* in 1730, to report the case of *Holt vs. Ward*. Later reports of cases in the 1770s referred to the suit as 'the breach of a marriage contract'.[21] The phrase 'breach of promise' was first mentioned in the *World and Fashionable Advertiser* in 1787, to describe an 'action of a most extraordinary kind'. The Burney Collection Newspapers at the British Library contain 127 references to 'breach of promise' between January 1787 and December 1799, pre-dating what legal scholars have described as the action's 'rise to cultural prominence' in the early 1800s.[22] Moralistic accounts of 'crowded' courtrooms, 'exemplary' damages, and virtuous female plaintiffs exploded in the early nineteenth century, with 101 articles mentioning the suit in

---

18 90 *ER* 1152; *Roebuck vs. Dunderdale* (1825) cited in Steinbach, 'Promises, Promises', 113–14.

19 *Chevely vs. Chevely*, DL/C/176, fols. 73v–83v, LMA.

20 Adam Komisaruk, 'The Privatization of Pleasure: Crim. Con. in Wollstonecraft's *Maria*', *Law and Literature* 16.1 (2004): 33–63, at 36; Susan Staves, 'British Seduced Maidens', *Eighteenth-Century Studies* 14.2 (1980–1): 109–34, at 110.

21 Based on keyword search of British Newspapers 1600–1900 on 9 November 2017. *Universal Spectator and Weekly Journal*, 13 June 1730, LXXXVIII; *Craftsman or Say's Weekly Journal*, 22 August 1772, 734. The number of articles mentioning 'breach of contract' is difficult to quantify, as the phrase was also used to describe housing, parliamentary, and mercantile contracts.

22 *World and Fashionable Advertiser*, 4 January 1787, 4. However, we should not assume that each example concerns a different case, as Issues 9627–54 of the *General Evening Post* between 13 June and 11 August 1795 each reprint the same account of *Brown vs. Harding* (1795). Lettmaier, *Broken Engagements*, 1.

Fig. 6.1. Thomas Rowlandson and Auguste Charles Pugin, *Court of Kings Bench. Westminster Hall*, from *The Microcosm of London*, plate 24, London, 1808, hand-coloured etching and aquatint, plate 23 cm × 27.5 cm, The Elisha Whittelsey Fund, The Metropolitan Museum of Art, New York, 59.533.1671(13).

the *Morning Chronicle*, 153 in the *Morning Post*, and 154 in *The Times* between 1800 and 1830.[23]

King's Bench lawyers even became celebrities in their own right, with Chief Justice Kenyon, Lord Thomas Erskine, and Chief Justice Ellenborough becoming the heroes and villains of pamphlets, newspaper reports, and satirical prints. These men had a significant impact upon the nature of breach of promise actions through their performances in court. The socially conservative Lloyd Kenyon, first Baron Kenyon (1732–1802) was Lord Chief Justice between 1788 and 1802 and was 'abrupt in speech and temper, often rude to counsel, not given to oratory unless it concerned an issue that touched him deeply'. One such issue was matrimony, where he actively encouraged juries to award large damages in suits for adultery and crim. con. Kenyon's stance undoubtedly encouraged the awarding of sizeable

---

[23] Quotes from *Forster vs. Hoblin* (1805) and *King vs. Chance* (1822). *The Morning Post and Gazetteer* was renamed *The Morning Post* in 1803. Based on keyword searches of British Newspapers 1600–1900 and *The Times* Digital Archive on 22 November 2017.

damages to plaintiffs in breach of promise suits during his time in office; in his fourteen years as Chief Justice the court only went against his recommendation on six occasions.[24] Even when a case was declared a nonsuit, he thought it fit to recommend compensation to plaintiffs, not 'in his character of Judge, but as a Man'.[25] Kenyon's protégée Thomas Erskine (1750–1823) was another notorious figure, whose famous defences in court were reprinted in multiple editions for an awed public, heaping him with praise as 'the first Orator of the British Bar'.[26] Erskine's oratory secured large damages for innumerable women, fixing the idea that 'if there was any case that more deserved attention than another, it was that which involved the consideration of an injury done to a woman.'[27] Kenyon was succeeded as Chief Justice by Edward Law, first Baron Ellenborough (1750–1818), who acted to diminish the level of damages awarded in crim. con. cases, which had been escalated by his predecessor. As Ellenborough warned the jury during *Storey vs. Eagle* (1802), 'in giving damages, the Jury should take care not utterly to ruin the defendant.'[28]

Cases could even be brought by the parents of individuals; when Cornelius Far promised to marry Mary Atkins in 1732, he executed a bond to her promising that if he did not marry her within twelve months, he would pay her £500. After Mary died, her mother brought a suit against Cornelius to recover the money, and won.[29] When the plaintiff in *Tawes vs. Jones* was nonsuited for breach of promise in 1796, her father was advised to bring a suit for seduction instead.[30] In 1814, jurors debated whether breach of promise cases should be available to the fathers of disappointed women. The issue arose during *Chamberlain vs. Williamson, Esq.*, as Chamberlain's daughter was 'thrown upon a sick bed, lost her reason, and died' after being deserted by John Williamson. Her death prevented her father from suing for seduction, as she 'did not live under the parental roof, and performed for him no personal service'. In response, he took out administration for his daughter, allowing him to sue for breach of promise. The judge directed that he should be awarded 'such damages as they would have given to the intestate herself, had she been alive to bring the action'.[31] Chamberlain's shift from a suit for seduction to one for breach of promise demonstrates the interconnected nature of the two actions, which were later brought concurrently in cases such as *Settle vs. Crumbleholme* (1820).

---

[24] Douglas Hay, 'Kenyon, Lloyd, first Baron Kenyon (1732–1802)', *Oxford Dictionary of National Biography*, online edition, October 2009, accessed 22 November 2017: http://www.oxforddnb.com.oxfordbrookes.idm.oclc.org/view/article/15431.

[25] *World and Fashionable Advertiser*, 4 January 1787, 4.

[26] *Sketches of the characters of the Hon. Thomas Erskine, and James Mingay, Esq.* (London, 1794), 3.

[27] *Morning Post and Gazetteer*, 12 December 1801, 10354.

[28] *Morning Post and Gazetteer*, 16 August 1802, 10566.   [29] 25 *ER* 1100.

[30] *The Sun*, 10 March 1796, 1078.

[31] *The Times*, 22 January 1814, 9125. One further action available to the fathers of seduced women was 'aggravated trespass', when the seducer came uninvited onto his property. Staves, 'British Seduced Maidens', 128.

BRINGING SUIT

The majority of breach of promise suits were fought between plaintiffs and defendants of the middling sort. The average individual bringing a breach of promise suit was inferior to members of the 'leisured, landed elite—esquires and above' bringing crim. con. actions, as well as many of the 'well-to-do' engaging in seduction actions after 1766, 'who could afford to keep their daughters at home'.[32] The gentry are also under-represented in breach of promise suits compared to canon-law matrimonial cases as a whole; Joanne Begiato has found that out of 119 matrimonial cases heard between 1660 and 1800, 41 per cent of couples were of titled or gentry rank, 23 per cent were relatively high-status manufacturers, shop owners, innkeepers, or master mariners, and 17 per cent were professionals, often attorneys and clergymen.[33] Conversely, participants in breach of promise cases remained steadfastly 'middling' into the nineteenth century, where 31 per cent of suits were between two lower middle-class people, and 21.3 per cent were between a lower middle-class plaintiff and a middle-class defendant.[34]

When used by contemporaries, the 'middling sort' constituted an 'impressionistic' social category used to denote people in the 'middle' of those of higher rank with landed wealth, and others such as 'journeymen, servants and labourers who lived off wages'. Nicholas Rogers has argued that in the seventeenth century, the group included 'independent small producers in agriculture and industry'. However, by the eighteenth century such men were largely classed as labourers, and 'middling' men were large-scale farmers and manufacturers and merchants in charge of distribution. To these he adds men in 'privileged urban occupations' such as merchants, tradesmen, substantial shopkeepers, and men in medicine, law, teaching, the civil service, and armed services. In addition were wealthier freeholders and tenant farmers.[35]

Records reveal that women bringing suits were engaged in running boarding houses, grocers, and confectioner's and chandler's shops, or were the daughters of shopkeepers, tobacconists, tradesmen, small-scale manufacturers, and attorneys. The plaintiff in *Hayden vs. Walker* (1791) ran her own boarding house, while the plaintiff in *Simpson vs. Burton* (1793) was the daughter of a shopkeeper. Others bringing suits in *Andrews vs. Morrison* (1801) and *Graves vs. Innocent* (1803) were described as the daughters of tradesmen. Women were usually defined by the profession of their fathers, who were frequently categorized as 'middle rank'. The *Morning Post* described the parties in *Vaile vs. Vandyk* (1821) as 'persons moving in the middle ranks of life; the Plaintiff lived in the house of her mother, and the Defendant, who was sent from Demerara, in the West Indies, to perfect himself in a knowledge

---

[32] This was following Lord Mansfield's ruling that a father 'could not sue for loss of his daughter's services if she had already left home to go into domestic service when the seduction and pregnancy occurred': Stone, *Road to Divorce*, 83. My findings correspond with Stone's argument that litigants were 'confined to a broad spectrum of the middling sort': 89.

[33] Bailey, *Unquiet Lives*, 13.

[34] Frost, *Promises Broken*, 189, note 3.

[35] Nicholas Rogers, 'The Middling Sort in Eighteenth-Century Politics', in *The Middling Sort of People*, ed. Barry and Brooks, 159–80, at 160–1.

of the commerce of this country'.[36] Members of the upper middling sort were singled out in reports as 'respectable', 'eminent', or 'master' tradesmen. For example, the plaintiff in *King vs. Chance* (1822) was the daughter of a fancy dress-maker and a 'respectable' manufacturer, who may have had pretensions to gentility. Other parties of the lower middling sort who did not occupy 'high or exalted situations of life' nonetheless worked in reputable professions, such as the parties in *Hunt vs. Smith* (1804), 'a decent woman keeping a small shop' and a stone cutter with two shops who was 'of her own rank and station'.[37] Similarly in *Simpson vs. Timperon* (1828), 'The station of life in which the parties moved was not very elevated; but it was respectable.'[38]

A small number of cases involved the gentry, including 'lesser esquires, men of respectable lineage who had lost their estates, the better class of professional men, retired military officers, former merchants, and the like'.[39] Only fourteen of the 180 parties (7.8 per cent) in Appendix 2 were described either as 'gentlemen' or a 'gentleman's daughter', while only seven men (7.8 per cent) styled themselves 'Esquire'. Terms such as 'wealthy', 'of property', and 'of fortune' were applied to thirty-three parties (18.3 per cent). The fortunes cited ranged enormously from 'small' or 'moderate' to 'plentiful' and 'large'. Cases such as *Bourdernelle vs. Bamfyld* (1819) were fought between a respectable foreign woman and a gentleman working as an army surgeon, while *Peake vs. Wedgwood* (1826) was between a gentleman's daughter and a man possessing a large landed estate and collieries. An unusual example of a case between the upper strata of the landed gentry is *Leeds vs. Cooke and Wife* (1803), brought by 'a young Gentleman of considerable property' against 'the daughter of a Gentleman of landed property'. After they had drawn up a marriage settlement and each party had advanced £4,000, Miss Cadanell eloped over the border to Gretna Green to marry her new lover Mr Cooke, purser on an East India Company ship.[40]

Nonetheless, the proportion of genteel participants was matched by the number of labouring parties. These include tanners, farmer's daughters, women working in milliners' shops, mantuamakers, and domestic servants. Newspaper reports further categorized plaintiffs into 'humble farmer's daughters' and 'respectable farmer's daughters' to indicate their relative social status.[41] Reports in 1802 argued that their 'humble situation in life' should not rule them out from receiving large damages, as 'the feelings of the humblest individual are not wantonly and barbarously to be outraged . . . without giving that individual a right to appear to a Jury for a compensation adequate to the injury sustained.'[42] The *Morning Post and Gazetteer*'s appeal may have been in response to comparatively low damages received by labouring women in previous cases, with the domestic servant in *Smith vs. Taylor* (1791), the milliner in *Williams vs. Harding* (1793), and the maidservant in *Storey vs. Eagle* (1802) each receiving only £50. The sum represented between three and five times

---

[36] *Morning Post*, 3 February 1821, 15565.
[37] *The Times*, 28 July 1804, 6085.
[38] *Morning Post*, 10 March 1828, 17857.
[39] Hunt, *The Middling Sort*, 17.
[40] *Morning Post*, 2 March 1803, 10736.
[41] For example, the plaintiff in *Rabbitts vs. West* (1824) was 'humble' whereas plaintiffs in *Forster vs. Hoblin* (1805) and *Capper vs. Orton* (1825) were 'respectable': *The Times*, 29 March 1805, 6293; *Morning Post*, 22 March 1825, 16927.
[42] *Morning Post and Gazetteer*, 16 August 1802, 10566.

their annual income, meaning that such women only received 'exemplary damages' of several hundred pounds in 'aggravated' cases involving pregnancy or the refusal of other suitors. While the mantuamaker in *Harris vs. Williamson* (1793) received £200 as she had refused the offers of two respectable tradesmen, the farmer's daughter in *Forster vs. Hoblin* (1805) was awarded £400 after being deserted while pregnant.[43] Courtships between parties of unequal social status were reasonably rare, prompting additional questioning in court over whether this was the cause of desertion. As Thomas Erskine asked the upwardly mobile banker's son Benjamin Barnard in 1792, 'You were not ashamed, Sir, to marry the daughter, though the mother was engaged in trade [as a milliner]?' to which he answered, 'Certainly not.'[44]

In exceptional cases where suits were brought by members of the nobility such as barons and earls, judges were reluctant to pry into the private lives of the elite. Calls to shield the nobility's relationships were not unique to breach of promise actions, with Mr Garrow appealing in the crim. con. trial of the Hon. Richard Bingham and Lady Elizabeth Howard in 1794 for the nobility to 'take heed to its own security' by letting 'Affection and Prudence lead the way' when selecting a spouse.[45] Only one of the parties in Appendix 2 had noble lineage—the plaintiff in *Murray vs. Gale, Esq.* (1794)—who was 'allied to many noble families'. In the case, a noble lady's daughter of 'great beauty' and 'accomplishment' sued a gentleman of significant fortune for breach of promise. Lord Chief Justice Kenyon revealed that he 'was sorry to have more of the veil withdrawn than was absolutely necessary' and was 'sorry so much of it had been withdrawn already', as 'such an exhibition seldom presented itself in a Court of Justice.'[46]

Plaintiffs and defendants were expected to be of a comparable age, with the *London Chronicle* expressing doubt in 1790 that a twenty-one-year-old had seriously courted a woman nearing forty who was 'old enough to be his mother'.[47] Two parties of a similar age were essential for the success of a case, with the judge in *Heyward vs. Arnold* (1796) ruling that 'there ought not to be too great a disparity in the ages of the parties.' Once again, the twenty-two-year-old defendant had been courting a forty-year-old woman.[48] More often, couples were drawn from the same age range, with an absolute maximum of twenty years between the two parties, such as a woman aged thirty and a man aged fifty. Such a large gap was only possible when the man was the elder party, due to the desirability of having a beautiful younger wife who was still able to bear children. Twenty-four parties in Appendix 2 were described as 'young', 'underage', or 'infant', compared to five parties described as 'old', and two of 'maturer age'. The average age of plaintiffs was thirty-four, compared to the average defendant aged forty-two.[49]

---

[43] *The Sun*, 2 May 1793, 184; *The Times*, 29 March 1805, 6293.

[44] *Trial for breach of promise of marriage, Miss Eleanor Palmer against Benjamin Barnard, Esq.* (London, 1792), 24.

[45] *The Trial of the Hon. Richard Bingham, for Crim. Con. with Lady Elizabeth Howard* (London, 1794), 40.

[46] *The Sun*, 29 December 1794, 703.   [47] *London Chronicle*, 19–21 August 1790, 5305.

[48] *The Sun*, 14 May 1796, 1134.

[49] Exact figures are 34.23 for plaintiffs and 41.98 for defendants. When a person was described as '20–22' or '35–40' the average figure was taken, while those 'nearly 18' or 'over 40' were taken as 18 and 40 respectively.

This figure is increased by the presence of nine defendants aged fifty and over compared to only four plaintiffs. Since over 80 per cent of defendants were male, this confirms our view of men as the elder party during courtship.

The presence of twenty-two parties aged forty or over reveals that breach of promise suits were not confined to the young, as high mortality rates meant that individuals often remarried several times. Widows and widowers display a strong presence in Appendix 2, with sixteen individuals either bringing or contesting suits. Cases were brought by plaintiffs of a wide age-range, including one woman 'in her *eighty-fifth* year' in 1797 and another nearing seventy in 1798.[50] However, older women were disadvantaged as both plaintiffs and defendants; judges argued that it was 'not to be endured, that a woman of full age, with ample time for deliberation, should be allowed thus to trifle with the feelings of a man'.[51] Those bringing suits also had their motives called into question, with Lord Alvanley (1744–1804) explaining during *Vaughan vs. Aldridge* (1801) that it was 'unlike a connection of youthful affection, where every future prospect in life might be blasted, and the object so deserted be left a sad memento of unrequited love'.[52] The Counsel for the Defendant blasted Miss Vaughan as a fortune hunter, arguing that if she was genuinely distraught at the loss of her suitor, '[L]ike other disappointed maidens, she would have been found at the tomb of Capulet, lamenting her lost Romeo…instead of which he perceived she was snugly seated in the gallery of the Court, waiting with greedy expectation the event of the verdict.'[53]

Despite the precedent set in *Harrison vs. Cage and Wife* (1698) that 'marriage is as much advancement to a man as it is to a woman', the proceedings of eighteenth-century suits made it increasingly clear that this was no place for a man.[54] This raises the issue of how legal precepts adapted to changing understandings of romantic hurt studied in Chapter 5. The scarcity of suits before 1771 demonstrates that it arose in this particular form in response to changing social and cultural mores. In all cases, a man was expected to have sacrificed his livelihood in order to justify bringing a suit against a woman. This meant that the women they sued had to be incredibly wealthy. In 1787, newspapers reported that a lieutenant of marines was expected to sue a foreign countess worth over £16,000 after she convinced him to sell his post before deserting him. Moreover, in 1796 a button-manufacturer retired from trade in expectation of his marriage to a widow about to inherit over £20,000.[55] No such requirement existed for women bringing breach of promise suits, who could be even wealthier than the parties they sued. The defendant in *Brown vs. Arnold* (1790) lived at the plaintiff's expense for fifteen months, and was 'a little embarrassed in his circumstances'.[56] Unfortunately for Mr Arnold, his

---

50 *True Briton*, 16 November 1797, 1528 and 6 December 1798, 1855.

51 *Morning Post*, 2 March 1803, 10736.

52 *Morning Post and Gazetteer*, 19 June 1801, 10237. The same sentiments were expressed in *Rabbitts vs. West* (1824).

53 Ibid.   54 87 *ER* 736.

55 *World and Fashionable Advertiser*, 4 January 1787, 4. Also see report of *Shaw[e] vs. Baker* where the plaintiff gave up his job as a distillery clerk in order to live independently as a gentleman: *Morning Post and Gazetteer*, 18 August 1800, 9966.

56 *London Chronicle*, 19 August 1790, 5305.

relative poverty in no way prevented his landlady Miss Brown from subsequently suing him for breach of promise.

Women dominated eighteenth-century breach of promise suits, with seventy-two of the cases in Appendix 2 brought by women (81.8 per cent), compared to only sixteen brought by men (18.2 per cent).[57] Men's under-representation was replicated in matrimonial suits in the church courts, where they initiated 30 per cent of suits for separation, restitution of conjugal rights, annulment, and jactitation between 1660 and 1800.[58] The number of men suing for breach of promise dropped remarkably over the nineteenth and early twentieth centuries. The later the period of study concludes, the further men's participation falls, dropping to 8 per cent between 1780 and 1920, and 3.7 per cent between 1800 and 1940.[59] The low number of men bringing eighteenth-century suits suggests that Ginger Frost's argument that men 'were quite as willing to bring actions as women' is hugely misleading.[60] However, while men were unlikely to bring suits for the most part of the century, this had become almost unthinkable by the early 1800s. This makes eighteenth-century suits unique for allowing marginally greater numbers of men to participate, witnessing their rapid decline as the nineteenth century progressed.

While men were less likely to bring suits, they were also less likely to win, with 84.7 per cent of women winning their cases, compared to only 53.3 per cent of men. Only two men and four women lost their cases, despite male plaintiffs being outnumbered by more than four to one. Many of these male 'victors' were subsequently awarded embarrassing damages of one shilling or one farthing, making it a hollow victory. The plaintiff in *Atcheson vs. Baker* was never actually paid the £4,000 he won on the retrial, after first being nonsuited, instead privately agreeing to an annuity of £200 per year. As James Atcheson found, men were more than four times as likely as women to be nonsuited or have their cases adjourned, referred to arbitration, settled, or withdrawn.[61] These figures again undermine Frost's argument that '[i]n its early stages...breach of promise was not biased in favour of one sex or the other.' Nonetheless, half of men did manage to win their cases between 1717 and 1830, a figure which falls to only 28 per cent in Steinbach's study of the period from 1780 to 1920.[62] These figures demonstrate how men gradually brought fewer suits over time, also winning them less frequently.

From the 1790s, romantic hurt was presented in court as a uniquely female grievance and was used by counsels to convince juries that women were seeking redress for emotional distress rather than greed. The shift demonstrates how the law gradually evolved to accommodate the changing understandings of romantic suffering that emerged at mid-century. Female plaintiffs were seen to suffer as

---

[57] This figure excludes the cases *Atkins vs. Far* (1738) and *Chamberlain vs. Williamson, Esq.* (1813) brought by women's parents.

[58] Bailey, *Unquiet Lives*, 14.

[59] Steinbach, 'Promises, Promises', 210; Lettmaier, *Broken Engagements*, 27.

[60] Frost, *Promises Broken*, 16.

[61] The exact figures are 6 out of 15 men (40%), compared to 7 out of 72 women (9.7%) (see Appendix 2). Case no. 10 was discounted as the verdict is unknown.

[62] Frost, *Promises Broken*, 15; Steinbach, 'Promises, Promises', 214.

their affections were 'deeply engaged' by dishonourable men, causing the women attending court to express their 'feelings of tenderness and pity' by crying over the maiden's plight.[63] Lawyers representing female plaintiffs were careful to invoke all of the hallmarks of the 'seduced maiden', emphasizing their client's simplicity, trustfulness, and affectionate nature.[64]

The archetypal woman bringing a breach of promise suit was also expected to be physically attractive. This reflected arguments in moral essays that the ideal wife should be beautiful—in addition to having a sufficient fortune and respectable family—as 'the object which is always before the eye, should not be disagreeable.'[65] It manifested itself in breach of promise and seduction trials where lawyers emphasized women's 'great beauty', 'personal beauty', 'extreme beauty', and 'great personal attraction' to aggravate men's wrongdoing. For example, the plaintiff in *Wilson vs. Powditch* (1799) was reported to be 'beautiful', while the plaintiff in *Hulme vs. Warbrick* (1809) was described as a 'young' woman 'of great personal attraction'.[66] Accounts of women's beauty increased the likelihood that men would want to debauch them, for 'nobody would want to seduce an ugly girl.'[67] The destruction of a woman's beauty necessitated higher damages; the plaintiff in *Belchier vs. Thompson* (1799) 'had been remarkably handsome, though her beauty was now impaired through distress and affliction of mind', prompting the jury to award the generous sum of £400.[68]

Miss Belchier was further afflicted as '[t]his ill treatment had materially affected her health and spirits.'[69] The same dialogue was repeated in numerous suits such as *Chapman vs. Shaw* (1790), *Marcom vs. Edgar* (1794), *Tyley vs. Deerhurst* (1796), *Wilson vs. Powditch* (1799), *Beattie vs. Pearson* (1820), and *Wait vs. Aspinall* (1824), where women were presented as having an inherently nervous disposition, causing them to fall into a mental disorder after their desertion. These parallel women's descriptions of mental agitation considered in Chapter 5. Witnesses deposed that romantic disappointment had caused plaintiffs acute mental strain in an attempt to prove aggravated circumstances and secure higher damages. In the case brought against William Shaw, Esq. by Elizabeth Chapman in 1790, the plaintiff's mother emphasized the mental disorder caused by her abandonment:

> [S]he was out of her mind. She kept her bed, and never slept for *seven days*. She was ill twice; and this illness was manifestly occasioned by Mr. Shaw's breaking off his visits... My daughter's illness was not a sore throat, nor fever: her's [*sic*] was a disorder of the mind. She was out of her senses two months.[70]

---

[63] *World and Fashionable Advertiser*, 30 March 1787, 77; *Belchier vs. Thompson*, in *Lloyd's Evening Post*, 15 May 1799, 6509.

[64] Staves, 'British Seduced Maidens', 118.

[65] Essay IXI, 'The Choice of a Partner for Life', in *Moral Essays, Chiefly Collected from Different Authors* (Liverpool, 1796), Vol. II, 22.

[66] *Oracle and Daily Advertiser*, 20 December 1799, 22173; *The Times*, 28 August 1809, 7760.

[67] Staves, 'British Seduced Maidens'; *Hulme vs. Warbrick* (1809), in *The Lancaster Gazette*, 9 September 1809, 430.

[68] *Belchier vs. Thompson*, in *Lloyd's Evening Post*, 15 May 1799, 6509.   [69] Ibid.

[70] *Trial for a Breach of Promise of Marriage. Miss Elizabeth Chapman, Against William Shaw. Esq; Attorney at Law. Before The Right Honourable Lord Kenyon, in the Court of King's-Bench, Westminster-Hall, On Saturday, The 22d of May, 1790* (London, 1790), 11–12.

Miss Marcom also won her case against the apothecary Devereux Edgar in 1794 after proving that her 'health and peace of mind had suffered' after being deprived of matrimony.[71] These discourses first emerged in breach of promise suits in the early 1790s, following new conceptualizations of romantic hurt. They reflect prevailing beliefs about women's beauty, fragility, nervousness, and mental instability, situating these suits firmly within contemporary notions of womanhood. Nancy Cott has also traced the ideology of female 'passionlessness' back to the 1790s, situating it within the Evangelical emphasis upon women's virtuous nature and lack of carnal motivation.[72] A related change took place in church court cases in the second half of the eighteenth century, where men found it less viable to claim abuse at the hands of their wives, who were 'recast as the "gentler sex"; inherently weak, naturally virtuous and sexually passive'. In turn, men were redefined as sexual predators.[73]

The role of men in breach of promise cases evolved simultaneously with the redefinition of female identity. Lawyers from the 1790s onwards increasingly characterized men as overly amorous due to their strong passions, like the suicidal men studied in Chapter 5 of this book. Young men were particularly likely to form inappropriate engagements, as they had not developed suitable 'discretion' and the ability to make prudent judgements. The 'very young' tradesman sued in *Williams vs. Harding* (1793) was said to be 'in the hey-day of blood, and likely to be suddenly prevailed upon to make promise of marriage [*sic*] in the moment of amorous passion; but which could not be supposed he would keep when reason and deliberation returned'.[74] The judge painted a similar picture of men's impulsive and imprudent nature during *Murray vs. Gale, Esq.* (1793):

> It did not very unfrequently happen...that young men, before they had arrived at the years of discretion, before they had emancipated themselves from the parental affection, had been driven from the impulse of their passions, to make imprudent promises with regard to the subject of marriage...the Law must consider them as responsible for the breach of such a promise, yet he should be ashamed of himself under such circumstances, to call for heavy damages.[75]

While recognising that young men must be held responsible for deserting their lovers, breach of promise suits provided a way for men to protect their reputation and excuse their ungallant behaviour by paying damages to protect a woman's virtue. The damages provided some form of compensation to women whose future prospects for marriage may have been significantly damaged.[76] Thomas Erskine presented the issue as a matter of honour and emotional sensibility in *Palmer vs. Barnard, Esq.*

[71] *Oracle and Public Advertiser*, 26 August 1794, 18782. A similar account of women's mental instability appeared five years later in *Wilson vs. Powditch* (1799): *Oracle and Daily Advertiser*, 20 December 1799, 22173.

[72] Nancy Cott, 'Passionlessness: An Interpretation of Victorian Sexual Ideology, 1790–1850', *Signs* 4.2 (1978): 219–36.

[73] Bailey, *Unquiet Lives*, 112, 129–31.   [74] *True Briton*, 18 March 1793, 66.

[75] *The Sun*, 29 December 1794, 703. For a further example, see *Page vs. Mont, Morning Chronicle*, 13 July 1813, 14412.

[76] For the relationship between male reputation and moral conduct, see Faramerz Dabhoiwala, 'The Construction of Honour, Reputation and Status in Late Seventeenth- and Early Eighteenth-Century England', *Transactions of the Royal Historical Society* 6 (1996): 201–13, at 204.

(1792), praising the (all-male) jury as 'gentlemen of honour' and imploring them to 'excite your sensibility' in comprehending Eleanor's loss.[77]

Changes in the nature of the action were hastened by emotional shifts as well as the redefinition of gender roles. The decreasing participation and success of male plaintiffs can be attributed to the fact that cases in the early 1800s came to rely more upon demonstrating the hurt *feelings* of spurned lovers. Although Staves has argued that breach of promise, seduction, and trespass actions each involved the demonstration of 'wounded feelings' rather than simply 'out of pocket losses', it was not until the early nineteenth century that this notion came to dominate suits. Earlier cases such as *Holt vs. Ward, Esq.* (1730) did not once mention the plaintiff's injured feelings, focusing on whether or not the defendant made an explicit promise of marriage. When a retrial of *Atcheson vs. Baker* was granted in 1797, the court was clear that the action 'was not brought for the loss of any affection', but solely concerned whether Mrs Baker had reneged upon her promise to marry James Atcheson within a specific time.[78] However, just three years later in *Shaw[e] vs. Baker* (1800), 'the injury done to individuals by the breach of a marriage contract consisted in the disappointment of expected happiness, the violation of their feelings.'[79] By the time the disappointed suitor Mr Leeds attempted to bring a case against his sweetheart and her new husband Mr Cooke in 1803, the case had come to centre upon the plaintiff's hurt feelings, which inevitably weighted proceedings in the favour of women. As Thomas Erskine admitted during his case for Mr Leeds, 'I do not mean to contend that when a man is thus deceived and disappointed, he suffers the like disparagement as when it happens to a female.'[80] During the trial, Lord Ellenborough explained the importance of the plaintiff's 'feelings' to the jury:

> There might be cases where even a man was entitled to a large compensation in damages for a breach of promise of marriage. In all cases of this sort, the Jury would consider the injury done to the feelings. If the party complaining were themselves indifferent to the event, or expressed gladness at their escape, the smallest compensation was sufficient.[81]

Despite his assertion that 'even a man' was theoretically entitled to sizeable compensation, men were never able to demonstrate the same emotional hurt described by women bringing suits, as they were not seen to suffer the same turmoil as women when a relationship ended. Thus while divorce, custody, and crim. con. actions favoured 'the already-propertied husbands', breach of promise actions provide a rare example of the courts favouring women.[82]

Lord Ellenborough's direction for juries to focus on 'the injury done to the feelings' provides a striking contrast to petitions for divorce on grounds of cruelty.[83] As Thomas Dixon has argued, parliamentary divorces based on cruelty required

---

[77] *Eleanor Palmer against Benjamin Barnard*, 8.
[78] *Evening Mail*, 3 May 1797 (no issue number available).
[79] *Morning Post and Gazetteer*, 18 August 1800, 9966. Also see Staves, 'British Seduced Maidens', 129.
[80] *Morning Post*, 2 March 1803, 10736.   [81] Ibid.
[82] Komisaruk, 'Privatization of Pleasure', 41.   [83] *Morning Post*, 2 March 1803, 10736.

expected or actual injury to 'life, limb, or health'. In contrast, the feelings of plaintiffs were marginalized, following Lord Stowell's oft-cited ruling in *Evans vs. Evans* (1790) that 'What merely wounds the mental feelings is in few cases to be admitted, where it is not accompanied with bodily injury, either actual or menaced.' Exceptions were only occasionally made in later cases, such as *Kelly vs. Kelly* (1869) where the petitioner invoked medical evidence attributing nervous disorders to their spouse's psychological cruelty.[84] Breach of promise cases in the early decades of the nineteenth century were therefore at odds with related matrimonial suits in their prioritizing of litigants' feelings. Judges presiding over breach of promise cases after 1800 repeatedly insisted that their key concern was the 'violation' of a plaintiff's 'feelings', that 'feelings' were not 'wantonly and barbarously to be outraged', and that no individual should be permitted to 'trifle with the feelings' of another.[85]

Damages were awarded based on injury to the plaintiff's reputation and their altered situation in life. Frost estimates that the average award in eighteenth-century cases was £500, which Steinbach raises to £620 2s. for successful female plaintiffs between 1780 and 1868.[86] While Frost's average is based on a negligible number of cases, Steinbach's is likely inflated by cases later in the nineteenth century. Of the ninety suits studied in this chapter, seventy-two record the damages ordered when settled or ruled for the plaintiff. These suits reveal average damages of £550 7s. 6d. between 1717 and 1830. Five defendants were also ordered to pay legal costs, and one child maintenance. However, this sum should not be taken as representative, as it is increased by exceptionally high awards of £4,000 in *Atcheson vs. Baker* (1796–7) and £5,000 in *Bishop vs. Robinson* (1810) and *Beattie vs. Pearson* (1820). A more accurate picture is provided by Table 6.1, which shows that the majority of damages were less than £250, with sums of £50, £100, and £140 regularly being awarded. While these are significantly lower than Steinbach's median award of £275, they would nonetheless have represented a significant sum for most middling people, who had incomes of between £50 and £2,000 per year, mostly concentrated between £80 and £150.[87] Higher damages of between £1,251 and £1,500 were equally as likely as derisory sums of less than a pound, including awards for 1s. in 1803 and 1f. in 1814. *Graves vs. Innocent* (1803) provides an example of a case with typical damages, as whilst Lord Ellenborough recognized that a promise of marriage had been breached, there were 'no circumstances of aggravation...She had not been deteriorated in her circumstances, nor degraded in her character. Nor had there been much public exhibition of her mortification.' Since it was only known to one of her acquaintances, she was awarded the average sum of £100.[88] Judges' continual reminders 'not utterly to ruin the defendant' and to respect their 'situation in life' presents a marked contrast to damages in

[84] Thomas Dixon, 'Feelings, Health, and Cruelty in 19th-Century Divorce Cases', Queen Mary History of the Emotions Blog, 10 May 2013: http://emotionsblog.history.qmul.ac.uk/?p=2388.
[85] *Morning Post and Gazetteer*, 18 August 1800, 9966 and 16 August 1802, 10566; *Morning Post*, 2 March 1803, 10736.
[86] Frost, *Promises Broken*, 16; Steinbach, 'Promises, Promises', Table Two, 212.
[87] Hunt, *The Middling Sort*, 15; Steinbach, 'Promises, Promises', Table Two, 212.
[88] *Morning Post*, 21 February 1803, 10728.

Table 6.1. Damages awarded in breach of promise trials 1717–1830, as sampled in Appendix 2

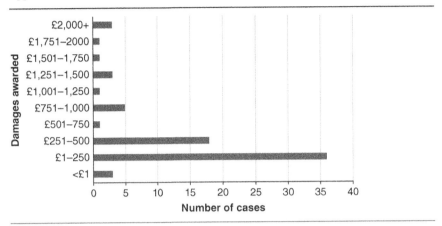

crim. con. trials, where juries did not concern themselves with the capacity of the defendant to pay.[89]

When it could be proven that a man was deliberately callous, the jury could be more unforgiving. During *Beattie vs. Pearson* (1820), the silk manufacturer Samuel Pearson was charged with deserting a woman and leaving her on the brink of insanity. He went on to behave 'in a similar manner towards another Lady', boasting that he could 'win any woman's heart' within one month. The jury were outraged, and 'convicted his folly' by forcing him to pay an enormous £5,000 damages, which only happened twice within the sample of cases in Appendix 2.[90] The damages were justified as Pearson was 'a gentleman of great opulence, at the head of an extensive silk manufactory', suggesting that he was able to afford such a sum.[91] Exceptional amounts worth over a year's wages were only charged in aggravated cases; other defendants in *Hayden vs. Walker* (1791) and *Storey vs. Eagle* (1802) were charged two and a half and one month's wages, respectively. This compares to the defendant in *Andrews vs. Morrison* (1801) who purchased a gold ring, a wedding licence, and furniture for the marital home before deserting his bride, justifying the inflated fine of sixteen months wages. Exorbitant damages remained the exception rather than the rule, only exceeding £3,000 in cases such as *Bishop vs. Robinson* (1810) and *Beattie vs. Pearson* (1820).

---

[89] *Morning Post and Gazetteer*, 12 December 1801, 10354; Stone, *Road to Divorce*, 90–1. For a similar formulation, see report of *Wilson vs. Powditch*, in *Oracle and Daily Advertiser*, 20 December 1799, 22173.

[90] *Morning Post*, 9 September 1820, 15439. The defendants in *Bishop vs. Robinson* (1810) and *Beattie vs. Pearson* (1820) were both ordered to pay £5,000, while the female defendant in *Atcheson vs. Baker* (1796–7) was ordered to pay £4,000, but never parted with the sum. See *Morning Post and Gazetteer*, 18 August 1800, 9966.

[91] *Trewman's Exeter Flying Post or Plymouth and Cornish Advertiser*, 14 September 1820, 2870.

Lawyers such as Mr Topping of the Lancaster Assizes proudly claimed that there were geographical variations in the amounts awarded, indicating the honourable character of particular regions. He argued during *Settle vs. Crumbleholme* (1818) that 'Lancashire juries were famed for setting no bounds to damages, in all cases that had any tendency of this kind.'[92] By 'this kind' he meant aggravated cases where the plaintiff had become pregnant before being deserted by her faithless suitor. Topping had enjoyed some degree of celebrity after winning £7,000 damages for the plaintiff in *Orford vs. Cole* (1818), who was from a 'well-known and respected' family. The case became a cause célèbre and ladies 'braved every danger' to gain admittance to the crowded 2,000-seater court.[93] However, detailed study of the damages awarded suggests that regional assizes conformed to the precedent set by the King's Bench, where most awards were for less than £250. Nominal amounts of £100 and £10 were regularly awarded in cases such as *Bird vs. Coupland* (1818) and *Duckworth vs. Johnson* (1824) at the Lancaster Assizes which did not feature aggravating circumstances.[94] Mr Topping was no doubt encouraged to make such an assertion to cement his growing reputation as the guardian of female virtue and chastity, which had become the defining features of the suit in the early decades of the nineteenth century.

The nature of the suit evolved over the long eighteenth century, as it drifted away from the principle established in *Holcroft vs. Dickenson* (1672–3) that romantic abandonment caused a temporal loss. The case held that 'the woman is preferred by marriage, and the loss of marriage hath always been reputed a damage.'[95] This remained the central tenet of cases such as *Hayden vs. Walker* (1791) where the defendant had agreed to settle £900 upon the plaintiff, causing her to lose a significant amount of money after her desertion. Losses could also be sustained by refusing other suitors, as in *Palmer vs. Barnard, Esq.* (1792), *Harris vs. Williamson* (1793), and *Murray vs. Gale, Esq.* (1794). However, in the early years of the nineteenth century, cases became less about remunerating actual financial loss and more about compensating women for their damaged virtue. The change represented a natural progression from the emerging emphasis in the 1790s upon women's affectionate nature, beauty, and nervous disposition. Feminine virtue became further entrenched within the suit in the early nineteenth century, with women first being compared to domestic 'angels' during *Andrews vs. Morrison* in 1801. As Thomas Erskine argued, 'Let her be as beautiful as an angel, and as accomplished as possible, she never could appear as she was before she became the object of such an insult.'[96] This represented a subtle change rather than an abrupt shift; while suffering from love was redefined in society as a whole from the 1750s, it became reflected in a legal context in the 1790s, leading to the legal entrenchment of the virtuous domesticated woman in the 1800s.

---

[92] *Lancaster Gazette*, 5 September 1818, 899.
[93] *The Derby Mercury*, 9 April 1818, 4483; *Liverpool Mercury*, 10 April 1818, 355.
[94] *The Lancaster Gazette*, 6 April 1816, 773.   [95] 89 *ER* 70.
[96] *Morning Post and Gazetteer*, 12 December 1801, 10354.

MATERIAL PROMISES

The social and emotional significance of objects did not cease immediately when a relationship came to an end, and they often proved decisive in securing a victory in court. While the courting couples studied in Chapters 3 and 4 of this book exchanged a cornucopia of gifts, only a select few were produced as evidence during breach of promise trials. These represent the items which plaintiffs believed unequivocally demonstrated that they were on the brink of matrimony. The four items which were uniformly produced by plaintiffs were love letters, wedding licences, wedding clothes, and furniture for the marital home.

The love letter was undoubtedly the most important object, used as proof in thirty-four out of ninety cases in Appendix 2 (37.8 per cent).[97] Isaac Cruikshank's etching *A New Chancery Suit removed to the Scotch Bar or more Legitimates* depicts the celebrated breach of promise lawyer Thomas Erskine marrying his mistress and housekeeper Sarah Buck (1771–1856) at Gretna Green in 1818, surrounded by their illegitimate children (Figure 6.2). Erskine is disguised as Sarah's mother, with

Fig. 6.2. Isaac Cruikshank, *A New Chancery Suit removed to the Scotch Bar or more Legitimates*, London, 1819, hand-coloured etching, 24.8 cm × 35.1 cm, British Museum, London, 1868,0808.8412. © The Trustees of the British Museum, All Rights Reserved.

---

[97] *Leeds vs. Cooke and Wife* (1803) was discounted as the case relied upon a letter sent after the desertion, as was *Shannon vs. Brandon* (1818) where the letter was a formal note using legal language, rather than a love letter. See *Morning Post*, 2 March 1803, 10736 and 29 June 1818, 14802.

his oversized bonnet invoking his wife's earlier trade as a bonnet maker. Hanging on the wall before them are 'Rings to fit all Hands', confirming the symbolism of rings as the emblem of married couples. Erskine holds a piece of paper in his right hand that reads 'Breach of Promise'. Yet he is not alarmed by his sweetheart running down the hill to interrupt the ceremony: 'she may do her worst since I have got my <u>Letters</u> back.' The woman cries 'Oh Stop Stop Stop, false Man, I will yet seek redress tho you have got back your letters', confirming the significance of love letters in attesting to a serious relationship in court.

When letters did not survive, domestic servants such as porters, chambermaids, and charwomen could be interrogated as to whether a correspondence had taken place. Such witnesses were asked whether the plaintiff had 'received any directed to her, from whom, by whom, and whether she heard them read', and even whether she gave her 'the liberty of perusing them?'[98] In 1730, a porter hired by the gentleman Knox Ward deposed that he was employed

> [I]n carrying letters frequently to the Plaintiff, Mrs. *Sarah Holt*, for which he was handsomely rewarded when he returned with an Answer to the Defendant, his good Master; but that he did not know what they contained, or what the Substance of them was, for that as he was only a hired Porter, his Business was only to carry the Letters, and bring back the Gentlewoman's Answers whenever she sent any...he could not be certain as to the particular Number, because he carry'd a great many, but verily believes them to be above two hundred.[99]

The frequency of exchanges between Knox and Sarah was significant, as the 'great many' letters they sent and received acted as a measure of their passion. The content of love letters provided further proof of their intentions and the implied contract between the couple, with the counsel for the plaintiff in *Chapman vs. Shaw, Esq.* (1790) attesting that 'You will find by his letters...it seemed impossible for him to enjoy any happiness in this world without marrying her.'[100] In other cases, the businesslike style of letters undermined the plaintiff's case, as they 'contained no expressions of love', prompting the court to rule for the defendant.[101]

At the turn of the nineteenth century, newspapers were increasingly willing to reprint a couple's love letters in full, scandalously revealing the intimate details of their relationship to a fascinated public. This was the fate of the parties in *Forster vs. Mellish* (1802) where the counsel for the plaintiff 'read an immense number of the Plaintiff's love letters in support of his reasonings', which were published as a pamphlet the same year.[102] The pamphlet ran to three editions in three months, despite the costly price of 5s.[103] This was astronomically expensive compared to crim. con. cases published during the same period, which were half the price at 2s.

---

[98] *A Collection of remarkable cases, for the instruction of both sexes, in the business of love and gallantry* (London, 1730), 17.

[99] *Tryal between Mrs Sarah Holt, and Knox Ward*, 5.

[100] *Elizabeth Chapman, Against William Shaw*, 2.

[101] *Brown vs. Arnold* (1790), *London Chronicle*, 19–21 August 1790, 5305.

[102] *Morning Chronicle*, 25 February 1802, 10224.

[103] *Morning Post and Gazetteer*, 1 March 1802, 10421.

6d. for a single trial pamphlet.[104] A similar fate was suffered by the parties in *Storey vs. Eagle* (1802) and *Compton vs. Winkworth* (1820), who had extracts from their letters published 'As a specimen of their style'.[105] The letters granted readers a teasing glimpse into their relationship, demonstrating public clamour in the early nineteenth century for every salacious detail of cases.

The Hardwicke Marriage Act required that couples wanting to be married needed either a licence or the calling of banns on three consecutive Sundays in their local parish. Licences would only be granted if one of the parties had resided in the parish for at least four weeks, but once granted the service could take place immediately.[106] Licences were regularly used as proof that a couple were about to marry, setting common law cases apart from church court cases before 1754, as licences were not previously required to exchange vows *per verba de praesenti*. In the temporal courts, licences were used to prove proximity to marriage by plaintiffs in *Horam vs. Humfreys* (1772), *Andrews vs. Morrison* (1801), *Barr[y] vs. Dixon* (1813), and *Duckworth vs. Johnson* (1828). Licences would usually have been obtained by men and presented to women as tangible proof of their intention to marry in the coming weeks. During *Andrews vs. Morrison* in 1801, Thomas Erskine described how Mr Morrison 'sanctioned his engagement by obtaining a licence from the Ecclesiastical Court: he presented her with the licence, and left it in her possession'. After changing his mind, he sent the beadle of the parish to retrieve it and 'foolishly supposed, as he had got the licence, there was an end of the contract'. The defendant's scheming saw him fined over a year's wages, as the licence demonstrated that the couple had 'looked upon each other as bound indissolubly together'.[107]

As the cost and spectacle of weddings grew over the late eighteenth and early nineteenth centuries, plaintiffs put increasing emphasis upon preparations for their nuptials. Eighteenth-century brides would generally have not expected to wear their dresses for a single occasion, and those on a limited budget would have worn their 'best' outfits for the ceremony.[108] The first use of wedding clothes to prove a couple's commitment was in *Holmes vs. Banbury* in 1791, where the innkeeper's daughter Miss Holmes spent £80 purchasing her outfit for the occasion, plus £24 for a gold watch. In the following years, marriage clothes acquired an increasingly prominent position in breach of promise trials. The ultimate insult was to purchase wedding clothes only to be forced to integrate them into your everyday wardrobe, with the disappointed bride in *Cooper vs. Everton* (1817) describing how 'I did buy wedding clothes, but I have now begun to wear them.'[109]

---

[104] Komisaruk, 'Privatization of Pleasure', 43.

[105] *The Lancaster Gazette and General Advertiser*, 8 January 1820, 969.

[106] While the Act forbade granting a licence in a parish where parties did not live, there were no sanctions for doing so, although surrogates had to give £100 security 'for the proper performance of their office'. Although marriages were void in the absence of a licence, there were no requirements that it had to be properly obtained: Probert, *Marriage Law and Practice*, 222–4, 232–3.

[107] Phrase used to describe the marriage contract drawn up by parties in *French vs. Keogh* (1813) at the King's Bench Dublin: *Morning Post*, 26 July 1813, 13265.

[108] Edwina Ehrman, *The Wedding Dress: 300 Years of Bridal Fashions* (London, 2011), 22–95.

[109] *The Times*, 4 August 1817, 10215.

The purchase of 'wedding habiliments' was especially scandalous when the men concerned were already married, such as the defendant in *Wait vs. Aspinall* (1824).[110] Steinbach has argued that preparations for a wedding compelled higher damages between 1780 and 1920 as it was expensive to purchase items such as dresses and bride-cake, whilst the cancelling of the ceremony added to the bride's humiliation.[111] The cases studied here demonstrate how the production of wedding clothes had become a central component of cases after 1791, as they unmistakably demonstrated a couple's intention to marry. However, these items lost their potency after a number of years, with the plaintiff in *Duckworth vs. Johnson* (1828) only awarded £10 despite choosing her bridesmaids and planning to marry the next day. The meagre sum was justified as Duckworth had waited three years to bring a suit, suggesting that she 'had not considered herself very grievously injured'.[112]

The purchase of furniture was also interpreted as clear evidence of proximity to marriage. Amanda Vickery has outlined how betrothed couples only weeks or days from marriage used the later stages of courtship as a gateway to 'setting up home'. The process involved purchasing domestic goods to furnish a new abode, signifying that a couple was on the 'threshold of matrimony'.[113] In 1801, the defendant in *Andrews vs. Morrison* aggravated his breach of promise by inviting the bride's mother 'to look at the house he had taken, and the furniture he had purchased for his intended bride', before leaving her for another woman.[114] The defendant in *Graves vs. Innocent* (1803) made similar plans for the marital home before deserting his bride, and 'During several visits he talked of the alterations he intended making in his house, and of the cloaths he wished to be purchased for his bride, for he said, he wished to pay every respect and attention.'[115] These purchases (actual and promised) were seen as aggravating the men's desertion, and they were fined £200 and £100, respectively, which represented roughly a year's wages. New houses and their attendant furnishings could evidently symbolize a promised marriage in court, even if that promise was subsequently broken.

CONCLUSION

This chapter has argued that breach of promise became progressively more popular over the eighteenth century before becoming inextricably associated with gendered notions of romantic suffering in its closing decades. The majority of cases were fought between individuals of the middling sort, the women being daughters of respectable manufacturers or running shops and boarding houses, and the men eminent tradesmen such as master bakers and landscape architects. Parties were

---

[110] *The Bury and Norwich Post*, 15 September 1824, 2203.
[111] Steinbach, 'Promises, Promises', 146.
[112] *The Lancaster Gazette*, 6 September 1828, 1421.
[113] Amanda Vickery, *Behind Closed Doors: At Home in Georgian England* (New Haven, CT and London, 2009), 88–105.
[114] *Morning Post and Gazetteer*, 12 December 1801, 10354.
[115] *Morning Post*, 21 February 1803, 10728.

not as young as we might expect, due to the high number of widows and widowers entering the court system. The damages awarded to plaintiffs were also far lower than historians have argued, usually remaining below £250 and only exceeding the equivalent of one year of the defendant's wages in aggravated cases.

The numerous shifts outlined in this chapter are united by the theme of gender identity in changing understandings of masculinity and femininity. These underpin the growing popularity of the suit from the 1790s, when cases came to hinge upon women's beauty, fragility, nervous disposition, and mental instability. In turn, men were characterized by their amorous nature, impetuosity, and passion. The purpose of the suit was to compensate women for their perceived physical and emotional trauma while excusing men for their ungallant behaviour. The chapter has shown how the law gradually adapted to new emotional norms, as while women became inextricably associated with suffering from love from the 1750s, it took almost half a century for this to emerge in a legal context.

Breach of promise suits also provide unique insight into the material culture of courtship by revealing which items provided incontrovertible proof of matrimony. While an abundance of gifts were exchanged by the courting couples studied in Chapters 3 and 4 of this book, only a small number were used to invoke proximity to marriage in court. These items changed over time, with wedding licences appearing after Hardwicke's Act was implemented in 1754, and wedding dresses after 1791. This tangible evidence also attests to the sheer power of love letters in symbolizing a couple's commitment. These small emotionally imbued missives had the power to prove a serious relationship even when not directly produced in court, as being seen to send, receive, and read love letters provided proof enough that a couple regarded themselves as bound indissolubly together.

Conclusion

This book has followed couples as they navigated the game of love over the long eighteenth century. Courtship was variously conceptualized as an exhilarating sport, a frenetic battlefield, a strategic game of chess, or a determined crossing of a stormy sea. In 1747, it was marketed as a new 'Entertaining Game for a large Company' titled *Courtship and Matrimony* (Figure 7.1). The game had been invented by the Society of Anatomists and could be purchased for one shilling from print and pamphlet shops.[1] Successful players were rewarded with a smile, a love letter, mutual passion, gaining the consent of friends, reaching a settlement, purchasing a marriage licence and wedding ring, and setting the date for nuptials. Players might land on a square worth £10,000, enough to live comfortably as a gentleman for twenty years.[2] After Hardwicke's Marriage Act came into force in 1754, the game was updated to enable couples to elope over the Scottish border to Gretna Green.[3] Like the courting couples studied in this book, players had to avoid hurdles such as a wounded heart, love rivals, disputes about money, and breaking off a relationship, which could send them back to the start of the board.

The central aim of this book has been to understand how men and women in Georgian England made sense of this emotionally fraught process—the making and breaking of courtships—in words and objects. To do so, it has examined how relationships were formed using the shared language of love, how love letters worked to create a reciprocal bond between couples and eventually secure an engagement, how sensory interaction with romantic gifts produced and intensified feelings of love, and how consumer goods were inscribed with affective meaning and adopted as objects of emotion. Yet not all courtships culminated in a church wedding, and this book has also explored the breaking of relationships through the return of letters and tokens, and the pursuit of damages for breach of promise in the civil courts.

Romantic relationships were guided by a porous script for love, which retained older references to Milton and Shakespeare, while gradually incorporating new allusions to Richardson and Rousseau, among others. This permeable lexicon also incorporated scientific advances to conceive of the chemistry and electricity of

---

[1] *London Evening Post*, 30 April 1747, 3041.

[2] Robert D. Hume, 'The Value of Money in Eighteenth-Century England: Incomes, Prices, Buying Power—and Some Problems in Cultural Economics', *Huntington Library Quarterly* 77.4 (2015): 373–416, at 377.

[3] *Bowles's New Invented and Entertaining Game of Courtship and Matrimony. To Be Played Not Only With Dice, as The Goose and Snake, But also with Cards, or an Index*, London, c.1795.

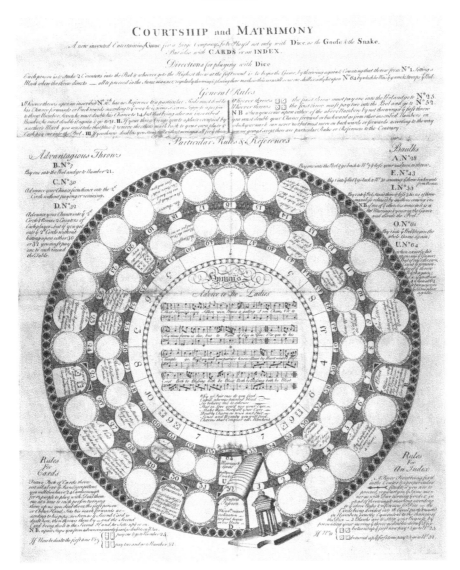

Fig. 7.1. *Courtship and Matrimony. A new invented Entertaining Game for a large Company*, London, 1747, copper engraving, 48 cm (W) × 60 cm (H), Ciompi/Seville 0978.

attraction. The language of love emerges from this study as a supremely adaptable lexicon, which evolved readily alongside social and cultural shifts. Romantic language was no mere affectation, but had a vital function in facilitating intellectual exchange, determining a couple's compatibility, shaping their emotions, and helping to make sense of their budding relationship. The creation and quotation of romantic verse also provided a way for men to set themselves apart from rival suitors by exhibiting their education and refinement. In the absence of this language, how could a couple have known for sure that they were engaging in courtship, as lovers and not just friends? In the words of one friend-turned-suitor, 'I have often wrote to you, but never in a strain like this.'[4] The shared language of love thus worked to bind couples together emotionally, to situate their exchanges clearly within the framework of courtship, and give their relationships an overarching trajectory.

The language of romantic love had widespread cultural reach, sweeping across social boundaries from the labouring classes (including humble labourers and individuals working in service) to the middling sorts (artisans, merchants, and tradesmen), the gentry (respectable businessmen, clergymen, lawyers, and politicians), and aristocracy. The adaptability of the language of love provided a popular theme in print culture, with series such as George Woodward's *Symptoms of the Shop* (1801) parodying the language used by suitors in different professions. The squat bookseller in Figure 7.2 entreats a sceptical taller woman that while he is 'but plainly bound' and not 'gilt or letter'd', his 'composition is good' and he hopes his 'Frontispiece' will not displease her. With her love, he hopes to 'rise from the sheets of Hymen a valuable unique not unworthy of a place in the Library of Love!!' Yet as we have seen, in practice the language used by men and women across social classes was remarkably uniform.

The eighteenth century witnessed a new celebration of romantic love in philosophy, literature, and visual and material culture, bound up with the rise of capitalism, sensibility, and more recognizably modern understandings of selfhood. As the barrister Charles Pratt put it, love was 'ye bond of all society, & production of all ye Good in this World'.[5] While pursuing partners of similar age, rank, fortune, religion, and disposition, the couples studied in this book clearly saw themselves as being in hot pursuit of love, particularly the distinct experience of 'falling in love' and remaining thereafter 'in love'. As evidenced throughout this book, being 'in love' was distinguished by anxiety, agitation, fear, happiness, blushes, sighs, trembling, weeping, and obsessive thoughts and dreams about a loved one, plus an attendant indifference to others. Under the influence of sensibility, love was transformed into a tender and refined sensation associated with a person's emotional sensitivity and delicacy of feeling. With a loving marriage now seen as essential to lasting and perfect happiness, it is no wonder that men and women felt duty bound to marry someone they were 'in love with', even as endogamy usually prevailed, and the gentleman courted the gentleman's daughter, and the merchant married the merchant's daughter.

Yet not all courtships ended at the altar, as courting couples were only too aware. This book has problematized the position of courtship in narratives of the life cycle by revealing that courtships could be transient, painful, and short-lived, rather than the first building block of matrimony. While previous studies have considered the breakdown of marriages through adultery, bigamy, cruelty, desertion, separation, or divorce, or the period immediately after courtship via illegitimacy, the relationships here fell apart as men and women simply changed their minds, fell out of love, or

---

[4] Jed. Strutt to Woollat, Blackwell, 3 February 1755, D5303/4/1, DRO.
[5] Pratt to Jeffreys, 22 July 1749, U840/C1/25, KHLC.

Fig. 7.2. George Woodward and Francis Sansom, *Symptoms of the Shop*, Plate 12, London, 1801, hand-coloured etching and engraving, roulette and stipple, plate mark 25.1 cm × 20.1 cm, Courtesy of the Lewis Walpole Library, Yale University, 801.04.01.04.

transferred their attentions to another. Some sought parental approval too late. Others were deserted on their wedding day. Particularly unlucky were women such as the novelist Mary Hays, whose suitor died during courtship. After a relationship came to an end, family and friends were there to pick up the pieces, demonstrating how the making *and* breaking of relationships were both aided by kin. Parents, siblings, and friends provided a crucial emotional support network after a courtship had come to an end, writing to apologize for faithless lovers, writing to the guilty to condemn their behaviour, and buoying the spirits of deserted parties. They worked to limit the potential social fallout by endeavouring to subdue gossip and organizing the retrieval of a woman's love letters as swiftly as possible. If a woman's health had been destroyed by her abandonment, parents could also take out administration for their daughters and sue faithless suitors for breach of promise.

The process of falling in and out of love was in part negotiated through objects; love, understood as a verb, is something that we *do*. A diverse range of objects could be designated conduits for romantic emotions, and therefore used to produce, affirm, and intensify feelings of love. Romantic love is not alone in being elicited by objects, and other forms of love, and other emotions, could also be productively studied in this way.[6] In moving beyond traditional approaches that quantify the relative popularity of different types of love tokens, the book has revealed how such items accrued affective meanings in practice.[7] We have much to gain from bringing together the fields of emotions history and sensory history, in order to explore how sight, sound, touch, smell, and taste operate as affective stimuli. This book has shown how rituals of gazing at, caressing, kissing, and smelling love tokens worked to cultivate particular feelings, summoning fond memories of loved ones and inspiring love letters and romantic poetry. Such objects could variously elicit pleasurable feelings of happiness, joy, comfort, and desire, but also pain at missing an absent lover. Items such as patch boxes did not necessarily possess any essential qualities as love tokens beyond the ways in which they were given, received, preserved, and used by lovers. Having said this, certain items such as ribbons, garters, gloves, and stay busks possessed particular value as quintessential romantic gifts, with rings acting as material emblems of the betrothed couple.

While this book has focused exclusively on courtships between men and women, a growing number of studies have examined the languages and practices used to build 'intimate partnerships', 'beloved friendships', and love affairs between same-sex couples.[8] Scholars reconstructing these histories must also grapple with

---

[6] For an introduction to the growing field of emotions and material culture, see Downes, Holloway, and Randles, 'A Feeling for Things', 8–23.

[7] The classic study quantifying types of gift is O'Hara, *Courtship and Constraint*, 57–98.

[8] On intimate relationships between women during this period, see Lillian Faderman, *Surpassing the Love of Men: Romantic Friendship and Love between Women from the Renaissance to the Present* (New York, 1981), Parts I & II; Margaret Hunt, 'The Sapphic Strain: English Lesbians in the Long Eighteenth Century', in *Singlewomen in the European Past 1250–1800*, ed. Judith M. Bennett and Amy M. Froide (Philadelphia, PA, 1999), 270–96; Valerie Traub, *The Renaissance of Lesbianism in Early Modern England* (Cambridge, 2002); Laura Gowing, 'The Politics of Women's Friendship in Early Modern England', in *Love, Friendship and Faith in Europe, 1300–1800*, ed. Laura Gowing, Michael Hunter, and Miri Rubin (Basingstoke, 2005), 131–49; Fiona Brideoake, *The Ladies of Llangollen: Desire, Indeterminacy, and the Legacies of Criticism* (Lewisburg, PA, 2017). On love between men, see George E. Haggerty, *Men in Love: Masculinity and Sexuality in the Eighteenth Century* (New York and Chichester, 1999); George E. Haggerty, 'Queering Horace Walpole', *Studies in English Literature, 1500–1900* 46.3 (2006): 543–62; Susan Gane, 'Common Soldiers, Same-Sex Love and Religion in the Early Eighteenth-Century British Army', *Gender & History* 25.3 (2013): 637–51.

the fragmentary nature of the evidence, the bias towards elite experiences, and the fact that much evidence (such as pamphlets and court cases) consists of antagonistic accounts by observers. Nonetheless, there are some notable parallels with the courtships studied in this book. Rachel Hope Cleves has studied the lives and loves of Charity Bryant (1777–1851) and Sylvia Drake (1784–1868) in eighteenth- and nineteenth-century America. In 1808, Charity presented Sylvia with a costly ring in order to formalize their relationship and 'establish the public face of their union'. While unable to marry in a legal sense, the couple used the language of matrimony to legitimize their union, with Charity acting as the head of the household and Sylvia her help-meet.[9] Similarly, when the Yorkshire heiress Anne Lister (1791–1840) bound herself 'by an irrevocable promise for ever' to Marianne Lawton (*née* Belcome) in 1821, Anne 'turned' a gold ring on Marianne's finger that she had previously given her as a gift, plus Marianne's wedding ring from her husband Charles.[10] Other rituals were more distinct to same-sex relationships; in 1812, Lister dreamed about presenting her love interest Miss Brown with a cor- nelian heart (a heart-shaped reddish pink quartz), echoing the token presented to Byron *c.*1805 by the choirboy John Edleston (d. 1811). Such objects, and others in the burgeoning material history of same-sex relationships, help to answer Robert Mills' question, 'what kinds of objects might stand in, metonymically, for the queerness of desire itself', without 'monumentalising gay identity, or treating it as a universal given'?[11]

The Game of Love in Georgian England forms one part of the broader story of the modernization and commercialization of romantic customs. Courting couples in Georgian England navigated their relationships both through more traditional gifts such as rings and a plethora of new or newly popular consumer goods such as books, perfume bottles, snuffboxes, muffs, epistolary accessories, souvenirs, and valentine cards. Such a study, situated at a key moment of change in our relationship with things, has wider implications for how we do emotions history using objects. It allows us to reconsider how emotions are inscribed in consumer objects, particularly objects given as gifts that have not been crafted by senders themselves. Further research is needed to ascertain how homemade, handmade, and machine-made objects differ in their emotional meanings, whether unique or uniform, individual or identical, and how these objects regulate and represent emotions in distinct ways. Particularly pertinent is how the emotional value of industrially produced goods endures over time, and whether they retain the same affective meanings even as patterns of consumption change. A further issue for future scholars is how

---

[9] Rachel Hope Cleves, *Charity and Sylvia: A Same-Sex Marriage in Early America* (Oxford, 2014), xi, 109, 131–6.

[10] Helena Whitbread, ed., *I Know my Own Heart: The Diaries of Anne Lister 1791–1840* (London, 1988), 23 and 28 July 1821, 159–60.

[11] Robert Mills, 'Queer is Here? Lesbian, Gay, Bisexual and Transgender Histories and Public Culture', *History Workshop Journal* 62.1 (2006): 253–63, at 260. Recent works in this growing field include Elizabeth Howie, 'Bringing Out the Past: Courtly Cruising and Nineteenth-Century American Men's Romantic Friendship Portraits', in *Love Objects*, ed. Moran and O'Brien, 43–52, and Jane Mackelworth, 'Sapphic Love and Desire in Britain, 1900–1950: In Texts, Objects, and Spaces' (unpublished PhD thesis, University of London, 2017).

anxieties about consumer capitalism figured in the marketplace of love, and to what extent 'romantic concerns about the loss of sincerity, authenticity, and self-expression' were in evidence before the nineteenth century.[12]

The languages and practices of love continued to change over the following centuries. By the mid-nineteenth century, writers came to express their love using the more familiar modern device of kisses, transcribed with an 'x'. The commercialization of romantic customs continued apace, in transitory fashions for novelty gifts such as acrostic brooches, lockets, and rings spelling out secret messages such as 'love', 'dearest', and 'regard' using gemstones.[13] The introduction of the Uniform Penny Post in 1840 saw an explosion in the popularity of valentine cards, which became ever more elaborate, coming with feathers, dried flowers, locks of hair, and even glass mirrors attached, steeped in perfume, with photographs of admirers affixed inside.[14] Daguerreotype photography was popularized after Richard Beard (1801–85) opened England's first portrait studio on Regent Street in 1841, enabling couples to have their photographs taken together. Ginger Frost has presented engagement rings, locks of hair, and photographs as the three universal gifts given by men in Victorian England, which would leave any woman 'perfectly justified' in expecting marriage.[15] While men collected exotic tokens during trips abroad, in anticipation of one day presenting them to their wives, women used objects such as prayer books as gifts in order to test the religious convictions of their betrothed.[16]

The twentieth century saw letter-writing assume new importance in sustaining relationships during wartime, with lovers utilizing a range of new acronyms, such as SWALK (Sealed With A Loving Kiss), HOLLAND (Hoping Our Love Lasts And Never Dies), and the more crude BYYGGI (Brace Yourself, You're Gonna Get It).[17] Convalescing soldiers during the First World War crafted objects such as 'sweetheart' pincushions to send home to their wives and girlfriends, made using commercially produced kits.[18] In the Second World War, pilots in the Royal Air Force flew with a range of talismans provided by their girlfriends as good luck charms, including silk stockings, chiffon scarves, and brassieres. Women shipped a range of homemade gifts to men in the forces—including luxury cashmere wristlets, jumpers, and scarves emblazoned with the men's initials—as both an emotional offering and a patriotic duty. The popularization of cinema as a medium disseminated glamorous

---

[12] Schmidt, 'The Fashioning of a Modern Holiday', 209.   [13] Phillips, *Jewels*, 67.

[14] Valentine card with applied photograph of a man, 1810–38, 34.170/360, MOL; 'Rimmel's perfumed valentine', 1860–75, 38.229/2, MOL; valentine card decorated with real hair, 1860–80, 34.170/892, MOL; sprung valentine card with dried grasses in centre, 1800–1900, DA2347, York Castle Museum (subsequently YCM); elaborate padded valentine with bouquet of fabric flowers, feathers, and glass beads, 1840–1900, DA2180, YCM; ornate valentine with silver and white fairies, decorated with feathers and cloth flowers, 1850–1900, DA2081, YCM; paper lace valentine with net windows and small mirror inside, 1860–1900, DA1903, YCM.

[15] Frost, *Promises Broken*, 64.

[16] Jane Hamlett, *Material Relations: Domestic Interiors and Middle-Class Families in England, 1850–1910* (Manchester, 2010), 76–7.

[17] Claire Langhamer, *The English in Love: The Intimate Story of an Emotional Revolution* (Oxford, 2013), 120.

[18] Sweetheart pincushion made by soldier in the Essex Regiment, World War One, EPH 4231, Imperial War Museum, London.

new models of cinematic romance, marketing new fantasies to couples through dashing heroes such as Clark Gable.[19] Post-war, an expanding range of new commercial gifts such as 'going steady rings' could signify that a relationship was serious.[20]

The language used by couples to navigate relationships today is no less culturally and historically specific (see 'breadcrumbing', 'benching', 'ghosting', 'sexting', 'Facebook Official', 'Netflix & Chill', and so on). Innovations such as emojis have provided wordless new ways to communicate our feelings, echoing the eighteenth-century vogue for hieroglyphic epistles.[21] Emojis can be used to add nuance to our messages, or add emphasis to particular statements like declarations of love.[22] No fewer than three versions of Jane Austen's *Pride and Prejudice* have been published in emojis, with the blurb asking readers, 'Mr Darcy *heart eyes emoji* Lizzie Bennet. But will she swipe right?'[23] The notion of swiping left or right on a potential partner is itself a product of the evolution of the language of love with the advent of dating apps. The formation of relationships online has profoundly altered the ways in which modern couples communicate and relate to one another; the philosopher Aaron Ben-Ze'ev has coined the term 'cyberlove' to describe romantic relationships conducted largely in cyberspace, 'consisting mainly of computer-mediated communication'. Even though individuals might be physically more remote and to some degree anonymous, he argues, the experience of love is no less intense.[24] In many ways, falling in love online has restored the pre-eminence of the written word in conducting a relationship, albeit words that can be copied and pasted, and sent and received instantaneously.[25]

While eighteenth-century rituals such as exchanging locks of hair might seem to us more remote, we continue to exchange gifts such as flowers, perfume, jewellery, books, and wedding rings, plus the latest sought-after consumer objects. We still keep certain precious items in order to preserve material histories of our relationships. For many, old love letters are too precious simply to throw away, particularly now that letter-writing is itself a dying art.[26] Such is the lasting emotional power of objects like wedding dresses that certain women choose to auction or destroy their dresses if an engagement is cut short or the marriage ends in divorce. Individuals can also donate relics to institutions such as the Museum of Broken Relationships as a means of catharsis and liberation, overcoming painful experiences by contributing

---

[19] Elizabeth Robinson, 'Women and Needlework in Britain, 1920–1970' (unpublished PhD thesis, University of London, 2012), 161–5; Martin Francis, *The Flyer: British Culture and the Royal Air Force 1939–45* (Oxford, 2008), Chs. 3 and 5.

[20] Langhamer, *The English in Love*, 128.

[21] See, for example, *The Tunbridge Love Letter* and *The Lady's Answer to The Tunbridge Love Letter* (London, 1794), 1861,0518.997, BM.

[22] Vyvyan Evans, *The Emoji Code: How Smiley Faces, Love Hearts and Thumbs Up are Changing the Way We Communicate* (London, 2017).

[23] *Pride and Prejudice & Emojis* (London: Pop Press, 2017).

[24] Aaron Ben-Ze'ev, *Love Online: Emotions on the Internet* (Cambridge, 2003), 4.

[25] Ibid., 7–8.

[26] 'I have letters from a man I fell in love with 50 years ago. Should I return them?', *The Guardian*, 28 July 2017, https://www.theguardian.com/lifeandstyle/2017/jul/28/letters-man-in-love-50-years-ago-while-married.

to a collective global emotional history.[27] Whether in the eighteenth century or the twenty-first, we make and break romantic relationships through the particular languages and social rituals available to us in a given historical moment, rituals that are in a continual process of change.

Scrutinizing the emotional experience of courtship provides us with a rare glimpse of how love was understood and enacted by couples, and by extension what it meant to craft a romantic relationship in Georgian England. A relationship once viewed as 'the happiest Circumstance' in a person's life could rapidly be transformed into 'the most unfortunate'.[28] It is only by scrutinizing the most intimate exchanges between courting couples, in both words and objects, that we can begin to understand the enormity of the question when posed by a suitor: 'Whither I appear to you in so favourable a Light that upon the whole you think you coud spend some Time agreeably with me?'[29]

---

[27] See the Museum of Broken Relationships online, https://brokenships.com, and Olinka Vištica and Dražen Grubišić, *The Museum of Broken Relationships: Modern Love in 203 Everyday Objects* (London, 2017).

[28] Gibbs to Vicary, undated (1740s), MS/11021/1/1, LMA. Elizabeth Woollat similarly wrote to Jedediah Strutt, to 'meet with proper Returns of affection from the person I love, in these circumstances no one coud be more Happy then myself; & of consequence proportionately distressing woud be the contrary condition', London, April 1755, D5303/4/3, DRO.

[29] Gibbs to Vicary, undated (1740s), MS/11021/1/1, LMA. He argued that his sweetheart's decision to marry 'ought to be determined by this single Question'.

APPENDIX 1

Relationships Consulted

This Appendix records the name, age, religious persuasion, and occupation or social rank of every individual consulted, plus the date and location of each of their relationships. It also lists the repositories where manuscripts can be located, and the types of sources—courtship and family letters, diaries, valentines (with named creators and/or recipients), and written proposals of marriage. The sources range in number from a single manuscript to several hundred per collection. Couples are arranged in roughly chronological order according to when a relationship began. The Appendix shows at a glance the distribution of sources over time, between different social and religious groups, and across England. Breach of promise cases are catalogued separately in Appendix 2.

	Name of man	Occupation or Social Rank	Religion	Name of woman	Occupation or Social Rank	Religion	Dates of Courtship	Location	Type of Source & Repository
1	'Oroondates'	Sailor		Mrs Ann Webb ('Statira')			Early 18th century	Rye, East Sussex	L—ESRO
2	Edward Hall (d. 1718)	Rector of Aspley Guise (1682–1718) & Hockliffe (1713–18)	A				1713	Aspley Guise, Bedfordshire	P—BAS
3	William Martin	Letters directed to Mr Watts, a packer in Cannon Street		Hannah Smith			1714	Cannon Street, London	L—HRO
4	William Denyer			Hannah Smith	Letters directed to Mr Denyer, a carpenter of Stoke Lane near Guildford		1716	Racton, West Sussex	L—HRO
5	Mr J. Gallant	Had 'care of' a shop		Mrs Mann (later Mrs Sibbs)	Addressed as 'your Ladyship' and notes her significant fortune		1717		L—NRO
6	Captain Martin Madan (1700–56)	Eldest son of the plantation owner Martin Madan of Nevis, West Indies and Penelope Madan (*née* Russell). Lieutenant and Captain of the Coldstream Guards (1717) and Captain of The King's Own Regiment of Horse (1721)		Judith Cowper (1702–81)	Poet. Only daughter of Spencer Cowper, Justice of the Common Pleas (1670–1728) and Pennington Cowper (*née* Goodere) of Herringfordbury Park (d. 1727)		1723	London & Hertfordshire	L—BLO
7	John Everard (b. c.1695)	Coachman to the Eccleston family		Isabella Eccleston (b. c.1710)	Daughter of John Eccleston, director of the East India Company	Q	1725–6	London & Amsterdam	L—BAS

	Name	Notes		Partner	Notes		Date	Place	Archive
8	Thomas Kirton (1709–57)	Flour merchant and dealer in timber, iron and nails	Q	Olive Lloyd (1707–75)	Daughter of the iron and steel merchant Charles Lloyd and his second wife Mary Lloyd, of an important Quaker family	Q	1734	Rimpton, Somerset	L—LSF
9	James Nicholson (1718–73)	Linen merchant from a respected merchant family	U	Elizabeth Seddon (1721–91)	Daughter of the gentleman Thomas Seddon of Seddon's House, Bickerstaff, Ormskirk	U	1738–40	Liverpool	L—JRL & LIRO
10	Philip Yorke (1720–90)	Eldest son of Lord Chancellor Philip Yorke, Baron Hardwicke (1690–1764) and Margaret Yorke (*née* Cocks) (1695–1761)		Lady Jemima Campbell (*c.*1722–97)	Only daughter of John Campbell, 3rd Earl of Breadalbane and Holland (1696–1782) and Lady Amabel de Grey (d. 1727)		1740	Cambridgeshire	P—BAS
11	William Bell	Sailor (unaware that Kitty had married during his four-year absence)	A	Catherine 'Kitty' Williamson (*née* Taylor)	First wife of Rector Edmund Williamson	A	1743	Aspley, Beaconsfield, & London	L—BAS
12	George Gibbs (*c.*1718–94)	Eldest surviving son of Abraham Gibbs of Topsham (1686–1726) and Mary Gibbs (*née* Moncke). Surgeon at the Royal Devon and Exeter Hospital	A	Ann 'Nanny' Vicary (1721/2–1800/3)	Daughter and co-heiress of the gentleman Anthony Vicary Esq. of Exeter (b. 1682) and Elizabeth Vicary (*née* Munckley)	A	1743–7	Exeter, Biddeford, & Exmouth	L—LMA
13	Charles Pratt (1714–94)	Third son of Lord Chief Justice Sir John Pratt (1657–1725) and his second wife Elizabeth Pratt (*née* Wilson) (d. 1728). Barrister (admitted to Middle Temple 1738	A	Elizabeth Jeffreys (*c.*1724–79)	Daughter of Nicholas Jeffreys & heiress of Brecon Priory, Wales	A	1745–9	London & the court circuit (Dorchester, Exeter, Lancaster, Taunton, Winchester, &c.)	L—KHLC

(continued)

Continued

Name of man	Occupation or Social Rank	Religion	Name of woman	Occupation or Social Rank	Religion	Dates of Courtship	Location	Type of Source & Repository
14 Richard How II (1727–1801)	Gentleman, eldest son of Richard How I (1689–1763) and Susanna How (née Briggins) (d. 1742).	Q	Elizabeth Johnson	Richard's cousin	Q?	c.1747–57	Aspley, Woburn, & Hamburg	L—BAS
15 Jedediah Strutt (1726–97)	Wheelwright, son of a small farmer	U	Elizabeth Woollat (1729–74)	Servant to Dr Ebenezer Latham (c.1688–1754), who ran a large Nonconformist academy in Findern	U	1748–55	Blackwell, Findern, Derby, Leicester, London, Mansfield, & Nottingham	L—DRO
16 Richard 'Neddy' Edgcumbe (1716–61)	Eldest son of Richard Edgcumbe, 1st Baron Edgcumbe, Capital burgess, Lostwithiel (1743) & Mayor (1744)		Lady Diana West (1731–66)	Daughter of John West, 1st Earl De La Warr (1693–1766) and his first wife Lady Charlotte (née MacCarthy) (d. 1735)		1750		L—LWL
17 Captain Henry Smith (1723–94)	Third son of the London merchant John Smith and Elizabeth Smith (née Griffith). Captain in the Royal Marines		Sarah Hurst (1736–1808)	Eldest child of the tailor Richard Hurst (1712–80) and Mary Tasker (1718–83), worked in the family's mercers shop. Marriage portion of £300	A	c.1751–62	Horsham, West Sussex	D—Pub & HM
18 Richard How II (1727–1801)	Gentleman, eldest son of Richard How I (1689–1763) and Susanna How (née Briggins) (d. 1742)	Q	Sally			1751	Aspley Guise, Bedfordshire	P—BAS

19	John Spencer (1734–83)	A	Only son of the landowner John Spencer (1708–46) and Georgiana Spencer (*née* Carteret) (1716–80). Great-grandson and heir of Sarah, Duchess of Marlborough (d. 1744)	Margaret Georgiana Poyntz (1737–1814)	Daughter of the diplomat and courtier Stephen Poyntz (1685–1750) of Midgham House, Berkshire, and Maid of Honour Anna Maria (*née* Mordaunt)	A	1754–5	London	L—BL
20	John Lovell	C	Apothecary	Sarah Harvey		C	1756–8	Bath & Cole Park, Malmesbury	L—WSA
21	J. H.			Catherine 'Kitty' Wood	Daughter of Thomas Wood of Beadnell, Northumbria		1763	Cumbria	L—CRO
22	Charles Ly–			Abigail Way (c.1746–93)	Daughter of the barrister Lewis Way of Richmond (1704–80)		1765	Richmond	L—ESRO
23	James Nelthorpe		Soldier	Abigail Way (c.1746–93)	Daughter of the barrister Lewis Way of Richmond (1704–80)		1765	London	L—ESRO
24	Dudley A. Sidney Cosby (c.1730–74)		Son of Pole Cosby of Stradbally, Queen's County, and Mary Cosby (*née* Dodwell). MP for Carrick (1763–8) and Minister Resident to Denmark (1763)	Abigail Way (c.1746–93)	Daughter of the barrister Lewis Way of Richmond (1704–80)		1766	Richmond	L—ESRO

(*continued*)

Continued

Name of man	Occupation or Social Rank	Religion	Name of woman	Occupation or Social Rank	Religion	Dates of Courtship	Location	Type of Source & Repository
25 Isaac Martin Rebow (1731–81)	Only surviving son of Isaac Lemyng Rebow (d. 1735) and Mary Rebow (*née* Martin) of Wivenhoe Park. Alderman, MP for Colchester, and Colonel in the East Essex militia	C	Mary Martin (*c.*1751–1804)	Gentlewoman. Third daughter and co-heiress of Thomas Martin of Alresford Hall, Essex	C	*c.*1767–72	Essex & London	L—ERO
26 Humphrey Senhouse III (1731–1814)	Fellow of Pembroke College, Cambridge (1756–68) and Lieutenant-Colonel of the Cumberland militia	C	Catherine 'Kitty' Wood	Daughter of Thomas Wood of Beadnell, Northumbria	C	1768	Cumbria	L—CRO
27 Alexander Chorley (1746–1801)	Ironmonger	Q	Elizabeth 'Betty' Fothergill (1752–1809)	Daughter of Joseph Fothergill of Warrington. Niece of the esteemed London physician, botanist, and philanthropist John Fothergill (1712–80)	Q	*c.*1769–70	Hardshaw & Warrington, Lancashire	D—LSF
28 Edward Leathes (1747–88)	Third son of the landowner and MP Carteret Leathes (1698–1780) and Loveday Leathes (*née* Garrod). Deacon of Norwich (1773) & Rector of Reedham and Freethorpe (1775–88)	A	Elizabeth 'Betsy' Reading (1748–1815)	Only child of Rev. James Reading (1721–90) and Elizabeth Reading (*née* Hoare)	A	1771–4	Strumpshaw & Woodstock, Oxfordshire	L—NRO
29 G. M. L.	Soldier? Leaving for Gibraltar					1775		L—NRO

30	John Cater (d. 1781)	Son of Margaret Cater of Kempston. Soldier in 89th Regiment		Charlotte Jackson	Friend of John's sister		1779	Portsmouth & Kempston	L—BAS
31	John Eccles (d. 1780)	No profession. Likely of inferior status to the Hays family	B	Mary Hays (1759–1843)	Writer. Daughter of John and Elizabeth Hays	B & U	1777–80	London	L—Pub
32	John Thomas			Elizabeth			1780	Kempley Court, Gloucestershire	V—V&A
33	Captain Richard Dixon (fl. 1782–5)	Captain of 85th Regiment of Foot, Richmond	Q	Esther Maria Cranmer (1760–1819)	Daughter of James Cranmer II (1719–1801), who owned the manor of Mitcham Canon in Surrey		1782	Bedford, Buxton, Epsom, London, & Mitcham	L—SHC
34	William Rathbone IV (1757–1809)	Eldest son of William Rathbone III (1726–89) and Rachel Rathbone (née Rutter). Ship-owner and merchant from a prominent Quaker family	Q	Hannah Mary Reynolds (1761–1839)	Daughter of the philanthropist and merchant Richard Reynolds and Hannah Reynolds (née Darby)	Q	1785–6	Liverpool	L—LUL
35	John Fawdington (1757–1817)	Bridle-maker (following his father and grandfather)		Jane 'Jenny' Jefferson (b. 1766)			1786–7	Asenby, North Yorkshire	L—NYRO
36	Joseph Strutt (1765–1844)	Cotton-trader and son of the wheelwright Jedediah Strutt (see no. 15)	C	Isabella Douglas (1769–1802)			1786–93	Derby & Sandy Brook, near Ashbourne	L—LOB
37	Samuel Whitbread II (1764–1815)	Gentleman, only son of the wealthy brewer and MP Samuel Whitbread I (1720–96) and Harriett Whitbread (née Hayton) (1733–64)	A	Elizabeth Grey (1765–1848)	Eldest daughter of the distinguished soldier Charles, 1st Earl Grey (1729–1807) and Elizabeth Grey (1744–1822)	A	1787–8	Cardington, Bedfordshire, & Fallodon, Northumberland	L—BAS

(continued)

Continued

	Name of man	Occupation or Social Rank	Religion	Name of woman	Occupation or Social Rank	Religion	Dates of Courtship	Location	Type of Source & Repository
38	Edward Peach, Esq. (d. 1805)	Gentleman, son of Rev. Edward Peach, Rector of Titsey, Surrey (d. 1772)	A	Elizabeth Leathes (née Reading) (1748–1815)	Widow of the vicar Edward Leathes (see no. 28)	A	1789–90	London, Norwich, & Sundridge, Kent	L—NRO
39	Captain Gilbert Imlay (1754–1828)	First Lieutenant in the Continental Army, land speculator, diplomat, and author	A	Mary Wollstonecraft (1759–97)	Writer, philosopher, schoolmistress, and governess. Eldest daughter of the gentleman farmer Edward Wollstonecraft (1736–1803) and Elizabeth Wollstonecraft (née Dixon) (1730–82)	A & U	1793–6	Paris & London	L—Pub
40	Reverend Charles Powlett (1764–1834)	Son of Percy Powlett (illegitimate son of the Duke of Bolton) and Elizabeth Powlett (née Packham), Rector of Winslade, Hampshire (1789–94), Blackford, Somerset (1794–6), and Chaplain in Ordinary to the Prince Regent	A	Anne Temple (1772–1827)	Eldest daughter of Reverend William Johnson Temple (1739–96), Vicar of St Gluvias, Cornwall. Marriage portion of approx £2,000	A	1790–6	St Gluvias, Cornwall	L & D—HRO
41	Lieutenant-General Charles O'Hara (c.1740–1802)	Illegitimate son of James O'Hara, Baron Kilmaine and 2nd Baron Tyrawley (1681/2–1773). Lieutenant and Captain in the Coldstream Guards (from 1756) and Lieutenant Governor of Gibraltar (from 1792)	C	Mary Berry (1763–1852)	Author. Eldest daughter of Robert Berry and Elizabeth Berry (née Seaton) (d. 1767)	C	1795–6	Kirkbride, North Yorkshire & London	L—Pub & BL

No.	Name		Description	Name	Description	A & U		Location	
42	William Godwin (1756–1836)	Ath	Philosopher and novelist. Seventh child of the nonconformist minister John Godwin (1723–72) and Anne Godwin (*née* Hull) (*c.*1723–1809)	Mary Wollstonecraft (1759–97)	Writer, philosopher, schoolmistress, and governess. Eldest daughter of the gentleman farmer Edward Wollstonecraft (1736–1803) and Elizabeth Wollstonecraft (*née* Dixon) (1730–82)		1796–7	London	L—Pub & BLO
43	David Bursell						*c.*1797	East Riding	V—ERA
44	Robert Lloyd (1778–1811)	Q	Stationer and Captain in the third battalion of the Loyal Birmingham Volunteers. Third son of the influential Quaker banker Charles Lloyd (1748–1828) and Mary Lloyd (*née* Farmer) (1750–1821)	Hannah Hart (1779–1842)	Daughter of the banker Francis Hart of Nottingham	Q	1803–4	Birmingham	L—LSF
45	Sir Gilbert Stirling (*c.*1779–1843)	C	Eldest son of the banker and Lord Provost of Edinburgh Sir James Stirling (*c.*1740–1805) and Alison Stirling (*née* Mansfield). 2nd baronet of Mansfield, Ayrshire	Anne Louisa Dalling (*c.*1784–1853)	Daughter and heiress of General Sir John Dalling, 1st baronet (*c.*1731–98) and his second wife Louisa (*née* Lawford) (d. 1824)	C	*c.*1803–5	Chelmsford, Southend, & Harley Street, London	L—NRO
46	Paul Moon James (1780–1854)	Q	Banker, magistrate of Worcestershire, and poet	Olivia Lloyd (1783–1854)	Second daughter of the influential Quaker banker Charles Lloyd (1748–1828) and Mary Lloyd (*née* Farmer) (1750–1821)	Q	1805–8	Birmingham	L—LSF

(continued)

Continued

Name of man	Occupation or Social Rank	Religion	Name of woman	Occupation or Social Rank	Religion	Dates of Courtship	Location	Type of Source & Repository
47 Francis Cobb Jr (1759–1831)	Banker, brewer, and shipping agent, only son of Francis Cobb Sr ('King of Margate') (1727–1802) and Elizabeth Cobb (née Sackett)	A	Charlotte Mary Curwen (d. 1823)	Daughter of a Baptist Minister (admitted to the Church of England in 1804)	A	1805	Fenstanton and Margate	L—KHLC
48 Richard Law	Former serge-maker and flax-dresser, follower of the prophetess Joanna Southcott (1750–1814)	S	Jane Townley (c.1761–1825)	Daughter of Colonel Richard Townley, High Sheriff of Lancashire. Companion, patron, and disciple of the prophetess Joanna Southcott (1750–1814)	S	c.1807–22	London	L—BL
49 John Dewey (b. c.1788)	Junior medical officer in the army, surgeon at the General Hospital in Lisbon		Charlotte Lambourne	Worked for a family, possibly as a governess		c.1809–16	Winchester, Southampton, & America	L—HRO
50 Henry Goulburn (1784–1856)	Eldest son of Munbee Goulburn of Amity Hall, Jamaica and Portland Place (1756/7–93) and Susannah Goulburn (née Chetwynd) (d. 1818). Tory politician and undersecretary of state for home affairs (1810)	A	Jane Montagu (d. 1857)	Fourth daughter of the politician Matthew Montagu (1762–1831) and Elizabeth Montagu (née Charlton) (d. 1817)	A	1811	Sandleford Priory, Newbury	L—SHC

No.	Name		Description	Spouse	Description		Dates	Place	Archive
51	Robert Garrett (1794–1869)	C	Eldest son of Captain John Garrett and Elizabeth Garrett (née Gore) of Thanet. Ensign by purchase in 2nd Regiment of Foot (1811)	Charlotte Georgina Sophia Cavendish-Bentinck (1789–1819)	Daughter of the politician Lord Edward Charles Cavendish-Bentinck (1744–1819) and Elizabeth Cavendish-Bentinck (née Cumberland)	C	1811–14	Ramsgate	L—KHLC
52	William Spencer (1790–1866)		Schoolmaster	Harriet Holmes	Daughter of John Holmes		c.1811–19	Derbyshire	V—V&A
53	William Calder		Merchant				1813		V—BLO
54	John Franklin (1786–1847)	A	Naval officer and Arctic explorer. Ninth child of the mercer Willingham Franklin (d. 1824) and Hannah Franklin (née Weekes)	Eleanor Anne Porden (1795–1825)	Poet. Youngest daughter of the distinguished architect William Porden (bap. 1755–1822) and Mary Porden (née Plowman) (d. 1819)		c.1818–23	London	L—DRO
55	Jason Humberstone			Mrs Jane Parker	Widow		1819	Campton and Steponly	P—BAS
56	John Keats (1795–1821)		Poet. Eldest child of the inn manager Thomas Keats (c. 1773–1804) and Frances Keats (née Jennings) (1775–1810)	Frances 'Fanny' Brawne (1800–65)	Eldest child of the businessman Samuel Brawne (1778–1810), and Frances Brawne (née Ricketts) (1772–1829)		1819–21	London	L—Pub
57	John Kerr (1794–1841)		Eldest son of William, 6th Marquess of Lothian and Lady Henrietta Hobart. Earl of Ancram (1815–24) and 7th Marquess of Lothian (from 1824)	Lady Elizabeth Grey (1798–1880)	Second daughter of the Whig politician Charles, 2nd Earl Grey (1764–1845) and Mary, Countess Grey (née Ponsonby) (1776–1861)		1823–4	Bothwell and London	L—BI

(continued)

Continued

	Name of man	Occupation or Social Rank	Religion	Name of woman	Occupation or Social Rank	Religion	Dates of Courtship	Location	Type of Source & Repository
58	Thomas Francis Cobb (1797–1882)	Son of the banker and brewer Francis Cobb Jr (see no. 47)	A	Miss Torre			1827	Margate and Cheltenham	P—KHLC
59	Anthony Hamond (1805–69)	Eldest son of Philip Hamond of Westacre, Norfolk. Deputy Lieutenant and Justice of the Peace for Norfolk	C	Mary Ann Musters (1806–1900)	Eldest daughter of John 'Jack' Musters (1777–1849) and Mary Ann Musters (née Chaworth) (1786–1832) of Colwick Hall	C	c.1828	Norfolk	L—NRO
60		Butler			Housekeeper		c.1830	Norfolk	L—NRO

Key

Repository		Religion		Type of Source	
BAS	Bedfordshire Archives Service, Bedford	A	Anglican	D	Diary
BI	Borthwick Institute, York	Ath	Atheist	L	Letters
BL	British Library, London	B	Baptist	P	Proposal
BLO	Bodleian Library, Oxford	C	Christian	V	Valentine
CRO	Cumbria Record Office, Carlisle	Q	Quaker		
DRO	Derbyshire Record Office, Matlock	U	Unitarian		
ERA	East Riding Archives, Beverley	N	Nonconformist		
ERO	Essex Record Office, Chelmsford	S	Southcottian		
ESRO	East Sussex Record Office, Brighton				
HM	Horsham Museum, West Sussex				
HRO	Hampshire Record Office, Winchester				
JRL	John Rylands Library, Manchester				
KHLC	Kent History and Library Centre, Maidstone				
LIRO	Liverpool Record Office, Liverpool				
LMA	London Metropolitan Archives, London				
LOB	Library of Birmingham				
LSF	Library of the Society of Friends, London				
LUL	Liverpool University Library, Liverpool				
LWL	Lewis Walpole Library, Farmington, CT				
NRO	Norfolk Record Office, Norwich				
NYRO	North Yorkshire Record Office, Northallerton				
Pub	Published				
SHC	Surrey History Centre, Woking				
V&A	Victoria and Albert Museum, London				
WSA	Wiltshire and Swindon Archives, Chippenham				

APPENDIX 2

Breach of Promise Cases in the Common Law Courts

This Appendix charts every record for 'breach of promise' and 'breach of contract' in British Newspapers 1600–1900 and *The Times* Digital Archive between 1717 and 1816, plus pamphlets and *English Reports*, a collection of judgements of the English Courts between 1220 and 1867. Due to the volume of cases reported after 1816, the Appendix uses the first article of every year in the *Morning Post* between 1817 and 1830. This newspaper was selected as it was published daily, had a wide circulation, and contained a substantial number of detailed assize reports. The Appendix reproduces the original language of reports where possible, in order to retain important nuances in the terms used by participants.

	Case	Date	Court(s)	Sex of Plaintiff	Age of Plaintiff During Trial	Occupation/Social Status of Plaintiff	Age of Defendant During Trial	Occupation/Social Status of Defendant	Verdict	Damages	Objects Used as Evidence	Source(s)
1	*Cork vs. Baker*	1717	CKB	F					P	£300		ER
2	*Holt vs. Ward, Esq.*	Feb. 1730	CKB	F	'Young'	'Had not a competent fortune'		'Squire' / Gentleman of 'plentiful fortune'	P	£2,000	Love letters	Plt/USWJ
3	*Atkins vs. Far*	1738 (OS)	CC	–					P	£500 + interest & costs	Bond for £500	ER
4	*Horam vs. Humfreys*	1771		F	'Young'	Daughter of a man in the board of works		Pawnbroker	P	£500	Licence	ER
5		1772	CBA	F	'Young'	Milliner who gave up a 'genteel and advantageous business'		'Wealthy farmer's son'	P	£500 + costs	Slide of the bride-cake produced in court	CSWJ
6	*Higgs vs. [?]*	July 1774	CCP	F				Brewer's clerk	P	£100		LC
7		1778	CKB	F		A 'lady of some property'		Son of an 'eminent weaver in Spitalfields'	P	£1,200 (as pregnant)		LPEP
8	*Schreiber vs. Frazer*	July 1780	CKB	M		'very respectable wealthy Merchant'		Widow of the late General Frazer, worth £24,000+	P	£600 + costs	House, horses, carriages, & suit of livery bought	LEP
9	*Morton vs. Fenn*	Feb. 1783	CKB	F	53 (widow)	'Poor' housekeeper	70 ('Old' & 'infirm')	Man of fortune in Jamaica	P	£500 (reduced from £2,000)		Plt/ER

10		Jan. 1787		M		Lieutenant of Marines		Widowed French Countess worth £16,000 exclusive of property	P			WFA
11		Mar. 1787	EA	F	'Young'	Young woman abandoned while pregnant		Gentleman of property	P			WFA
12	*Forster/Fosset vs. Rowe*	Aug. 1789	NWA	F					P	£500		W/OBNW
13	*Chapman vs. Shaw, Esq.*	May 1790	CKB	F	'Young Lovers'	'very respectable family'	'Young Lovers'	'very respectable parents', Attorney at Law	P	£20		Plr/W/ WEP/T
14	*Brown vs. Arnold*	Aug. 1790		F	Nearly 40—'old maid'	Maiden lady who ran a lodging house	Just turned 21	Lived in Miss Brown's lodging house at her expense for 15 months	D		Love letter & 'preliminary articles' for marriage	LC/WEP
15	*Holmes vs. Banbury*	Feb. 1791	CKB	F	'Young'	Daughter of a 'respectable' innkeeper		Widower & grocer	P	£150	Wedding clothes worth £80 & gold watch worth £24	T
16	*Andrews vs. Jolly & Wife*	June 1791	CKB	M	30	'Master carman' of no property in £110 debt	c.40	Married to 'an industrious clerk in an office'	JW		Wedding garments	T

(continued)

Continued

	Case	Date	Court(s)	Sex of Plaintiff	Age of Plaintiff During Trial	Occupation/Social Status of Plaintiff	Age of Defendant During Trial	Occupation/Social Status of Defendant	Verdict	Damages	Objects Used as Evidence	Source(s)
17	Smith vs. Taylor	June 1791	CKB	F	c.43 (came to London aged 40)	Domestic servant, farmer's daughter, & distant relative of celebrated mathematical instrument maker	c.30	Young mechanic who had recently acquired a business from a brasier & tinman	P	£50		W/O
18	Hagen [or Hayden] vs. Walker	Dec. 1791	CKB	F	c.30	Quaker 'of undoubted credit and character' who kept a boarding house	c.50	Methodist earning £250–£300 per annum	P	£50		T/W
19	Palmer vs. Barnard, Esq.	Dec. 1792	GH	F	23	Tradesman's daughter	29	Banker's son	P	£1,000		Plt
20	Davis vs. Saunders	Jan. 1792	CCP	F	c.28	Educated farmer's daughter working as a milliner & mantuamaker		'Widower of some property'	P	£100	Love letters	DWR
21	Williams vs. Harding	Mar. 1793		F	'Young'	Milliner of 'exemplary character for prudence, virtue and industry'	'Very young'	Tradesman in the city	P	£50	Large settlement declined by woman	TB
22	Sands vs. Sayer and Wife	May 1793	CKB	M	22	Respectable man who was bred up a planner and layer out of gardens and pleasure grounds'	22	Niece of eminent coachmaker who had left her a 'considerable fortune'	JW	Parties paid their own costs	Love letters	T/LC

												S
23	*Harris vs. Williamson*	May 1793	CKB	F	20	Mantuamaker			P	£200		
24	*Simpson vs. Burton*	Sept. 1793	GA	F		Daughter of a 'respectable shopkeeper'		Army Lieutenant	N		Love letters	W
25	*Watts vs. Johnson*	Nov. 1793	CKB	F	c.25	Milliner and mantuamaker	c.40	Master of a haberdashery business who suffered occasional fits of 'insanity'	P	£20	Love letters	MC/PA
26	*Marcom vs. Edgar*	Aug. 1794	NA	F		Independent fortune of £5,000		Apothecary and surgeon	P	£500	Love letters	OPA
27	*Gay vs. Harlington*	Oct. 1794		F		'not a lady of strict chastity'			P	£30		OPA
28	*Murray vs. Gale, Esq.*	Dec. 1794	CKB	F	Under 18—'infant'	Daughter of noble lady & baronet		Gentleman of 'very large fortune'	D		Mother gave him picture of her daughter	LPEP/S
29	*Taylor vs. Norton*	Dec. 1794	CCP	F	Fifteen years older than D	'not a lady distinguished for her chastity'			D			CEG
30	*Brown vs. Harding*	June 1795	CCP	F		Widow of 'exemplary prudence'	Younger than P	Propertied tradesman	P	£20	'Preliminaries'	GEP/S
31	*Jones vs. Gordon*	July 1796	CCP	F	'Young'	Young woman 'of virtue and correct demeanour'		Tradesman 'of some eminence', with a father 'of considerable property'	P	£50	Love letters	TB/WEP/OPA

(continued)

Continued

Case	Date	Court(s)	Sex of Plaintiff	Age of Plaintiff During Trial	Occupation/Social Status of Plaintiff	Age of Defendant During Trial	Occupation/Social Status of Defendant	Verdict	Damages	Objects Used as Evidence	Source(s)
32 *Atcheson vs. Baker*	1796 & 1797 (R)	CKB	M	70–2 (R)	Respectable button-manufacturer earning £300 per annum, retired expecting marriage	60–2 (R)	Wealthy widow worth £24,000	N/P (R)	£4,000 (but never paid)		TB/WEP/EM/Tel
33 *Tauves vs. Jones*	Mar. 1796	CCP	F			'Young'	'Gentleman of fortune'	N			OPA/S
34 *Heyward vs. Arnold*	May 1796	CCP	F	c.40	Woman of 'levity of conduct'	c.22		N			S
35 *Jones vs. Gordon*	July 1796	CCP	F	'Young'			Tradesman 'of some eminence' whose father had 'considerable property'	P	£50	Love letters	OPA
36 *Tyley vs. Deerhurst*	Sept. 1796	EA	M	'Young'	Man of 'respectable family and connections' and a 'polished life'		Woman with 'equally respectable connections'	N			OPA
37 *Bennet vs. Handcocks*	Nov. 1796	CCP	M	Over 40	'Respectable tradesman's son'	22		D		Love letters	S
38 *Bond vs. Oliver*	Dec. 1798	CKB	M			Nearly 70	Lady	S			TB

39	*Belchier vs. Thompson*	May 1799	CKB	F	Young	Daughter of a deceased gentleman who was an officer in the navy and widow who took the City of London inn in Dover		Son of a wine merchant who owned his own business as a 'Wine-merchant and Woolstapler' and was in 'a great way of business'	P	£400	Love letters	ODA/SJC
40	*Wilson vs. Powditch*	Dec. 1799	CCP	F				'Captain of a Ship trading to the Baltic Seas' who had 'failed in trade' so was worth no more than £600	P	£500	Love letters	ODA
41	*Harris vs. Surry*	Apr. 1800	CHA	F		Schoolmistress			P	£20		MPG
42	*Jones vs. Brock Wood, Esq.*	Aug. 1800	GA	F					P	£1,000		LPEP
43	*Shaw[e] vs. Baker* (second case brought against Mrs Baker, after *Atcheson vs. Baker*, no. 32)	Aug. 1800	SRA	M	*c.*30	Managing Clerk of distillery earning £200 per year. 'Middling but decent and respectable rank of life'	68 (MPG) more than 70 (ODA)	'widow Lady of very considerable property' with fortune of approx. £30,000	D		Draft marriage settlement	MPG/ODA/MC
44	*Fowkes vs. Selway*	Dec. 1800	CKB	F	'maturer age' than usual	Widow who had 'lived in trade', kept a shop and lodgers	'maturer age' than usual	Widower who had 'been in trade' but was 'comfortable'	D			S

(continued)

Continued

	Case	Date	Court(s)	Sex of Plaintiff	Age of Plaintiff During Trial	Occupation/ Social Status of Plaintiff	Age of Defendant During Trial	Occupation/ Social Status of Defendant	Verdict	Damages	Objects Used as Evidence	Source(s)
45	Prothero vs. Evans/Jones	Jan. 1801	CKB	F	28		60 (MPG) 60–70 (BG)	Methodist preacher, publican, and farmer	P	£50	Love letters	MPG/BG
46	Vaughan vs. Aldridge	June 1801	CCP	F	50		75	Lived on his income independent of trade, but now confined in an asylum	P	£10	Love letters & 'other evidence'	MP
47	Andrews vs. Morrison	Dec. 1801	CKB	F		Daughter of a deceased tradesman		Respectable tradesman worth £150 per year independent of his business	P	£200	Wedding ring, licence, & furniture	MC/MPG
48	Forster vs. Mellish	Feb. 1802	CKB	M	c.27	Respectable gentleman 'in the medical line' with an income of £800–£900 per year	'Young'	Daughter of 'a person of considerable property' with a fortune of £13,900	P	£200	Love letters, house, & 'marriage clothes'	MPG/MC
49	Hand vs. Kisten	July 1802	CCP	F	37	Sister of a 'respectable tradesman'	'might almost be her son'	Apprentice to P's brother	P	£100	Love letters	MC
50	Storey vs. Eagle	Aug. 1802	YA	F		Humble maidservant		Humble hostler, becoming an innkeeper worth £600	P	£50	Love letters	MPG/T

No.	Case	Date	Court	M/F	Description	Age	Description	Age	P/S	Amount	Evidence	Outcome
51	*Graves vs. Innocent*	Feb. 1803	CKB	F	Daughter of a 'very respectable tradesman'		Goldsmith, jeweller, & dealer in curiosities		P	£100	Love letters	MP
52	*Leeds vs. Cooke and Wife*	Mar. 1803	CKB	M	'young Gentleman of considerable property'	'Young'	Daughter of a 'Gentleman of landed property'	'Young'	P	1s.	Letters sent after desertion	MP
53	*Martin vs. Jeffery*	Mar. 1803	DCA	F	'Servant girl'		Tanner		P	£80		IJ
54	*Hunt vs. Smith*	July 1804	KA	F	A 'decent woman keeping a small shop' (a grocer's & chandler's)	c.35	Stone-cutter who kept two shops	c.35	P	£10		T/MC
55	*Greenwood vs. Bradshaw*	Aug. 1804	LNA	F	'humble station'		'humble station' with only £100 and a house		P	£80		MP
56	*Forster vs. Hoblin*	Mar. 1805	WA	F	Daughter of a 'respectable farmer' deserted while pregnant		Farmer in same county 'considered a man of substance'		P	£400		T/MP
57	*Montgomery vs. Evans*	Aug. 1805	WXA	M	Reverend		Niece of Admiral Sir Peter Parker		S	Defendant paid £100 + costs	Love letters	T/MP
58	*Balls vs. Gardener*	Aug. 1806	SFA	F			Miller, maltster, and brickmaker		P	£300	Love letters	BNP
59	*Forrester vs. Lyons*	July 1808	CCP	F	Farmer's daughter		Master baker		S	£50 + costs + maintenance for child		MP

(continued)

Continued.

Case	Date	Court(s)	Sex of Plaintiff	Age of Plaintiff During Trial	Occupation/Social Status of Plaintiff	Age of Defendant During Trial	Occupation/Social Status of Defendant	Verdict	Damages	Objects Used as Evidence	Source(s)
60 *Howells vs. Charles*	Dec. 1808	CKB	F		Farmer's daughter		Farmer and timber merchant with estate worth £100 per year	P	£150		MC
61 *Corham vs. Bulteel (née Pinson)*	Apr. 1809	EA	M		Ensign in the Devonshire militia			P	£400	Love letters	BNP
62 *Hulme vs. Warbrick*	Aug. 1809	LNA	F	'Young'	Woman of 'great personal attraction' who ran a confectioners shop		Had previously been 'in trade', but Miss Hulme helped purchase a commission in the Dragoons	AR		Love letters	T/LG
63 *Millis vs. Flower*	Mar. 1810	CKB	F		Daughter of a 'respectable ribbon manufacturer'	'Old fool'	Wholesale ribbon merchant & manufacturer 'in a respectable situation in life'	P	£500	Love letters	MP/IJ/ YH/BNP
64 *Blankney vs. Temps*	July 1810	CKB	F	18–19	Woman with 'wandering inclinations' and a 'love of pleasure'		In 'a very comfortable situation in life as an art engraver'	JW	Each side paid their own costs	Love letters	MP

No. & Case	Date										MP/HP/BNP
65 *Bishop vs. Robinson*	Aug. 1810	CKB	F	'Young'	'Young Lady of respectable family and connections' with a 'small fortune'	'Young'	A 'merchant of London, and a man of great opulence, having therefore ample means to pay any damages'	P	£5,000	Love letters	MP/HP/ BNP
66 *Archer vs. Hinches*	Mar. 1812	BA	F	23	'the daughter of an Attorney'	23	'Young man of credit'/'Person of respectability'	S			T/LM
67 *Sherriff vs. Godbold*	Dec. 1812	CKB	F	30 (BNP) 30–40 (MC & OJ)	Captain's widow	c.50 (MC & BNP) 50–60 (OJ)	Gentleman of 'considerable property', proprietor of 'Vegetable Balsam'	P	40s.	Love letters	MC/BNP/ OJ
68 *Chamberlain vs. Williamson, Esq*	Sept. 1813	GA	–		Overseer of the poor house—daughter ran a 'little school'	'Considerably older' than her	'ample fortune' from trade	P	£200	Love letters	MP
69 *Barr[y] vs. Dixon*	Dec. 1813	CKB	F	Young Lady	Orphan of 'moderate fortune, but of very good connection'		Coal merchant making £400 per annum	P	£300	Marriage licence & plate given as wedding present	T/MP
70 *O'Neil vs. Evans, Clerk and Wife*	Mar. 1814	OA	M		Drawing master	Relationship began when she was underage	Daughter of J. Ireland, Esq.	P	1f.	Love letters	IJ

(continued)

Continued

	Case	Date	Court(s)	Sex of Plaintiff	Age of Plaintiff During Trial	Occupation/ Social Status of Plaintiff	Age of Defendant During Trial	Occupation/ Social Status of Defendant	Verdict	Damages	Objects Used as Evidence	Source(s)
71	*Pilgrim vs. Weston*	Mar. 1814	TA	F	c.17–18	Servant		Bailiff	P	£150		BNP
72	*Page vs. Mont*	July 1815	HA	F	'Young' but 'considerably older' than D	'Daughter of an Innkeeper'	c.22 (Under 18 when married in 1810)	grocer and cheesemonger	P	£500	Love letters	MC
73	*Badeley vs. Mortlock*	Feb. 1816	CCP	M	Over 40	Attorney	Over 40		P	1s.		BNP/EFP
74	*Long vs. Peyton*	June 1816	CKB	F		Widow 'of considerable attraction'		Son of Admiral Peyton, holding a Lieutenant's commission in the Navy	P	300 g.		E/BNP/ RCG
75	*Lancey vs. Hunter, Esq.*	June 1816	CKB	F		Daughter of a Mathematical Professor at Greenwich Hospital School and Governess to the defendant's daughters	51–2	'a widower, and a Gentleman of considerable fortune'	P	£1,500	Love letters	BNP/YH/ HP
76	*Matchiff/ Mathers vs. Dixie/Dixey*	Aug. 1816	DA	F		Sister of a grocer	17–18 during courtship	Apprentice surgeon and apothecary; becoming a baronet before trial with a 'not large' fortune	P	£1,500		MP/BNP

77	*Evans vs. Jones*	May 1817	CKB	F		Daughter of Excise Collecter	c.27	Labourer in lead mine who unexpectedly came into property	P	£1,000		MP
78	*Shannon vs. Brandon*	June 1818	CCP	F	Young Jewish Lady			Jewish merchant in Goodman's Fields	P	£500	Letters	MP
79	*Bourdernelle vs. Bamfild*	July 1819	CCP	F		Respectable foreigner		Gentleman/army surgeon	P	£100	Love letters	MP
80	*Beattie vs. Pearson*	Sept. 1820	LNA	F		Widow		Silk manufacturer	P	£5,000		MP
81	*Vaile vs. Vandyk*	Feb. 1821	CKB	F	18	'Middle rank'	25	'Middle rank'	P	£100		MP
82	*King vs. Chance*	Apr. 1822	GA	F	32	Fancy dress-maker & respectable manufacturer's daughter		Gentleman of considerable fortune with accomplished manners. Ex-Lieutenant in the South Gloucestershire Militia	P	£800	Love letters	MP
83	*Ester vs. Hiatt*	Jan. 1823	CKB	F	40	Daughter of a brewery clerk	36	American possessing large property	P	£980		MP
84	*Rabbitts vs. West*	Apr. 1824	SMA	F	30–40	Humble farmer's daughter	c.70	Farmer of considerable property	P	£200		MP

(continued)

Continued

	Case	Date	Court(s)	Sex of Plaintiff	Age of Plaintiff During Trial	Occupation/ Social Status of Plaintiff	Age of Defendant During Trial	Occupation/ Social Status of Defendant	Verdict	Damages	Objects Used as Evidence	Source(s)
85	*Horner vs. Wood*	Feb. 1825	CKB	F					P	£100		MP
86	*Peake vs. Wedgwood*	Mar. 1826	STA	F		Gentleman's daughter		Man possessing large landed estate & collieries	P	£1,500		MP
87	*Levers vs. Faulkes*	Mar. 1827	NTA	F	Nearly 35 by trial			Gentleman worth c.£15,000	P	£1,600		MP
88	*Simpson vs. Timperon*	Mar. 1828	CLA	F	'old'	'The station of life in which the parties moved was not very elevated; but it was respectable'	'old'	Butcher, farmer, and 'man of considerable property' worth about £120 per annum	P	£350		MP
89	*Foot vs. Ottuay*	Mar. 1829	SLA	F		One 'of four orphan daughters'	c.21 (under 18 in 1825)	Coachmaker	P	£100	Love letters	MP
90	*Cooper vs. Bunning*	Feb. 1830	CCP	M	65	Widowed surgeon		Widow	P	£140	Love letters	MP

Key

Abbreviation	Court
BA	Bury Assizes
CBA	Cambridge Assizes
CHA	Chelmsford Assizes
CLA	Carlisle Assizes
CC	Court of Chancery
CCP	Court of Common Pleas
CKB	Court of King's Bench
DA	Derby Assizes
DCA	Dorchester Assizes
EA	Exeter Assizes
GA	Gloucester Assizes
GH	Guildhall
HA	Hertford Assizes
KA	Kent Assizes
LNA	Lancaster Assizes
NA	Norwich Assizes
NTA	Nottingham Assizes
NWA	Newcastle Assizes
OA	Oxford Assizes
SFA	Suffolk Assizes
SLA	Salisbury Assizes
SMA	Somerset Assizes
SRA	Surrey Assizes
STA	Stafford Assizes
TA	Thetford Assizes
WA	Warwick Assizes
WXA	Wexford Assizes
YA	York Assizes

Abbreviation	Verdict
A	Adjourned
AR	Referred to arbitration
D	Rule for the Defendant
JW	Juror Withdrawn
N	Nonsuit
P	Rule for the Plaintiff
(R)	Retrial
S	Settlement reached

Abbreviation	Source
BG	*E. Johnson's British Gazette and Sunday Monitor*
BNP	*The Bury and Norwich Post*
CEG	*Courier and Evening Gazette*
CSWJ	*Craftsman or Say's Weekly Journal*
DWR	*Diary or Woodfall's Register*
E	*The Examiner*
EFP	*Trewman's Exeter Flying Post*
EM	*Evening Mail*

Abbreviation	Source
ER	*English Reports*
GEP	*General Evening Post*
HP	*The Hull Packet*
IJ	*The Ipswich Journal*
LC	*London Chronicle*
LEP	*Lloyd's Evening Post*
LG	*Lancaster Gazette and General Advertiser*
LM	*Leeds Mercury*
LPEP	*London Packet or New Lloyd's Evening Post*
MC	*The Morning Chronicle*
MP	*The Morning Post*
MPG	*The Morning Post & Gazetteer*
O	*Oracle*
OBNW	*Oracle Bell's New World*
ODA	*Oracle and Daily Advertiser*
OJ	*Jackson's Oxford Journal*
OPA	*Oracle and Public Advertiser*
PA	*Public Advertiser*
Plt	Pamphlet
RCG	*Royal Cornwall Gazette*
S	*Sun*
SJC	*Saint James's Chronicle*
T	*The Times*
TB	*True Briton*
Tel	*Telegraph*
USWJ	*Universal Spectator and Weekly Journal*
W	*World*
WEP	*Whitehall Evening Post*
WFA	*World & Fashionable Advertiser*
YH	*The York Herald*

Select Bibliography

1. MANUSCRIPTS

(i) Local Archives and Museums

Bedfordshire Archives Service, Bedford (BAS)
Copy of proposal of marriage from Edward Hall, 1713, HW66.
Letters concerning the elopement of Isabella Eccleston and John Everard, 1725–46, HW86.
Proposal of marriage from Philip Yorke to Lady Jemima Campbell, 1740, L30/9/113.
Letters from William Bell to Catherine 'Kitty' Williamson (*née* Taylor), 1743, M/10/3/1–4.
Letters between Elizabeth Johnson and Richard How II, *c.*1747–57, HW87/223–5.
Proposal of marriage from Richard How II to Sally, 1751, HW87/182.
Letters from John Cater to Mrs Williamson concerning Charlotte Jackson, 1779, M/10/4/16–18.
Letters from Samuel Whitbread II to Elizabeth Grey, 1787–8, W1/6546–612.
Proposal of marriage from Jason Humberstone to Mrs Jane Parker, and letter seeking support from Jason Humberstone to Mrs Ann Ireland, 1819, Z742/36–7.

Bodleian Library, Oxford (BLO)
Letters between Judith Cowper and Martin Madan, 1723, MS Eng. Lett. c. 284.
Letters between Mary Wollstonecraft and William Godwin, 1796–7, MS Abinger c40.
Engraved Writing Blanks (uncatalogued), Educational Folder 4, John Johnson Collection (JJC).
Valentines (uncatalogued), Boxes 1 and 2, John Johnson Collection (JJC).

Borthwick Institute, York (BI)
Mascall vs. Watson, 1743–5, Consistory Court of York, appealed from Consistory Court of Durham, TRANS.CP.1744/5.
Letters in the broken love affair of the Earl of Ancram and Lady Elizabeth Grey, 1823–4, HALIFAX/A1/4/30.

Cornwall Record Office, Truro
Folded heart-shaped valentine created as part of a lottery, *c.*1750, X54/1.

Cumbria Record Office, Carlisle (CRO)
Love letters from 'J. H.' and Humphrey Senhouse III to Catherine Wood, 1763 and 1768, D/SEN 5/5/1/9/1/1 and 5/5/1/9/1/5.

Cumbria Record Office, Kendal
'An Acrostick on the Amiable Miss Carus, Beck-head, Kirkby Lonsdale Westmorland', 18th–19th century, WDBIG/1/113.

Derbyshire Record Office, Matlock (DRO)
Letters between Jedediah Strutt and Elizabeth Woollat, 1748–55, D5303/1–4.
Letters between Eleanor Anne Porden and John Franklin, 1821–2, D3311/8/1.
'Inventory & Valuation of Pictures, Busts, Books, Prints, Wines, Household Goods and Furniture, Horses & Carriage &c bequeathed to Mrs Galton under the Will of the Late Joseph Strutt Es^{re} deced', 1844, D3772/EL2/2/3.

East Riding Archives, Beverley
Heart-shaped paper valentine by David Bursell, *c.*1797, DDX114/8.

East Sussex Record Office, Brighton (ESRO)
Letters from Oroondates to Statira (Mrs Ann Webb), early 18th century, FRE/5411–18.
Love letters from Charles Ly–, James Nelthorpe, Dudley A. Sidney Cosby, and two further anonymous suitors to Abigail Way, 1765–6, SPK 1/3/2.
Incomplete puzzle purse, *c.*1820, HMU 1/1/3.

Essex Record Office, Chelmsford (ERO)
Photocopies of letters from Mary Martin to Isaac Martin Rebow, *c.*1767–76, A12691, Box 1, Vols. I–III.

Hampshire Record Office, Winchester (HRO)
Love letters from W[illia]m Martin and William Denyer to Mrs Hannah Smith, 1714 and 1716, 3M51/684–5.
Photocopy of valentine from J.E. to a 'Fair Lady', 1729, 2M37/608.
Letters from Charles Powlett to Anne Temple, and Journal of Anne Temple, 1790–6, 72M92.
Letters to John Dewey from various correspondents, *c.*1805–18, 32M77/F/C1–29, and John Dewey's letter book, *c.*1811–17, 32M77/F/C30.

Horsham Museum, West Sussex (HM)
Diaries of Sarah Hurst, 1755–62, MS 3542–5, accession no. 1991.1131.

John Rylands Library, University of Manchester (JRL)
Letters from Elizabeth Seddon to James Nicholson, 1738–9, Nicholson Papers, GB133 Eng. MS 1041 (Box 1).

Kent History and Library Centre, Maidstone (KHLC)
Letters between Charles Pratt and Elizabeth Jeffreys, 1745–9, Pratt Manuscripts, U840/C/9 and U840/C/1.
Letters between Francis Cobb and Charlotte Mary Curwen, 1805, EK/U1453/C287 and EK/U1453/C2, Bundle A.
Letters from Robert Garrett to Charlotte Bentinck, 1811–14, R/U888/C11 & R/U888/C14.
Proposal of marriage from Thomas Cobb to Miss Torre, 1827, R/U11/C39–40.

Library of Birmingham (LOB)
Letters between Joseph Strutt and Isabella Douglas, 1786–92, Galton Papers, MS 3101/C/E/4/8 and MS3101/C/E/5/16.

Library of the Society of Friends, London (LSF)
Letter from Thomas Kirton to Olive Lloyd, 1734, TEMP MSS 210/2/96.
Diaries of Elizabeth 'Betty' Fothergill, 1769–70, MS. Vol. 5, 51/1–3.
Letters from Robert Lloyd to Hannah Hart, 1803–4, TEMP MSS 210.
Letters and poems from Paul Moon James to Olivia Lloyd, 1805–8, TEMP MSS 403/9/19/1.

Liverpool Record Office, Liverpool (LIRO)
Letters between James Nicholson and Elizabeth Seddon, 1738–63, 920 NIC/5–6.

Liverpool University Library, Liverpool (LUL)
Letters concerning the marriage of William Rathbone IV and Hannah Reynolds, 1785–6, RP. II. 1 and RP. III. 1.

London Metropolitan Archives (LMA)
Letters from George Gibbs to Ann Vicary, *c.*1743–7, MS/11021/1.

Museum of London (MOL)
Lace paper and watered silk valentine card by Dobbs with applied photograph of a man inside, 1810–38, 34.170/360.

Flower cage valentine of a rose marked 'Dobb's Patent', 1813–16, A28549/53.

'Rimmel's perfumed valentine of the language of flowers', 1860–75, 38.229/2.

Lace paper valentine card printed with a portrait of a young woman, decorated with real hair, 1860–80, 34.170/892.

Norfolk Record Office, Norwich (NRO)

Copy of love letter from Mr J. Gallant to Mrs Mann (later Mrs Sibbs), 1717, WKC7/450/10.

Copy of love letter from 'G. M. L.', 1775, FEL 616, 554 × 1.

Letters between Elizabeth Reading and Edward Leathes, 1772, BOL 2/4.

Letters between Elizabeth Leathes (*née* Reading) and Edward Peach, 1789–1804, BOL 2/140, 740 × 4.

Letters between Gilbert Stirling, Andrew Stirling, and William Dalling, 1805, MEA 10/110, 662 × 6.

Letters from Anthony Hamond to Mary Ann Musters, *c*.1828, HMN 5/95.

Copy of love letter from a butler to a housekeeper, watermark 1830, BUL 13/5, 619 × 5.

North Yorkshire Record Office, Northallerton (NYRO)

Letters from John Fawdington to Jane 'Jenny' Jefferson, 1786–7, Z. 640.

Surrey History Centre, Woking (SHC)

Letters from Richard Dixon to Esther Maria Cranmer, 1782, 8215/1/9 and 8215/7.

Letters between Henry Goulburn and Jane Montagu, 1811, 304/A4/Box 1 and 304/D/Box 2.

The Postal Museum, London (TPM)

Francesco Bartolozzi, 'Sailor's Farewell' valentine, *c*.1800, OB1996.9.

Embossed flower cage valentine, *c*.1820, OB1995.28.

Hand-coloured printed valentine with lady stealing arrows from a sleeping Cupid, *c*.1820, OB1996.85.

Victoria & Albert Museum, London (V&A)

True love knot from John Thomas of Kempley Court to his future wife Elizabeth, *c*.1780, E.767–1985.

Circular cut-paper valentine to 'Mary', 1810–20, E.1035–1970.

Acrostic valentine from William Spencer to his future wife Harriet Holmes, 1811–14, E.1207–1925.

Embossed valentine stamped 'Dobb's patent', 1814, E.1534–1929.

Wiltshire and Swindon Archives, Chippenham (WSA)

Letters from John Lovell to Sarah Harvey and her aunt, Mrs Smith, Lovell of Cole Park Collection, 1756–8, 161/102.

Cut-paper valentine by John Lovell for 'ES' and 'PHL', 1778, 161/133.

York Castle Museum (YCM)

Sprung valentine card with dried grasses affixed in the centre, 1800–1900, DA2347.

Elaborate padded valentine with bouquet of fabric flowers, feathers and glass beads, 1840–1900, DA2180.

Ornate valentine with silver and white fairies, decorated with feathers and cloth flowers, 1850–1900, DA2081.

Paper lace valentine with net windows and small mirror inside, 1860–1900, DA1903.

(ii) National Archives and Museums

British Library, London (BL)

Letters from Georgiana Poyntz to Theadora Cowper concerning her relationship with John Spencer, 1754–5, Althorp collection, Add MS 75691.

Letters between Mary Berry, Charles O'Hara, Anne Damer, and Mrs Chomeley, 1795–6, Berry Papers, Vol. II, Add MS 37727.
Letters from Richard Law to Jane Townley, Ann Underwood, and Joanna Southcott, 1816–22, Southcott Papers, Vol. III, Add MS 47796.

British Museum, London (BM)
Heal Collection of trade cards.

(iii) International Archives and Museums
Huntington Library, California
Letters from Elizabeth Montagu to Margaret Cavendish, Duchess of Portland, *c*.1740, MSS MO 295.

Lewis Walpole Library, Farmington, CT (LWL)
Letters from Charles Hanbury Williams to his daughters, 1748, MSS Vol. 181, 11391.
Letters from Henry Fox to Charles Hanbury Williams concerning the love affair of Richard Edgcumbe and Lady Diana West, 1750, CHW10902/52.
Misc. poems on love and marriage by Princess Amelia, MSS Vol. 14.

Metropolitan Museum of Art, New York (MET)
Flower cage valentine of a cupid in a rose, watermark Smith & Allnutt, 1816, 1981.1136.529.
Flower cage valentine of a parrot tulip and moss rose, marked 'Dobbs Patent', watermark Smith & Allnutt, 1819, 1981.1136.525.

2. PRINTED PRIMARY SOURCES

A Collection of remarkable cases, for the instruction of both sexes, in the business of love and gallantry (London, 1730).
A complete edition of the poets of Great Britain (London, 1792), Vol. IV.
A desertation wherein the meaning, duty and happiness of kissing are explained, from Genesis (London, 1780).
A Fifth grand selection of music. As performed at the Theatre-Royal in Covent-Garden (London, 1793).
A practical treatise of saving faith (London, 1730).
Adair, James Makittrick, *Commentaries on the principles and practice of physic* (London, 1772).
Aikin, John, *Letters from a father to his son, on various topics, relative to literature and the conduct of life* (London, 1793).
Aikin, John, *Principles of midwifery, or puerperal medicine* (Edinburgh, 1784).
Alexander, Adam, *Classical Biography* (Edinburgh, 1800).
An account of the various systems of medicine (London, 1788).
An essay on the nature and conduct of the passions and affections (London, [1728] 1730).
An inquiry into the original of our ideas of beauty and virtue (London, [1725] 1738).
Ancient songs, from the time of King Henry the Third, to the Revolution (London, 1790).
Anecdotes of polite literature (London, 1764).
Apollo's Cabinet: or the muses delight (Liverpool, 1757).
As you like it, a poem, addressed to a friend (London, 1785).
Austen, Jane, *Emma* (Oxford, [1816] 2003).
Austen, Jane, *Persuasion* (London, [1818] 2008).
Austen, Jane, *Sense and Sensibility* (London, [1811] 2000).
Behn, Aphra, *The Land of Love. A Poem* (London, 1717).

Blair, Hugh, *Essays on Rhetoric, Abridged Chiefly From Dr. Blair's Lectures on that Science,* fourth edition (London, 1801), 298.

Blair, Hugh, *Lectures on rhetoric and belles lettres* (London, 1785), Vol. III.

Bourne, Henry, *Antiquitates Vulgares, or the Antiquities of the Common People* (Newcastle, 1725).

Burney, Frances, *Camilla: or, A Picture of Youth* (Cambridge, [1796] 1999).

Burney, Frances, *Evelina, or The History of a Young Lady's Entrance into the World* (Cambridge, [1778] 1996).

Burrell, Lady Sophia, *Poems. Dedicated to the Right Honourable the Earl of Mansfield* (London, 1793).

Captain Wedderburn's courtship to Lord Roslin's daughter. to which is added, Bess of Bedlam (Glasgow, 1780).

Cobb, William Francis, *Memoir of the Late Francis Cobb, Esq. of Margate* (Maidstone, 1835).

Cobbold, Elizabeth, *Cliff's Valentines* (Ipswich, 1813).

Cooke, Thomas, *The Universal Letter-Writer; Or, New Art of Polite Correspondence* (London, 1788).

Descartes, René, *The Passions of the Soul*, trans. Stephen Voss (Cambridge, [1649] 1989).

Devonshire, Georgiana Cavendish, Duchess of, *The Sylph*, third edition (London, 1779), Vol. I.

Djabri, Susan C., ed., *The Diaries of Sarah Hurst 1759–1762: Life and Love in Eighteenth Century Horsham* (Stroud, 2009).

Dossie, Robert, *The Handmaid to the Arts* (London, 1758).

Edgeworth, Maria, *Belinda* (Oxford, [1801] 2008).

Ellis, George, *Specimens of the early English poets* (London, 1790).

Every Lady's Own Valentine Writer, in Prose and Verse, for the Year 1794 (London, 1794).

Fielding, Henry, *The History of Tom Jones, A Foundling* (Ware, [1749] 1999).

Forman, Harry Buxton, ed., *Letters of John Keats to Fanny Brawne* (London, 1878).

Gaskell, Elizabeth, *Cranford* (New York, 1853).

Goethe, Johann Wolfgang von, *The Sorrows of Young Werther* (Oxford, [1774] 2012).

Gregory, John, *A Father's Legacy to his Daughters* (London, 1774).

Gregory, John, *Elements of the practice of physic* (Edinburgh, 1772).

Halford, W. and C. Young, *A Jewellers' Book of Patterns in Hair Work* (London, c.1850).

Haller, Albrecht von, *Dr Albert Haller's physiology; being a course of lectures upon the visceral anatomy and vital oeconomy of human bodies* (London, 1754), Vol. I.

Hays, Mary, *Memoirs of Emma Courtney* (Oxford, [1796] 2009).

Haywood, Eliza, *Love in Excess; Or The Fatal Enquiry, A Novel* (London, 1719–20).

Ingpen, Roger, ed., *The Love Letters of Mary Wollstonecraft to Gilbert Imlay* (London, 1908).

Jerusalem Delivered; An Heroic Poem: Translated from the Italian of Torquato Tasso, by John Hoole, fourth edition (London, 1772).

Johnson, Samuel, *A Dictionary of the English Language: In Which the Words are Deduced from their Originals, and Illustrated in their Different Significations by Examples from the Best Writers*, first edition (London, 1755), Vols. I–II.

Letters of Abelard and Héloïse. To which is prefix'd, A Particular Account of their Lives, Amours, and Misfortunes. Extracted chiefly from Monsieur Bayle. Translated from the French, fourth edition (London, 1722).

Locke, John, *An Essay Concerning Humane Understanding. In Four Books* (London, 1690).

Love given over: or, a Satyr against the Pride, Lust and Inconstancy, &c. of Woman (London, 1690).

Love in a Village; A Comic Opera. As it is Performed at the Theatre Royal in Covent-Garden, ninth edition (London, 1764).

M. Misson's Memoirs and Observations in his Travels over England (London, 1719).

McGuire, Kelly, ed., *The History of Suicide in England, 1650–1850* (London, 2012), Vol. IV.

Mandeville, Bernard, *The Virgin Unmask'd: Or, Female Dialogues Betwixt an Elderly Maiden Lady, and Her Niece, On Several Diverting Discourses of the Times* (London, 1709).

Manley, Delarivier, *The Power of Love. In Seven Novels* (London, 1720).

Martin, W., *The Hair Worker's Manual* (London, c.1840s).

Matthews, William, ed., *The Diary of Dudley Ryder 1715–1716* (London, 1939).

Melville, Lewis, ed., *The Berry Papers; being the correspondence hitherto unpublished of Mary and Agnes Berry (1763–1852)* (London, 1914).

Millar, John, *The Origin of the Distinction of Ranks; or, An Inquiry into the Circumstances which Give Rise to Influence and Authority in the Different Members of Society*, third edition (London, 1781).

Milton, John, *Paradise Lost. A Poem, In Twelve Books* (London, [1667] 1788).

Moir, John, *Female Tuition; or, An Address to Mothers, on the Education of Daughters*, second edition (London, 1786).

Moral Essays, Chiefly Collected from Different Authors (Liverpool, 1796).

Perry, Charles, *A mechanical account and explication of the hysteric passion, under all its various symptoms and appearances* (London, 1755).

Pope, Alexander, *A collection of Essays, Epistles and Odes* (London, 1758).

Pulteney, Richard, *A General View of the Writings of Linnaeus* (London, 1781).

Reuben, or, The Suicide (London, 1787).

Richardson, Samuel, *Clarissa, or The History of a Young Lady* (London, [1747–8] 1985).

Richardson, Samuel, *Pamela; or, Virtue Rewarded* (Oxford, [1740] 2001).

Richardson, Samuel, *The History of Sir Charles Grandison, In a Series of Letters*, sixth edition (London, [1753–4] 1770).

Rinaldo; A New Serious Opera (London, 1780).

Rochefoucauld, François de La, *Maxims and Moral Reflections* (Edinburgh, [1665] 1798).

Rousseau, Jean-Jacques, *Eloisa: or, a Series of Original Letters* (Dublin, 1766), Vol. I.

Rousseau, Jean-Jacques, *Emilius; or, A Treatise of Education* (Edinburgh, 1768).

Scott, Grant F., ed., *Selected Letters of John Keats* (Cambridge, MA and London, 2002).

Shaftesbury, Anthony Ashley Cooper, third Earl of, *Characteristicks of men, manners, opinions, times* (London, [1711] 1732), Vol. II.

Shakespeare, William, *The Works of Shakespear* (London, 1725).

Sharman, Ruth, ed., *The Cansos and Sirventes of the Troubadour Giraut de Borneil: A Critical Edition* (Cambridge, 1989).

Sketches of the characters of the Hon. Thomas Erskine, and James Mingay, Esq. (London, 1794).

Solomon, Robert C. and Kathleen M. Higgins, eds, *The Philosophy of (Erotic) Love* (Lawrence, KS, 1991).

Sterne, Laurence, *A Sentimental Journey through France and Italy* (Dublin, 1768).

Sylvius, Aeneas, *The History of the Amours of Count Schlick, Chancellor to the Emperor Sigismund, and a Young Lady of Quality of Sienna* (London, 1708).

The Arcana of polite literature (Dublin, 1789).

The Art of Courtship; or the School of Love (London, c.1775).

The attic miscellany; and characteristic mirror of men and things (London, 1791).

The Beauties of Shakespeare Selected from his Plays and Poems (Dublin, 1783).

The Cautious Maid's Garland (Bristol, c.1755).

The Complete Valentine Writer: Or, The Young Men and Maidens Best Assistant (London, 1780?).

The Dictionary of Love. In which is contained, The Explanation of most of the Terms used in that Language (London, 1753).

The Frighted West-Country Man's Garland (London, c.1705).

The Golden Glove's Garland, Containing a Choice Collection of New Songs (Newcastle, c.1785).

The Hampshire Syren: or, Songster's Miscellany (Southampton, 1794).

The history of Miss Harriot Fitzroy, and Miss Emilia Spencer (Dublin, 1767).

The Lady's Preceptor. Or, a Letter to a Young Lady of Distinction upon Politeness, Taken from the French of the Abbé d'Ancourt, And Adapted to the Religion, Customs, and Manners of the English Nation, second edition (London, 1743).

The Memoirs of Charles-Lewis, Baron de Pöllnitz. Being the Observations he Made in his Late Travels from Prussia thro' Germany, Italy, France, Flanders, Holland, England, &c. In Letters to his Friend (London, 1739).

The New English Valentine Writer, Or The High Road to Love; for Both Sexes (London, 1784).

The New lover's instructor; or, Whole art of Courtship (London, c.1780).

The poetical epitome (London, 1791 and 1792).

The Poetical Love-Token. By the editor of the 'Forget-Me-Not' (London, 1850).

The political farrago: being a miscellaneous assemblage of epigrams and other jeux d'espirit (London, 1794), Vol. II.

The Trial of the Hon. Richard Bingham, for Crim. Con. with Lady Elizabeth Howard (London, 1794).

The Tunbridge Love Letter and *The Lady's Answer to The Tunbridge Love Letter* (London, 1794).

The Universal Dictionary of Trade and Commerce (London, 1774).

The Whole Proceedings on the Tryal between Mrs. Sarah Holt, and Knox Ward, Esq; upon a Promise of Marriage, On Wednesday, February 25, 1729–30 (London, 1730).

Trial for a Breach of Promise of Marriage. Miss Elizabeth Chapman, Against William Shaw. Esq; Attorney at Law. Before The Right Honourable Lord Kenyon, in the Court of King's-Bench, Westminster-Hall, On Saturday, The 22d of May, 1790 (London, 1790).

Trial for breach of promise of marriage, Miss Eleanor Palmer against Benjamin Barnard, Esq. (London, 1792).

Wardle, Ralph M., ed., *Godwin & Mary: Letters of William Godwin and Mary Wollstonecraft* (London, 1967).

Wedd, A. F., ed., *The Love-Letters of Mary Hays* (London, 1925).

West, Moses, *A Treatise Concerning Marriage. Wherein the Unlawfulness of Mixt-Marriages is Laid Open* (London, 1732).

Wetenhall Wilkes, *A Letter of Genteel and Moral Advice to a Young Lady. In which is digested, into a new and familiar Method, a System of Rules and Informations, to qualify the Fair Sex to be useful and happy in every State*, second edition (Dublin, 1741).

Winstanley, William, *The new help to discourse or, Wit, mirth, and jollity* (London, 1680).

Wollstonecraft, Mary, *A Vindication of the Rights of Woman* (London, 1792).

3. DATABASES

British and Irish Women's Letters and Diaries (BIWLD), https://alexanderstreet.com/products/british-and-irish-womens-letters-and-diaries.

British Newspapers 1600–1900, https://www.connectedhistories.org/resources/bu/

English Broadside Ballad Archive (EBBA), https://ebba.english.ucsb.edu.

Old Bailey Online (OBO), https://www.oldbaileyonline.org.

Oxford Dictionary of National Biography (*ODNB*), http://www.oxforddnb.com.
Oxford English Dictionary (online) (*OEDO*), http://www.oed.com.
The Times Digital Archive, https://www.gale.com/uk/c/the-times-digital-archive.

4. SECONDARY SOURCES

Abelove, Henry, 'Some Speculations on the History of Sexual Intercourse during the Long Eighteenth Century in England', *Genders* 6 (1989): 125–30.

Adams Day, Robert, *Told in Letters: Epistolary Fiction before Richardson* (Ann Arbor, MI, 1966).

Ahmed, Sara, *The Cultural Politics of Emotion*, second edition (Edinburgh, 2004).

Ahmed, Sara, 'Happy Objects', in *The Affect Theory Reader*, ed. Melissa Gregg and Gregory J. Seigworth (Durham, NC and London, 2010), 29–51.

Allan, David, *A Nation of Readers: The Lending Library in Georgian England* (London, 2008).

Appadurai, Arjun, 'The Thing Itself', *Public Culture* 18.1 (2006): 15–21.

Ayto, John, ed., *Brewer's Dictionary of Phrase and Fable*, seventeenth edition (London 2007).

Backscheider, Paula R., *Eighteenth-Century Women Poets and Their Poetry: Inventing Agency, Inventing Genre* (Baltimore, MD, 2005).

Backscheider, Paula R. and Catherine E. Ingrassia, eds, *British Women Poets of the Long Eighteenth Century: An Anthology* (Baltimore, MD, 2009).

Bailey, Joanne [Begiato], *Parenting in England 1760–1830: Emotion, Identity, and Generation* (Oxford, 2012).

Bailey, Joanne [Begiato], *Unquiet Lives: Marriage and Marriage Breakdown in England, 1660–1800* (Cambridge, 2003).

Bannet, Eve Tavor, *British and American Letter Manuals, 1680–1810*, Vol. I, *Academies of Complement, 1680–1806* (London, 2008).

Bannet, Eve Tavor, *Empire of Letters: Letter Manuals and Transatlantic Correspondence, 1680–1820* (Cambridge, 2009).

Barclay, Katie, 'Emotions, the Law and the Press in Britain: Seduction and Breach of Promise Suits, 1780–1830', *Journal for Eighteenth-Century Studies* 39.2 (2016): 267–84.

Barclay, Katie, *Love, Intimacy and Power: Marriage and Patriarchy in Scotland 1650–1850* (Manchester, 2011).

Barclay, Katie and Rosalind Carr, 'Women, Love and Power in Enlightenment Scotland', *Women's History Review* 27.2 (2018): 176–98.

Barker-Benfield, G. J., *The Culture of Sensibility: Sex and Society in Eighteenth-Century Britain* (Chicago, IL and London, 1992).

Barry, Jonathan and Christopher Brooks, eds, *The Middling Sort of People: Culture, Society and Politics in England, 1550–1800* (London, 1994).

Barthes, Roland, *A Lover's Discourse: Fragments*, trans. Richard Howard (London, [1977] 2002).

Bendall, Sarah Anne, 'To Write a Distick upon It: Busks and the Language of Courtship and Sexual Desire in Sixteenth- and Seventeenth-Century England', *Gender and History* 26.2 (2014): 199–222.

Ben-Ze'ev, Aaron, *Love Online: Emotions on the Internet* (Cambridge, 2003).

Berg, Maxine, *Luxury and Pleasure in Eighteenth-Century Britain* (Oxford, 2005).

Berg, Maxine, '"The Merest Shadows of a Commodity": Indian Muslins for European Markets 1750–1800', in *Goods from the East, 1600–1800: Trading Eurasia*, ed. Maxine Berg, with Felicia Gottmann, Hanna Hodacs, and Chris Nierstrasz (Basingstoke, 2015), 119–34.

Berg, Maxine and Elizabeth Eger, eds, *Luxury in the Eighteenth Century: Debates, Desires and Delectable Goods* (Basingstoke, 2003).

Berry, Helen, *The Castrato and his Wife* (Oxford, 2011).

Berry, Helen, *Gender, Society and Print Culture in Late Stuart England* (Aldershot, 2003).

Berry, Helen, 'Polite Consumption: Shopping in Eighteenth-Century England', *Transactions of the Royal Historical Society* 12 (2002): 375–94.

Berry, Helen, 'Queering the History of Marriage: The Social Recognition of a Castrato Husband in Eighteenth-Century Britain', *History Workshop Journal* 74.1 (2012): 27–50.

Berry, Helen and Elizabeth Foyster, eds, *The Family in Early Modern England* (Cambridge, 2007).

Blair, Kirstie, '"Proved on the Pulses": Heart Disease in Victorian Culture, 1830–1860', in *Framing and Imagining Disease in Cultural History*, ed. George Rousseau, Miranda Gill, David Haycock, and Malte Herwig (Basingstoke, 2003), 285–302.

Bloch, Ruth H., 'Changing Conceptions of Sexuality and Romance in Eighteenth-Century America', *The William and Mary Quarterly* 60 (2003): 13–42.

Boddice, Rob, 'The Affective Turn: Historicizing the Emotions', in *Psychology and History: Interdisciplinary Explorations*, ed. Cristian Tileagă and Jovan Byford (Cambridge, 2014), 147–65.

Boettcher, Graham C., ed., *The Look of Love: Eye Miniatures from the Skier Collection* (London, 2012).

Borsay, Peter, ed., *The Eighteenth-Century Town: A Reader in English Urban History 1688–1820* (New York and London, 2014).

Bound Alberti, Fay, 'Emotions in the Early Modern Medical Tradition', in *Medicine, Emotion and Disease, 1700–1950*, ed. Fay Bound Alberti (Basingstoke, 2006).

Bound Alberti, Fay, *Matters of the Heart: History, Medicine, and Emotion* (Oxford, 2010).

Bound [Alberti], Fay, 'Writing the Self? Love and the Letter in England, c.1660–c.1760', *Literature & History* 11.1 (2002): 1–19.

Bourdieu, Pierre, *The Logic of Practice* (Stanford, CA, [1980] 1990).

Brewer, John and Roy Porter, eds, *Consumption and the World of Goods* (London and New York, 1994).

Certeau, Michel de, *Culture in the Plural*, trans. Tom Conley (Minneapolis, MN and London, [1974] 1997).

Certeau, Michel de, *The Practice of Everyday Life* (Berkeley and Los Angeles, CA, [1984] 2011), Vol. I.

Cleves, Rachel Hope, *Charity and Sylvia: A Same-Sex Marriage in Early America* (Oxford, 2014).

Cott, Nancy, 'Passionlessness: An Interpretation of Victorian Sexual Ideology, 1790–1850', *Signs* 4.2 (1978): 219–36.

Crawford, Patricia and Sara Mendelson, 'Sexual Identities in Early Modern England: The Marriage of Two Women in 1680', *Gender and History* 7.3 (1995): 362–77.

Cressy, David, *Birth, Marriage and Death: Ritual, Religion, and the Life-Cycle in Tudor and Stuart England* (Oxford, 1997).

Dabhoiwala, Faramerz, 'The Construction of Honour, Reputation and Status in Late Seventeenth- and Early Eighteenth-Century England', *Transactions of the Royal Historical Society* 6 (1996): 201–13.

Dabhoiwala, Faramerz, *The Origins of Sex: A History of the First Sexual Revolution* (London, 2013).

Dant, Tim, 'Fetishism and the Social Value of Objects', *Sociological Review* 44.3 (1996): 495–516.

Dawson, Lesel, *Lovesickness and Gender in Early Modern English Literature* (Oxford, 2008).

Daybell, James, 'Female Literacy and the Social Conventions of Women's Letter-Writing in England, 1540–1603', in *Early Modern Women's Letter Writing, 1450–1700*, ed. James Daybell (Basingstoke, 2001), 59–76.

Deigh, John, 'Concepts of Emotions in Modern Philosophy and Psychology', in *The Oxford Handbook of Philosophy of Emotion*, ed. Peter Goldie (Oxford, 2010), 17–40.

Dixon, Thomas, '"Emotion": The History of a Keyword in Crisis', *Emotion Review* 4.4 (2012): 338–44.

Dixon, Thomas, *From Passions to Emotions: The Creation of a Secular Psychological Category* (Cambridge, 2003).

Dixon, Thomas, *Weeping Britannia: Portrait of a Nation in Tears* (Oxford, 2015).

Dixon, Thomas, 'Why I am Angry: The Return to Ancient Links between Reason and Emotion', *Times Literary Supplement*, 1 October 2004.

Dorfles, Gillo, 'The Man-Made Object', in *The Man-Made Object*, ed. Gyorgy Kepes (New York, 1966), 1–8.

Downes, Stephanie, Sally Holloway, and Sarah Randles, eds, *Feeling Things: Objects and Emotions through History* (Oxford, 2018).

Duggan, Holly, *The Ephemeral History of Perfume: Scent and Sense in Early Modern England* (Baltimore, MD, 2011).

Dyer, Serena, 'Shopping, Spectacle & the Senses', *History Today* 65.3 (2015): 30–6.

Easton, Fraser, 'Gender's Two Bodies: Women Warriors, Female Husbands and Plebeian Life', *Past & Present* 180 (2003): 131–74.

Ehrman, Edwina, *The Wedding Dress: 300 Years of Bridal Fashions* (London, 2011).

Ellison, Julie, 'Sensibility', in *A Handbook of Romanticism Studies*, ed. Joel Faflak and Julia M. Wright (Chichester, 2016), 37–54.

Erickson, Amy, 'Mistresses and Marriage: or, a Short History of the Mrs', *History Workshop Journal* 78.1 (2014): 39–57.

Eustace, Nicole, '"The cornerstone of a copious work": Love and Power in Eighteenth-Century Courtship', *Journal of Social History* 34.3 (2001): 517–46.

Eustace, Nicole, *Passion is the Gale: Emotion, Power, and the Coming of the American Revolution* (Chapel Hill, NC, 2010).

Eustace, Nicole, Eugenia Lean, Julie Livingston, Jan Plamper, William Reddy, and Barbara Rosenwein, 'AHR Conversation: The Historical Study of Emotions', *American Historical Review* 117.5 (2012): 1487–531.

Evans, Vyvyan, *The Emoji Code: How Smiley Faces, Love Hearts and Thumbs Up are Changing the Way We Communicate* (London, 2017).

Feldman Barrett, Lisa, *How Emotions are Made: The Secret Life of the Brain* (London, 2017).

Finn, Margot, 'Men's Things: Masculine Possession in the Consumer Revolution', *Social History* 25.2 (2000): 133–55.

Fisher, Helen, *Anatomy of Love: A Natural History of Mating, Marriage, and Why We Stray* (New York and London, [1992] 2016).

Fisher, Helen, *Why We Love: The Nature and Chemistry of Romantic Love* (New York, 2004).

Fletcher, Anthony, *Gender, Sex and Subordination in England 1500–1800* (New Haven, CT and London, 1995).

Foyster, Elizabeth, 'Sensory Experiences: Smells, Sounds and Touch', in *A History of Everyday Life in Scotland, 1600 to 1800*, ed. Elizabeth Foyster and Christopher Whatley (Edinburgh, 2010), 217–33.

Frances, Catherine, 'Making Marriages in Early Modern England: Rethinking the Role of Family and Friends', in *The Marital Economy in Scandinavia and Britain 1400–1900*, ed. Maria Ågren and Amy Louise Erickson (Aldershot, 2005), 39–55.

Freud, Sigmund, *On Sexuality: Three Essays on the Theory of Sexuality and Other Works*, ed. Angela Richards, trans. James Strachey (London, 1977), Vol. 7, 65–8.

Frevert, Ute, *Emotions in History—Lost and Found* (Budapest and New York, 2011).

Friedman, Emily C., *Reading Smell in Eighteenth-Century Fiction* (Lanham, MD, 2016).

Frost, Ginger S., *Promises Broken: Courtship, Class, and Gender in Victorian England* (Charlottesville, VA and London, 1995).

Geertz, Clifford, 'Thick Description: Toward an Interpretive Theory of Culture', in *The Interpretation of Cultures* (New York, 1973), 310–23.

Gibson, Kate, 'Marriage Choice and Kinship among the English Catholic Elite, 1680–1730', *Journal of Family History* 41.2 (2016): 144–64.

Gibson, William and Joanne Begiato, *Sex and the Church in the Long Eighteenth Century* (London and New York, 2017).

Giese, Loreen, *Courtships, Marriage Customs, and Shakespeare's Comedies* (New York, 2006).

Gillis, John, *For Better, For Worse: British Marriages, 1600 to the Present* (Oxford, 1985).

Girouard, Mark, *The Return to Camelot: Chivalry and the English Gentleman* (London, 1981).

Goldie, Peter, 'Love for a Reason', *Emotion Review* 2.1 (2010): 61–7.

Goodman, Dena, *Becoming a Woman in the Age of Letters* (Ithaca, NY and London, 2009).

Goody, Jack, *The Theft of History* (Cambridge, 2006).

Gowing, Laura, *Domestic Dangers: Women, Words and Sex in Early Modern London* (Oxford, 1996).

Green, Juana, 'The Sempster's Wares: Merchandising and Marrying in *The Fair Maid of the Exchange* (1607)', *Renaissance Quarterly* 53.4 (2000): 1084–118.

Griffiths, Paul, *What Emotions Really Are: The Problem of Psychological Categories* (Chicago, IL and London, 1997).

Hamlett, Jane, *Material Relations: Domestic Interiors and Middle-Class Families in England, 1850–1910* (Manchester, 2010).

Harvey, Karen, *Reading Sex in the Eighteenth Century: Bodies and Gender in English Erotic Culture* (Cambridge, 2004).

Heal, Felicity and Clive Holmes, *The Gentry in England and Wales, 1500–1700* (London, 1994).

Herman, Bernard L., *The Stolen House* (London, 1992).

Hindle, Steve, 'The Problem of Pauper Marriage in Seventeenth-Century England', *Transactions of the Royal Historical Society* 8 (1998): 71–89.

Hitchcock, Tim, 'Redefining Sex in Eighteenth-Century England', *History Workshop Journal* 41 (1996): 72–90.

Hollingsworth, T. H., 'The Demography of the British Peerage', Supplement to *Population Studies* 18.2 (1964).

Houston, R. A., *Bride Ales and Penny Weddings: Recreations, Reciprocity, and Regions in Britain from the Sixteenth to the Nineteenth Centuries* (Oxford, 2014).

Howard, Vicki, 'A "Real Man's Ring": Gender and the Invention of Tradition', *Journal of Social History* 36.4 (2003): 837–56.

Howes, David, 'Culture Tunes Our Neurons', in *Empire of the Senses: The Sensual Culture Reader*, ed. David Howes (Oxford, 2005), 21–4.

Hughes, Therle, *English Domestic Needlework 1660–1860* (London, 1961).

Hume, Robert D., 'The Value of Money in Eighteenth-Century England: Incomes, Prices, Buying Power—and Some Problems in Cultural Economics', *Huntington Library Quarterly* 77.4 (2015): 373–416.

Hunt, Margaret, *The Middling Sort: Commerce, Gender, and the Family in England, 1680–1780* (London, 1996).

Ingram, Allan with Michelle Faubert, *Cultural Constructions of Madness in Eighteenth-Century Writing: Representing the Insane* (Basingstoke, 2005).

Ingram, Martin, *Church Courts, Sex and Marriage in England, 1570–1640* (Cambridge, 1990).

Jager, Eric, *The Book of the Heart* (London, 2000).

Jankowiak, William R. and Edward F. Fischer, 'A Cross-Cultural Perspective on Romantic Love', *Ethnology* 31.2 (1992): 149–55.

Jones, Kathryn, 'The "Irresistible Tide of Luxury"', in *The First Georgians: Art & Monarchy 1714–1760*, ed. Desmond Shawe-Taylor (London, 2014), 394–439.

Kavanagh, Declan, *Effeminate Years: Literature, Politics, and Aesthetics in Mid-Eighteenth-Century Britain* (Lewisburg, PA, 2017).

Keymer, Thomas, *Richardson's Clarissa and the Eighteenth-Century Reader* (Cambridge, 1992).

Keymer, Thomas, ed., *Samuel Richardson's Published Commentary on Clarissa 1747–65* (London, 1998), Vol. I.

Keymer, Thomas and Peter Sabor, *Pamela in the Marketplace: Literary Controversy and Print Culture in Eighteenth-Century Britain and Ireland* (Cambridge, 2005).

Komisaruk, Adam, 'The Privatization of Pleasure: Crim. Con. in Wollstonecraft's *Maria*', *Law and Literature* 16.1 (2004): 33–63.

Kwint, Marius, 'Material Memories: A History of the Souvenir', *Tate: The Art Magazine* (1998), 45–9.

Labanyi, Jo, 'Doing Things: Emotion, Affect, and Materiality', *Journal of Spanish Cultural Studies* 11.3–4 (2010): 223–33.

Lambert, Julie Anne, *A Nation of Shopkeepers: Trade Ephemera from 1654 to the 1860s in the John Johnson Collection* (Oxford, 2001).

Lambert, Susan, *Prints: Art and Techniques* (London, 2001).

Lamy, Lubomir, 'Beyond Emotion: Love as an Encounter of Myth and Drive', *Emotion Review* 8.2 (2016): 97–107.

Langhamer, Claire, *The English in Love: The Intimate Story of an Emotional Revolution* (Oxford, 2013).

Laqueur, Thomas, *Making Sex: The Body and Gender from the Greeks to Freud* (Cambridge, MA, 1990).

Lemmings, David, 'Marriage and the Law in the Eighteenth Century: Hardwicke's Marriage Act of 1753', *The Historical Journal* 39.2 (1996): 339–60.

Lettmaier, Saskia, *Broken Engagements: The Action for Breach of Promise of Marriage and the Feminine Ideal, 1800–1940* (Oxford, 2010).

Lindblom, Ina, 'The Botany of Friendship and Love', *Scandinavian Journal of History* 41.3 (2016): 410–26.

Lyons, Martyn, 'Love Letters and Writing Practices: On *Écritures Intimes* in the Nineteenth Century', *Journal of Family History* 24.2 (1999): 232–9.

Lystra, Karen, *Searching the Heart: Women, Men, and Romantic Love in Nineteenth-Century America* (New York and Oxford, 1989).

MacColla, Charles J., *Breach of Promise: Its History and Social Considerations* (London, 1879).

McGuire, Kelly, *Dying to be English: Suicide Narratives and National Identity, 1721–1814* (London, 2012).

McKendrick, Neil, John Brewer, and J. H. Plumb, *The Birth of a Consumer Society: The Commercialization of Eighteenth-Century England* (London, 1983).

McNeil, Peter and Giorgio Riello, 'Luxury and Fashion in the Long Eighteenth Century', in *Treasured Possessions from the Renaissance to the Enlightenment*, ed. Victoria Avery, Melissa Calaresu, and Mary Laven (Cambridge, 2015), 153–61.

Manning, Susan, 'Sensibility', in *The Cambridge Companion to English Literature 1740–1830*, ed. Thomas Keymer and Jon Mee (Cambridge, 2004), 80–99.

Massumi, Brian, 'The Autonomy of Affect', *Cultural Critique* 31 (1995): 83–109.

Mauss, Marcel, *The Gift: Forms and Functions of Exchange in Archaic Societies*, trans. Ian Cunnison (London, [1954] 1970).

Mews, Constant J., *Abelard and Heloise* (Oxford, 2005).

Miller, Daniel, *The Comfort of Things* (Cambridge, 2008).

Milligan, Edward H., *Quaker Marriage* (Kendal, 1994).

Milsom, S. F. C., *Historical Foundations of the Common Law* (London, 1969).

Moran, Anna and Sorcha O'Brien, eds, *Love Objects: Emotion, Design, and Material Culture* (London, 2014).

Mui, Lorna H. and Hoh-Cheung Mui, *Shops and Shopkeeping in Eighteenth-Century England* (London, 1989).

Novak, Maximillian, 'Sex, Madness, and Suicide in Sir Herbert Croft's *Love and Madness*', in *Sex and Death in Eighteenth-Century Literature*, ed. Jolene Zigarovich (Basingstoke, 2013), 165–82.

O'Day, Rosemary, 'Tudor and Stuart Women: Their Lives through their Letters', in *Early Modern Women's Letter Writing, 1450–1700*, ed. James Daybell (Basingstoke, 2001), 127–42.

O'Hara, Diana, *Courtship and Constraint: Rethinking the Making of Marriage in Tudor England* (Manchester, 2000).

Oppenheim, Janet, '*Shattered Nerves*': Doctors, Patients, and Depression in Victorian England* (Oxford, 1991).

Pearsall, Sarah, *Atlantic Families: Lives and Letters in the Later Eighteenth Century* (Oxford, 2008).

Perkin, Joan, *Women and Marriage in Nineteenth-Century England* (London, 2002).

Perkins, David, 'How the Romantics Recited Poetry', *Studies in English Literature, 1500–1900* 31.4 (1991): 655–71.

Pinto, Edward H., *Treen and Other Wooden Bygones: An Encyclopaedia and Social History* (London: G. Bell & Sons, 1969).

Plamper, Jan, *The History of Emotions: An Introduction*, trans. Keith Tribe (Oxford, 2015).

Pointon, Marcia, *Brilliant Effects: A Cultural History of Gem Stones & Jewellery* (New Haven, CT and London, 2009).

Pointon, Marcia, '"Surrounded with Brilliants": Miniature Portraits in Eighteenth-Century England', *The Art Bulletin* 83.1 (2001): 48–71.

Preston, John, '*Les Liaisons Dangereuses*: Epistolary Narrative and Moral Discovery', *French Studies* 24.1 (1970): 23–36.

Probert, Rebecca, *Marriage Law and Practice in the Long Eighteenth Century* (Cambridge, 2009).

Prown, Jules David, *Art as Evidence: Writings on Art and Material Culture* (New Haven, CT and London, 2001).

Reddy, William, *The Navigation of Feeling: A Framework for the History of Emotions* (Cambridge, 2001).

Reinarz, Jonathan, *Past Scents: Historical Perspectives on Smell* (Urbana, IL, 2014).

Retford, Kate, *The Art of Domestic Life: Family Portraiture in Eighteenth-Century England* (New Haven, CT and London, 2006).

Rickards, Maurice and Michael Twyman, *The Encyclopedia of Ephemera* (London, 2000).

Riello, Giorgio, 'Asian Knowledge and the Development of Calico Printing in Europe in the Seventeenth and Eighteenth Centuries', *Journal of Global History* 5 (2010): 1–28.

Rivers, Isabel, *Reason, Grace and Sentiment: A Study of the Language of Religion and Ethics in England 1660–1780* (Cambridge, [1991] 2000), Vols. I–II.

Rivers, Isabel, ed., *Books and their Readers in Eighteenth-Century England*, Vol. II *New Essays* (London and New York, 2003).

Rushton, Peter, 'The Testament of Gifts: Marriage Tokens and Disputed Contracts in North-East England, 1560–1630', *Folk Life* 24.1 (1985): 25–31.

Sant, Ann Jessie van, *Eighteenth-Century Sensibility and the Novel: The Senses in Social Context* (Cambridge, 2004).

Sartre, Jean-Paul, *Being and Nothingness: An Essay on Phenomenological Ontology*, trans. Hazel E. Barnes (London and New York, [1943] 2003).

Scarisbrick, Diana, *Historic Rings: Four Thousand Years of Craftsmanship* (Tokyo, 2004).

Scheer, Monique, 'Are Emotions a Kind of Practice (And is That What Makes Them Have a History)? A Bourdieuian Approach to Understanding Emotion', *History and Theory* 51.2 (2012): 193–220.

Schmidt, Leigh Eric, 'The Fashioning of a Modern Holiday: St. Valentine's Day, 1840–1970', *Winterthur Portfolio* 28.4 (1993): 209–45.

Schneid Lewis, Judith, *In the Family Way: Childbearing in the British Aristocracy, 1760–1860* (New Brunswick, NJ, 1986).

Serres, Michel, *The Five Senses: A Philosophy of Mingled Bodies*, trans. Margaret Sankey and Peter Cowley (London, [1985] 2016).

Shank, Barry, *A Token of My Affection: Greeting Cards and American Business Culture* (New York and Chichester, 2004).

Showalter, Elaine, *The Female Malady: Women, Madness and English Culture, 1830–1980* (London, 1985).

Small, Helen, *Love's Madness: Medicine, The Novel, and Female Insanity 1800–1865* (Oxford, 1996).

Staff, Frank, *The Valentine and its Origins* (London, 1969).

Staves, Susan, 'British Seduced Maidens', *Eighteenth-Century Studies* 14.2 (1980–1): 109–34.

Steedman, Carolyn, *Dust: The Archive and Cultural History* (Manchester, 2001).

Steinbach, Susie, 'From Redress to Farce: Breach of Promise Theatre in Cultural Context, 1830–1920', *Journal of Victorian Culture* 13.2 (2008): 247–76.

Steinbach, Susie, 'The Melodramatic Contract: Breach of Promise and the Performance of Virtue', *Nineteenth-Century Studies* 14 (2000): 1–34.

Stobart, Jon, 'Shopping Streets as Social Space: Leisure, Consumerism and Improvement in an Eighteenth-Century County Town', *Urban History* 25.1 (1998): 3–21.

Stone, Lawrence, *The Family, Sex and Marriage in England, 1500–1800* (London, 1977).

Stone, Lawrence, *Road to Divorce: England 1530–1987* (Oxford, 1990).

Tadmor, Naomi, *Family and Friends in Eighteenth-Century England: Household, Kinship, and Patronage* (Cambridge, 2004).

Tadmor, Naomi, 'Women and Wives: The Language of Marriage in Early Modern English Biblical Translations', *History Workshop Journal* 62.1 (2006): 1–27.

Tague, Ingrid, 'Love, Honour and Obedience: Fashionable Women and the Discourse of Marriage in the Early Eighteenth Century', *Journal of British Studies* 40.1 (2001): 76–106.

Thatcher Ulrich, Laurel, Ivan Gaskell, Sara J. Schechner, and Sarah Anne Carter, *Tangible Things: Making History through Objects* (Oxford, 2015).

Trentmann, Frank, *Empire of Things: How We Became a World of Consumers, from the Fifteenth Century to the Twenty-First* (London, 2016).

Tresidder, Jack, ed., *The Complete Dictionary of Symbols in Myth, Art and Literature* (London, 2004).

Trumbach, Randolph, *Sex and the Gender Revolution*, Vol. I, *Heterosexuality and the Third Gender in Enlightenment London* (Chicago, IL and London, 1998).

Tuite, Clara, 'Tainted Love and Romantic Literary Celebrity', *English Literary History* 74.1 (2007): 59–88.

Twyman, Michael, *Lithography 1800–1850* (London, 1970).

Vickery, Amanda, *Behind Closed Doors: At Home in Georgian England* (New Haven, CT and London, 2009).

Vickery, Amanda, *The Gentleman's Daughter: Women's Lives in Georgian England* (New Haven, CT and London, 1998).

Vištica, Olinka and Dražen Grubišić, *The Museum of Broken Relationships: Modern Love in 203 Everyday Objects* (London, 2017).

Volk, Katharina, 'Ovid on Love as a Cultural Construct', in *The Art of Love: Bimillennial Essays on Ovid's Ars Amatoria and Remedia Amoris*, ed. Roy Gibson, Steven Green, and Alison Sharrock (Oxford, 2006), 235–51.

Vries, Jan de, *The Industrious Revolution: Consumer Behaviour and the Household Economy, 1650 to the Present* (Cambridge, 2008).

Walsh, Claire, 'Shop Design and the Display of Goods in Eighteenth-Century London', *Journal of Design History* 8.3 (1995): 157–76.

Walsham, Alexandra, ed., 'Relics and Remains', *Past & Present Supplement* 5 (2010).

Watt, Jeffrey R., ed., *From Sin to Insanity: Suicide in Early Modern Europe* (New York, 2004).

Weiner, Annette B., *Inalienable Possessions: The Paradox of Keeping-While-Giving* (Oxford, 1992).

Whitbread, Helena, ed., *I Know my Own Heart: The Diaries of Anne Lister 1791–1840* (London, 1988).

Whyman, Susan, *The Pen and the People: English Letter Writers 1660–1800* (Oxford, 2009).

Wilce, James M., *Language and Emotion* (Cambridge, 2009).

Wrigley, E. A., R. S. Davies, J. E. Oeppen, and R. S. Schofield, *English Population History from Family Reconstitution 1580–1837* (Cambridge, 1997).

Zhivov, Victor, 'Love à la mode: Russian Words and French Sources', in *French and Russian in Imperial Russia*, ed. Derek Offord, Lara Ryazanova-Clarke, Vladislav Rjéoutski, and Gesine Argent (Edinburgh, 2015), Vol. II, 214–41.

5. UNPUBLISHED THESES

Mackelworth, Jane, 'Sapphic Love and Desire in Britain, 1900–1950: In Texts, Objects, and Spaces' (PhD thesis, University of London, 2017).

Robin, Sarah Ann, 'Pictures, Posies and Promises: Love and the Object: The English in the Seventeenth Century' (PhD thesis, Lancaster University, 2016).

Robinson, Elizabeth, 'Women and Needlework in Britain, 1920–1970' (PhD thesis, University of London, 2012).

Smith, Heather, 'Women and Marriage in the Eighteenth Century: Evidence from the Church Courts, 1730–1780' (PhD thesis, University of Bristol, 2000).

Steinbach, Susie, 'Promises, Promises: Not Marrying in England 1780–1920' (PhD thesis, Yale University, 1996).

Index

Printed and bound by CPI Group (UK) Ltd, Croydon, CR0 4YY